9/92

Critical Essays on
Eudora Welty

Critical Essays on Eudora Welty

W. Craig Turner
Lee Emling Harding

G.K. Hall & Co. • Boston, Massachusetts

Library of Congress Cataloging in Publication Data

Critical essays on Eudora Welty / [edited by] W. Craig Turner,
    Lee Emling Harding.
        p.   cm.—(Critical essays on American literature)
    Includes index.
    ISBN 0-8161-8888-2 (alk. paper)
        1. Welty, Eudora, 1909-   —Criticism and interpretation.
    I. Turner, W. Craig. II. Harding, Lee Emling. III. Series.
PS3545.E6Z63   1989   88-24737
813′.52—dc19   CIP

This publication is printed on permanent/durable acid-free paper
MANUFACTURED IN THE UNITED STATES OF AMERICA

CRITICAL ESSAYS ON AMERICAN LITERATURE

This series seeks to anthologize the most important criticism on a wide variety of topics and writers in American literature. Our readers will find in various volumes not only a generous selection of reprinted articles and reviews but original essays, bibliographies, manuscript sections, and other materials brought to public attention for the first time.

This volume of reviews and essays traces the critical reputation of Eudora Welty, offering a sizable gathering of early reviews and a broad selection of more recent scholarship, including essays on each of Welty's books. Among the noted reviewers are Louise Bogan, Lionel Trilling, John Crowe Ransom, Louis D. Rubin, Jr., and Margaret Marshall. The authors of reprinted articles include Robert Penn Warren, Granville Hicks, Reynolds Price, Marilyn Arnold, Bev Byrne, and Ruth M. Vande Kieft. In addition to an extensive introduction by editors W. Craig Turner and Lee Emling Harding are four original essays commissioned specifically for publication in this volume by Pearl Amelia McHaney, Albert J. Devlin, Merrill Maguire Skaggs, and Suzanne Marrs. We are confident that this book will make a permanent and significant contribution to American literary study.

James Nagel, GENERAL EDITOR

Northeastern University

To our parents,
Sybil and A. C. Turner, and
Jane and Ed Emling

CONTENTS

INTRODUCTION

In her remarkably prescient introduction to *A Curtain of Green and Other Stories* (1941), Katherine Anne Porter quotes Eudora Welty as having commented: "I haven't led a literary life at all. . . . But I do feel that the people and things I love are of a true and human world, and there is no clutter about them."[1] Indeed, through more than a half century of writing short stories, novels, criticism, and autobiography, Welty has consistently presented her readers with fundamental truths and essential humanity, all the while avoiding the unnecessary clutter of fads, fancies, ideologies, and inanities. Like her nineteenth-century literary progenitor Robert Browning, she has focused on the human soul in action, developing dramatic moments of character confrontation in which the speakers and actors typically reveal far more than they realize; and like her twentieth-century Mississippi neighbor William Faulkner, she has been especially interested in "the human heart in conflict with itself."

As for her having missed a literary life, Welty has conscientiously resisted the notion of having her private life invaded for scholarly dissection, maintaining that the only important biography is that life which is contained in her works. Thus, no full-length biography has been written and, for the time being at least, the chronology in Ruth Vande Kieft's *Eudora Welty* (1962; 1987), used in conjunction with the anecdotal reminiscences of the autobiographical *One Writer's Beginnings* (1984), provides essential biographical highlights.[2] Welty has, however, been gracious and relatively open in granting interviews for publication, twenty-six of which are collected in Peggy W. Prenshaw's *Conversations With Eudora Welty* (1984).[3] Her literary papers—manuscripts, literary correspondences, unpublished writings, and so forth—are collected primarily in two repositories: the Mississippi Department of Archives and History in Jackson and the Harry Ransom Humanities Research Center of the University of Texas at Austin. Much of the correspondence, however, remains in private hands, and other uncollected letters and manuscripts are scattered about in colleges and universities throughout the United States.

1

Bibliographical aids for Welty study begin with Noel Polk's "A Eudora Welty Checklist," published in a special Welty issue of *Mississippi Quarterly* in 1973, which includes the most extensive listing of her works up to that year.[4] Polk continues to work toward publication of a complete descriptive bibliography. Until then, Victor H. Thompson's *Eudora Welty: A Reference Guide* (1976) offers a comprehensive compilation of secondary materials, including reviews from 1936 to 1976 of Welty's fiction, as well as listings of biographical materials and of her nonfiction, exclusive of reviews.[5] Updates of Polk's "Checklist" have periodically appeared in the *Eudora Welty Newsletter*. Begun in 1977 and edited by W. U. McDonald, Jr., the *Newsletter* provides an ongoing clearinghouse of information for both primary and secondary Welty materials. Peggy W. Prenshaw has prepared the most useful and important descriptive bibliography to date for *American Women Writers: Bibliographical Essays* (1983).[6] Helpful in tracking Welty's early reputation, Bethany C. Swearingen's *Eudora Welty: A Critical Bibliography, 1936–1958* (1984) presents a complete annotated listing of primary and secondary sources for that period.[7] A more recent updating of Polk's 1973 "Checklist" is Pearl Amelia McHaney's "A Eudora Welty Checklist: 1973–1986" that appeared in a second *Mississippi Quarterly* special Welty number in 1986.[8] Suzanne Marrs's annotated bibliography of the extensive Welty collection at the Mississippi Department of Archives and History was scheduled for fall 1988 publication by the University Press of Mississippi.

The first, and in many ways still the most important, full-length study of Welty's work is Ruth M. Vande Kieft's *Eudora Welty,* originally published in 1962 as part of Twayne's United States Authors Series. In it, Vande Kieft established the standard work against which all later studies have been measured. She attempts to convey the inner life of Welty's fiction by offering a series of careful and telling interpretive readings. Drawing on Robert Penn Warren's seminal essay, "The Love and the Separateness in Miss Welty,"[9] Vande Kieft stresses the ingredients of dualities of experience, experimentation, and lyricism in Welty's works. She calls attention to the great variety, both of form and content, in the fiction, and proceeds to examine most of what have become the standard points of critical discussion: the importance of place; the evolving technical virtuosity; the use of comedy, dream, and fantasy; and the ability to arrive at the universal—the essence behind the reality—while working with the materials of the particular. Finally, Vande Kieft attempts to trace patterns of relationships among the various works. In 1987 Vande Kieft offered a revised and updated edition that includes analysis of Welty's work since 1962, as well as a substantially revised chapter on *The Bride of the Innisfallen,* and that maintains both the general methods and the high standards of the earlier volume.

Michael Kreyling, in his *Eudora Welty's Achievement of Order* (1980), shifts the focus to technique as the unifying and vivifying force in Welty's fiction.[10] Continuing the emphasis on her work as more lyrical than narrative, Kreyling moves behind close interpretive readings of individual works and beyond the tracing of regional, mythological, and folk roots in an attempt to identify the unique voice that characterizes Welty's art. In this first full-length study to include discussion of her work through *The Optimist's Daughter* (1972), he traces Welty's growth in artistic sensibility into what he considers her most encompassing aesthetic achievement, *Losing Battles* (1970). Kreyling's sensitive and subjective approach offers an intelligent and stimulating counterbalance to Vande Kieft's more analytical criticism.

Drawing on Welty's own insistence upon the importance of place working on the author's imagination, Albert J. Devlin's *Eudora Welty's Chronicle* (1983) attempts to clarify and trace the historical aesthetic in her fiction as it is rooted in her home state of Mississippi.[11] Devlin finds an essential underlying cultural unity in the fiction that is informed by the cumulative effect of her historical imagination. Agreeing with Kreyling that formalist and mythological readings do not closely enough approach Welty's overriding vision, he posits that "The intense subjectivity that Welty portrays in her most characteristic work may indeed be historic in origin." After mapping Welty's Mississippi chronicle from the beginnings of the territory to the present day, Devlin concludes by sketching her literary kinship with modernist writers such as Yeats, Joyce, and Virginia Woolf.

A number of less significant book- and monograph-length studies of Welty's work have also appeared. Alfred J. Appel, Jr., published *A Season of Dreams* (1965) as the first volume in Louisiana State University Press's Southern Literary Series.[12] It is a highly derivative book based heavily on Vande Kieft and several other important essays, such as Warren's "Love and Separateness." Marie Antoinette Manz-Kunz presented a very uneven study—at times provocative, at times mundane—in her *Eudora Welty: Aspects of Reality in Her Short Fiction* (1971). Zelma Turner Howard's *The Rhetoric of Eudora Welty's Short Stories* (1973) applies Wayne Booth's techniques in *The Rhetoric of Fiction* to discussions of Welty's artistry in the short fiction. *A Tissue of Lies: Eudora Welty and the Southern Romance* (1982), by Jennifer Lynn Randisi, locates Welty in the tradition of Southern romance writing, particularly stressing the importance of place in her work. Carol Sue Manning's *With Ears Opening Like Morning Glories: Eudora Welty and the Love of Story Telling* (1985) stresses Welty's love affair with story telling as the basis for her extensive and comic depiction of the South's oral culture. Though not focusing exclusively on Welty, Louise Westling's *Sacred Groves and Ravaged Gardens: The Fiction of Eudora Welty, Carson Mc-Cullers, and Flannery O'Conner* (1985) traces the traditions of Southern womanhood and their impact on the fiction of the three writers. Her chapter on Welty is perhaps her most successful at demonstrating her thesis, but she considers in detail only *Delta Wedding, The Golden Apples,* and *The Optimist's Daughter.*[13]

Three shorter monographs, or pamphlets, on Welty have appeared as part of established series. J. A. Bryant, Jr., in *Eudora Welty* (1968) provides a brief general introduction to Welty as part of the Minnesota American Writers Series. Neil Isaacs's *Eudora Welty* (1969), in the Steck-Vaughn Southern Writers Series, presents a more advanced and focused—and at times more forced—reading of Welty's use of mythology and archetypes. Elizabeth Evans's *Eudora Welty* (1981), part of the Ungar Modern Literature Series, offers a sympathetic and mainstream approach to Welty's work without much spark or challenge. A series of introductory pamphlets issued by the Mississippi Library Commission includes titles by Kreyling, Gayle Goodin, Prenshaw, and Robert L. Phillips, Jr.[14]

Increasingly, collections of essays and special issues of scholarly journals have been devoted to Welty and her work. First among these is a special issue of *Shenandoah* (1969) edited by James Boatwright and containing essays by astute readers such as Robert B. Heilman, Joyce Carol Oates, and Reynolds Price, as well as brief tributes by other such distinguished writers as Walker Percy, Allen Tate, and Robert Penn Warren.[15] The fall 1973 issue of *Mississippi Quarterly,* edited by Lewis P. Simpson and also dedicated to Welty, contains significant essays by Vande Kieft, dealing with Welty's vision embodying dualities of theme and structure; Kreyling, treating the dualities of mythical and historical consciousnesses in *Losing Battles;* Cleanth Brooks, examining Welty's treatments of history in *The Optimist's Daughter;* and Thomas L. McHaney, presenting an in-depth study of myth in *The Golden Apples.* Also noteworthy is Polk's inclusive "Checklist" mentioned above.[16]

John F. Desmond has gathered ten articles for *A Still Moment: Essays on the Art of Eudora Welty* (1978), perhaps the best of which is a slightly revised reprint of J. A. Allen's "Eudora Welty: The Three Moments."[17] *Eudora Welty: A Form of Thanks* (1979), edited by Louis Dollarhide and Ann J. Abadie, is the published proceedings of a symposium held at the University of Mississippi in 1977. In it Cleanth Brooks discusses the American Southern idiom and folk culture as vital links to earlier English dialects and relates their threatened demise to forces seen in *The Optimist's Daughter.* Peggy W. Prenshaw presents a reading of heroism and women's roles in

Welty's fiction, while William Jay Smith draws attention to Welty's poetic vision by emphasizing her genius for metaphor making. Noel Polk offers a close reading of the imagery in several later stories and relates them to *The Optimist's Daughter*. Reynolds Price contributes an affectionate tribute praising Welty for her lifegiving example.[18]

The largest, and most important, such collection to date is Peggy Prenshaw's *Eudora Welty: Critical Essays* (1979). Among the initial nine pieces that are labeled "General Studies," particularly noteworthy is Chester Eisinger's "Traditionalism and Modernism in Eudora Welty," an extension of his earlier treatment of Welty's significant relationships with both the moderns and the Eliot-Bloom sense of literary heritage. Also, John A. Allen employs an innervating mythological approach to the novels, especially *Delta Wedding, The Golden Apples,* and *Losing Battles,* in his "The Other Way to Live: Demigods in Eudora Welty's Fiction." "The Recovery of the Confident Narrator: *A Curtain of Green* to *Losing Battles*," by J. A. Bryant, Jr., discusses Welty's artful use of narration as examples both of her modernist technique and of her ability to escape from its solipsistic prison by commanding an attitude of acceptance from her readers. Among other notable contributions in later sections of this landmark volume is "Eudora Welty's Mississippi," an attempt by Albert J. Devlin to locate Welty and her early fiction in the solid world of the South with its temporality, causality, and social pressures. Merrill Maguire Skaggs treats Welty's imagery and symbolism as illustrative of the coherence of *The Golden Apples* in her "Morgana's Apples and Pears." Seymour Gross's "A Long Day's Living: The Angelic Ingenuities of *Losing Battles*" takes the thoughtful tack of choosing not to side with any of the novel's contending factions, but instead to emphasize the novel's overriding sense of irony. Michael Kreyling and Ruth Vande Kieft close the volume with essays probing Welty's criticism: Kreyling focuses on her important recurring critical terms as aids in reading the fiction, while Vande Kieft treats *The Eye of the Story* as, finally, less revealing of Welty's artistic vision of life than *The Optimist's Daughter*.[19]

Prenshaw has also edited a special Welty issue of *The Southern Quarterly* (1982) that contains pieces by Devlin, Elizabeth Evans, and W. U. McDonald, Jr., as well as an interview by Martha Van Noppen. Also appearing in that volume are Kreyling's "Modernism in Welty's *A Curtain of Green and Other Stories*," and Vande Kieft's "Eudora Welty and The Question of Meaning."[20]

Mississippi Quarterly issued a second special Welty number in 1986 celebrating the fiftieth anniversary of her initial publication. Edited by Albert J. Devlin, it includes an interview of Welty by Devlin and Prenshaw; essays by Vande Kieft, Mary Hughes Brookhart and Suzanne Marrs, Louise Westling, Kreyling, Prenshaw, and others;

and a checklist by Pearl Amelia McHaney updating Polk's 1973 work.[21] It has been published as a book—*Welty: A Life in Literature*—by the University Press of Mississippi in 1987, with Polk's "Checklist" reprinted along with McHaney's supplement. A symposium entitled "Eudora Welty: Eye of the Storyteller" was held at the University of Akron in the fall of 1987, with proceedings promised from Kent State University Press.

As the ongoing and ever-increasing scholarly attention paid to her work attests, Eudora Welty remains at the forefront of American literature. She did not, however, always enjoy this place. Michael Kreyling, in a speech given at the Southern Literary Festival in 1984 to celebrate Welty's seventy-fifth birthday, noted that the climate—literary and otherwise—was not conducive when *A Curtain of Green* appeared in 1941: war was beginning, so a first collection of short stories could not expect to command much attention. Further, Welty was a regional writer from an area whose "typical" authors were William Faulkner and Erskine Caldwell, and her early fiction would not readily fit those molds. Several of those who did review the stories, like Louise Bogan, talked of the Southern Gothicism of her work and noted parallels between her stories and Gogol's.[22]

Much attention was then, and has since, been focused on the introduction to the collection by Katherine Anne Porter who hailed Welty at the beginning of her career and warned against her being forced into producing "The Novel." Other critics since have emphasized the skill of her technique, such as Robert J. Griffin in "Eudora Welty's *A Curtain of Green*" who summarizes critical points concerning the poetic style, theme, and symbol. Albert J. Devlin in Prenshaw's *Critical Essays* mentioned above makes a significant contribution to understanding social and historical foundations of the stories. In his chapter on Welty in *Savages and Naturals: Black Portrayals by White Writers in Modern American Literature*, John R. Cooley discusses a special aspect of the stories. Individual stories in the collection have been examined in noteworthy pieces such as Robert B. Heilman's "Salesmen's Deaths: Documentary and Myth" and Charles E. May's "Why Sister Lives at the P.O.," which uses R. D. Laing's theories to give a psychological approach. Other representative studies include A. R. Coulthard's " 'Keela, the Outcast Indian Maiden': A Dissenting View" and Robert Deitweiler's "Eudora Welty's Blazing Butterfly: The Dynamics of Response" on "Old Mr. Marblehall." Kreyling, forty years after Porter's introductory comments, calls for a revision in Welty criticism, recognizing that many "have stressed the technique of Welty's stories and sacrificed their connections with the times. . . . Welty probed the complex growth of the malaise . . . and presented alternatives."[23]

The Robber Bridegroom—a novella Welty called "A Fairy Tale," certainly not The Novel—appeared in 1942. Indeed the typical critical response to *The Robber Bridegroom* has been through its connection to fairy tale. Early reviewers Marianne Hauser, Alfred Kazin, and Lionel Trilling take this approach, while Marilyn Arnold takes a contrary but intriguing position and labels *The Robber Bridegroom* a parody of the traditional fairy tale motif. Charles C. Clark explores the literary and historical sources, as well as themes, in "*The Robber Bridegroom:* Realism and Fantasy on the Natchez Trace." Merrill Maguire Skaggs expands examination of the work and links it to the Southwest humor tradition in "The Uses of Enchantment in Frontier Humor and *The Robber Bridegroom.*" Bev Byrne makes an interesting connection between this work and Welty's latest novel in "A Return to the Source: *The Robber Bridegroom* and *The Optimist's Daughter.*" Byrne notes "the currents of 'doubleness' have run as surely and deeply through Welty's fiction as the Mississippi River and the Natchez Trace have run."[24]

In 1943 a collection of eight Welty short stories entitled *The Wide Net and Other Stories* was published. By this time, many critics seemed ready to fault writers from the South for any hint of adhering to the Southern past and for stories appearing fantastical rather than realistic. Diana Trilling's shrill criticism in the *Nation* that Welty had "developed her technical virtuosity to the point where it outweighs the uses to which it is put and her vision of horror to the point of nightmare" was one reason Robert Penn Warren felt compelled to write the essay "The Love and the Separateness in Miss Welty." Ostensibly a review of *The Wide Net* collection, this essay helped to establish several of the critical approaches to Welty that continue to be followed today. On the one hand, Warren writes, are those characters who are "cut off, alienated, isolated from the world" and who either try to "escape into the world" or at the very least become aware of—or make the reader aware of—"the nature of the predicament." There is also, Warren points out, the theme of Innocence and Experience, opposing poles around which the sparks of conflict may fly. Essays on the collection as a whole since then have tended to emphasize the historical background and the depiction of the artist in the stories as indicative of Welty's own concept of the artist. Daniel Curley, in "Eudora Welty and the Quondam Obstruction," gives a sound stylistic analysis of the stories while focusing on "A Still Moment" and positing that the character of Audubon is best able to synthesize "acceptance and seeking . . . silence and communication" and therefore "offers a way of living, a hope of knowing, which is denied those who refuse to accept their own humanity . . . and . . . to accept the necessity of otherness." Devlin concentrates on this story also, along with "First Love," to discuss Welty's procedures of selection and transformation of historical matter into fiction. Suzanne

Marrs has contrasted Welty's and Robert Penn Warren's portrayals of John James Audubon in "John James Audubon in Fiction and Poetry: Literary Portraits by Eudora Welty and Robert Penn Warren," while Carol S. Manning contrasts Welty with Ellen Glasgow in her discussion of "The Winds" in "Little Girls and Sidewalks: Glasgow and Welty on Childhood's Promise." Pearl McHaney in a new essay in this collection carefully traces historical sources and inspirations for several of the stories.[25]

Delta Wedding, a full-length novel published in 1946, was often greeted with the same "here we go again" criticism—another stereotyped picture of Southern plantation life, such as, again, by Diana Trilling in the *Nation.* John Crowe Ransom, though, rejected such a critique in his penetrating review. He sees beyond the setting and characters and praises Welty's skill with the actual telling of the story as she alternates between "drama of dialogue and external action, on the one hand, and interior monologue on the other." Peggy W. Prenshaw shows Welty's portrayal of the complex social structure of the twentieth-century South to be anything but stereotyped in "Cultural Patterns in Eudora Welty's *Delta Wedding* and 'The Demonstrators.' " John Edward Hardy's 1952 essay on "*Delta Wedding* as Region and Symbol" sees Welty at her best in this novel, focusing on her skill at conveying the meaning of her novel "in the whole particularity of the moment, the single, illuminating still act of private *perception.*" The idea of seeing appears and reappears in the writing of Welty critics, and in Welty herself, probably reaching its culmination in *One Writer's Beginnings* when Welty entitles her pivotal middle chapter "Learning to See." Other approaches have been through a study of family, especially women, in such essays as those by Bolsteri, Bradford, and Hinton in Prenshaw's *Critical Essays,* and myth, as in "Demeter, and Kore, Southern Style" by Louise Westling.[26]

By the 1949 publication of *The Golden Apples,* more and more criticism was being focused on Welty's remarkable command of narrative technique. Though less negative criticism is typical of this period, Margaret Marshall's review for the *Nation* continues the complaint that "Miss Welty . . . has indulged herself in finespun writing that becomes wearing" and introduces a note that continues to be sounded: "one is scarcely ever made aware of the mixed racial background which must surely affect the quality of life." Interestingly enough, Katherine Anne Porter in her introduction to *A Curtain of Green* eight years earlier had identified and answered this criticism: "But there is an ancient system of ethics, an unanswerable, indispensable moral law, on which she is grounded firmly, and this, it would seem to me, is ample domain enough; these laws have never been the peculiar property of any party or creed or nation, they relate to that true and human world of which the artist is a living part; and when he disassociates himself from it in favor of a set of political, which is to say, inhuman, rules, he cuts himself away from his proper society—living men." Others since Porter have also answered Marshall, such as Suzanne Marrs in "The Metaphor of Race in Eudora Welty's Fiction." Since the publication of "Where is the Voice Coming From?" in 1963 and "The Demonstrators" in 1966, both in the *New Yorker,* acknowledgment has been widespread of Welty's concern for and gift of expressing the racial conflicts of the region. Vande Kieft in her revised study goes so far as to call "The Demonstrators" "possibly the greatest story to come out of the Civil Rights era."[27]

Much of the criticism of *The Golden Apples* has focused on Welty's use of myth. Vande Kieft's longest chapter in both editions of her book examines *The Golden Apples,* with mythic motifs receiving much of the attention. Thomas L. McHaney in "Eudora Welty and the Multitudinous Golden Apples" traces Greek and Celtic mythological references and surveys criticism of the work up to 1973. Patterns of initiation are the subject of Carol S. Manning's "Male Initiation, Welty Style" with emphasis on "Moon Lake." J. A. Bryant, Jr., like Hardy in his essay on *Delta Wedding,* examines *The Golden Apples* and finds "a special way of seeing, or perceiving . . . of most of the principal characters and which . . . may drive them to go on strange quests." He links this perception motif to much of Welty's fiction before and after *The Golden Apples,* such as *The Robber Bridegroom.* Merrill M. Skaggs in a new essay uses the occasion of a discussion about Katherine Anne Porter that included Welty to show how much Welty reveals about her own work when reminiscing about Porter. Skaggs relates these revelations to *The Golden Apples* in particular. Moving in a new direction, Patricia S. Yaeger in " 'Because a Fire Was in My Head': Eudora Welty and the Dialogic Imagination" uses Mikhail Bakhtin's linguistic theories to discuss *Golden Apples,* "a beautifully crafted and gender-preoccupied novel whose emphasis on sexuality and intertextuality has not been fully comprehended."[28]

In 1954 *The Ponder Heart* was published to mostly complimentary reviews and was awarded the William Dean Howells Medal of the Academy of Arts and Letters the next year. William Peden read it as a masterful tour de force revealing Welty at her best. In "Dialogue as a Reflection of Place in *The Ponder Heart,*" Robert B. Holland observes in an early review an important quality that can easily be seen in later Welty characters, especially the Renfros and Beechams of *Losing Battles* and Fay of *The Optimist's Daughter:* the people of Clay have "no love for originality, either in words or in ideas." More widely reviewed than any of Welty's previous works, *The Ponder*

Heart in recent years has received less attention. Discussion of the novel's use of language and of humor is often included with more general studies, such as Nell Ann Pickett's "Colloquialism as a Style in the First-Person-Narrator Fiction of Eudora Welty" and Cleanth Brooks's "Eudora Welty and the Southern Idiom." Seymour L. Gross's "Eudora Welty's Comic Imagination" comments on the joyful comedy in *The Ponder Heart* as well as in other works by Welty.[29]

A collection of seven stories entitled *The Bride of the Innisfallen and Other Stories* appeared in 1955. Certainly the least critically explored of all of Welty's fiction, *The Bride of the Innisfallen* has recently been receiving more attention. In the preface to her revised edition of *Eudora Welty,* Vande Kieft notes that her chapter on this volume is "substantially revised," unlike the ones on *Delta Wedding* and *The Golden Apples.* Louis D. Rubin, Jr., in an early article, "Two Ladies of the South," interprets the stories as being about the characters' discovery of self through discovery of the meaning of the moment. A detailed analysis of myth and mythic design can be found in "Eudora Welty's Circe: A Goddess Who Strove with Men" by Andrea Goudie. Alun R. Jones discusses three of the stories in the special issue of *Shenandoah* mentioned above. In "Water, Wanderers, and Weddings: Love in Eudora Welty," Noel Polk focuses on the title story and "No Place for You, My Love," while also commenting on Welty's treatment of love throughout her fiction. Lorraine Liscio in "The Female Voice of Poetry in 'The Bride of the Innisfallen' " analyzes the title story to show a "power theme that inconspicuously gives breadth to the narrator's vision" and a "poetic, female journey . . . amplified in the theme of childbirth."[30]

Losing Battles (1970) has proven a favorite Welty novel for critical discussion. For example, five essays in Prenshaw's *Critical Essays* alone deal specifically with *Losing Battles.* Jonathan Yardley, reviewing it in the *New Republic,* commented on "the sheer variety" of Welty, her unparalleled use of simile, while allowing the novel "is too long and a trifle out of focus." Other reviewers used the opportunity of Welty's first publication in fifteen years to survey her overall achievement. Louise Y. Gossett, for example, in "Eudora Welty's New Novel: The Comedy of Loss" uses the concept of the pairing of opposites to examine themes and narrative methods throughout Welty's fiction. Larry J. Reynolds also discusses narrative structure and theme in "Enlightening Darkness: Theme and Structure in Eudora Welty's *Losing Battles*" and points the reader "beneath its entertaining surface where the story of an intense struggle for survival is subtly and carefully told." Criticism of the novel has frequently focused on the family and / or the family-versus-Julia Mortimer, as in James Boatwright's "Speech and Silence in *Losing Battles*" and William McMillen's "Conflict and Resolution in *Losing Battles.*"

Suzanne Marrs has written three articles that trace the development of characters and plot: "The Making of *Losing Battles:* Jack Renfro's Evolution"; "The Making of *Losing Battles:* Judge Moody Transformed"; "The Making of *Losing Battles:* Plot Revision."[31]

The Optimist's Daughter appeared in book form in 1972 and won the Pulitzer Prize for Fiction. The work received almost unanimous praise by critics in early reviews, including Granville Hicks, who in "Universal Regionalist" writes of being "awed by the novella's richness." Reynolds Price welcomed it as "Welty's strongest, richest work." Later articles on *The Optimist's Daughter* deal with the novel's treatment of the past and the present, of life examined and unexamined, such as Brooks's "The Past Reexamined: *The Optimist's Daughter.*" Naoka Fuwa Thornton continues the mythic criticism of Welty's work in "Medusa-Perseus Symbolism in Eudora Welty's *The Optimist's Daughter.*" Marilyn Arnold traces the imagery, in particular the bird imagery, in the novel to show the characters,' especially Laurel's, revelations about freedom and evading the past. Lucinda H. MacKethan examines *The Optimist's Daughter,* along with *Delta Wedding, Golden Apples,* and *Losing Battles,* and synthesizes many of the main modes of Welty criticism as she discusses place, sense of identity, relationships, time, and perception. She feels that the characters' "main challenge" in these works "is to perceive, understand, and transmit the moments when place yields up its 'extraordinary' values." She notes a greater "sense of fragmentation" in *The Optimist's Daughter* because of Welty's new treatment of the "insider" character; Becky McKelva's control comes as a reminder, not as a live person.[32]

In 1952 Granville Hicks offered a general estimate of Welty's career to that point in which he notes the persistent themes in the variety of stories. He discusses her interest in the mystery of personality and in the mystery of what brings people together and holds them apart. Elmo Howell, echoing Hicks, notes that Welty "does not take much to isolation" and "feels keenly the plight of the individual." Thirty years after Hicks, Vande Kieft cautions critics who overvalue Welty's comic mood and misemphasize it, thereby overlooking her tragic view, especially apparent in later works such as *The Optimist's Daughter.* She reminds us, though, that Eudora Welty's "motives for writing are celebration and love."[33]

Nonfiction works by Welty have provided valuable information and insights for readers and critics alike. *One Time, One Place* (1971), Welty's collection of some of the photographs she took in Mississippi during the depression, also includes a foreword by Welty that reviewers commented on. The remainder of those photographs, housed in the Mississippi Department of Archives and History, will be valuable resources for studies such as Suzanne Marrs's "Eudora Welty's Photography: Images into Fiction." In her essay written for this collection, Marrs explores Welty's photography and finds important images and techniques used later in her writing. The foreword to *One Time, One Place* is also included as one of the essays in Welty's *The Eye of the Story* (1978), a collection of book reviews, biographical sketches of people and places, and essays, that has been praised and studied for its revelations about the workings of the writer's mind. Victoria Glendinning in her review called the volume "prescribed reading for all literary critics." The publication of three lectures that Welty had delivered at Harvard University as *One Writers's Beginnings* (1984) has opened up much new information to Welty scholars. Reviewers were ecstatic, and the book provided Harvard University Press with its first best-seller. In a recent article, Peggy Prenshaw notes the "deep affinities and correspondences that link" Elizabeth Bowen and Welty based on her reading of Bowen's *Pictures and Conversations* and *One Writers's Beginnings* and "that the daring, inward way was the necessary destination all along for both Elizabeth Bowen and Eudora Welty."[34]

In more than five decades since her first story was published in 1936, Eudora Welty has created a large, varied, and most impressive body of prose that continues to appeal to readers and to challenge critics. Our brief survey of the scholarship surrounding her canon is merely suggestive, certainly not exhaustive. For, as Welty's literary stature continues to grow, scholarly examinations of her works and her career have begun to multiply exponentially.

The essays in this volume reflect both that explosion of criticism and its growing maturity: from its precocious infancy in review essays such as Warren's and Ransom's, to its fecund adolescence in Vande Kieft's *Eudora Welty* and essays such as those reprinted here by Hardy, Hicks, and Holland, to its powerful young adulthood in *Critical Essays*, the books by Kreyling and Devlin, and studies collected here by Arnold, Kreyling, Howell, and Vande Kieft. The new essays by Devlin, Marrs, McHaney, and Skaggs further point to the breadth and vigor that Welty studies currently enjoy. Still, as Peggy Prenshaw has noted in concluding her bibliographic essay on Welty, "despite the considerable study of structure and technique, poetic and colloquial language, plot and character, the fiction of Eudora Welty has not yet received the scale and depth of critical analysis that it warrants."

If we believe, as Eudora Welty says she does in *One Writer's Beginnings,* that "emotions do not grow old," (52) then the emotions of love and hate, of hope and fear, that inform her impressive volumes will remain forever new and will continue to provoke still more such studies as those collected here. For Miss Welty's writings, as the criticism so richly attests, "seem not meteors but comets; they have a course of their own that brings them around more than once; they reappear in their own time in the sense that they reiterate their meaning and show a whole further story over and beyond their single significance."[35]

W. CRAIG TURNER
LEE EMLING HARDING

Mississippi College

Notes

1. Katherine Anne Porter, introduction to *A Curtain of Green and Other Stories* (New York: Harcourt, Brace, Jovanovich, 1979), xiii.

2. Ruth M. Vande Kieft, *Eudora Welty* (Boston: G. K. Hall, 1962; rev. 1987); Eudora Welty, *One Writer's Beginnings* (Cambridge, Mass.: Harvard University Press, 1984).

3. Peggy W. Prenshaw, ed., *Conversations with Eudora Welty* (Jackson: University Press of Mississippi, 1984).

4. Noel Polk, "A Eudora Welty Checklist," *Mississippi Quarterly* 26 (Fall 1973):663–94.

5. Victor H. Thompson, *Eudora Welty: A Reference Guide* (Boston: G. K. Hall, 1976).

6. Prenshaw, "Eudora Welty," in *American Women Writers: Bibliographical Essays,* ed. Maurice Duke, Jackson R. Bryer, and M. Thomas Inge (Westport, Conn.: Greenwood Press, 1983), 233–67.

7. Bethany C. Swearingen, *Eudora Welty: A Critical Bibliography, 1936–1958* (Jackson: University Press of Mississippi, 1984).

8. Pearl Amelia McHaney, "A Eudora Welty Checklist: 1973–1986," *Mississippi Quarterly* 39 (Fall 1986):651–97.

9. Robert Penn Warren, "The Love and the Separateness in Miss Welty," *Kenyon Review* 6 (Spring 1944):246–59; rpt. in *Selected Essays* (New York: Vintage Books, 1958), 156–69.

10. Michael Kreyling, *Eudora Welty's Achievement of Order* (Baton Rouge: Louisiana State University Press, 1980).

11. Albert J. Devlin, *Eudora Welty's Chronicle: A Story of Mississippi Life* (Jackson: University Press of Mississippi, 1983).

12. Alfred J. Appel, Jr., *A Season of Dreams: The Fiction of Eudora Welty* (Baton Rouge: Louisiana State University Press, 1965).

13. Marie Antoinette Manz-Kunz, *Eudora Welty: Aspects of Reality in Her Short Fiction* (Berne: Francke Verlag, 1971); Zelma Turner Howard, *The Rhetoric of Eudora Welty's Short Stories* (Jackson: University and College Press of Mississippi, 1973); Jennifer Lynn Randisi, *A Tissue of Lies: Eudora Welty and the Southern Romance* (Washington: University Press of America, 1982); Carol Sue Manning, *With Ears Opening Like Morning Glories: Eudora Welty and the Love of Story Telling* (Westport, Conn.: Greenwood Press, 1985): Louise Westling, *Sacred Groves and Ravaged Gardens: The Fiction of Eudora Welty, Carson McCullers, and Flannery O'Connor* (Athens, Ga.: University of Georgia Press, 1985).

14. J. A. Bryant, Jr., *Eudora Welty* (Minneapolis: University of Minnesota Press, 1968); Neil Isaacs, *Eudora Welty* (Austin, Tex.: Steck-Vaughan, 1969); Elizabeth Evans,

Eudora Welty (New York: Frederick Ungar, 1981); Kreyling, *Eudora Welty* (Jackson: Mississippi Library Commission, 1976); Gayle Goodin, *An Introduction to Eudora Welty's "Losing Battles"* (Jackson: Mississippi Library Commission, 1976); Prenshaw, *An Introduction to Eudora Welty's "The Optimist's Daughter"* (Jackson: Mississippi Library Commission, 1977); Robert L. Phillips, *An Introduction to Eudora Welty's "The Golden Apples"* (Jackson: Mississippi Library Commission, 1977).

15. *Shenandoah* 20 (Spring 1969).

16. *Mississippi Quarterly* 26 (Fall 1973): Vande Kieft, "The Vision of Eudora Welty," 517–42; Kreyling, "Myth and History: The Foes of *Losing Battles*," 639–50; Cleanth Brooks, "The Past Reexamined: *The Optimist's Daughter*," 577–88; McHaney, "Eudora Welty and the Multitudinous Golden Apples," 589–624.

17. John F. Desmond, ed., *A Still Moment: Essays on the Art of Eudora Welty* (Metheun, N.J.: Scarecrow Press, 1978).

18. Louis Dollarhide and Ann J. Abadie, eds., *Eudora Welty: A Form of Thanks* (Jackson: University Press of Mississippi, 1979): Brooks, "Eudora Welty and the Southern Idiom," 3–24; Prenshaw, "Woman's World, Man's Place: The Fiction of Eudora Welty," 46–77; William Jay Smith, "Precision and Reticence: Eudora Welty's Poetic Vision," 59–70; Polk, "Water, Wanderers, and Weddings: Love in Eudora Welty," 95–122; Reynolds Price, "A Form of Thanks," 123–28.

19. Prenshaw, ed., *Eudora Welty: Critical Essays* (Jackson: University Press of Mississippi, 1979): Chester Eisinger, 3–25 [Eisinger's earlier identification of Welty as a writer of "new fiction" is in his *Fiction of the Forties* (Chicago: University of Chicago Press, 1963)]; John A. Allen, 26–55; Bryant, 68–82; Devlin, 157–78; Merrill Maguire Skaggs, 220–41; Seymour L. Gross, 325–40; Kreyling, "Words into Criticism: Eudora Welty's Essays and Reviews," 411–22; Vande Kieft, "Looking with Eudora Welty," 423–44. A baker's dozen of essays from this collection have been reprinted by Prenshaw as *Eudora Welty: Thirteen Essays* (Jackson: University Press of Mississippi, 1983).

20. Prenshaw, ed., *The Southern Quarterly* 20 (Summer 1982); Devlin, "Jackson's Welty," 54–91; Evans, "Eudora Welty: The Metaphor of Music," 92–100; W. U. McDonald, "An Unworn Path: Bibliographical and Textual Scholarship on Welty," 101–8; Martha Van Noppen, "A Conversation with Eudora Welty," 7–23; Kreyling, 40–53; Vande Kieft, 24–39.

21. Devlin, ed., *Mississippi Quarterly* 39 (Fall 1986); Devlin and Prenshaw, "A Conversation with Eudora Welty, Jackson, 1986," 431–54; Vande Kieft, "Eudora Welty; Visited and Revisited," 453–80; Mary Hughes Brookhart and Suzanne Marrs, "More Notes on River Country," 507–20; Westling, "The Loving Observer of *One Time, One Place*," 587–604; Kreyling, "Subject and Object in *One Writer's Beginnings*," 627–38; Prenshaw, "The Antiphonies of Eudora Welty's *One Writer's Beginnings* and Elizabeth Bowen's *Pictures and Conversations*," 639–50; Pearl Amelia McHaney, "A Eudora Welty Checklist: 1973–1986," 651–97.

22. Lousie Bogan, "The Gothic South," *Nation* 153 (6 December 1941):572.

23. Robert J. Griffin, "Eudora Welty's *A Curtain of Green*," in *The Forties: Fiction, Poetry, Drama,* ed. Warren French (Deland, Fla.: Everett / Edwards, 1969), 101–10; John R. Cooley, *Savages and Naturals: Black Portrayals by White Writers in Modern American Literature* (Newark: University of Delaware Press, 1982), 124–37; Robert B. Heilman, "Salesmen's Deaths: Documentary and Myth," *Shenandoah* 20 (Spring 1969):20–28; Charles E. May, "Why Sister Lives at the P.O.," *Southern Humanities Review* 12 (Summer 1978):243–49; A. R. Coulthard, " 'Keela, the Outcast Indian Maiden': A Dissenting View," *Studies in Short Fiction* 23 (Winter 1986):35–41; Robert Deitweiler, "Eudora Welty's Blazing Butterfly: The Dynamics of Response,"

Language and Style 6 (Winter 1973):58–71; Kreyling, "Modernism in Welty's *A Curtain of Green and Other Stories,*" *The Southern Quarterly* 20 (Summer 1982):40–53.

24. Maryanne Hauser, "Miss Welty's Fairy Tale," *New York Times Book Review,* 1 November 1942, 6; Alfred Kazin, "An Enchanted World in America," *NYHTB,* 25 October 1942, 19; Lionel Trilling, "American Fairy Tale," *Nation,* 19 December 1942, 686–87; Marilyn Arnold, "Eudora Welty's Parody," *Notes on Mississippi Writers* 11 (Spring 1978):15–22; Charles C. Clark, "*The Robber Bridegroom:* Realism and Fantasy on the Natchez Trace," *Mississippi Quarterly* 26 (Fall 1973):625–38; Skaggs, "The Uses of Enchantment in Frontier Humor and *The Robber Bridegroom,*" *Studies in American Humor* 3 (October 1976):96–102; Bev Byrne, "A Return to the Source: *The Robber Bridegroom* and *The Optimist's Daughter,*" *The Southern Quarterly* 24 (Spring 1986):74–85.

25. Trilling, "Fiction in Review," *Nation* 157 (2 October 1943):386–87; Daniel Curley, "Eudora Welty and the Quondam Obstruction," *Studies in Short Fiction* 5 (Spring 1968):209–24; Devlin, "Eudora Welty's Historicism: Method and Vision," *Mississippi Quarterly* 30 (Spring 1977):213–34; Marrs, "John James Audubon in Fiction and Poetry: Literary Portraits by Eudora Welty and Robert Penn Warren," *Southern Studies* 20 (Winter 1981):378–83; Manning, "Little Girls and Sidewalks: Glasgow and Welty on Childhood's Promise," *The Southern Quarterly* 21 (Spring 1983):67–76.

26. Trilling, "Fiction in Review," *Nation,* 11 May 1946, 578; John Crowe Ransom, "Delta Fiction," *Kenyon Review* 8 (Summer 1946):503–7; Prenshaw, "Cultural Patterns in Eudora Welty's *Delta Wedding* and 'The Demonstrators,'" *Notes on Mississippi Writers* 3 (Fall 1970):51–70; John Edward Hardy, "*Delta Wedding* as Region and Symbol," *Sewanee Review* 60 (Summer 1952):397–417; Westling, "Demeter, and Kore, Southern Style," *Pacific Coast Philology* 19 (November 1984):101–7.

27. Margaret Marshall, "Notes by the Way" *Nation,* 10 September 1949, 2; Marrs, "The Metaphor of Race in Eudora Welty's Fiction," *Southern Review* 22 (Autumn 1986):697–707.

28. Manning, "Male Initiation, Welty Style," *Regionalism and the Female Imagination* 4, no. 2 (1978):53–60; Bryant, "Seeing Double in *The Golden Apples,*" *Sewanee Review* 82 (Spring 1974):300–15; Patricia S. Yaeger, " 'Because a Fire Was in My Head': Eudora Welty and the Dialogic Imagination," *Mississippi Quarterly* 39 (Fall 1986):561–86; rpt. in rev. form from *PMLA* 99 (October 1984):955–73.

29. William Peden, "A Trial With No Verdict," *Newsweek,* 11 January 1954, 83; Robert B. Holland, "Dialogue as a Reflection of Place in *The Ponder Heart,*" *American Literature* 35 (November 1963):352–58; Nell Ann Pickett, "Colloquialism as a Style in the First-Person-Narrator Fiction of Eudora Welty," *Mississippi Quarterly* 26 (Fall 1973):559–76; Gross, "Eudora Welty's Comic Imagination," in *The Comic Imagination in American Literature,* ed. Louis D. Rubin, Jr., (New Brunswick, N.J.: Rutgers University Press, 1973), 319–28.

30. Rubin, "Two Ladies of the South," *Sewanee Review* 63 (Autumn 1955): 671–81; Andrea Goudie, "Eudora Welty's Circe: A Goddess who Strove with Men," *Studies in Short Fiction* 13 (Fall 1976):481–89; Alun R. Jones, "A Frail Travelling Coincidence: Three Later Stories of Eudora Welty," *Shenandoah* 20 (Spring 1969):40–53; Lorraine Liscio, "The Female Voice of Poetry in 'The Bride of the Innisfallen,'" *Studies in Short Fiction* 21 (Fall 1984):357–62.

31. Jonathan Yardley, "The Last Good One?" *New Republic* 162 (9 May 1970):33–36; Louise Y. Gossett, "Eudora Welty's New Novel: The Comedy of Loss," *Southern Literary Journal* 3 (Fall 1970):122–37; Larry J. Reynolds, "Enlightening Darkness: Theme and Structure in Eudora Welty's *Losing Battles,*" *Journal of Narrative Technique* 8 (Spring 1978):133–40; James Boatwright, "Speech and Silence in *Losing Battles,*" *Shenandoah* 25 (Spring 1974):3–14; William McMillen, "Conflict and Res-

olution in *Losing Battles*," *Critique* 15 (1973):110–24; Marrs, "The Making of *Losing Battles:* Jack Renfro's Evolution," *Mississippi Quarterly* 37 (Fall 1984):469–74; Marrs, "The Making of *Losing Battles:* Judge Moody Transformed," *Notes on Mississippi Writers* 17 (1985):47–53; Marrs, "The Making of *Losing Battles:* Plot Revision," *Southern Literary Journal* 18 (Fall 1985):40–49.

32. Granville Hicks, "Universal Regionalist: A Review of Eudora Welty's *The Optimist's Daughter*," *New Leader* 55 (7 August 1972):19; Reynolds Price, "The Onlooker, Smiling: An Early Reading of *The Optimist's Daughter*," *Shenandoah* 20 (Spring 1969):58–73; Naoka Fuwa Thornton, "Medusa-Perseus Symbolism in Eudora Welty's *The Optimist's Daughter*," *The Southern Quarterly* 23 (Summer 1985):64–76; Marilyn Arnold, "Images of Memory in Eudora Welty's *The Optimist's Daughter*," *Southern Literary Journal* 14 (Spring 1982):28–38; Lucinda H. MacKethan, "To See Things in Their Time: The Act of Focus in Eudora Welty's Fiction," *American Literature* 50 (May 1978):258–75; rpt. in *The Dream of Arcady* (Baton Rouge: Louisiana State University Press, 1980), 181–206.

33. Hicks, "Eudora Welty," *College English* 14 (November 1952):69–76; Elmo Howell, "Eudora Welty and the City of Man," *Georgia Review* 33 (Winter 1979):770–82; Vande Kieft, "Eudora Welty: The Question of Meaning," *The Southern Quarterly* 20 (Summer 1982):24–39.

34. Victoria Glendinning, "Eudora Welty in Type and Person," *New York Times Book Review*, 7 May 1978, 7; Prenshaw, "The Antiphonies," 650.

35. Eudora Welty, "Looking at Short Stories," in *The Eye of the Story: Selected Essays and Reviews* (New York: Random House, 1978), 85–106. Miss Welty was making the comment about Faulkner's short stories.

A Curtain of Green and Other Stories

The Gothic South

The definite Gothic quality which characterizes so much of the work of writers from the American South has puzzled critics. Is it the atmosphere of the *roman noir,* so skillfully transferred to America by Poe? Or is it a true and indigenous atmosphere of decaying feudalism? Faulkner treats the horrifying and ambiguous situations thrown up by a background which has much in common with nineteenth-century Russia in a style darkened and convoluted by, it would seem, the very character of his material. Eudora Welty, who is a native and resident of Mississippi, in the stories of this volume has instinctively chosen another method which opens and widens the field and makes it more amenable to detached observation. She proceeds with the utmost simplicity and observes with the most delicate terseness. She does not try mystically to transform or anonymously to interpret. The parallel forced upon us, particularly by those of Miss Welty's stories which are based on an oblique humor, is her likeness to Gogol.

The tramp musicians, the inhabitants of a big house (either mad, drunk, or senile), the idiots and ageless peasant women, the eccentric families tyrannized over by an arch-eccentric, the pathetic and ridiculous livers of double lives, even the Negro band leader with his sadism and delusion of grandeur—all these could come out of some broken-down medieval scene, and all could be treated completely successfully—with humorous detachment, combined with moments of tenderness and roaring farce—by the author of "The Inspector General" and "Dead Souls." Like Gogol, Miss Welty opens the doors and describes the setting, almost inch by inch. She adds small detail to small detail: the fillings in people's teeth, the bright mail-order shirts of little boys, the bottles of Ne-Hi, the pictures of Nelson Eddy hung up like icons. We see what happens to representatives of an alien commercial world—here, traveling salesmen: how they become

* Reprinted with permission from the *Nation,* 6 December 1941, 572. Copyright 1941 by The Nation Company, Inc.

entangled against their will in this scene, which goes on under its own obscure decomposing laws; or dissolve back into it, symbolically enough, in delirium and death. Even the women in the beauty parlor have a basic place in the composition; they are not so much modernly vulgar as timelessly female—calculating, shrewd, and sharp. Miss Welty's method can get everything in; nothing need be scamped, because of romantic exigencies, or passed over, because of rules of taste. Temperamentally and by training she has become mistress of her material by her choice of one exactly suitable kind of treatment, and—a final test of a writer's power—as we read her, we are made to believe that she has hit upon the only possible kind. But it is a method, in Miss Welty's hands, only suitable for her Southern characters on their own ground. The one story dealing with the North, Flowers for Marjorie, goes completely askew.

Katherine Anne Porter, in her preface, surveys with much insight the nature and scope of and the dangers attendant upon the specialized talent of the writer of short stories. She warns against "the novel," a form held up to the short-story writer as a baited trap. She does not warn against the other trap, the commercial short story, and the other tempter, "the agent." It seems impossible that Miss Welty, equipped as she is, should fall into line and produce the bloated characters and smoothed-out situations demanded by "commercial" publications. But other finely equipped persons have given in. As for the novel, she needs only the slenderest unifying device, something analogous to "a smart *britchka,* a light spring-carriage of the sort affected by bachelors, retired lieutenant colonels, staff captains, landowners possessed of about a hundred souls," to produce one whenever she wishes.

Modernism in Welty's
A Curtain of Green and Other Stories
Michael Kreyling*

"Every age has its mannerisms," wrote Jacques Barzun in *Classic, Romantic, and Modern* (1943).[1] Those mannerisms are preserved, lively fossils, in the works of the artists of every age. Among the obligations of criticism is the recovery of these mannerisms and the interpretation of them for a later age. Recovering and interpreting the "modernism" in Eudora Welty's first volume of short stories, *A Curtain of Green and Other Stories,* enables us to see a facet of her

* Reprinted with permission from *The Southern Quarterly* 20 (Summer 1982):40–53.

work often overlooked: its relationship to the modern period that envelops the Southern material of which she is an acknowledged master. Consideration of Welty's early stories through the lens of modernism shows us that Welty's domain is decidedly not provincial (in the pejorative sense), and that her artistic voice addresses her age's moral and philosophical dilemmas as directly as anyone else's. Many critics, myself included, have stressed the technique of Welty's stories and sacrificed their connections with the times. It is time for some re-vision.

Welty's first seventeen stories, collected in *A Curtain of Green* in 1941, are works in the modern temper. That elusive thing, resulting from the gauging of the human spirit and the morale of civilization in the interval between the world wars, provides readers of these stories with a fresh context. "Modern," wrote Joseph Wood Krutch, "designated a complex of ideas which [had] never been analyzed. . . ."[2] Yet the word "modern," along with its synonym "sophistication," were magnets for the imaginations of writers across a wide spectrum. Sophistication and modernism occupied writers as polished and erudite as Krutch, Bertrand Russell, and Jacques Barzun, as well as lesser writers such as Ted Olson, author of "Sophisticate's Progress," a short parable for the modern reader of *Harper's Magazine* for March 1925. Fitzgerald's sophisticated young men and flappers were, in one sense, designer originals. But the market for sophistication was by no means Fitzgerald's monopoly. In the 1930s, as Fitzgerald's reputation foundered, so did stock in his brand of sophistication. Several essayists took up the topic only to renounce modernism and all its works. Modernism was indicated for a full bill of civilization's problems: "hatred of sentimentality," despair in ideals after the débâcle of World War I, movie-induced "foppish" pretense to urbanity, pessimism, alcoholism, and the decline of marriage and the rise of divorce. The modern could not feel; he or she practiced too many hours on the finesse needed to keep mundane human emotions or miseries at bay. Taking a longer cultural view, Barzun diagnosed the modern malaise more severely: ". . . the modern ego has lost its faith, and with it the willingness to take risks."[3] Everywhere, according to the critics, Western civilization was in retreat.

By the close of the decade George Jean Nathan, after expressing doubt that any observer of trends in art and culture should venture to announce the death of any mode, ventured nevertheless to yank sophistication from the stage. His obituary contains a useful description of the deceased:

> By sophistication, I mean, if any explanation is necessary, the superficial attitude which makes a philosophical virtue of boredom and a critical vice of interest, which accepts with a languid resignation

what is normally regarded with enthusiasm, and which views with worldly disdain the affectionate beliefs and little incidents of the common run of mankind.[4]

Joseph Wood Krutch, in *The Modern Temper* (1929), went beyond description to the thoroughness of an anatomy of the modern. He depicted the moderns as mere husks of former vital generations, and sadly prophesied that the necessary vitality to renew civilization's faith in itself was likely to come from a wave of barbarians from beyond the pale of polite refinement. Sophistication, Krutch wrote, was the death mask of a civilization bereft of values and buried under an avalanche of scientific knowledge that earlier stages of civilization had organized through faith in poetry, mythology, religion, or philosophy. For Krutch, as for Barzun, Russell, and others, the crisis of the times was a crisis of morale, of faith in civilization's strength to prevail in the accelerating wave of knowledge and event. Modern man, through stages of increasing sophistication, had become fatally distanced from the well-springs of human vitality. His doom was imminent.[5]

These are the times of Welty's early stories, and the stories themselves are natural parts of those times in ways we have seldom noticed. We have, indeed, no difficulty in seeing their connection with the South of the Great Depression; Welty's own photographs reinforce the conviction that her early fiction records her time and place for the outer eye. But the inner eye, on which the more complex images of the artist's world are recorded, must not be slighted. In the images recorded on the inner eye we can trace "the very close affinity with its time and place"[6] that distinguishes fiction from the work of the journalist or the historian, and establishes certain fiction crucially in a culture's portrait of itself. With special attention to the context of "modern," we can see *A Curtain of Green and Other Stories* as the author has suggested: as responses to "their own present time."[7]

The starting point is crucial. In the recent *The Collected Stories of Eudora Welty*, a moment in "The Hitch-Hikers" commands attention, for it seems to be a moment that combines the general problem of the modern temper with the particular problem of artistic response to it.

Tom Harris, the protagonist of the story and one of several itinerant moderns in *A Curtain of Green*, has picked up two hitch-hikers in the Mississippi Delta. One of the men carries a guitar and chats incessantly; the other, Sobby by name, is morose and opens his mouth only to complain. Late in the afternoon, Harris leaves the pair in his car while he goes into the Dulcie Hotel to reserve a room for the night. When he returns he finds Sobby in the custody of two bystanders; the guitar player, still in the back seat of the car, is bleeding profusely from a head wound. Harris looks into his car at the wounded man:

> It was the man with the guitar. The little ceiling light had been turned on. With blood streaming from his broken head, he was slumped down upon the guitar, his legs bowed around it, his arms at either side, his whole body limp in the posture of a bareback rider. (*CS,* p. 66)

This act of seeing is not simply that of the outer eye, that is, descriptive of the world impinging on the beholder. Harris, the modern, sees not only the injured guitar player. He also sees through a painting, Picasso's "The Old Guitarist," in which the figure of the guitarist cradles an instrument with bowed and crossed legs, and whose posture is as slumped and limp as that of the hitchhiker in Harris's car.[8]

This is the crucial moment in "The Hitch-Hikers" when the complex examination of the modern temper, through which these stories echo the temper of their time, discovers its first complication. Harris, faced with an act of brutality all too common in life, shows us that his sensing apparatus operates with a buffer that shields him from naked contact with the world. Brutality is distanced by style; the simple human act of looking is modified so that fear, danger, blood, mortality are all distanced from Harris. Harris's vision is temptingly akin to that of the young Picasso himself. Art critic John Canaday describes the style of "The Old Guitarist," coincidentally, as "a style of great sophistication" through which a volatile subject is cooled to "pathos."[9] The buffering function of vision—automatically and perhaps unconsciously performed by Harris—is characteristic of the modern who, as his critics claim, cuts himself off from the vitality of life.

From the beginning of "The Hitch-Hikers" Harris acts like a man fending off life. He initially picks up the pair of hitchhikers when, in a moment of trance at the wheel of his car, he feels a kind of disorientation or vertigo that makes "his stand very precarious and lonely" (p. 62). Later, after taking the injured man to a hospital, Harris goes on to a party and fends off one woman, Ruth, while a younger girl, Carol, flatters him with the names "angel" and "hero." Like the typical modern, Harris avoids frank emotions. For Welty's Harris, as for Bertrand Russell's "modern," ardor of any kind "seems a trifle crude."[10]

Alone in his hotel room after the party, Harris turns on the ceiling fan to protect himself from the silence and the glaring bulb. Carol appears outside his window, in a drizzle, and he reluctantly takes her to an all-night drugstore. She wants to tell him how she has had a crush on him since the summers years ago when he had played the piano at a Gulf Coast resort. He had played with enviable assurance, and Carol had been moved. But, ducking all flattery, Harris sends the girl home in a taxi. The next morning, learning that the guitarist has died, Harris flees Dulcie and its entanglements. He drops the guitar with a black boy who asks him for it.

Harris, as modern, has been partially described by Barzun, whose modern type is one who systematically distrusts his own desires and "hides its wounds under an affectation of toughness and expresses its uneasiness by bravado."[11] Harris is, at the core, a sophisticated young man who has dismissed belief and thereby has committed himself to hiding and false toughness. He emits an atmosphere that "cools" all reality to temperatures at which he can safely handle it.

Harris's smooth handling of Ruth and Carol demonstrates sophistication in personal relationships, an aspect of modern behavior much discussed by the critics of the times. Ted Olson's modest takeoff on Bunyan, "Sophisticate's Progress," finds the stereotypical modern male secure within "the shell of his haughty isolation."[12] Harris's deflection of Carol's approaches, showing what Olson had called "wisdom cool and aseptic," also bears out Irvin Edman's diagnosis of the modern. Edman wrote:

> Enter the modern. . . . He will not talk love or admit it. He will not believe in the Good Life or be publicly seen leading it. He will have no nonsense about religion or believe that relic of primitive mentality still exists. He will be "anesthetized to all that Jesus or that Plato prized." He will have little patience with politeness or allow himself to practice it. He will try to be a tough mind gaily indifferent in a tough world. The last obscenity he will permit himself will be nobility. The last weakness he will indulge in will be to be sweet or soft.[13]

Not quite as suave as Hammett's Nick Charles, nor as savvy as Sam Spade, Welty's Harris is nevertheless a brother in that fraternity of modern, private souls. Questions of personal involvement are, with finesse, kept at bay; questions of sentiment (jettisoning the guitar) are simply evaded when there are no witnesses.

"Death of a Traveling Salesman" steps forward immediately into this discussion of the modern in Welty's stories. R. J. Bowman, Harris's elder colleague, is a figure whose shadow can be found in Krutch's *The Modern Temper:* physically and emotionally "debilitated" and "enfeebled" (Krutch's words) by the great machine of civilization that he serves, Bowman is sick unto death.[14] On the first page of the story we know that Bowman's basic humanity has been infected by the virus of modern commercialism. He has hated his bout with influenza because illness forces him back upon his mortal humanity. He tries to declare his recovery perfect by paying the hotel doctor.

And he attempts to quit his debt to his nurse similarly: "He had given the nurse a really expensive bracelet, just because she was packing up her bag and leaving" (*CS*, p. 119). Neither gesture is meaningful, however, and Bowman goes off on his last trip with a doomed heart. He is a dying and emotionally powerless man; his feeble heart acts as emblem of both.

In Bowman's encounter with Sonny and his wife, the doom of the modern man is clearly discernible. Krutch writes that the modern wastes his life in "the successive and increasingly desperate expedients by means of which [he], the ambitious animal, endeavors to postpone the inevitable realization that living is merely a physiological process with only a physiological meaning and that it is most satisfactorily conducted by creatures who never feel the need to attempt to give it any other."[15] When Bowman meets Sonny and his wife, their creatures (mule and dogs), and their contentment within a closed circle of food, warmth, procreation, and work, he is stricken with the simplicity of the other life: "A marriage, a fruitful marriage. That simple thing. Anyone could have had that" (p. 129). Yet there is nothing more remote from the reach of Bowman's flickering life, and never was. In feeble gratitude for their sharing, he can think only of footwear and money. In his solitary death, the modern is warned of his eventual death as well.

The character of Howard in "Flowers for Marjorie" is Harris and Bowman *in extremis*. "Flowers for Marjorie" is set in the metropolis of New York City during the Depression. Howard stumbles through this modern maze from one unreal bumper of "civilization" to another: slot machine, W. P. A. office, Radio City Music Hall. He is driven mad in the unreal city; he can no longer distinguish actuality from hallucination. Modern civilization has mechanized his time and his world. The clock which he throws out the window cannot be discarded so easily; the ticks grow "louder and louder" as he attempts to flee from them.

Howard has drifted into a radical estrangement from the world of pure natural vitality. His wife Marjorie, swelling with their child, growing as fragrant as the pansy she finds on the pavement, is Howard's antithesis. She is as confident of survival as he is anxious about it. Her confidence drives him to hatred of her, and ultimately to a murder: "Away at his distance, backed against the wall, he regarded her world of sureness and fruitfulness and comfort, grown forever apart, safe, hopeful in pregnancy, as if he thought it strange that his world, too, should not suffer" (*CS*, p. 101).

Howard, whose work is paving, continues to obliterate his standing in the natural world. His marriage to Marjorie is, in microcosm, the condition of modern civilization in its direst trouble. An abyss separates Howard from the "world of sureness and fruitfulness," as it surely does modern man from the origins of his existence with all other created nature. It is one of Krutch's chief points that, whatever past ages might have lacked in intellectual rigor, they made up for in "physical and emotional vigor which is, unlike critical intelligence, analogous to the processes of nature."[16] When Howard murders Marjorie (whether in reality or in hallucination) he commits his own suicide as well.

Usually Welty reserves for her black characters the function of expressing this purely vital, sure and fruitful, way of living which modern man has either lost or denied. Phoenix Jackson, perhaps the most famous character in *A Curtain of Green,* brings to the doctor's office in Natchez—and also into the camp of those who embrace the science of living, living mediated by modern thinking about living— simple vitality. Because of her associations with the phoenix of antique myth, Phoenix Jackson represents the condition of the human race before "enfeebling" layers of civilization anesthetized it. Although primitive, Phoenix is centered in and directed toward the value of life, the path worn by the habit of hope. She possesses that vitality without which, Krutch says, faith would not be possible.[17]

"Powerhouse" presents us with a more elaborated figure of vitality, but a more useful counterpoint to Harris and company. "You can't tell what he is. 'Negro man?'—he looks more Asiatic, monkey, Jewish, Babylonian, Peruvian, fanatic, devil. He has pale gray eyes, heavy lids, maybe horny like a lizard's, but big glowing eyes when they're open. He has African feet of the greatest size, stomping, both together, on each side of the pedals" (*CS,* p. 31). Powerhouse suggests all that predates in history and in imagination the white audience for whom he plays. He is power and vitality—a powerhouse not only for his own band, but also for the white audience who might as well be in another hemisphere.

The meaning of Powerhouse's life is the taking of risks. This requires a courage that most of Welty's white, male moderns lack. Barzun's words provide a gloss on Powerhouse: "Another way of summarizing these lacks would be to say that the modern ego has lost its faith, and with it the willingness to take risks. It looks for certainties, guarantees of permanence and safety without, often, be- lieving that they exist."[18] Powerhouse's jazz is the essence of risk- taking, for he never knows just how each number will be played. Nothing is certain in his music or in his life, yet he faces each moment heroically. He is a hero among heroes in the small diner where he and his men go on their break. The lesser hero whom the black patrons present to him is fitly offered for Powerhouse's blessing.

In the story of Uranus Knockwood, formally a superb rendition in prose of the dynamics of ensemble jazz, Powerhouse faces and masters the absence of certainty and order that the modern avoids.

He imagines his wife unfaithful to him the second he leaves the apartment in New York. He spares himself no degree of loneliness on tour. He describes the gory details of his wife's imagined suicide. Facing each moment of his fear, pain, anxiety, and loneliness, Powerhouse thrusts himself into life. Unlike Harris, who once knew how to play the piano but surrendered his control and power, Powerhouse not only finds the central risk, the "essential" thing lacking in Harris's modern life, but also becomes the center for his sidemen, for the blacks in the sad diner, and for the whites at the dance who, by and large, fail to find their connection with him.

Holding and imparting vitality for life is a gift few white characters in *A Curtain of Green* seem to possess. Even in the one case in which the white stranger of "The Key" appears to have a gift, the imparting of it is complicated by impediments that seem peculiarly modern.

The young man who "gives" two keys to the deaf mute couple Albert and Ellie Morgan, is a very complex modern ego:

> The man was still smoking. He was dressed like a young doctor or some such person in the town, and yet he did not seem of the town. He looked very strong and active; but there was a startling quality, a willingness to be forever distracted, even disturbed, in the very reassurance of his body, some alertness which made his strength fluid and dissipated instead of withheld and greedily beautiful. His youth by now did not seem an important thing about him; it was a medium for his activity, no doubt, but as he stood there frowning and smoking you felt some apprehension that he would never express whatever might be the desire of his life in being young and strong, in standing apart in compassion, in making any intuitive present or sacrifice, or in any way of action at all—not because there was too much in the world demanding his strength, but because he was too deeply aware. (*CS*, p. 33)

Unlike Powerhouse, who sees all of the uncertainties in human existence but nevertheless rushes to accept them, the young stranger hesitates. He sees too much ever to act spontaneously.

Albert Morgan, on the other hand, in his enthusiasm to possess the first key ("present or sacrifice") rushes undeterred to the interpretation of the symbol. Albert believes without caution and, as the young stranger's somber presence seems to tell us, will eventually be duped. Ellie, "with her suspicions of everything," is more skeptical. Albert's enthusiastic faith in the first key as a freely signifying symbol is a sore spot for her. "Yes, she must regard it as an unhappiness lying between them, as more than emptiness" (p. 35). The first key raises Albert's hope, but Ellie had already circumscribed hope within the bounds of the likely—a modern trait. The impulsive in human nature, that which is premodern, seeks the center, and will invent it if need be. That need—so the somber young man's mood tells us—is often invoked. And thus man lurches from one fictive center of permanence and certainty to another, says the modern, never really discovering the genuine center. Better to remain "apart in compassion," like the young stranger, or simply apart, like Harris, than to be duped into chimaeric searches with the likes of Phoenix and Powerhouse.

The stranger of "The Key" is another counterpoint to the vital. Like the modern he stands still, but unlike the modern he generates some passion in his stillness:

> He stood and stared in distraction at the other people; so intent and so wide was his gaze that anyone who glanced after him seemed rocked like a small boat in the wake of a large one. There was an excess of energy about him that separated him from everyone else, but in the movement of his hands there was, instead of the craving for communication, something of reticence, even of secrecy, as the key rose and fell. You guessed that he was a stranger in town; he might have been a criminal or a gambler, but his eyes were widened with gentleness. His look, which traveled without stopping for long anywhere, was a hurried focusing of a very tender and explicit regard. (p. 30)

Like the reticent and vulnerable young girl of "A Memory," this stranger emerges as the type of the artist: the individual who has transformed the apparently passive act of "regard" into an act of passionate involvement in life. For the moderns of Welty's early stories, this is the breakthrough that parallels Powerhouse's. But for this modern artist, and for the artist *manqué*, Harris, the breakthrough at best leads to a tortured ambivalence. This is clearly dramatized in the ending of "The Key."

The story concludes on a dissonant note that echoes the imperfect resolution in both plot and theme. As Albert cherishes the first key, a symbol of freely assignable meaning (for we are told of no lock it might open), the young stranger drops a second key into Ellie's hand. This key has one meaning ("Star Hotel, Room 2") and no other. It is appropriately placed in Ellie's hand, for the possible multideterminancy of signs always brings her to sadness. The young man then leaves, giving the Morgans a contradictory look, "both restless and weary, very much used to the comic" (p. 37). The final sentence of the story hits the intriguing note: "You could see that he despised and saw the uselessness of the thing he had done." Does he despise the losing of the first key—freely assignable symbol—or the giving of the second—restricted symbol? Does he regret his intrusion into the secret lives of the two deaf mutes? As he goes out "abruptly into the night" seeking oblivion and relief from the trials of human company, he manifests in a supercharged way the spiritual confusion of the race of moderns in these stories. For all of his knowledge of the human plight, summed up in his "comic" expression, the stranger has learned very little about himself.

Barzun also made this observation about the modern: "The first striking trait of the modern ego is self-consciousness. I say self-consciousness rather than self-awareness, because I believe that in spite of much heart-searching, the modern ego is more concerned with the way it appears in others' eyes than with learning fully about itself and admitting its troubles fearlessly."[19] The stranger of "The Key" is, then, as much the subject of the story as he is its point of view.

Movement toward reattachment to the world comes in the story that gives its title to the collection, "A Curtain of Green." Welty dissents from Krutch's pessimistic opinion that a renewal of vitality will only come from outside modern civilization, for her protagonist Mrs. Larkin makes a breakthrough from the modern into the vital and the original. Many of Krutch's ideas and images find fictional expression in this story, as they do in "Death of a Traveling Salesman."

Krutch argues that modern man needs to return, by some means, to the spirit in which he felt himself continuous with the natural world. The legacy of Baconian thinking, he writes, has been to make man master of Nature but to estrange him from all that is metaphysical—to leave man, like the stranger in "The Key," with nothing to believe and with no interest in the activity of believing.[20] Mrs. Larkin breaks through this impasse of unbelief and renews her continuity with the natural world.

Having seen her husband "accidentally" crushed by a falling tree in their own safe driveway, Mrs. Larkin is rattled out of the trance of the modern ego. Bertrand Russell, responding to Krutch's study of the modern, describes the resultant misery:

> But the modern man, when misfortune assails him, is conscious of himself as a unit in a statistical total; the past and the future stretch before him in a dreary procession of trivial defeats. Man himself appears as a somewhat ridiculous strutting animal, shouting and fussing during a brief interlude between infinite silences.[21]

Krutch had envisioned the remedy: reintegration. This seems a simple cure, thus captured in a single word, but it is, as the several stories of *A Curtain of Green* persuade us, densely complicated in practice. Welty has placed certain black characters in the original state of continuousness with nature, and most white characters adrift. Mrs. Larkin is the character who makes the passage, perhaps not totally willfully, through the "curtain of green" (Krutch had called it a "*door* into the unseen world") into a flourishing garden (called by Krutch a world where "religion might well *flourish* quite as luxuriantly as it did in former times" and where other saving human beliefs "would once more come to seem living realities").[22] Welty no more effectively achieves connection with her times than by this shared pattern of imagery: the world the modern is exiled from is fertile, flourishing, natural. To enter it Mrs. Larkin must trade her self-consciousness, in Barzun's terms, for self-awareness and must surrender as well the ego that keeps her apart.

The death of her husband had thrust upon Mrs. Larkin the fact that nature is not accountable to man in terms that the rational human mind accepts as satisfactory. "The cause in oblivion" for her husband's death is Mrs. Larkin's way of realizing that, as a creature within— not apart from—nature, man is subject to its "ends-less" operations. The characters of *A Curtain of Green* who know this in the blood, Phoenix Jackson, for example, or Ruby Fisher in "A Piece of News," live within nature's cycles. But Mrs. Larkin needs ends, explanations, a rationale. This is symptomatic of the modern predicament. Krutch writes:

> To those who study her, Nature reveals herself as extraordinarily fertile and ingenious in devising *means,* but she has no *ends* which the human mind has been able to discover or comprehend. Perhaps, indeed, the very conception of an end or ultimate purpose is exclusively human. . . .[23]

As Mrs. Larkin seeks refuge in her flowers she is drawn to this truth. Appearing at dawn, vanishing inside her house at dusk, working in overalls stained with the green stuff of her plants, Mrs. Larkin is becoming, even as her human will holds out, increasingly natural, swept up in means. She had gone into seclusion from the human world because ends had been denied her. Now she is drawn into the flourishing world that, in Krutch's view, stands opposite the modern.

When Mrs. Larkin faints, drops to the ground of her garden, she becomes one of her own cultivations. Her apartness breaks (and a summer storm breaks overhead as if to commemorate the moment) and she enters, or reenters, the unseen world where, as Krutch had said, the lost intangibles of vital human existence would once again appear as "living realities."

Krutch, among many others, had much to say about the malady of modernism. Welty's voice can be clearly heard in the chorus. Although she uses the language of fiction, she shares much with all of the writers who took modernism and its ills as their subject. Between Welty's fiction and the plentitude of nonfictional works on the subject of modernism there are many marks of kinship and "affinity."

To any reading and interpretation of the stories of *A Curtain of Green* we must add the "modern" dimension. What Krutch, Barzun,

Russell and others probed and decried and surveyed in our now bygone modern years, Welty worked into fiction. Her early stories significantly, albeit not exclusively, address us on the topic of the modern. As a writer of fiction Welty probed the complex growth of this malaise, rendered its peculiar evils in the figures of fiction, and presented alternatives—other ways to live. Welty herself suggests that some such ongoing address and response is the lively rhythm of fiction. In her review of Elizabeth Bowen's *Collected Stories,* Welty singled out "the close affinity with its time" that keeps a work of fiction pulsating with life. In her reading of others Welty has given us, once again, directions on how to read her own work.

Notes

1. Jacques Barzun, *Classic, Romantic, and Modern* (1943; rpt. Garden City, N. Y.: Anchor Books, 1961), p. 116.

2. Joseph Wood Krutch, *The Modern Temper* (1929; rpt. New York: Harcourt, Brace, 1956), p. 19.

3. Barzun, p. 128.

4. George Jean Nathan, "Exit 'Sophistication,'" *American Mercury,* 52 (Feb. 1941), p. 227.

5. Krutch, pp. 6–13.

6. Eudora Welty, rev. of *The Collected Stories of Elizabeth Bowen, New York Times Book Review,* 8 Feb. 1981, p. 3.

7. Eudora Welty, *The Collected Stories of Eudora Welty* (New York: Harcourt Brace Jovanovich, 1980), p. x.

8. Welty's use of Picasso's paintings as jumping off places for her own fiction is not a new idea. She has acknowledged that viewing "Les Saltimbiques" might have had something to do with the story "Acrobats in a Park," an early version of "A Memory." See Eudora Welty, *Acrobats in a Park* (Northridge, Ca.: Lord John Press, 1980).

9. John Canaday, *Mainstreams of Modern Art* (New York: Holt, Rinehart and Winston, 1959), pp. 451–52. Italics mine.

10. Bertrand Russell, "Why Is Modern Youth Cynical?" *Harper's Magazine,* 160 (May 1930), p. 721.

11. Barzun, pp. 117, 118.

12. Ted Olson, "Sophisticate's Progress," *Harper's Magazine,* 150 (March 1925), p. 301.

13. Irvin Edman, "How To Be Sweet Though Sophisticated," *Century,* 117 (Jan. 1929), p. 331.

14. Krutch, pp. 81, 162.

15. Krutch, pp. 159–60.

16. Krutch, p. 13.

17. Krutch, p. 13.

18. Barzun, p. 128.

19. Barzun, p. 117.

20. Krutch, p. 138.
21. Russell, p. 722.
22. Krutch, p. 151. Italics Mine.
23. Krutch, pp. 81–82. Italics are Krutch's.

The Robber Bridegroom

American Fairy Tale Lionel Trilling[*]

Eudora Welty's little fairy-tale novel has been greeted with considerable reserve. The reviewers have given it the respect obviously due a book by the author of "A Curtain of Green," and they have expressed great admiration for its prose. But most of them have been disappointed, and some of them have attributed Miss Welty's lack of success to the impossibility or the impropriety of what she has tried to do. For "The Robber Bridegroom" translates the elements of European fairy tales into the lore of the American frontier—its princess is a Mississippi girl who gathers pot herbs at the edge of the indigo field, its mild father-king is a planter, its bridegroom with a secret that must not be pried into is a river bandit, its giant is the fabulous flatboatman Mike Fink, its Rumpelstiltskinesque creature of earth is a white-trash boy, its spirits of air are Indians.

It seems to me that we cannot judge on principle the possibility or the propriety of this transmogrification. To be sure, there is a hint of quaintness in the conception; still, if it were well done it could be done, and if it has not been well done by Miss Welty it might yet be done by someone else who thought it worth trying. But what I find disappointing in the book is not its conception but its manner— exactly that element which has been generally exempted from blame, Miss Welty's prose. This is in the fashion of sophisticated Celtic simplicity—the jacket blurb speaks accurately of its connection with "The Crock of Gold"—and it aims at an added piquancy by introducing American idioms. It is sometimes witty, it is always lucid and graceful, and it has the simplicity of structure that is no doubt the virtue of modern prose. But its lucidity, its grace, and its simplicity have a quality that invalidates them all—they are too conscious, especially the simplicity, and nothing can be falser, more purple and "literary," than conscious simplicity. This is prose whose eyes are a little too childishly wide; it is a little too conscious of doing something daring and difficult. Miss Welty is being playful and that is perfectly all right, but she is also aware of how playful she is and that is

[*] Reprinted with permission from the *Nation*, 19 December 1942, 686–87. Copyright 1942 by The Nation Company, Inc.

31

wearisome. She has used the manner of a secret archly shared but (ah!) even more archly not shared, for although she seems to have attached no specific meanings to her fantastic episodes, the whole work has the facetious air of having a profound meaning for herself. In short, she has written one of those fabrications of fantasy which have so tempted two other gifted women of our time—Elinor Wylie with her "The Venetian Glass Nephew" and her "Mr. Hazard and Mr. Hodge," and Virginia Woolf with her "Orlando," very artful and delicate works, very remote and aloof, though passionately connected, in secret ways, with the lives of the authors themselves, and very exasperating in their inevitably coy mystification.

Eudora Welty's Parody   Marilyn Arnold°

Those of us who regularly read and reread Eudora Welty find ourselves asking just as regularly, what is she up to in *The Robber Bridegroom?* There have been some helpful discussions on that work in recent years,[1] but Welty's purpose in writing it nevertheless keeps eluding us. We might be persuaded that she wrote the book for pure enjoyment; she has admitted that writing it was fun, filled as it is with things "I've liked for as long as I can remember."[2] Granted, *The Robber Bridegroom* gives Welty a chance to romp happily through countless fairy tales, innumerable pieces of folklore, and a variety of myths, but it is surely more than an exercise in literary virtuosity. In this narrative of romance and terror along the Natchez Trace, Welty uses scores of stock fairy tale devices and even the fairy tale form itself, a form which by her own declaration is antithetical to good fiction. She has said in no uncertain terms that "there are only four words, of all the millions we've hatched, that a novel rules out: 'Once upon a time.' " Those words, she says, "make a story a fairy tale by the simple sweep of the remove—by abolishing the present and the place where we are, instead of bringing them to us. Fiction is properly at work on the here and now. . . ."[3] Thus, Welty has apparently set out deliberately to write what is by her own definition a non-novel, a book that, as a fairy tale, cannot be significant fiction. The question is, why would she do that?

I have begun to suspect that *The Robber Bridegroom* is not so much an attempt to imitate the fairy tale as it is an attempt to create a parody of the fairy tale. With incredible skill, Welty manipulates

° Reprinted with permission from *Notes on Mississippi Writers* 11 (Spring 1978):15–22. Copyright Notes on Mississippi Writers, 1978.

the form to make it mock itself. But then the question arises, could Welty do that to something she loved as much as she loved fairy tales? My answer is yes, if she thought today's adult readers and writers were believing and perpetuating the inherent lies which fairy tales tell about human life and experience. Delightful as fairy tales are, they are not great fiction; they are not the stuff life is made of. And sometime, we as readers and writers must mature beyond the simplistic, if tantalizing, life-view presented in fairy tales. What better way to reveal the shallowness of fairy tale vision than to expose that shallowness through parody?

A quick plot summary demonstrates to some degree how much Welty relied on fairy tale form and material in writing her book. The story opens when Clement Musgrove, a wealthy but innocent planter, and Jamie Lockhart, a handsome dandy and secret bandit, meet on a stormy night. They are forced to share lodgings with a legendary Mississippi flatboatman named Mike Fink. Jamie learns with great interest of Clement's wealth, eagerly accepting the planter's invitation to dine with Clement and to meet his beautiful daughter Rosamond, and his second wife, the greedy Salome. Jamie and Rosamond, however, meet sooner than Clement had expected. As she is gathering herbs in the woods one morning, he appears in his berry-stain disguise and robs her of her clothing. The next day at dinner, Rosamond acts so silly and appears so disheveled that Jamie does not recognize her, nor does she recognize his unstained face. The following morning he snatches Rosamond away on his magnificent horse, Orion, and robs her of more than her clothing. Discovering that she loves the bold bandit, Rosamond voluntarily takes up residence with Jamie and his robber gang in the woods. Clement, believing she has been kidnapped, searches frantically for her, even engaging Jamie in the search by promising Rosamond to him in marriage. Jamie agrees, craving her inheritance, not knowing that his sweetheart of the woods is actually the lost Rosamond. After many trials, including threats from Indians and rival bandits, Rosamond and Jamie are finally safely wed in New Orleans. The book is fairly jammed with fairy tale stage properties— wicked stepmother, mistreated daughter, talking bird, magic horse, hidden cottage, difficult tasks, handsome hero and heroine, secret potion, and so on.

Welty's parody works simultaneously on several fronts as she introduces complexities of character, plot, action, tone and theme unheard of in fairy tales. Using what appear on the surface to be standard characters and motifs, Welty creates standard expectations in the reader; but she does not fulfill them. Instead, she subverts, reverses, burlesques, and just generally scatters asunder the fairy tale's sacrosanct notions about the agenda for happily-ever-after living. Among the cherished fairy tale doctrines which *The Robber Bride-*

groom cheerfully demolishes is the idea that wealth, position, and "royal" marriage are the highest expressions of human happiness, and that personal worthiness is inevitably rewarded with such plums. In fairy tales wealth is the answer to all of life's problems. The most valuable things are made of gold—golden fish, golden lilies, golden foals, golden children, golden hair, golden fruit, golden rain, golden dresses, golden kingdoms. Not so in Welty's tale. Instead of winning the princess and the kingdom as one prize, Welty's hero gets the princess only after he willingly abandons the kingdom. Welty insists that the hero's desire for wealth and position is evidence of a flawed character; the prize he should rightly seek is human understanding.

Another doctrine taught implicitly in fairy tales is that clarity is always possible, that good and evil are easily distinguished, and that people can be readily defined and labeled. Welty pretends to follow the fairy tale pattern by adopting a simple manner, by allowing her characters to assume that there are simple solutions to life's problems, and by labeling these characters in fairy tale fashion as "the innocent Clement and the greedy Salome and the mad Little Harp and the reproachful Rosamond."[4] It is clear that for Welty, however, life's complexities cannot be sidestepped by the writer of fiction. *The Robber Bridegroom,* in spite of what it appears to do at first glance, actually says implicitly what Welty has said explicitly in an essay: "Great fiction, we very much fear, abounds in what makes for confusion; it generates it. . . . It is very seldom neat, . . . is capable of contradicting itself. . . . There is absolutely everything in great fiction but a clear answer." She says further that the fiction writer simply cannot "set people to acting mechanically or carrying placards to make their sentiments plain. People are not Right and Wrong, Good and Bad, Black and White personified." Human beings "have to be treated as real, with minds, hearts, memories, habits, hopes, with passions and capacities like ours." Therefore, she says, and this is crucial, "novelists begin the study of people from within." They must "throw away the labels."[5]

On nearly every page of *The Robber Bridegroom* Welty undercuts the pat-answer world of the fairy tale. Jamie Lockhart is not the single-minded, morally pure fairy tale hero. Both handsome lover and greedy bandit, he is caught in the ambiguities of his own nature. Typically seeing things in terms of either-or, insisting that "there is nothing midway" about most matters, Jamie is unwilling to face his own doubleness. Poor Clement Musgrove decides that he cannot risk killing the bandit for fear of destroying the bridegroom. Rosamond, too, is not the simple, forthright person we expect as heroine of a fairy tale. Beautiful and loving, she is also an incurable liar and a scheming wife. Clement, who *is* simple and forthright, nevertheless has to learn through terrible suffering that easy labels and easy answers hide rather than reveal truth. Nature teaches him that evil cannot be defeated in an open battle as it often is in fairy tales, and it teaches him that ambiguity abounds. He observes that men on the Mississippi can be "arrogant by day," yet "wakeful and dreamless by night," in a time when "all is first given, then stolen away." He cries in anguish, "Wrath and love burn only like the campfires. And even the appearance of a hero is no longer a single and majestic event like that of a star in the heavens, but a wandering fire soon lost" (p. 143).

While Jamie and Rosamond and Clement learn something about accepting life's ambiguities, Salome clings to her either-or fairy tale mentality and is destroyed. On a rampage to ensnare Jamie, she cries, "Punishments and rewards are in order!" The Indians are able to capture her because "her eye, from thinking of a golden glitter, had possibly gotten too bright to see the dark that was close around her now, and while she scanned the sky the bush at her side came alive, and folded her to the ground" (pp. 144–145).

Perhaps the clearest indication that *The Robber Bridegroom* is a parody of the fairy tale lies in Welty's treatment of the romance between Jamie and Rosamond. The two of them have all the physical characteristics and even many of the adventures of fairy tale lovers, but their courtship and marriage would be an absolute scandal in any proper fairy tale. The first time Jamie and Rosamond meet he is interested only in the monetary value of her clothing, so he steals her clothes and leaves her naked. Thus dishonored, a true fairy tale heroine would probably beg for death, and Jamie gives Rosamond that virtuous option. But Rosamond, caring nothing for fairy tale niceties, replies, ". . . before I would die on the point of your sword, I would go home naked any day" (p. 50). The second time they meet, Jamie rapes Rosamond, an event which clearly disqualifies them as fairy tale lovers. The third time they meet, Rosamond is a mess— unrecognizably dirty from house and yard chores, careless in serving dinner, mustard-stained on her mouth. No southern Cinderella, she is not discovered by her prince. Nevertheless, our expectations rise when Rosamond finds the robbers' cabin where Jamie lives. Fairy tales and fairy tale fiction have trained us to suppose that now the two will marry and live happily ever after. Not so. They live together without the benefit of marriage vows, and Rosamond fabricates an ingenious wedding story to ease her father's mind.

Granted, Welty surrounds Jamie and Rosamond with a degree of felicity while they are living together in the woods, but, again, she does this in order to laugh all the more effectively at simplistic fairy tale notions of romance. The lovers are scarcely living alone in marital bliss. In fact, they share quarters with Jamie's whole band of dirty, rowdy robbers for whom the blushing "bride" must cook and sew and clean. The pair are separated and captured by Indians, and in constant jeopardy from Little Harp as well. Finally, in a devastating shock to fairy tale propriety, Welty tells us that Rosamond is pregnant. The prospective mother catches up with Jamie and a preacher just "in the time's nick" (p. 181). Whoever heard of a fairy tale heroine delivering twins just moments after her wedding?

As if her point were not already solidly made, Welty also creates a loony subplot that is clearly a parody of the principal love affair, producing, in effect, a double parody. Little Harp, an ugly, crude caricature of Jamie the robber chief, decides that he too must have a bride. Salome's grotesque mercenary, Goat, sees an opportunity to marry off one of his sisters and brings her to Little Harp. Their "courtship" is a riot of comedy and terror.

Surely the serious writer has something to say that fairy tales simply never say, and Welty's aim is to publish their deficiency. She very pointedly refuses to punish or even seriously acknowledge some of the lovers' most obvious sins, sins that would merit ample attention in a fairy tale. In describing the rape scene, for example, Welty says only that Jamie "robbed her of that which he had left her the day before" (p. 65). Fornication and cohabitation are largely ignored. Rosamond's lying is treated more as a delightful quirk of personality than as a serious flaw. Jamie's banditry is never very real. Whatever standard sins her characters may commit, it is faithlessness and lack of trust in human relationships that Welty condemns. Her parody of the fairy tale focuses on the problems of human relationship that complicate great fiction, a subject that the authentic fairy tale consistently ignores and a subject which Welty insists is basic to fiction. In "Must the Novelist Crusade?" she says emphatically that "morality as shown through human relationships is the whole heart of fiction, and the serious writer has never lived who dealt with anything else" (p. 105).

Rosamond and Jamie love each other, but they hide their identities from each other, fearing to extend trust with their love or make permanent commitments to each other. They also exercise power over each other in threatening ways—he by reminding her that he is pledged to a wealthy heiress for whom he might leave her at any time, she by warning him that one squawk from her could bring six bold brothers and a fierce father upon his head. Rosamond is so curious about Jamie's identity that, like Psyche, she risks losing him to learn who he is. And Jamie, like Cupid, values the secret of his identity so much that he deserts Rosamond once she learns it. Both have much to learn about human trust and understanding; and in the course of the book, they do learn—she "that names were nothing and untied no knots" (p. 150), he that Rosamond means more to him than money or name or reputation.

That Welty's first priority is concern over how human beings treat each other becomes still more evident in her delightful parody of the standard fairy tale device of "natural morality."[6] Since in fairy tales nature is often a sensitized field which reacts hostilely to the presence of evil, we might expect that after Rosamond's apparently enjoyable loss of virtue, nature would react harshly to her. But when Rosamond enters the woods the next day, nature is instead lush and wonderful and kind. Even things that might at first glance seem threatening turn out to be benign. So long as Rosamond acts out of love and faith, nature smiles upon her; but when she violates Jamie's trust and plots with the evil Salome to learn his identity, nature becomes fearsome and hostile. As she enters the woods with an evil design in her heart, she feels alone and afraid. She stumbles, her hair gets tangled by a whirlwind, the squirrels shriek, and the air turns cold. Rosamond loses her Eden not when she loses her maidenly virtue, but when she conspires against someone who loves her.

Once the idea that *The Robber Bridegroom* is a parody of the fairy tale begins to tease the mind, then everything in the book seems to support that interpretation—the rich, figurative language that renders fairy tale rhetoric pale by comparison; the rollicking humor that seems to mock the self-seriousness of the fairy tale;[7] the recognition that the dark side of experience is something to be valued and accepted rather than defeated and dismissed;[8] the somewhat tentative ending that sends Clement on his way alone and reveals that Rosamond has not been completely cured of her lying (". . . it was all true but the blue canopy"); the bold stroke that collides crude American folk characters and humor, not to mention Indians, with every fairy tale a person could call up at one sitting; and finally, the relentless insistence that people and circumstances can change by degrees, a fact unrecognized by the fairy tale, which lives in a world where change is instantaneous and externally wrought.

If *The Robber Bridegroom* is indeed a parody, and I think it is, it is probably the warmest and most loving parody ever written. No writer has ever loved her subject more or exposed its limitations more tenderly. The fairy tale, of course, has never pretended to be great fiction, but some of us have pretended that it represents a valid system of morality and tells the truth about human experience. Eudora Welty is simply reminding us, in every way she can think of, that it does not.

Notes

1. See Charles C. Clark, *"The Robber Bridegroom:* Realism and Fantasy on the Natchez Trace," *The Mississippi Quarterly,* 26 (Fall 1973), 625–638, and Gordon E.

Slethaug, "Initiation in Eudora Welty's *The Robber Bridegroom*," The *Southern Humanities Review*, 7 (Winter 1973), 77–87. For years, except for Eunice Glenn's discussion in Allen Tate's *A Southern Vanguard*, the book was largely ignored, though Faulkner spoke of it some years ago as "the worthwhile one" of Welty's books (see Frederick L. Gwynn and Joseph L. Blotner, eds., *Faulkner in the University*, p. 24).

2. Robert van Gelder, "An Interview with Eudora Welty," *New York Times Book Review* (June 14, 1942), p. 2.

3. "Place in Fiction," *Three Papers on Fiction* (Northampton, Mass.: Smith College, 1962), p. 2.

4. *The Robber Bridegroom* (New York: Atheneum, 1963, first published 1942), p. 147. All citations are from this edition.

5. "Must the Novelist Crusade?" *Atlantic*, 206 (October 1965), 105.

6. Alfred and Mary Elizabeth David, in "A Literary Approach to the Brothers Grimm," *Journal of the Folklore Institute*, 1 (1964), 183–187, state that the Grimms saw nature as the "source of all good," that they believed in and incorporated into the tales they collected a "natural morality" in which nature is kind to the good but "punishes whatever is unnatural and evil."

7. In "Must the Novelist Crusade?" p. 105, Welty asserts that great fiction "is not impervious to humor."

8. Criticizing the crusader-novelist, Welty says that he errs in that his "blueprint for sanity and of solution for trouble leaves out the dark. (This is odd, because surely it was the dark that first troubled us.)," "Must the Novelist?" p. 106. The fairy tale does not leave out the dark, but does suggest that the dark is always evil and can invariably be overcome (and cast out) by good.

The Wide Net and Other Stories

Fiction in Review

Diana Trilling°

In her latest collection of short stories, *The Wide Net* (Harcourt, Brace, $2.50), Eudora Welty has developed her technical virtuosity to the point where it outweighs the uses to which it is put, and her vision of horror to the point of nightmare. Of course even in her earlier work Miss Welty had a strong tendency toward stylism and "fine" writing; she liked to move toward the mythical, and she had a heart for decay and an eye for the Gothic in detail. But she also had a reliable and healthy wit, her dialogue could be as normally reportorial of its world as the dialogue of Ring Lardner, and for the most part she knew how to keep performance subservient to communication; she told her story instead of dancing it, and when she saw horror, it could be the clear day-to-day horror of actual life, not only the horror of dreams. There was plenty of surrealist paraphernalia, if you will, in a story like "The Petrified Man"—the falling hair of the customer, the presence of the three-year-old boy amid the bobbie-pins and sexual confidences of the beauty parlor, the twins in a bottle at the freak show, or even the petrified man himself. But compare to "The Petrified Man" the story "Asphodel" from Miss Welty's current volume, with its Doric columns and floating muslins, its pomegranate stains and blackberry cordial and its "old goats and young," and you will recognize the fancy road up which Miss Welty has turned her great talents.

The title story of Miss Welty's new volume is its best story, but not typical. An account of a river-dragging party which starts out to recover the body of a supposed suicide but forgets its mission in the joys of the occasion, "The Wide Net" has its share of the elements of a tour de force, but it has more communicated meaning than the rest of the stories in the book, and it best fuses content and method. Of the six other stories "Livvie" is the only one which I like at all, and the only story, in addition to "The Wide Net," which I feel I understood. Yet the volume as a whole has tremendous emotional impact, despite its obscurity. However, this seems to me to be beside

° Reprinted with permission from the *Nation*, 2 October 1943, 386–87. Copyright 1943 by The Nation Company, Inc.

the point, for the fear that a story or a picture engenders is likely to be in inverse proportion to its rational content: witness the drawings of children or psychotics, or most of surrealist art; and Miss Welty employs to good effect the whole manual of ghostliness—wind and storm, ruined buildings, cloaks, horses' hooves on a lonely highway, fire and moonlight and people who live and ride alone. But the evocation of the mood of horror or of a dreamlike atmosphere has become an end in itself, and if, for each story, there is a point of departure in narrative, so that I can report, for instance, that "First Love" is about a deaf-and-dumb boy who falls in love with Aaron Burr, or that "Asphodel" is about a tyrannical half-mad Southern gentlewoman, or that "A Still Moment" is a legend of Audubon, still the stories themselves stay with their narrative no more than a dance, say, stays with its argument. This, indeed, is the nature of *The Wide Net:* it is a book of ballets, not of stories; even the title piece is a *pastorale macabre.*

Now I happen to think that to make a ballet out of words is a perversion of their best function, and I dislike—because it breeds exhibitionism and insincerity—the attitude toward narrative which allows an author to sacrifice the precise meaning of language to its rhythms and patterns. The word sincerity has lost caste in the criticism of serious writing, I know. But this seems to me unfortunate. We live in a very crafty literary period in which what aims to be art but is only artful is too often mistaken for the real thing. When an author says "Look at me" instead of "Look at it," there is insincerity, as I see it. The test of sincerity is wasted in the sphere of popular art, where criticism has sent it; most popular art is nothing if not sincere, and where it is not, it is usually because it is aping the manners of its betters. In these new stories Miss Welty's prose constantly calls attention to herself and away from her object. When she writes, ". . . Jenny sat there . . . in the posture of a child who is appalled at the stillness and unsurrender of the still and unsurrendering world," or "He walked alone, slowly through the silence, with the sturdy and yet dreamlike walk of the orphan," she is not only being falsely poetic, she is being untrue. How does the walk of an orphan differ in its sturdiness and in its dream quality from the walk of a child with two parents? How would you even explain "unsurrender" to a child, and wouldn't a child be appalled precisely by the *surrender* of the world, if the concept could reach him? This is the sin of pride—this self-conscious contriving—endemic to a whole generation of writers since Katherine Mansfield and most especially to the women of that generation.

Somewhere between Chekhov and Katherine Mansfield the short story certainly went off its trolley. I think it is Miss Mansfield who must be held responsible for the extreme infusion of subjectivism and private sensibility into the short fiction of our day. In Miss Welty's case the subjectivism takes the form, as I say, of calling attention to herself by fine writing; in stories for a magazine like the *New Yorker,* which happily has no taste for fine writing, the form it takes is rather more subtle—the calling of attention to oneself for one's fine moral perceptions. This is a point I shall develop next week in discussing several other current collections of short stories, including those of Sylvia Townsend Warner.

I have spoken of the ballet quality of Miss Welty's stories: In this connection I am reminded of the painter Dali and—via Dali— of the relationship between the chic modern department store and much of modern fiction. (One day I should like, in fact, to trace what I see to be the direct line of descent from Miss Mansfield to Bonwit Teller.) Although the suspicion intrudes itself that Dali works with his tongue in his cheek, Miss Welty's dedication is of course un-questionable: this should be said at once. Still, the resemblance in performance and the subtle cultural kinship between the two is striking. Both Dali and Miss Welty are mythologists and creators of legend, both take their metaphor from dreams, and yet both are devoted naturalists; and each has a mother-country—Dali, Spain; Miss Welty, the Natchez country—whose atmosphere and superstition permeate his work and whose confines are determining beyond the power of travel or maturer experience to enlarge them. Rather more suggestive, however, than these similarities is their common service to what amounts to a myth of modern femininity.

For if it seemed a strange day for both art and commercialism when Bonwit Teller engaged Dali to do its windows, actually it was not so revolutionary as it looked. In the making of modern myths, the American department store has been at least abreast of the American artist. The chic department-store mannequin is surely one of the great metaphors of our time; the displays of merchandise one of the great abstractions, based upon naturalism, of our art. But more fundamental, we recall the slogan created a few years ago by Bonwit Teller, "Have you that cherished look?" and we realize that it was the department store which stated most unmistakably (so unmistak-ably, indeed, that the slogan was dropped) the modern woman's dream of herself. Here in all its economic nakedness is the narcissism which is so widely supported in current female writing, including Miss Welty's. This mythologizing of the feminine self, whether by means of clothes or prose, is as far from femininity as from feminism.

There is now running in the magazines an advertisement for a Schiaparelli product, "Shocking Radiance," the illustration painted by Dali. "Shocking Radiance," it appears, is four oils—for the body, the face, the eyelids, and the lips—and to promote its sale Dali has painted a Venus rising from her shell, attended by a trio of sprites, one of whom pours a libation on her breast, while another holds before her the mirror of her self-regard. Even at the risk of satirizing Miss Welty's stories, I suggest a study of this Schiaparelli-Dali advertisement to see the *reductio ad absurdum* of the elements in Miss Welty's latest work which have no place in such a serious and greatly endowed writer.

The Love and the Separateness in Miss Welty
Robert Penn Warren[*]

> He could understand God's giving Separateness first and then giving Love to follow and heal in its wonder; but God had reversed this, and given Love first and then Separateness, as though it did not matter to Him which came first.—"A Still Moment."

If we put *The Wide Net,* Eudora Welty's present collection of stories, up against her first collection, *A Curtain of Green,* we can immediately observe a difference: the stories of *The Wide Net* represent a specializing, an intensifying, of one of the many strains which were present in *A Curtain of Green.* All of the stories in *A Curtain of Green* bear the impress of Miss Welty's individual talent, but there is a great variety among them in subject matter and method and, more particularly, mood. It is almost as if the author had gone at each story as a fresh start in the business of writing fiction, as if she had had to take a new angle each time out of a joy in the pure novelty of the perspective. There is the vindictive farce of "The Petrified Man," the nightmarish "Clytie," the fantastic and witty "Old Mr. Marblehall," the ironic self-revelation of "Why I Live at the P. O.," the nearly straight realism of "The Hitch-Hikers," the macabre comedy and pathos of "Keela, the Outcast Indian Maid." The material of many of the stories was sad, or violent, or warped, and even the comedy and wit were not straight, but if read from one point of view, if read as a performance, the book was exhilarating, even gay, as though the author were innocently delighted not only with the variety of the world but with the variety of ways in which one could look at the world and the variety of things which stories could be and still be stories. Behind the innocent delight of the craftsman, and of the admirer of the world, there was also a seriousness, a philosophical cast of mind, which gave coherence to the book, but on the

[*] Originally published in the *Kenyon Review* 6 (Spring 1944):246–59; reprinted in *Selected Essays* (Random House, 1958), 156–69. Copyright 1958 by Robert Penn Warren. Reprinted with permission of the author.

surface there was the variety, the succession of surprises. In *The Wide Net* we do not find the surprises. The stories are more nearly cut to one pattern.

We do not find the surprises. Instead, on the first page, with the first sentence, we enter a special world: "Whatever happened, it happened in extraordinary times, in a season of dreams . . ." And that is the world in which we are going to live until we reach the last sentence of the last story. "Whatever happened," the first sentence begins, as though the author cannot be quite sure what did happen, cannot quite undertake to resolve the meaning of the recorded event, cannot, in fact, be too sure of recording all of the event. This is coyness, of course; or a way of warning the reader that he cannot expect quite the ordinary direct lighting of the actual event. For it is "a season of dreams"—and the faces and gestures and events often have something of the grave retardation, the gnomic intensity, the portentous suggestiveness of dreams. The logic of things here is not quite the logic by which we live, or think we live, our ordinary daylight lives. In "The Wide Net," for example, the young husband, who thinks his wife has jumped into the river, goes out with a party of friends to dredge for the body, but the sad occasion turns into a saturnalian fish-fry which is interrupted when the great King of the Snakes raises his hoary head from the surface of the river. But usually, in the present stories, the wrenching of logic is not in terms of events themselves, though "The Purple Hat" is a fantasy, and "Asphodel" moves in the direction of fantasy. Usually the events as events might be given a perfectly realistic treatment (Dreiser could take the events of "The Landing" for a story). But in these cases where the events and their ordering are "natural" and not supernatural or fantastic, the stories themselves finally belong to the "season of dreams" because of the special tone and mood, the special perspective, the special sensibility with which they are rendered.

Some readers, in fact, who are quite aware of Miss Welty's gifts, have recently reported that they are disturbed by the recent development of her work. Diana Trilling, in her valuable and sobering comments on current fiction, which appear regularly in the *Nation*, says that the author "has developed her technical virtuosity to the point where it outweighs the uses to which it is put, and her vision of horror to the point of nightmare." There are two ideas in this indictment, and let us take the first one first and come to the second much later. The indictment of the technique is developed along these lines: Miss Welty has made her style too fancy—decorative, "falsely poetic" and "untrue," "insincere." ("When an author says 'look at me' instead of 'Look at it,' there is insincerity . . .") This insincerity springs from "the extreme infusion of subjectivism and private sensibility." But the subjectivism leads not only to insincerity and fine writing but to a betrayal of the story's obligation to narrative and rationality. Miss Welty's stories take off from a situation, but "the stories themselves stay with their narrative no more than a dance, say, stays with its argument." That is the summary of the argument.

The argument is, no doubt, well worth the close attention of Miss Welty's admirers. There is, in fact, a good deal of the falsely poetic in Miss Welty's present style, metaphors that simply pretend to an underlying logic, and metaphors (and descriptions) that, though good themselves, are irrelevant to the business in hand. And sometimes Miss Welty's refusal to play up the objective action—her attempt to define and refine the response rather than to present the stimulus—does result in a blurred effect. But the indictment does not treat primarily of such failures to fulfill the object the artist has set herself but of the nature of that object. The critic denies, in effect, that Miss Welty's present kind of fiction is fiction at all: "It is a book of ballets, not of stories."

Now is it possible that the critic is arguing from some abstract definition of "story," some formalistic conception which does not accommodate the present exhibit, and is not concerning herself with the question of whether or not the present exhibit is doing the special job which it proposes for itself, and, finally, the job which we demand of all literature? Perhaps we should look at a new work first in terms of its effect and not in terms of a definition of type, because every new work is in some degree, however modest, wrenching our definition, straining its seams, driving us back from the formalistic definition to the principles on which the definition was based. Can we say this, therefore, of our expectation concerning a piece of literature, new or old: that it should intensify our awareness of the world (and of ourselves in relation to the world) in terms of an idea, a "view." This leads us to what is perhaps the key statement by Diana Trilling concerning *The Wide Net:* she grants that the volume "has tremendous emotional impact, despite its obscurity." In other words, she says, unless I misinterpret her, that the book does intensify the reader's awareness—but *not* in terms of a presiding idea.

This has led me to reread Miss Welty's two volumes of stories in the attempt to discover the issues which are involved in the "season of dreams."[1] To begin with, almost all of the stories deal with people who, in one way or another, are cut off, alienated, isolated from the world. There is the girl in "Why I Live at the P. O."—isolated from her family by her arrogance, meanness, and sense of persecution; the half-witted Lily Daw, who, despite the efforts of "good" ladies, wants to live like other people; the deaf-mutes of "The Key," and the deaf-mute of "First Love"; the people of "The Whistle" and "A Piece of News," who are physically isolated from the world and who make their pathetic efforts to reestablish something lost; the travelling-salesman and the hitch-hikers of "The Hitch-Hikers" who, for their different reasons, are alone, and the travelling-salesman of "Death of a Travelling Salesman" who, in the physically and socially isolated backwoods cabin, discovers that he is the one who is truly isolated; Clytie, isolated in family pride and madness and sexual frustration, and Jennie of "At the Landing," and Mrs. Larkin of "A Curtain of Green," the old women of "A Visit of Charity" and the old Negro woman of "A Worn Path"; the murderer of "Flowers for Marjorie" who is cut off by an economic situation and the pressure of that great city; Mr. Marblehall in his secret life; Livvie, who, married to an old man and trapped in his respectable house, is cut off from the life appropriate to her years; Lorenzo, Murrell, and Audubon in "A Still Moment," each alone in his dream, his obsession; the old maids of "Asphodel," who tell the story of Miss Sabina and then are confronted by the naked man and pursued by the flock of goats. In some of the cases, the matter is more indirectly presented. For instance, in "Keela, the Outcast Indian Maid," we find, as in "The Ancient Mariner," the story of a man who, having committed a crime, must try to re-establish his connection with humanity; or in the title-story of *The Wide Net,* William Wallace, because he thinks his wife has drowned herself, is at the start of the story cut off from the world of natural joy in which he had lived. "The Petrified Man" and "A Memory" present even more indirect cases, cases which we shall come to a little farther in the discussion.

We can observe that the nature of the isolation may be different from case to case, but the fact of isolation, whatever its nature, provides the basic situation of Miss Welty's fiction. The drama which develops from this basic situation is of either of two kinds: first, the attempt of the isolated person to escape into the world; or second, the discovery by the isolated person, or by the reader, of the nature of the predicament. As an example of the first type, we can remember Clytie's obsessed inspection of faces ("Was it possible to comprehend the eyes and the mouth of other people, which concealed she knew not what, and secretly asked for still another unknown thing?") and her attempt to escape, and to solve the mystery, when she lays her finger on the face of the terrified barber who has come to the ruinous old house to shave her father. Or there is Jennie, of "At the Landing," or Livvie, or the man of "Keela." As an example of the second type, there is the new awareness on the part of the salesman in "The Hitch-Hikers," or the new awareness on the part of the other salesman in the back-country cabin. Even in "A Still Moment" we have this pattern, though in triplicate. The evangelist Lorenzo, the outlaw Murrell, and the naturalist and artist Audubon stand for a still moment and watch a white heron feeding. Lorenzo having seen a beauty greater than he could account for (he had earlier "accounted for" the beauty by thinking, "Praise God, His love has come visible"), and with the sweat of rapture pouring down from his forehead, shouts into the marshes, "Tempter!" He has not been able to escape from his own obsession, or in other words, to make his definition of the world accommodate the white heron and the "natural" rapture which takes him. Murrell, looking at the bird, sees "only whiteness ensconced in darkness," and thinks that "if it would look at him a dream penetration would fill and gratify his heart"—the heart which Audubon has already defined as belonging to the flinty darkness of a cave. Neither Lorenzo nor Murrell can "love" the bird, and so escape from their own curse as did, again, the Ancient Mariner. But there remains the case of Audubon himself, who does "love" the bird, who can innocently accept nature. There is, however, an irony here. To paint the bird he must "know" the bird as well as "love" it, he must know it feather by feather, he must have it in his hand. And so he must kill it. But having killed the bird, he knows that the best he can make of it now in a painting would be a dead thing, "never the essence, only a sum of parts," and that "it would always meet with a stranger's sight, and never be one with the beauty in any other man's head in the world." Here, too, the fact of the isolation is realized: as artist and lover of nature he had aspired to a communication, a communion, with other men in terms of the bird, but now "he saw his long labor most revealingly at the point where it met its limit" and he is forced back upon himself.

"A Still Moment," however, may lead us beyond the discussion of the characteristic situation, drama, and realization in Miss Welty's stories. It may lead us to a theme which seems to underlie the stories. For convenience, though at the risk of incompleteness, or even distortion, we may call it "Innocence and Experience." Let us take the case of Audubon in relation to the heron. He loves the bird, and innocently, in its fullness of being. But he must subject this love to knowledge; he must kill the bird if he is to commemorate its beauty, if he is to establish his communion with other men in terms of the bird's beauty. There is in the situation an irony of limit and contamination.

Let us look at this theme in relation to other stories. "A Memory," in *A Curtain of Green,* gives a simple example. Here we have a young girl lying on a beach and looking out at the scene through a frame made by her fingers, for the girl can say of herself, "To watch everything about me I regarded grimly and possessively as a need." (As does Audubon, in "A Still Moment.") And further: "It did not matter to me what I looked at; from any observation I would conclude that a secret of life had been nearly revealed to me. . . ." Now the girl is cherishing a secret love, a love for a boy at school about whom she knows nothing, to whom she has never even spoken, but whose wrist her hand had once accidentally brushed. The secret love had made her watching of the world more austere, had sharpened her demand that the world conform to her own ideas and had created a sense of fear. This fear had seemed to be realized one day when, in the middle of a class, the boy had a fit of nose-bleed. But that is in the past. This morning she suddenly sees between the frame of her fingers a group of coarse, fat, stupid, and brutal people disporting themselves on the sand with a maniacal, aimless vigor which comes to climax when the fat woman, into the front of whose bathing suit the man had poured sand, bends over and pulls down the cloth so that the lumps of mashed and folded sand empty out. "I felt a peak of horror, as though her breasts themselves had turned to sand, as though they were of no importance at all and she did not care." Over against this defilement (a defilement which implies that the body, the breasts which turn to sand, had no meaning), there is the refuge of the dream, "the undefined austerity of my love."

"A Memory" presents the moment of the discovery of the two poles—the dream and the world, the idea and nature, innocence and experience, individuality and the anonymous, devouring life-flux, meaning and force, love and knowledge. It presents the contrast in terms of horror (as do "The Petrified Man" and "Why I Live at the P. O." when taken in the context of Miss Welty's work), and with the issue left in suspension, but other stories present it with different emphases and tonalities. For instance, when William Wallace, in "The Wide Net," goes out to dredge the river, he is acting in terms of the meaning of the loss of his wife, but he is gradually drawn into the world of the river, the saturnalian revel, and prances about with a great cat-fish hung on his belt, like a river-god laughing and leaping. But he had also dived deep down into the water: "Had he suspected down there, like some secret, the real true trouble that Hazel had fallen into, about which word in a letter could not speak . . . how (who knew?) she had been filled to the brim with that elation that they all remembered, like their own secret, the elation that comes of great hopes and changes, sometimes simply of the harvest time, that comes with a little course of its own like a tune to run in the head, and there was nothing she could do about it, they knew—and so it had turned into this? It could be nothing but the old trouble that William Wallace was finding out, reaching and turning in the gloom of such depths." This passage comes clear when we recall that Hazel, the wife who is supposed to have committed suicide by drowning, is pregnant: she had sunk herself in the devouring life-flux, has lost her individuality there, just as the men hunting for the body have lost the meaning of their mission. For the river is simply force, which does not have its own definition; in it are the lost string of beads to wind around the little negro boy's head, the cat fish for the feast, the baby alligator that looks "like the oldest and worst lizard," and the great King of the Snakes. As Doc, the wise old man who owns the net, says: "The outside world is full of endurance." And he also says: "The excursion is the same when you go looking for your sorrow as when you go looking for your joy." Man has the definition, the dream, but when he plunges into the river he runs the risk of having it washed away. But it is important to notice that in this story, there is not horror at the basic contrast, but a kind of gay acceptance of the issue: when William Wallace gets home he finds that his wife had fooled him, and spanks her, and then she lies smiling in the crook of his arm. "It was the same as any other chase in the end."

As "The Wide Net," unlike "A Memory," does more than merely present the terms of contrast, so do such stories as "Livvie" and "At the Landing." Livvie, who lives in the house of wisdom (her infirm husband's name is Solomon) and respectability (the dream, the idea, which has withered) and Time (there is the gift of the silver watch), finally crosses into the other world, the world of the black buck, the field-hand, in his Easter clothes—another god, not a river god but a field god. Just after Solomon's death, the field-hand in his gorgeous Easter clothes takes Livvie in arms, and she drops the watch which Solomon had given her, while "outside the redbirds were flying and criss-crossing, the sun was in all the bottles on the prisoned trees, and the young peach was shining in the middle of them with the bursting light of spring."

If Livvie's crossing into the world of the field god is joyous, the escape of Jennie, in "At the Landing," is rendered in a different tonality. This story assimilates into a new pattern many of the elements found in "A Memory," "The Wide Net," "Livvie," and "Clytie." As in the case of Clytie, Jennie is caught in the house of pride, tradition, history, and as in the case of Livvie, in a house of death. The horror which appears in "A Memory," in "Clytie," re-appears here. The basic symbolisms of "Livvie" and especially of "The Wide Net" are again called into play. The river, as in "The Wide Net," is the symbol of that world from which Jennie is cut off. The grandfather's dream at the very beginning sets up the symbolism which is developed in the action:

> The river has come back. That Floyd came to tell me. The sun was shining full on the face of the church, and that Floyd came around it with his wrist hung with a great long catfish. . . . That Floyd's catfish has gone loose and free. . . . All of a sudden, my dears— my dears, it took its river life back, and shining so brightly swam through the belfry of the church, and downstream.

Floyd, the untamed creature of uncertain origin, is William Wallace dancing with the great catfish at his belt, the river god. But he is also, like the buck in "Livvie," a field god, riding the red horse in a pasture full of butterflies. He is free and beautiful, and Jennie is drawn after him, for "she knew that he lived apart in delight." But she also sees him scuffling playfully with the hideous old Mag: the god does not make nice distinctions. When the flood comes over the Landing (upsetting the ordered lives, leaving slime in the houses), Floyd takes her in his boat to a hill (significantly the cemetery hill where her people are buried), violates her, feeds her wild meat and fish (field and river), and when the flood is down, leaves her. She has not been able to talk to him, and when she does say, "I wish you and I could be far away. I wish for a little house," he only stares into the fire as though he hadn't heard a word. But after he has gone she cannot live longer in the Landing; she must set out to find him. Her quest leads her into the woods (which are like an underwater depth) and to the camp of the wild river people, where the men are throwing knives at a tree. She asks for Floyd, but he is not there. The men put her in a grounded houseboat and come in to her. "A rude laugh covered her cry, and somehow both the harsh human sounds could easily have been heard as rejoicing, going out over the river in the dark night." Jennie has crossed into the other world to find violence and contamination, but there is not merely the horror as in "Clytie" and "A Memory." Jennie has acted out a necessary role, she has moved from the house of death, like Livvie, and there is "gain" as well as "loss." We must not forget the old woman who looked into the dark houseboat, at the very end of the story, and understands when she is told that the strange girl is "waiting for Billy Floyd." The old woman nods, "and nodded out to the flowing river, with the firelight following her face and showing its dignity."

If this general line of interpretation is correct, we find that the stories represent variations on the same basic theme, on the contrasts already enumerated. It is not that there is a standard resolution for the contrasts which is repeated from story to story; rather, the contrasts, being basic, are not susceptible to a single standard resolution, and there is an implicit irony in Miss Welty's work. But if we once realize this, we can recognize that the contrasts are understood not in mechanical but in vital terms: the contrasts provide the terms of human effort, for the dream must be carried to, submitted to, the world, innocence to experience, love to knowledge, knowledge to the fact, individuality to communion. What resolution is possible is, if I read the stories with understanding, in terms of the vital effort. The effort is a "mystery," because it is in terms of the effort, doomed to failure but essential, that the human manifests itself as human. Again and again, in different forms, we find what we find in Joel of

"First Love": "Joel would never know now the true course, or the true outcome of any dream: this was all he felt. But he walked on, in the frozen path into the wilderness, on and on. He did not see how he could ever go back and still be the boot-boy at the Inn."

It is possible that, in my effort to define the basic issue and theme of Miss Welty's stories, I have made them appear too systematic, too mechanical. I do not mean to imply that her stories should be read as allegories, with a neat point-to-point equating of image and idea. It is true that a few of the stories, especially some of those in the present volume, such as "The Wide Net," do approach the limit of allegory, but even in such cases we find rather than the system of allegory a tissue of symbols which emerge from, and disappear into, a world of scene and action which, once we discount the author's special perspective, is recognizable in realistic terms. The method is similar to the method of much modern poetry, and to that of much modern fiction and drama (Proust, James, Kafka, Mann, Isak Dinesen, Katherine Anne Porter, Pirandello, Kaiser, Andreyev, O'Neill, for example); but at the same time it is a method as old as fable, myth, and parable. It is a method by which the items of fiction (scene, action, character, etc.) are presented not as document but as comment, not as a report but as a thing made, not as history but as idea. Even in the most realistic and reportorial fiction, the social picture, the psychological analysis, and the pattern of action do not rest at the level of mere report; they finally operate as expressive symbols as well.

Fiction may be said to have two poles, history and idea, and the emphasis may be shifted very far in either direction. In the present collection the emphasis has been shifted very far in the direction of idea, but at the same time there remains a sense of the vividness of the actual world: the picnic of "The Wide Net" is a real picnic as well as a "journey," Cash of "Livvie" is a real field-hand in his Easter clothes as well as a field god. In fact, it may be said that when the vividness of the actual world is best maintained, when we get the sense of one picture superimposed upon another, different and yet somehow the same, the stories are most successful.

The stories which fail are stories like "The Purple Hat" and "Asphodel" in which the material seems to be manipulated in terms of an idea, in which the relation between the image and the vision has become mechanical, in which there is a strain for atmosphere, in which we do find the kind of hocus-pocus deplored by Diana Trilling.

And this brings us back to the criticism that the volume "has tremendous emotional impact, despite its obscurity," that the "fear" it engenders is "in inverse ratio to its rational content." Now it seems to me that this description does violence to my own experience of literature, that we do not get any considerable emotional impact unless we sense, at the same time, some principle of organization, some view, some meaning. This does not go to say that we have to give an abstract formulation to that principle or view or meaning before we can experience the impact of the work, but it does go to say that it is implicit in the work and is having its effect upon us in immediate aesthetic terms. Furthermore, in regard to the particular work in question, I do not feel that it is obscure. If anything, the dream-like effect in many of the stories seems to result from the author's undertaking to squeeze meaning from the item which, in ordinary realistic fiction, would be passed over with a casual glance. Hence the portentousness, the retardation, the otherworldliness. For Miss Welty is like the girl in "A Memory":

> . . . from any observation I would conclude that a secret of life had been nearly revealed to me, and from the smallest gesture of a stranger I would wrest what was to me a communication or a presentiment.

In many cases, as a matter of fact, Miss Welty has heavily editorialized her fiction. She wants us to get that smallest gesture, to participate in her vision of things as intensely meaningful. And so there is almost always a gloss to the fable.

One more word: It is quite possible that Miss Welty has pushed her method to its most extreme limit. It is also possible that the method, if pursued much farther, would lead to monotony and self-imitation and merely decorative elaboration. Certainly, the tendency to decorate elaboration is sometimes present. Perhaps we shall get a fuller drama when her vision is submitted more daringly to the fact, when the definition is plunged into the devouring river. But meanwhile *The Wide Net* gives us several stories of brilliance and intensity; and as for the future, Miss Welty is a writer of great resourcefulness, sensitivity, and intelligence, and can probably fend for herself.

Notes

1. Limitation of space has prohibited any discussion of the novelette, *The Robber Bridegroom*, but I do not feel that it breaks the basic pattern of Miss Welty's work.

Historical Perspectives in "A Still Moment"

Pearl Amelia McHaney[*]

"A Still Moment," first published in 1942 and one of the eight stories of *The Wide Net* (1943), is one of Eudora Welty's historical fictions. The story is grounded in the lives of three historical characters: Lorenzo Dow, Methodist minister; James Murrell, bandit of the southwest; and John James Audubon, ornithologist and painter. Each traveling alone on the Natchez Trace, the three meet for a still moment as a white heron alights to feed and each man reflects on his life and future. After Audubon shoots the bird in order to paint its portrait, Dow and Murrell leave the clearing confused and still alienated.

In 1940–41 Welty was deeply immersed in reading and writing about the history of the Natchez Trace, and, with the encouragement of her agent Diarmuid Russell and her early editor John Woodburn, she completed her writing of *The Robber Bridegroom* in October 1940. Letters to Russell are filled with her enthusiasm for the local spirit and demonstrate that she was reading Robert Coates's *Outlaw Years,* Lorenzo Dow's journals, and books about Audubon and Aaron Burr.[1] An examination of Welty's possible sources and influences for "A Still Moment" illustrates how adept she is at the selection and adaptation of such historical detail. Its rich historical background also gives the still moment on the Natchez Trace a validity that makes the story all the more acceptable to readers who enjoy realistic fiction as opposed to metaphysical positing.

Initial considerations should focus on how and why Welty chose these particular "real" men as models for her characters. First, she was familiar with the travels and associations in the Natchez region of all three. For example, she found report of Murrell among the same information where she had encountered Mason, Hare, and the Harpe brothers for *The Robber Bridegroom.* She certainly was acquainted with the work of Audubon: he had traveled in the Natchez area and had taught art and dancing at Jefferson College and the Elizabeth Female Academy in Washington, Mississippi, just outside Natchez.[2] In fact, had her interest been particularly piqued for Audubon, she might even have viewed several of his bird sketches at the New York Historical Society during her school years at Columbia, 1930–31. Furthermore, MacMillan's edition of Audubon's *Birds of America,* published in 1937, had made his remarkable pictures available to the general public. Lorenzo Dow, who had had his journals

[*] This essay was written specifically for this volume and is published here by permission of the author.

published in the 1830s, had also frequented the Natchez country. Indeed, at one time Welty had intended to write a story just about Dow, and she had mused to Russell about the abundance of fascinating characters who had roamed the Trace.[3]

More specifically, *Mississippi: A Guide to the Magnolia State,* compiled and written by the Federal Writers Project of the Works Progress Administration as one of the *American Guide Series,* by its existence, its contents, and Welty's own work on it may have prompted her to combine the personalities of these three colorful men. As publicity agent for the WPA from 1933 to 1936, Welty had traveled throughout Mississippi taking photographs, and three of her pictures were published in the 1938 *Guide.* It is important to note that all three men are incorporated into this work, which served as a history of Mississippi as much as a tour guide. In the *Guide* itself, Lorenzo Dow receives the lengthiest treatment among Welty's trio: he is included among the "diviners, circuit riders, missionaries, itinerant evangelists and camp-meeting crusaders" who worked the Mississippi Frontier.[4] As a famous itinerant preacher he traveled throughout the "Natchez country, where, undaunted by rebuffs, he made up in zeal and resourcefulness what he lacked in education."[5] The work of "John James Audubon" and "the journal of Lorenzo Dow" are, in fact, even mentioned in the same sentence in the *Guide.*[6] Perhaps the visual juxtaposition of the two men's names helped to trigger Welty's later choice of characters for her historical story. Murrell, too, is mentioned in the *Guide,* grouped first with the other infamous southwestern outlaws, and then described more specifically: "In him the passion of the others rose high enough to envisage empire," a reference to the Mystic Rebellion mentioned in "A Still Moment."[7] Welty's story, of course, gives each man a much more complete treatment than the *Guide,* but since her familiarity with this work is accepted, and since no other obvious source published prior to "A Still Moment" mentions all three men, it is probable that her choosing these three particular personalities for a Natchez Trace encounter was influenced by the *Guide.*

Such a relationship is further supported by her mention of one of Dow's eccentric methods of evangelism illustrated in the *Guide:* a little Negro boy, hidden in a tree above the camp-ground crowds, was schooled to blow his tin horn in syncopation with Lorenzo's call for the Final Judgment.[8] This anecdote is recalled in "A Still Moment" by Welty's line, "they would all be gathered in by his tin horn blasts."[9] Further, Welty dramatizes two other incidents that the *Guide* only mentions: Lorenzo's flight from the Indians' entrapment and a Reverend Mr. Foster's concealment in the mud to evade Indians, which she attributes to Dow.

The stories in "A Still Moment" of Lorenzo's escape from the circle of Indians (also mentioned in the *Guide*), his Spanish race horse to be paid for in November, and the Roman-Irish taunts of "mind the white hat!" are adapted from Lorenzo Dow's journals. The horse reference and the Indian story even appear in consecutive entries. En route to Tennessee, Lorenzo records in entry 601, "I left my horse with brother Gibson, and took a Spanish race horse, which he was to be responsible for, and I was to remit him the money by post, when it should be due on my arrival in Georgia in November." The next entry concerns his escape from the Choctaw Indians: "602. June 20. [1803] . . . I set off alone, and rode the best part of twenty miles, when I saw a party of Indians within about a hundred feet of me: I was in hopes they would pass me, but in vain, for [they] surrounded me." Lorenzo considers a few alternatives, recalls God's protection during his trials in Ireland, and observes that the "Indians had ramrods in the muzzles of their guns . . . my horse started and jumped sideways . . . I gave my horse the switch, and leaned down on the saddle, so that if they shot I would give them as narrow a chance as I could to hit me, as I supposed they would wish to spare and get my horse."[10] Welty's adaptation makes Lorenzo more heavenly inspired in his escape. One senses, as Welty intends, the animated, passionate nature of the itinerant preacher who struggles to move beyond his human mortality.

A third borrowing from Lorenzo's journals concerns his second trip to Ireland in 1806. His first visit, from 31 October 1799 to 2 April 1801, had been to improve his health and to preach to the Irish. Since he was in Ireland without the consent of the Methodist Conference, fellow Methodists proved to be his enemies; they wished to dictate his work or to prevent him from speaking at all. For the second trip, on which he was accompanied by his wife, Peggy, Lorenzo's journal records an increase in both speaking engagements and physical harassments. On neither trip did Lorenzo find much sympathy from the Catholic Dubliners:

> 837. Tuesday, September 2d. [1806] The devil viewing the danger of his kingdom, began to work in the minds of the people, and to raise confusion and disturbance; however, on my return from meeting, I took a street out of my customary way, by which means I escaped the rabble, who were in pursuit: one of whom was heard to say, *"Now for the life of Lorenzo,"* another cried, *"mind the white hat."*[11]

It appears that Welty chose to borrow from this particular entry for ironic purposes. Lorenzo was usually dressed in drab, worn, black clothes. The white hat was a short-lived costume, perhaps abandoned after such episodes as mentioned above in which he was too easily recognized and taunted. Lorenzo's successful escapes from the Indians and from the angry mobs illustrate for him the belief that he was among God's chosen. Therefore, he pursues immortality, all the while acknowledging death as the entrance to God's Kingdom. Ironically, however, he flees both death and the mental anguish that his mortal quickness causes him. The only other mention of white garments for Lorenzo occurs in his record of a dream in which he appears robed in "white, fine unspotted linen" as one of God's angels at the door of a poor villager whose son in turn had dreamed of two angels instructing him to welcome an approaching traveler.[12] In his dream, Lorenzo is both the angel-messenger and the traveler—again, perhaps, a confusion of the contrary states that he valued so.

In addition to these specific details garnered from Lorenzo's journals, Welty seems to have gleaned an understanding of the itinerant preacher's sensibilities. The opening pages of the journals describe an earnest and bewildered young man suddenly struck by God's call to serve. He describes himself as "one wondering and benighted in an unknown wilderness, who wants both light and a guide" and goes on to reflect, in words appropriate to Welty's story, "Soon I became like a speckled bird, among the birds of the forest, in the eyes of my friends."[13] Lorenzo's sensitivity to nature, his love of birds, his dreams and voices are noted frequently in his journals. As in "A Still Moment," he seeks solace in the wilderness even while being confronted by the unknown therein. Once when he doubted his salvation he "loaded a gun, and withdrew into a wilderness."[14] In another passage, Lorenzo writes, "I dreamed that I was walking in the solitary woods beside a brook . . . I heard a voice over my head. . . ."[15] From these early pages of Lorenzo's journals, Welty apparently felt Lorenzo's passionate kinship with nature. She even uses the very images with which Lorenzo so frequently describes himself in his own journals. Perhaps the most startling incident he records is a boyhood memory that Welty is sure to have remembered from her reading: "One day I was the means of killing a bird, and upon seeing it gasp, I was struck with horror; and upon seeing any beast struggle in death it made my heart beat hard, as it would cause the thoughts of my death to come into my mind."[16] Welty translates the emotions Lorenzo then felt into the horror he feels when Audubon shoots the heron in "A Still Moment."

It is quite likely that in addition to Lorenzo's journals Welty was also familiar with Charles Coleman Sellers's biography *Lorenzo Dow: Bearer of the Word* (1928). From Sellers, Welty may have gleaned further suggestions for her characterization of Lorenzo. In two instances, Welty seemingly quotes directly from Sellers. In a sermon quoted by Sellers to demonstrate the highly charged, punctuated style of Lorenzo's delivery, Lorenzo shouts, "Man, who was an inhabitant of time; is now disembodied and become an inhabitant of eternity!"[17]

Welty uses the same phrase—"Inhabitants of Time!"—in "A Still Moment."[18] Also, as Welty tells the story of Lorenzo's unorthodox courtship and eventual marriage to Peggy Holcomb, she quotes his proposal, "Would she accept of such an object as him?"[19] This third person approach is taken from Sellers rather than from Lorenzo's own journal in which he records the proposal in the first person, "Do you think you could accept such an object as me?"[20] Sellers also reports that Lorenzo commonly sought counsel from dreams and voices,[21] as does Welty's character. Furthermore, the characterization of Lorenzo in "A Still Moment" is compatible with Sellers's descriptions of Lorenzo's appearance, mannerisms, sermon tricks, and wearying travel schedule.

Finally, Sellers makes an interesting conclusion about Lorenzo's name: "He always referred to himself as 'Lorenzo.' And indeed, the plebian Dow was frequently dropped from his name—an earthly clod unbefitting his unusual character."[22] Perhaps Sellers's observation and his own use of the evangelist's first name prompted Welty also to call Lorenzo by his first name alone.

For the characterization of Murrell, Welty probably had three sources in addition to the Mississippi *Guide:* the first is *The History of Virgil A. Stewart and his Adventures in capturing and exposing the great "Western Land Pirate,"* compiled by H. R. Howard, 1836; the second is *The Life and Adventures of John A. Murrell, The Great Western Land Pirate,* assumed to be by H. R. Howard, 1847, and containing essentially the same information as *The History of Stewart;* and the third is *The Outlaw Years: The History of the Land Pirates of the Natchez Trace,* by Robert Coates, 1930. All three detail the life of the criminal who traveled the Natchez Trace taking advantage of anyone he happened upon. Both Howard and Coates tell of Virgil A. Stewart's pursuit of Murrell in order to retrieve two stolen slaves owned by Stewart's Methodist friend Rev. Henning. After Stewart approaches Murrell on the trail, the outlaw strikes up an astonishing conversation, telling Stewart of the murders and thefts of a rogue who "directs the operations of the banditti . . ." and who "so paves the way to all his offences that the law cannot reach him."[23] Stewart's wilderness companion much later reveals himself as Murrell. Welty portrays the outlaw similarly, heightening the drama by making him "the silent man who would have done a piece of evil, a robbery or a murder, in a place of long ago," who tells his potential victim the story, "and it was all made for the revelation in the end that the silent man was Murrell himself."[24]

Several specific characterizations of the Murrell in "A Still Moment" appear in the legends recorded by Stewart and more recently by Coates. In 1832 Murrell was convicted of a single instance of horse theft. His sentence was a year's imprisonment, thirty lashes in public, and two hours a day in a pillory for three days. He was also "branded on the left thumb with the letters 'H. T.' in the presence of the Court."[25] Welty mentions the brand—for Horse Thief—as Murrell shades his eyes to study the white heron, but never reveals the meaning of the "H. T." The image of the "H. T." and the heron meld in his sight and confuse Murrell's dreams of what Welty calls the Mystic Rebellion, something a frenzied Murrell supposedly concocted during his year in jail, "that fantastic scheme of his, for the Mystic Confederacy and the negro rebellion."[26]

This "Mystic Rebellion"[27] also has some historical validity, although it seems to have been readily thwarted. As Murrell described the plan to Stewart, his clan of nearly "two thousand"[28] plotted

> to excite a rebellion among the negroes throughout the slave-holding states. Our plan is to manage so as to have it commence everywhere at the same hour. We have set on the 25th of December, 1835, for the time to commence our operations. We design having our companies so stationed over the country, in the vicinity of the banks and large cities, that when the negroes commence their carnage and slaughter, we will have detachments to fire the towns and rob the banks while all is confusion and dismay.[29]

Murrell's clan held elaborate ceremonies with sworn oaths and secret handshakes. "Many a noble plot was concerted"[30] in their headquarters, a lone cabin on an island in the Mississippi. In "A Still Moment" Welty recounts the rebellion through Murrell's vision:

> . . . he stood looking proudly, leader as he was bound to become of the slaves, the brigands and outcasts of the entire Natchez country, with plans, dates, maps burning like a brand into his brain, and he saw himself proudly in a moment of prophecy going down rank after rank of successively bowing slaves to unroll and flaunt an awesome great picture of the Devil colored on a banner.[31]

As a result of Stewart's testimony, Murrell was captured and sentenced to ten years for slave stealing, but the clan persevered and moved the date of the negro uprising up to 4 July 1835. Plantation by plantation the slaves would revolt, kill their masters, and regroup until they numbered enough to capture Natchez. Without Murrell leading them, however, the clansmen fumbled, argued, and failed. More than a dozen leading landowners, doctors, and tradesmen were exposed and hanged. Murrell himself survived his ten-year sentence and left prison a free but crazed man who disappeared from history.[32]

In "A Still Moment," as his opportunity to kill Lorenzo is interrupted by Audubon's appearance, Murrell remembers that "he had disguised himself once as an Evangelist, and his final words to his victim would have been, 'One of my disguises was what you are.' "[33] This frequent masquerading as a Methodist minister is documented by all three previously noted sources. Murrell had studied the Scriptures, and, after delivering sermons, he would accept offerings, pass or request change for counterfeit bills, and "borrow" fellow-preachers' horses or mules with the intent to make payment on his return circuit.

In his record of the confessions of Murrell, Stewart often notes Murrell's techniques of murder and theft on the Trace. Of one incident Murrell told Stewart, "As soon as he [the victim] fell, I drew out my knife and ripped open his belly and took out his guts. Then I scooped up a lot of sand, stuffed it in the vacant stomach and sunk the body in the creek."[34] Thus, as Welty's Murrell has a moment of remorse for his past he considers the evolution of time that would render "all these trees . . . cut down, and the Trace lost, then my Conspiracy that is yet to spread itself will be disclosed, and all the stone-loaded bodies of murdered men will be pulled up, and all everywhere will know poor Murrell."[35] In "A Still Moment" Murrell recognizes Time as his enemy, but historically he had no prescience of Virgil Stewart's revelation of the Western Land Pirate's plots.

Historians continue to debate the reality of the slave rebellion maneuvered by Murrell and a secret clan. Edwin Miles quotes the *United States Telegraph* of 24 September 1935 as acknowledging the goal of the insurrection to be one of *"plunder,"* not freedom for slaves.[36] However, Jonathan Daniels (*The Devil's Backbone: The Story of the Natchez Trace*, 1962) is quite skeptical of the existence of the rebellion. Daniels finds more truth in the conclusion of Mississippi historian J. F. H. Claiborne that Murrell and Stewart were both scoundrels and that Stewart invented his "confessions" as a personal revenge against Murrell.[37] A 1981 publication researched and written by James Lal Penick, Jr., argues that Murrell was not a clan leader at all, but rather a product of legend that has become accepted as history. Court records suggest that although Murrell was sentenced to be branded, that portion of the punishment was never actually carried out. Furthermore, Penick concludes that Murrell was worth more to others after his death and was more notorious in legend than he ever was in life.[38] Whether the Mystic Rebellion was fact or fiction in Murrell's time, it is certainly a real and vital part of the Natchez Trace lore that has been told and retold. Welty's use of Murrell as one of her characters for "A Still Moment" is grounded in both that local lore and the history of the Trace as Welty believed it. That which she reveals to us of Murrell may be fictional, but it does not contradict the legendary history.

Welty's depiction of John James Audubon also evolves from historical accounts of his character and actions. Audubon was no less a stranger to the Trace than was either Dow or Murrell. His story is recorded in his own journals and in his life work, *Birds of America*.

Originally printed as part of the volumes of *Birds,* Audubon's *Delineations of American Scenery and Character* was published separately in 1926. Also in separate editions, *Ornithological Biography, or an account of the habits of the birds of the United States of America* was published in five volumes from 1831 to 1839. These personal accounts of Audubon's adventures and efforts to find and paint his subjects and then to sell his bird portraits were most likely available for Welty's research. It is also important to remember that Macmillan's edition of *The Birds of America with an Introduction and Descriptive Text by William Vogt* was first published in 1937, five years prior to the publication of "A Still Moment." Vogt's legend for the "Snowy Egret," plate 242, notes that "when feeding, will stir mud vigorously with foot."[39] This clause's similarity to Welty's description, "When it feeds it muddies the water with its foot,"[40] strongly suggests her use of the Macmillan edition as a source. Some critics have erroneously attributed this information to Audubon himself, rather than to William Vogt's text for the Macmillan publication.

In addition to *The Birds of America* and Audubon's journalistic descriptions, two other sources appear likely for Welty's research. In 1917 Francis H. Herrick published the definitive *Audubon the Naturalist: A History of his Life and Time.* Ornithologists and historians regard this work as the most authoritative Audubon biography. Perhaps Herrick's most important contribution is the substantiation of Audubon's birth at Les Cayes, Santo Domingo, 26 April 1785, the natural son of Lieutenant Jean Audubon and a French Creole woman named Rabin. At various times the child was called Jean Jacques Fougere (French for "fern"), Jean Rabin, and of course, Jean Jacques (or John James) Audubon. He was formally adopted in Nantes, France, 1794, by his father, Jean Audubon, and his wife, Anne Maynet.[41] The legends of Audubon's birth and subsequent birthrights are nearly as renowned as his paintings. Reflecting this, the Audubon character in "A Still Moment" is greatly concerned with his origins and the rumors that he might be the Lost Dauphin of France. While Herrick's work seeks to eradicate such royal notions, Constance Rourke's biography *Audubon* (1936) nevertheless concentrates throughout on the possibility that the great ornithologist may have had an earlier claim to celebrity.

Rourke's first chapter is a lengthy discussion of Audubon's heritage, parentage, and names. Unlike other biographers who suggest failures or personal faults as the cause for Audubon's departure from France for America, Rourke offers his questionable parentage as reason enough. She notes that the lost Dauphin and Audubon are of "precisely the same age" and that "the small son of Louis XVI and Marie Antoinette was generally believed to have been spirited out of prison, and was said to be living obscurely in France, in England, or even

America." She quotes Audubon as saying, "My own name I have never been permitted to speak. . . . Accord me that of Audubon, which I revere, as I have cause to do"; and at another time, "Her name [an old boat sunk by storm on the Ohio] like mine, is only a shadow."[42] Mid-story, Rourke again interprets Audubon's doubts about his origins. Following bankruptcy, business failures, and the death of his father, Audubon, she says, "must have raised questions once more in his own mind and perhaps that of others as to his birth and early life, leaving him with a sense of uncertainty that was acute. Who was he? What were his true origins? And how could he emerge from the narrow possibilities that lay before him?"[43] Even in her final note after acknowledging Herrick's rather definitive statement of Audubon's birth, Rourke raises further queries and coincidental facts to keep the legend alive. The uncertain, ever-questioning Audubon depicted by Rourke is also the Audubon of "A Still Moment." He writes a journal, "not wanting anything to be lost the way it had been, all the past"[44]; he queries, "If my origin is withheld from me, is my end to be unknown too?"[45] Audubon seeks to "discover at last, though it cannot be spoken, what was thought hidden and lost."[46] Welty's thoughts for Audubon are mere hints of his preoccupation with his birthright: "Audubon in each act of life was aware of the mysterious origin he half-concealed and half-sought for. People along the way asked him in their kindness or their rudeness if it were true, that he was born a prince, and was the Lost Dauphin, and some said it was his secret, and some said that that was what he wished to find out before he died."[47] Although the doubtful, introspective figure of the Audubon of "A Still Moment" seems modeled after Rourke's characterization, Welty amplifies the particular, personal questions to universalize Audubon's ponderings.

Other particulars of the Audubon portrayed in "A Still Moment" appear to be historical also. "His long playing on the flute"[48] and the pictures drawn to communicate with the Indians are noted by Rourke.[49] In "A Still Moment," however, Audubon's entries "Only sorry that the sun sets" and "The Mocking Birds so gentle that they scarcely move out of the way" are quoted directly from his actual journals of 1821 and are not in Rourke.[50]

While Welty characterizes the Trace with various significant sounds, colors, and wildlife, clearly the most important animal of "A Still Moment" is the snowy heron. The *Birds of America* plate 242 is entitled "Snowy Egret" but is described "Snowy Heron or White Egret . . . Adult Male Spring plumage. Rice Plantation, South Carolina. 1835 . . . *Habitat:* Swamps and marshes." Although the evidence in "A Still Moment" suggests late summer or early fall as a time frame, "a plumicorn on its head, its breeding dress extended in rays"[51] does match the heron pictured in *Birds of America*. Also,

Welty's snowy heron is a female as Audubon "had thought it to be."[52] While the heron after which Audubon modeled his final portrait was studied in South Carolina and not Mississippi, Audubon describes another sighting in his snowy heron biography:

> While I was at Charleston, in March 1831, few had arrived from the Floridas by the 18th of that month, but on the 25th thousands were seen in the marshes and rice fields, all in full plumage . . . On the Mississippi they seldom reach the low grounds about Natchez, where they also breed, earlier than the period at which they appear in the Middle States.[53]

The rarity of the single snowy heron "out of its flock"[54] as far north and inland as the overgrown Natchez Trace is matched by the extraordinary meeting of the three travelers in "A Still Moment" beneath the "great forked tree."[55]

The initial choice of a heron for her story may have been suggested to Welty by the confessions of Joseph Thompson Hare, one of Murrell's fellow bandits of the southwest. Albert J. Devlin believes Hare's recorded vision of "a beautiful white horse, as white as snow, his ears stood straight forward, and his figure very beautiful,"[56] may be the germ for the snowy white heron of "A Still Moment." Devlin suggests that some aspects of Welty's Murrell are transposed from Hare's self-characterization, including their impostures as both ministers and devils to extract money from unsuspecting travelers.[57] Hare's confession also reveals that he and his fellow thieves hid in a cave described much like Cave-in-Rock. Unlike Murrell in the historical biographies or in "A Still Moment," however, Hare professes to be opposed to murder: "I told him [fellow thief] murder will out: that God never forgave a murder: that nobody ever led a quiet life, that had anything to do with murder."[58] While convincing evidence that Welty had read Hare's confession is not available, the "white horse" text is quoted by Coates in *The Outlaw Years,* which Welty had read. Devlin makes a strong argument that Hare's vision is a probable text for physical, but not thematic, suggestion for her character of the snowy heron. A possible inspiration for Welty's tone and stylistic description of the heron alighting has been suggested by Suzanne Marrs who has noted that an encounter of an ornithologist with a white heron as recorded in a 1936 issue of *Bird-Lore* bears remarkable resemblance to Welty's fictional moment on the Trace.[59]

The Birds of America introduction makes note of Audubon's "devotion to the swamps of the Mississippi valley."[60] This description is in accord with the portrayal of Audubon in "A Still Moment." As he appears to be a sensitive, dedicated artist, the reader may be shocked when the ornithologist kills the heron. Numerous sources, however, explain that Audubon habitually shot his birds like prey, then strung them up with twigs and wild flowers in order to achieve a lifelike, though stationary, model. He refused to stuff the birds, though that was his colleagues' common practice. The shooting in "A Still Moment" is somewhat foreshadowed when Audubon enters the Trace with "crayon and paper, a gun, and a small bottle of spirits"[61]; but the reader, like Audubon's two companions, is still surprised by the suddenly violent act of the man perceived to be the most passive of the story's trio.

Welty has remained historically accurate in much of her story: Lorenzo, Murrell, and Audubon are carefully drawn to agree with their own accounts of their lives. Also, historians recording the early years and personages of the Trace provide a wealth of detail from which Welty accurately and artistically selects. The sounds and sights, especially of the birds heard and seen, are believable. Only a few historical inconsistencies present themselves in "A Still Moment," and these are not significant. Lorenzo's wife, Peggy, did not reside in Massachusetts during his circuit days of absence, but in New York where her family had settled. Although Peggy's letter of acceptance of Dow's proposal certainly may have existed, it is not mentioned in either Dow's journals or Sellers's biography.

Some discrepancy also arises when Welty tries to assign a date to the story's setting. In a 1981 interview with Scot Haller for the *Saturday Review* she recalls "A Still Moment" as one of her favorite stories. She describes it as "the one about the three figures meeting in the woods, about Lorenzo Dow, John James Audubon, and Murrell the Bandit, back in 1798."[62] Her label for Murrell associates him with her studies of the Trace outlaws, but the date she erringly assigns the story is historically impossible: Lorenzo's travels in Mississippi were not until the early 1800s; Audubon would have been only thirteen and still in France; and Murrell was not born until 1804. The year 1798 is by coincidence the date Welty gives the events of *The Robber Bridegroom* when discussing the novel in her 1975 essay "Fairy Tale of the Natchez Trace."[63] In her autobiographical *One Writer's Beginnings*, Welty describes the scene of "A Still Moment" as "the Mississippi wilderness in the historic year 1811—'anno mirabilis,'" the year the stars fell on Alabama and lemmings, or squirrels perhaps, rushed straight down the continent and plunged into the Gulf of Mexico, and an earthquake made the Mississippi River run backwards and New Madrid, Missouri, tumbled in and disappeared."[64] In his journals Lorenzo also mentions the *anno mirabilis* and the destruction at New Madrid.[65] While 1811 is still an unrealistic date for Welty's story because of the birth dates of the three men, "A Still Moment" is yet another of the type of incredible occurrences that may have happened during the "*anno mirabilis*," and therefore 1811 is quite fitting for Welty to have chosen for the story's setting.

Although Welty chooses historical characters, selecting details from among the many available, her story is in no way bound to or inhibited by the historical framework. On the contrary, she successfully uses the history to enrich her story rather than to restrict it. Thus, in a 1965 interview Welty said, "In the course of my work [for the WPA and Mississippi Advertising Commission] I had to do a lot of reading on the Natchez Trace. I'm not a writer who writes fiction by research, but reading these primary sources, such as Dow's sermons, Murrell's diary and letters of the time, fired my imagination."[66] Source materials are discernible for each of the characters Welty has chosen for this auspicious moment on the Natchez Trace, and it is helpful to read these background works for what they add to the reader's awareness of Welty's skill in selection and dramatization of the real characters. But what is evident in the story is not that the characters are real or fictional, but that their passions and dilemmas are real.

In a 1972 interview in response to a question regarding the influence of any particular psychologists or philosophers (such as Freud or Jung), Welty insists that the writer's

> influences are by way of the imagination only. . . . I don't think any ideas come to you from other people's minds, when you're writing, as directives. You can't take hints and suggestions from this person and that to know where you're going. It's just outside the whole process of writing a story. . . . It doesn't mean that you haven't read things and understood things through reading and come to think things through reading that don't filter down and apply.[67]

Lest this emphasis upon imagination mislead us, Welty also avowedly takes care to place her characters in an appropriate time and place: "And I don't use anything that couldn't happen, that wouldn't be right for that part of the country or that kind of family, that time in history."[68] Welty appears to have been fully conscientious in creating the verisimilitude of "A Still Moment," and perhaps her use of historical persons demanded even more attention to details that could accompany or fill out her narrative than would have been the case with totally invented characters.

One larger question also deserves attention: why did Welty turn to historical characters during this period of her writing? In November 1940 Welty's future editor suggested she write "an entire book of Mississippi stories, some realistic, some in the unicorn-mood . . . ," and in a later correspondence dated 24 January 1941 he asks again for a future book ". . . on the Natchez Trace."[69] *The Robber Bridegroom,* written in 1940 and published in 1942, combined historical and fictional characters in a "Fairy Tale of the Natchez Trace." Furthermore, in February 1942 "First Love," a boy's dreamy admiration of Aaron Burr, appeared in *Harper's Bazaar;* again, as in *The Robber Bridegroom,* the characters were a combination of history and fiction. With excitement and anxiousness about her work with historical characters, Welty had written to Russell, "Do I have to have honest to goodness people?" They had already reveled together about Coates's *Outlaw Years,* and Welty had listed a cast of people from the Trace who fascinated her. As noted earlier, at one point she had intended to do "a story just about Lorenzo Dow himself."[70] "A Still Moment," first published in spring 1942, however, became a story of three fully historical characters: Welty chose to create a story of real personages only—with no entirely fictional character. Still, her own comment in *One Writer's Beginnings* that she invents her characters "along with the story that carries them"[71] would suggest that the notion of the chance meeting and the image of a heron had initiated the story, which in turn may have dictated her choice of characters. Welty further describes her story as "a fantasy, in which the separate interior visions guiding three highly individual and widely differing men marvelously meet and converge upon the same single exterior object."[72] She acknowledges that all the characters "were actual persons who had lived at the same time, who would have been strangers to one another, but whose lives had actually taken them at some point to the same neighborhood."[73] It would appear that following her model of *The Robber Bridegroom,* Welty was experimenting with another historical fantasy, the fairy tale influence in her early novel being replaced by a historical one. Though such observations do not altogether answer our question, they do substantiate that Welty at this point in her career consciously and purposefully used history in her stories.

The essence of a writer's objectives is to seek answers to man's meaning and existence, and Welty's approach in this fiction is to study the past. Welty notes several times in *One Writer's Beginnings* that it was only after her parents' deaths that she realized many truths about their feelings and motivations. Perhaps she wished to look into the history of the people and the region she knew, which was the background for characters she had already created, to understand what had made them as they were.

Welty believes in the strength and truth in the past, and in her essay on time in fiction she quotes Faulkner's theory: ". . . no man is himself, he is the sum of the past. There is no such thing really as was, because the past is. It is a part of every man, every woman, and every moment."[74] The validity of the past is more easily recognized than that of the present:

> Indians, Mike Fink the flatboatman [character in *The Robber Bridegroom*], Burr, and Blennerhassett [from "First Love"], John James

Audubon, the bandits of the Trace, planters, and preachers ["A Still Moment"]—the horse fairs, the great fires—the battles of war, the arrivals of foreign ships, and the coming of floods: could not all these things still move with their true stature into the mind here, and their beauty still work upon the heart?[75]

Referring to *The Robber Bridegroom,* Welty has written:

Fantasy is no good unless the seed it springs from is a truth, a truth about human beings. The validity of my novel has to lie in the human motivations apparent alike in the history of time and in the timeless fairy tale. In whatever form these emerge, they speak out of the same aspirations—to love, to conquer, to outwit and overcome the enemy, to reach the goal in view. And, in the end, to find out what we all wish to find out, exactly who we are and who the other fellow is, and what we are doing here all together.[76]

Specifically then, why does Welty use historical characters for "A Still Moment"? First, her choices lend verisimilitude to the story. She is already using a real place, the Natchez Trace, and she has said that she begins with place. It seems a logical followup to use historical characters, since so many are available. Certainly having three real people meet gives the story intrigue: Could it have truly happened? But back to our original consideration: Why Dow, Murrell, and Audubon? She had already written of Aaron Burr in "First Love," and of the Harpe brothers in *The Robber Bridegroom.* Many other travelers are recorded in Trace history and even in the *Mississippi Guide:* why not Joseph Hare instead of Murrell, if Hare's confession gave her an idea for the story's heron? Why not John McGrady, who painted Negro subjects; humorist A. B. Longstreet; Tobias Gibson, a rather militant Methodist, or Baptist Richard Curtis, both of whom lead Mississippi in its transition from Catholicism?[77] Any of these men might have been used for "A Still Moment." One wonders if Welty chose Dow, Murrell, and Audubon precisely because both the first- and secondhand source material that intrigued her was available.

Albert Devlin hypothesizes that Welty's choices evolve from the "historical crosscurrents of hope and despair"[78] in which the three men were caught during their individual years on the Trace. Careers, finances, ambitions, or personal goals put Lorenzo, Murrell, and Audubon in pivotal situations so that they were related not by physical time or place, but by mental state.

Other serendipitous connections among the men can be found. Both Lorenzo and Audubon had sought success in England after being disappointed in America where their peers and colleagues had failed to give them either moral or financial support. Murrell's mother was "married to an itinerant preacher who only waited for his absence to make money as eager whore and avaricious thief,"[79] and Murrell's disguises as a Methodist preacher are well substantiated. Audubon records an encounter with runaway slaves and later with the regulators who had caught the outlaw Mason,[80] illustrating that Audubon was familiar with the bandits of the Trace, if not with Murrell in particular. In addition, Audubon and Murrell are individually associated with Cave-in-Rock: Audubon had sketched it in 1820,[81] and on a 1911–14 map the cave is misnamed "Murrell's Cave," though Murrell's visits to the spot are not verifiable.[82] Beyond Coates's *Outlaw Years* and Dow's journals we do not know precisely what else Welty had read about Dow, Murrell, or Audubon. But this ultimately diminishes as a problem, because what evolves in "A Still Moment" is a constant refining of the relationships within the fictional triad. It is not important whether or not these three could have met historically. In fact, in "A Still Moment," Welty herself writes, "No one could say the three had ever met, or that this moment of intersection had ever come in their lives."[83] Indeed, it can be verified that the three were not traveling the Trace at the same time, and certainly Welty was aware of this. In fact, she probably would not have wanted them to be "available" for a historic meeting. Her story is, finally, fiction, not biography.

What is important is whether or not the reader can believe Welty's incident, accepting the time, place, and people chosen by Welty to tell her tale. Her premise is that a real place gives the story "actuality" and that believing the place to be real, the reader can then accept the story itself. Of place in the novel, Welty has written, "The moment the place in which the novel happens is accepted as true, through it will begin to glow, in a kind of recognizable glory, the feeling and thought that inhabited the novel in the author's head and animated the whole of his work."[84] We can safely conclude that in this regard "A Still Moment" is successful. The reader requires little suspension of disbelief to accept the occurrences on the Trace that day and to enjoy the glow of feeling and thought that shines through it. The reader does not need to know more about Audubon, Murrell, or Dow to enjoy or to understand the story, but his understanding and enjoyment are both enhanced by the available background information. No doubt a completely separate story might have been successfully told with three fully imaginary characters, but Welty enriches her art by using what was historically "available" to her Natchez Trace setting in the early nineteenth century.

Notes

1. Michael Kreyling, "The Benevolent Intermediary: Diarmuid Russell, Eudora Welty's Literary Agent," Symposium: Eudora Welty: Eye of the Storyteller, Akron, Ohio, 18 September 1987 (proceedings to be published).

2. *Mississippi: A Guide to the Magnolia State*, Federal Writers Project of the Works Progress Administration (New York: Viking Press, 1938), 333, 335.

3. Kreyling, "Benevolent Intermediary."

4. *Mississippi*, 115.

5. Ibid., 115–16.

6. Ibid., 139.

7. Ibid., 85.

8. Ibid., 116.

9. Eudora Welty, "A Still Moment," in *The Collected Stories of Eudora Welty* (New York: Harcourt, Brace, Jovanovich, 1980), 191.

10. Lorenzo Dow, *The Dealings of God, Man, and the Devil, as Exemplified in the Life, Experience, and Travels of Lorenzo Dow* (Norwich: Wm. Faulkner, 1833), 115, 116.

11. Ibid., 235–36.

12. Ibid., 85.

13. Ibid., 11.

14. Ibid., 12.

15. Ibid., 22.

16. Ibid., 29.

17. Charles Coleman Sellers, *Lorenzo Dow: Bearer of the Word* (New York: Minton, Balch and Company, 1928), 131.

18. "A Still Moment," 191.

19. Ibid., 190.

20. Dow, *Dealings of God*, 179.

21. Sellers, *Bearer of the Word*, 32, 91.

22. Ibid., 74.

23. H. R. Howard, *The History of Virgil A. Stewart* (New York: Harper and Bros., 1836), 18.

24. "A Still Moment," 192.

25. Robert M. Coates, *The Outlaw Years: The History of the Land Pirates of the Natchez Trace* (New York: The Literary Guild of America, 1930), 238.

26. Ibid., 239.

27. "A Still Moment," 195.

28. Howard, *History of Stewart*, 60.

29. Ibid., 54–55.

30. Ibid., 89.

31. "A Still Moment," 195.

32. Coates, *Outlaw Years*, 301.

33. "A Still Moment," 194.

34. Coates, *Outlaw Years*, 214; see also 186 and Howard, *History of Stewart*, 66, 106.

35. "A Still Moment," 196.

36. Edwin A. Miles, "The Mississippi Slave Insurrection Scare of 1835," *Journal of Negro History* 42 (January 1957):60.

37. Jonathan Daniels, *The Devil's Backbone* (New York: McGraw-Hill, 1962), 245.

38. James Lal Penick, Jr., *The Great Western Land Pirate: John A. Murrell in Legend and History* (Columbia: University of Missouri Press, 1981), 20, 30–31.

39. John James Audubon, *The Birds of America* (New York: Macmillan Company, 1937), plate 242.

40. "A Still Moment," 196.

41. Francis H. Herrick, *Audubon the Naturalist: A History of His Life and Time*, vol. 1 (1917; rpt. New York: Dover Publications, 1968), xxix.

42. Constance Rourke, *Audubon* (New York: Harcourt, Brace and Company, 1936), 9.

43. Ibid., 131.

44. "A Still Moment," 194.

45. Ibid., 195.

46. Ibid.

47. Ibid., 197.

48. Ibid., 194.

49. Rourke, *Audubon*, 10, 77–78.

50. John James Audubon, *Journal of John James Audubon 1820–1821*, ed. Howard Corning (Cambridge, Mass.: The Business Historical Society, 1929), 121, 108.

51. "A Still Moment," 196.

52. Ibid., 197.

53. John James Audubon, *Ornithological Biography, or an account of the habits of the birds of the United States of America*, vol. 3 (Edinburgh: Adam Black, 1835), 317.

54. "A Still Moment," 195–96.

55. Ibid., 193.

56. Joseph Thompson Hare, *The Dying Confession of Joseph Hare*, 2nd ed. (Baltimore: [Edward J. Coole], 1818), 13.

57. Albert J. Devlin, "From Horse to Heron: A Source for Eudora Welty," *Notes on Mississippi Writers* 10, no. 2 (Winter 1977):65.

58. Hare, *Dying Confession*, 8.

59. Suzanne Marrs, "Eudora Welty's Snowy Heron," *American Literature* 53 (January 1982):723–25.

60. Audubon, *Birds*, v.

61. "A Still Moment," 194.

62. Scot Haller, "Creators on Creating: Eudora Welty," *Saturday Review*, June 1981, in *Conversations with Eudora Welty*, ed. Peggy W. Prenshaw (Jackson: University Press of Mississippi, 1984), 314.

63. Eudora Welty, *The Eye of the Story: Selected Essays and Reviews* (New York: Random House, 1978), 302.

64. Eudora Welty, *One Writer's Beginnings* (Cambridge, Mass.: Harvard University Press, 1984), 89.

65. Dow, *Dealings of God*, 292–94.

66. "An Interview with Eudora Welty," *Comment Magazine*, 16 October 1965, in Prenshaw, *Conversations*, 24. In reference to Murrell, Welty probably recalls Stuart's writings since Murrell himself left no diaries or letters.

67. Charles T. Bunting, " 'The Interior World': An Interview with Eudora Welty," in Prenshaw, *Conversations*, 58.

68. Bunting, "Interior World," 51.

69. This material was related in a letter from Noel Polk, 25 August 1983.

70. Kreyling, "Benevolent Intermediary."

71. *One Writer's Beginnings,* 99.

72. Ibid., 89.

73. Ibid.

74. Frederick L. Gwynn and Joseph L. Blotner, eds., *Faulkner in the University* (New York: Vintage Books, 1965), 84, and quoted by Welty in "Some Notes on Time in Fiction" in Welty, *Eye,* 171.

75. "Some Notes on River Country," in *Eye,* 299.

76. "Fairy Tale of the Natchez Trace," in *Eye,* 311.

77. *Mississippi,* 113.

78. Albert J. Devlin, *Eudora Welty's Chronicle: A Story of Mississippi* (Jackson: University Press of Mississippi, 1983), 54.

79. Daniels, *Devil's Backbone,* 204.

80. John James Audubon, *Delineations of American Scenery,* ed. Francis Robert Herrick (New York: G. A. Baker, 1926), 20–21, 117–23.

81. Rourke, *Audubon,* 139, 70.

82. Otto A. Rothert, *The Outlaws of Cave-in-Rock* (1924; rpt. Freeport, New York: Books for Library Press, 1970), 318.

83. "A Still Moment," 196.

84. "Place in Fiction," in *Eye,* 121.

Delta Wedding

Delta Fiction
John Crowe Ransom°

Miss Welty's stature as an artist increases continually. We knew her last as the author of "The Wide Net" and its companion short stories, and very substantial these short stories were. She gave us rural characters who contrasted with the norms of their society by being earthy, and scandalous; they were pagans, descendants of the people in myths and folk-tales. Robert Penn Warren described their curious behaviors in this light. Their role was to retain the primitive attitudes to nature, and their vagaries were in the service of natural religion. Each was worth a good story. But not worth a novel; quaint characters become simply and painfully repetitious in a long narrative. And now, in her fourth book, we have from Miss Welty a full-length formal novel, with a content which is really capable of sustained presentation. She writes here according to some of the solidest canons of fiction.

The characters are so many as to confuse us at first, but soon they begin to compose with great clarity into what the English would call a county family. I should be prepared to suppose that a novel, ideally, is like an epic in that the individual actions are seen against the background of the cultus, the social establishment. Here a single family supplies that establishment, though the assumption would be that it is a representative family. The restriction greatly reduces the scope of the action as compared, let us say, with that of a novel by Jane Austen—who liked to take a simple theme but to involve in it a whole cluster of families. The plot has to do only with a wedding in the family, and the preparations and brief aftermath last but a week. Nor are the Welty characters turned out as handsomely as those in Austen. Indeed they are not English, they are Southern; they are the Fairchilds of that Deep South which is the Delta country of Mississippi. I am glad that Miss Welty did not want them aristocratic and picturesque, as if to perpetuate some tradition of Southern novelists, or as if to produce a commodity in characters fit to sell to some movie firm. They have a cotton plantation, and from their

° From the *Kenyon Review* 8 (Summer 1946), 503–7. Copyright by Kenyon College. Reprinted with permission of the author's daughter and the *Kenyon Review*.

71

economic status follows a certain social status. The time, however, is 1923, not eighty years earlier.

What a family sense they have! They look at each other with little starts of love and understanding. They stop to be glad for their own happiness, and then for their faults and failures if necessary, confident that everything is according to the mysterious requirements of the family, as well as knowing that an unvarying beatitude might dull the sense for happiness, which has to run perilously close to the tragic sense. It is needless to remark that this is a woman's book— I don't think the same inference was prompted by the short stories— and a modern one. Miss Welty in her present phase resembles Virginia Woolf more than does any other novelist of my acquaintance; the Fairchilds' wedding is the perfect analogue for Mrs. Dalloway's party. I am sure the resemblance is fortuitous. Miss Welty's prose, like her people, is her own; it is every bit as clean as Virginia Woolf's, and if it is not quite so flexible it does not need the literary range of a Bloomsbury style. Both writers confer an extreme self-consciousness upon their characters when these have recourse to their interior monologue. A scene or action is doubly beautiful when the observer stops to register it in that sense; or perhaps becomes then truly beautiful, and bears an unexpected testimony to Kant's idea that first we take a spontaneous pleasure in the object, and only presently find the object beautiful when we introvert our attention and discover the pleasure it gave us. Being an admirer of the beauties thus attested in Mrs. Woolf's books, I admire also the autochthonous beauties now achieved similarly by our own writer. Both like to take firm possession of what is beautiful, though it has to be caught on the wing; as if this were what their civilizations had trained them for, and invited them to. Their technique, if it makes us think of Kant, reminds us also of Wordsworth, who was always memorizing in his verse some specimen moment of happiness which might go, so to speak, into his winter album.

The Fairchilds are a gentle, spirited, and interesting family, perfectly realized. If there seems to be a preponderance of females, that is lucky for the special grade of communication that has to be made to the reader. They even do most of the reporting upon the males, though it is not of the management of the plantation or the ordering of business that they tell, much less of political discussions. They show the objective contribution of the males to the scene and theatre of the piece; they even read and translate for us the masculine sensibilities, these being remarkably acute though not so fine as their own.

Since I have slipped into a dramatic locution, I must say that Miss Welty's narrative method is not technically dramatic. She passes continually back and forth between the drama of dialogue and external action, on the one hand, and interior monologue on the other. But the figure of drama occurs to me at this point as useful in another way. The Fairchilds have so much self-consciousness along with their naturalness that it is as if they were actors, and their common life the drama they enacted daily. They are brought up to have this sense of themselves, and it affects them with a certain sophistication, and a public responsibility. The Fairchild servants share it. So they all enact a comedy of love together. Each actor must improvise his lines, since the development of the action is never wholly of his determination and cannot be foreseen. But he knows he must register in the right tone, and give generous leads to the other actors. The language which they address to each other is not specially remarkable in any literary sense, but there are other ways than language in which to register dramatic effect. The total effect is complex and rich.

II

But we come now to a kind of critical sequel which is not comedy. It is certain that Miss Welty's book is going to meet with many animadversions; probably we could categorize them, the several varieties of them, in advance. And though my own admiration is explicit, I am going to admit to fears and reservations which distress me a great deal.

Her objectors will stand on the authority of American life as they know it. Some will not be able to give credence to her exhibit of so exotic a minority culture in action down in the South. Others will project themselves into it faithfully, but even if they find it not too disagreeable they will have to disapprove it on principle.

Perhaps I had better disclose that I must have lived more than as long if not as deep in the South as has Miss Welty, and spent besides some fifteen years at one time or another looking at the South from points outside it, i.e., *ex partibus infidelium.* These points may be vantage points for the critic; who accordingly may devote himself to problems in Southern life which in theory are extremely pressing, but in fact are far from irrupting incessantly into the consciousness of Southerners at home.

How can Miss Welty's Fairchilds afford to live so casually on their sensibilities, seizing expertly upon the charming experiences that life brings them yet apparently heedless of the moral and material shortcomings of their establishment? I have been careful to intimate that in the background of the Fairchild behaviors, if rarely brought to explicit attention, there is the sense of a material culture, i.e., an objective economic and social establishment. The planter family is a microcosm of the collective society. To its members their establishment seems strong enough, with provisions that are adequate in some fashion from day to day; it has been going a long time. There is no particular worrying about it, nor idea of overhauling it. But this is not the same as saying that it is really too early for them to be worrying, and even re-ordering; nor as saying that when they do begin on the repairs there will only be a little tinkering needed. It has been a favorite conviction of mine that there can hardly be an art of living where there is not moral and material security, like a capital fund stored up by original thrift. I have no doubt that the Fairchilds have a high art, but I am inquiring about what looks like the obsolescence of their capital investment.

It would be political sense which would look after this sort of investment. Now Miss Welty's characters have copious vitality but they do not waste it on politics. The energy they have put into sensibility is not available when presently they might be projecting new models for society. I believe this has always been the way of the South. Political interest is occasional; it is intense when a polity has to be founded, but afterwards only as emergency requires; it makes a formal recovery periodically at election times, when it proceeds cheerfully to delegate the routine of departmental government. And so far as I am concerned this is not a bad political philosophy, relegating politics as it does to a certain "place"; but only provided the political interest does not die of inanition over the interim periods, which is quite a proviso. In other words, I think politics is the means and not the end of life, like some other activities such as war, or even money-making, which it is barbarous to pursue beyond your need of them. This is not the occasion to argue that position, but I want to assure Miss Welty of one reader's philosophical rapport with her.

I feel sure that the pattern of Southern life as Miss Welty has it is doomed. The Delta establishment will be disestablished, and at a time not far off. Like any artist, Miss Welty must be given to pondering her literary strategy in the light of the climate of public discussion. Where will she find the material of her further novels? The time of *Delta Wedding* was 1923, but that is already long ago. Her reader will probably identify it as the time of her childhood— if ignorant of the biographical data on Miss Welty as I am—and the child Laura, who is one of the precocious juvenile reporters in fiction, as herself; and he might even conclude that there was no strategic conception behind this novel other than that Miss Welty was nostalgic for a kind of life that already had passed beyond recognition, and had to go back to it in imagination. But at any rate the mechanical cotton-picker had not been made and marketed then; nor had the mechanical cultivators broken into the cotton patch; they are among the instruments of revolution. Nor were relations between the black folk and the white folk strained as now, even in the Delta, they are coming to be. Both races accepted the Fairchild establishment; they had tolerances on both sides, and made mutual accommodations. But the distribution of the material benefits of this society was wholly arbitrary, even if strictly according to pattern, and the handsome sensibility of the Fairchilds was at the expense of the shabbiest kind of moral obtuseness. I expect the readjustment of racial relations in the South to be the more painful in the degree of its belatedness. But there will be many innovations, and all that cut deep into ancient habit will be painful.

In short, I am forced to wonder if *Delta Wedding* may not be one of the last novels in the tradition of the old South.

Delta Wedding as Region and Symbol
John Edward Hardy*

The reputation of Eudora Welty is beginning to outrun criticism of her work. We need something comprehensive in the way of a study, something less hasty than the review and something at once more objective and not so essentially condescending as the bon voyage essay. Wherever it was she was going, I think it will be generally agreed that Miss Welty has by now arrived—perhaps for the second or third time—and it would be no longer very discerning to treat the seasoned traveler as if she were the young Isabel Archer.

But, such is the nature of her work itself, a study that is to be really comprehensive must be most particular. We will have to take one thing—or one thing at a time, anyway. The Welty reader too should be lessoned with the characterizing refrain-phrase of E. M. Forster's little essay on Virginia Woolf—"one thing—one." And the one thing I want to consider here is *Delta Wedding*. A great many critics seem to think that Miss Welty is at her best in the shorter forms; and perhaps she feels so too, to judge from the continued emphasis of her work. But this novel, it seems to me, is not only still the biggest thing, but still the most rigidly restricted, disciplined. It has most characteristically developed that sense of the symbolic particularity of things, of a place and a time and people, which can make the good regionalist the most universal of artists—or of novelists, at any rate. It is the most "one"—whole.

I mean to suggest, then, that the most important thing about the novel is its formal structure. But if the nature of its design has,

* From *Sewanee Review* 60 (Summer 1952):397–417. Copyright 1952 by The University of the South. Reprinted with permission of the editor.

perhaps, escaped many readers, the reasons are not hard to find. There is considerable prejudice against a "serious" novelist's treating material of this kind with such an attitude of sympathy as Miss Welty assumes. Certainly it was obvious from the start, to a reader with any sensitivity at all, that *Delta Wedding* was not simply another Mississippi plantation, "historical" novel, designed for a bosom-and-columns dust jacket. But, if the author's irony is felt from the first sentence, its essence is very subtle. And the patience of a good many of the liberal reviewers a few years ago was pretty short.

If Miss Welty wasn't starry-eyed in quite the usual way about "the South," she wasn't indignant either, or even decently tough and realistic now and again. She had distinctly her own version of what Wyndham Lewis called Faulkner's "whippoorwill tank"; but it might have seemed only unfortunately less manageable than his. The novel *was,* after all, historical—that its time was only about twenty and not seventy-five or a hundred years past was calculated to allay suspicion only slightly. Few eyebrows were raised particularly over the treatment of the Negroes in the novel; but they might well have been. The darkies were sometimes just a little too charmingly typical. And where the attitude went beyond one of placid acceptance—this remains, I think, one of the most genuinely distressing flaws of the novel—it often became only half-heartedly apologetic, with a rather strong suggestion of the old "well, at least they had *status*" routine. What Miss Welty could do with Negroes at her best in some of the short stories seemed rather sadly absent here. And one could go only so far in justifying it on grounds of dramatic propriety, that the author was bound to the point-of-view of the white characters of the story; simply for purposes of realism, it might easily have been made a little *more* apparent how severely restricted that outlook was in this regard.

And yet the immediate inferences from all this are, clearly, not correct. And perhaps the best way of getting at *why* they are not correct is simply to allow the novel to establish for itself the per-spective in which we are to look at its features.

One has first to see that Miss Welty is not taking *any* attitude toward "the South." The story is about the Delta, at the most—not the South, not even Mississippi. Yankees, of course, are unthinkable; but Ellen, the Virginian, is acutely conscious all her life of *her* difference from the Delta family she mothers. And the circle is drawn even closer; Troy Flavin, who is largely responsible for the significance of the wedding as a symbol of threatened disruption, is alien by virtue of being a *hill-country* Mississippian. And (disregarding for the moment Laura McRaven, whose case is rather special), Robbie Reid, whom the family wisely regard as a far greater threat to the insularity of their world even than Troy, is foreign as a native of the *town* of Fairchilds, as distinguished from the plantation.

The psychological basis of the relationship of the characters one to another here is simple enough, of course. The barrier between Robbie Reid and the Fairchilds is greatest for several reasons—simply that she is a woman, that she is the unworthy wife of the darling of the family, but most important of all, that she *is* a lifelong near neighbor. In any society, of course, class distinctions are always, though ironically, most keenly appreciated by native members of the immediate community. Troy Flavin, not so much out of mere stupidity as simply because his origins are more remote, finds nothing so terribly formidable in the family he is "marrying into"—as he puts it with a confidence which dismays and amuses those who know the Fairchilds. And in the face of his naïve assurance, the family are fairly constrained to be gentle with him, though they make little effort to hide their feelings from Dabney. But the point I want to make just now is that this narrowing of the circle is carried so far that it finally excludes emphasis upon the kind of typicality, the true provincialism, in character and situation, which is characteristic of the commonplace regional novel. The Fairchilds are finally most typical, if at all, in their very singularity. And it is at this point that the principle of exclusiveness almost ceases, or for the reader's purposes in understanding the novel ought almost to cease, to be a social principle at all. It becomes, rather, the *formal* principle, and the principle of sensibility, in a version of pastoral which has been before only vaguely hinted at in the Southern novel.

Miss Welty's awareness of the classic elements of pastoral in the situation she is dealing with is quite evident. One may take as an initial statement of the conventional "paradox" of pastoral, the familiar principle of inversion of values, one of Laura's early reflections— "Jackson was a big town, with twenty-five thousand people, and Fairchilds was just a store and a gin and a bridge and one big house, yet she was the one who felt like a little country cousin when she arrived. . . ."

But it is just the awareness it reveals which is most important about a passage like this. What it says, the statement of the pastoral "formula" in these terms, is only a starting point. The tradition of the Southern novel has been all but exclusively pastoral from the start, of course—and in a great many different ways, both naturalistic and romantic. But there has been before no such fully *conscious* exploring of the implications of the mode as Miss Welty's, an insight which finally carries beyond the significance of the form for the *mores* of the society which produced it.

(Something of this sort—its wit, its merging of realism and magic, its delicacy, its formal and elegiac ironies, its universal mythiness, and basic to all the rest its struggle between anonymity and self-consciousness—is inevitable toward the *end* of any cycle of pastoral. And the reader might well have to go back to the Sixteenth and Seventeenth centuries of English literature for instructive parallels.)

Miss Welty's depiction of the Delta society and its structure, of the family as the typical unit of that society, is studiedly accurate, right, always in substance and, with the exception of a few distressing lapses into an over-precious style, nearly always in tone. The rightness of it meets the test of communication certainly even to the reader unfamiliar with the actuality. And the structure of the society, in the pattern of the novel as well as in fact, clearly produces and supports the kind of hyper-developed individuality which the characters severally manifest. But it is one of the basic paradoxes of the novel—one of which several of the characters are keenly aware—that the strength of the society to support is entirely the dynamic of the personality's constant and tireless struggle with it. And the center of interest, finally, is in the exercise of entirely private sensibilities—not so much in the relationships abstractly as such among the various people, as in the way in which each person privately *sees* those relationships.

Indeed, at the beginning of the novel, and again qualifiedly at the end, it is not even people and their relationships which are *seen*—but *things,* rather. Laura comes into the Delta country with the bemused aloneness of the adventurer into an enchanted forest. Other people, as people, are secondary realities—the signs of their existence, to the extent that she is aware of them at all, becoming talismans of a significance entirely private to her, the ticket she had stuck in her hat band, "in imitation of the drummer across the aisle." It is things that are most alive—the fields, the train itself becoming a creature of the fields. And then the train "seemed to be racing with a butterfly."

The vision is not quite ecstatic. The sun which in its sinking momentarily obliterates the most basic distinction—"all that had been bright or dark was now one color"—is a real sun. It sinks, and Laura arrives, and is met by the Fairchild cousins, real, other people. The last word on Laura before the conductor cries "Fairchilds!" is simply that she "felt what an arriver in a land feels." And though there has been fair warning that the land is to be much more than a land—"the clouds were large . . . larger than anything except the fields the Fairchilds planted"; "the Delta buzzards . . . seemed to wheel as high and wide as the sun"; "the west was a milk-white edge, like the foam of the sea"—it is only a warning so far. There is no immediate plunge to that depth of the private consciousness in which the particular becomes the universal. If the reader constructs a cloud-cuckoo land here, it is his own doing. Miss Welty has no unrealistic intention of giving away her story in one lyric offering. Certain pertinent, practical facts stick in Laura's mind. She knows where she came from and where she is going and why. She is conscious of time—and her reality in it—she has been here before. (The fact that the visit, to "nature," out of the life of the city, is a *return,* functions similarly to the same fact in Wordsworth's *Tintern Abbey,* for example). Even in her vision of the immensity of the clouds it is not just the fields that they are compared to, but the fields "that the Fairchilds planted." The fields belong to them, and not simply as a matter of economics either, we are soon to discover. The myth is theirs too. The train was a legendary creature, it had its name of the Yellow Dog, in *their* consciousness before hers. Their baffling otherness, their exclusiveness possessiveness, threatens both to invade and to shut her out at every level of her sensibility.

But what we do get in this opening passage is just enough of the ecstatic to reassure us that Laura's personal emotional problem doesn't *matter* a great deal. (The reader is never permitted actually to "feel sorry" for Laura; the "poor Laura, little motherless girl" greeting which she anticipates has only a ritualistic solemnity, no real sadness). And, conversely, we are assured that the personal "problems" of the others aren't going to matter a great deal either—which, in turn, is further assurance on Laura's account. We get, in other words, the symbolic sense—we begin to see things with a great, though not quite a whole, measure of aesthetic distance (This, by the way, accounts I think for the time-setting of the novel. Aside from the fact that the early Twenties actually were a period of significant social and economic transition—the slight, but only slight, removal in time makes it easier for the author to put the emphasis just where she wants it, upon probability rather than upon the kind of mere possibility which our generation demands not only of the immediately contemporary novel but of the usual historical one as well.) The action takes on from the beginning, and never quite loses, even at the highest pitch of visual excitement, the somewhat cool, formal tone of the conscious pastoral.

One feels from the beginning that it is not actions, but reactions, which are to count. A few things do manage to happen in the course of the novel—Dabney and Troy do marry, Robbie comes back to George, it is decided that Laura will stay at Shellmound, at least for a time. But this is not a great deal, after all. And—the marriage is the most obvious example—it is perfectly clear that none of these things is of great moment in itself. The word "wedding" in the title is important. It is in a sense with the wedding, the ritual, not the marriage, that Miss Welty is concerned. The ritual sense is private, of course; the ceremony itself is passed over in a few words—"Mr. Rondo married Dabney and Troy." Mr. Rondo's status, the status of the church in the Fairchild world, perfectly defines the more than baronial self-sufficiency of the family, their superiority to any larger public, institutional significance of their affairs. But, private both in the sense that the family has its peculiar rituals and even more in the sense that each individual has his own in which the others do not participate, it is ritual nonetheless. There are no raw emotions in the novel—and little of a structure of personal involvements, conflicts, as we have observed, about the center of a "problem" which is carried through to some resolution in action. Nor is it that the story is actionless simply in the sense of being introspective—with much private examination of motives, intentions, much logical self-analysis. No one has time for much introspection in this usual sense. There is, in fact, a great deal *going on* all the time. But the incidents are important mainly as points of refraction, from which light is cast back upon various moments of symbolic perception in the minds of the several characters.

This is where Miss Welty is at her best, and where one has to start looking for the "meaning" of the novel, in the whole particularity of the moment, the single, illuminating, still act of private *perception*. It is where one has to look for the truth about the characters, severally. They don't communicate much of themselves to one another, however much they are in a sense involved with one another, and mutually dependent.

The thing is stated over and over again, this impregnable, at times reassuring, at times to one or another hopelessly baffling, privacy of the consciousness of every person, of the being of every thing which the consciousness entertains, even of every separate *moment* of consciousness. There are the various lights, with the obvious significance of light, especially of light *inside* something. The lamp which the aunts give to Dabney, a *night*-light, notably, itself an object of family tradition but, given to Dabney, becoming the prime symbol of her independence, her private rebellion of indifference when she carelessly breaks it, carrying out the theme of general disaster which the very flame itself, the intended source of light and comfort, draws out upon the shade—"The picture on it was a little town. Next, in the translucence, over the little town with trees, towers, people, windowed houses, and a bridge, over the clouds and stars and moon and sun, you saw a redness glow and the little town was all on fire, even to the motion of fire, which came from the candle flame drawing." The same lamp in India's perception, precious and cherished, but in infinite secrecy, and so again a symbol of impenetrable isolation, the magic circle of her privacy—"India made a circle with her fingers, imagining she held the little lamp"—the vessel of light filled, paradoxically, "with the mysterious and flowing air of night." The light on the back porch, when Shelley comes in alone for a moment away from the dancers, and "the moths spread upon the screens, the hard beetles knocked upon the radius of light like an adamant door," as she falls into musing; the light in her room, as she sits writing in her diary, with the beetle again clawing at the screen.

The various places of hiding and retreat. The seemingly innumerable rooms of the house itself. The wood in which Ellen walks, with its mysteriously ageless, directionless paths. The privilege, if it is a privilege altogether, is denied not even to the Negroes. Partheny, in the chinaberry-hidden fastness of her house in Brunswicktown, retiring into the undisturbed, unquestioned and unanswerable, mystery of her "mindlessness." Aunt Studney, with her jealously guarded sack that is to the children perhaps the source of life itself, the place where babies come from—her very existence hardly more, as the reader is permitted to perceive it, than a legendary creation of the family's very love of the eternal secret, than the name which puns her one, uncommunicative phrase—"Ain't studyin' you."

Or simply the sudden, isolated moments of private illumination. Dabney's ride in the morning, when she sees Marmion, sees it first *reflected* in the river, "and then the house itself reared delicate and vast, with a strict tower, up from its reflection," sees it defiantly and exultantly alone, "while they never guessed, she had seen Marmion . . . all had been before her eyes when she was all by herself." The loneliness of Laura, abandoned during the game of hide-and-seek, in which she perceives the necessity of George's isolation. "Then she saw Uncle George walk out of the house and stare out into the late day. She wanted to call out to him, but . . . something told her . . . that it was right for him to stand apart, and that when he opened an envelope in a room no one should enter. Now she felt matter-of-factly intimate with it, with his stand and his predicament."

Or, more definitive still, the sound of Mary Lamar Mackey's piano—the constant music which is a figure of the author's omnipresence, proceeding from an all but invisible source (we get only one brief close-up of Mary Lamar), only now and again distinctly heard at some chance pause in the activity, but always there. At a moment of tense silence during the first hours of Robbie's visit, Mary Lamar "was playing a nocturne—like the dropping of rain or the calling of a bird the notes came from another room, effortless and endless, isolated from them, yet near, and sweet like the guessed existence of mystery. It made the house like a nameless forest, wherein many little lives lived privately, each to its lyric pursuit and shy protection. . . ." The momentary perfection of the pastoral vision.

And it is this sort of thing, of course, that gives the novel its first appearance of disorder. The characters seem hopelessly unpredictable, their actions unmotivated and obscure, without intelligible issue; the transitions, from one scene to another, from the reflections of one character to another, appear entirely capricious. It would seem at first glance that Miss Welty has sacrificed an order of the whole entirely in the interest of an illusion of life in the details. But it ought to be apparent from the very symbols, and symbolic instances, of the privacy of consciousness given here, that there is order of a kind. The lives, the thoughts, of all the characters are intensely private—but because they are ritualistic too, and ritual is always inevitable, they fall into patterns which transcend the privacy, with or without the consciousness of the particular character. And, if the characters themselves are not often conscious of the pattern, the author is clearly conscious of it. It emerges, beyond its inevitability, as a principle of deliberate and controlled artistry, in an order of *recurrence* which informs the whole action of the novel. The order of the novel is a poetic order—of recurrent themes, symbols, and motives of symbolic metaphor. And it must be close-read, as a poem.

Perhaps the thread nearest the center of the design is that of the story, told and re-told, again and again reflected upon and alluded to, of George and Maureen on the railroad trestle. Certain reasons for the importance of the story to the Fairchilds are immediately apparent. It was just after the incident on the trestle that Troy and Dabney had "gone on up the railroad track and got engaged"—thus beginning the latest threat to the solidarity of the Fairchild world. It was then that Robbie Reid, providing the climax to the story with her accusation, "George Fairchild, you didn't do this for *me!*," brought into the open the whole complex of bitter feelings which the Fairchilds entertain for this earlier, and even more significant than Dabney's, "bad match"—their resentment at the love of poor, common little Robbie for George, George who is the universally acknowledged, living embodiment of their ideal of Fairchild man, their infuriated amusement at her daring to intrude the voice of her "rights" even against his defense of what is even more holy to the Fairchilds than George or any *living* thing, the memory of the dead Denis. Robbie's thinking of herself at that moment, her indignation at George's willingness to sacrifice himself for the semi-idiotic Maureen, defines perfectly for the Fairchild *women* especially her hopeless failure to understand their vision of themselves—and their investment of that vision in Denis, of whom nothing remains but his daughter Maureen, the crazy Virgie Lee, a few vague stories and a little pathetic "poetry," but who in their minds is the more dignified by the "tragedy" of indignities, and who finally is beyond reproach (as even George cannot be) simply by virtue of being dead, who as the symbol of the holy past is worthy of *any* sacrifice. Robbie's behavior at the trestle is all of a piece with the absurdity, the hopeless childishness, of her taunt that the Fairchilds are "not even rich!"—her failure to comprehend the myth of their aristocracy.

This much, then—beyond what is simply their love, aristocratically both pious and hilariously irreverent, for a *story,* any story, which involves the family—all the Fairchilds understand, in one way or another. They understand also something of how important it is that the train was the familiar Yellow Dog, the train that is almost itself their property—so that it *could not* actually have killed George (thus the whole thing became absurd enough for amusement), and yet, faithful servitor, provides enough of the thrill of danger, of death, for the purposes of their ritual.

Ellen, who retains enough of the attitude of an outsider always to see (or to have to see, to figure out consciously) a little more than the others, understands also what it meant for Robbie—she is a little daunted, even, seeing that Robbie has had a vision, a vision of *fact,* that makes the Fairchilds' prattling over their legend a little ridiculous. She understands that a train on that track *can* kill, that it has killed the astonishingly beautiful girl she met in the woods, and that if her daughters are spared it is only perhaps because they are *not* that beautiful, not beautiful enough to be heroines of a genuine tragedy. And she understands, finally, George's role in all of it. In a way that no one else can be, because no one else knows about the lost girl, she is at once both grateful and ashamed at the implications of George's constant sacrifice. She comprehends the simple fact that George is a man, that he has reacted simply as a man to the beauty of the girl when he "took her over to the old Argyle gin and slept with her." She understands that it is with his possession and his knowledge of such facts, literally the facts of life, that he defends the Fairchilds *against* the intrusion of fact, against all that comes, like the train, bearing down upon them. She suspects, perhaps, that the Fairchild women are vaguely aware of the condescension in his nobility, aware that he can *afford* to indulge them in their disparagement and ignorance of fact, the fact of the outside world which begins at Memphis, simply because he does know it so well and because the knowledge is supremely self-sufficient. She suspects that it is out of chagrin at this element of his attitude, at their own half-realized envy of his knowledge, his knowledge of life present and real, that they continue to shade his glory under the image of the dead Denis. She knows that he has worked the device of disparagement on her, in telling her what he has done with the girl, protecting *her* from too sudden a vision of what beauty it is (not the garnet pin!) that is lost in the wood, that she has lost and the world knows; but she knows also that George's act has *not* degraded the girl's beauty, that if anything it has enhanced it. In short, she knows George—George the unknowable.

But beyond all of this even, beyond Ellen's or all the characters' conscious experience of it together, the legend serves as a unifying force. Basically, the train and the bridge (trestle) are communication symbols. In Ellen's case, the relationships she discovers in the light of the incident result in the one most nearly perfect personal communication of the story. The separate incidents of the trestle episode itself and of her meeting with the girl in the wood are brought together in her mind, after the photographer has told the wedding party of the girl his train has killed on the way down from Memphis, in a single, comprehensive vision which opens the way to her wordless communication with George at the dance. But the most important significance of her experience in the whole purposes of the novel is not for our interest in her, her effort to know George personally; her insight is important, rather, simply as an example of the kind of structural relationships that are to be seen. We have to go on to see that the Yellow Dog is also the train that has brought Laura to Shellmound—still another visitant from the outside world, and a permanent one, since she is heiress to Marmion. It brings even the shepherd crooks, ironically, and other furnishings for the wedding, from Memphis. We have to see, further, that the symbols, characteristically, work both ways. That is, the legend for some means the failure of communication—for Robbie with the family, as we have seen, and for Shelley with Dabney, the engagement to Troy having closed a door upon Shelley's understanding of her sister, perhaps even upon her sympathy with the entire family.

   Or, another way of putting it is that Ellen's "knowing" George is, after all, only a final understanding of the fact of his independence, the fact that he *is* unknowable. The legend makes George himself a symbol. Ellen specifically repudiates her "young girl's love of symbols" in her final attitude toward George—that is, the sort of thing that the Fairchilds make of him. Hers is a vision of the unmanageable *fact* of him. But Ellen's, perhaps, is a schoolgirl's understanding of the term. And in the larger purposes of the novel he remains a symbol; not entirely the Fairchilds' symbol—but his very factuality itself becomes symbolic. It is notable that none of the *men* in the novel admit the reader very often to their minds. Such is the Fairchild women's notion of their men, which the author accepts as a technical principle, that they are a kind of serviceable gods—infinitely capable, having access to wonderful powers of the outer world, and always *decently* keeping their own counsel. And if one uneasily suspects, with Ellen, that George is actually godlike in his manhood, that his stalwart impenetrability is not a matter of decency, but of *having* some counsel to keep, an unsearchable purpose—still this is only the excess of heroic typicality. As the reader has to know him, as he functions in the novel, the legend has made him—with the final qualification only that it has made all the Fairchilds too, and not, as they sometimes suppose, they the legend. (This is the point, of course, of Shelley's realization, when she runs the car across the tracks in front of the Yellow Dog, that it won't do to try "contriving" it.)

As an example of George's symbolic function, we may consider again Laura's experience. Ellen's, in fact, is not quite so exclusive an understanding of George as it might at first appear. At her childish level, Laura has entertained the same vision—of his necessary isolation, we will remember, and felt "matter-of-factly intimate" with the fact of the isolation, with him. And potentially this experience is a basis of sympathy between Laura and Ellen in the little girl's effort to make herself a part of the family. But George has "brought them together" without any conscious intention, without any rational understanding even of what is happening in the situation, either on his part or theirs. There is no willed, in the usual sense, *personal* communication anywhere in the relationship. George functions here, then, precisely in the way that the various symbolic *objects* function to establish, and to illuminate, certain relationships. George is, in fact, the ultimate embodiment of the author's subtle conception of the subject-object relationship which is symbol—the object *informed* by, inseparable from, an always quickening, always manifest, but always inscrutable intelligence.

The people, then, as well as things, are carried out of themselves by the legend. And, finally, the significance of the particular story carries outside itself to other stories; every legend is all legend. The way in which we have seen the thread of the trestle incident becoming involved with Ellen's reflections upon the fate of the girl she met wandering in the woods—the girl and the meeting figure in the statement of what might be followed out as a distinct, major theme in itself, the theme of loss—is but one illustration of the complexity of the structure. The symbols of the trestle story are actually parts of certain larger, extended motives. The train is one of several means of transportation which have a symbolic function, more or less explicit, wherever they appear. The horses—Troy's horse, the horse which George gives to Dabney (having thought of it, significantly, when Robbie took his car to run away in), the horse which Dabney rides on her visit to her aunts (carrying a "wedding-present home on horseback"); the cars too—George's car which Robbie has wrecked, the new Pierce Arrow (all cars are still comparatively new), the darkened car which Dabney and Troy ride away in after the wedding, the lighted car in which the mayor and his family arrive for the reception. And so on. The trestle, over Dry Creek, is closely related to what may be loosely defined as the *water* motive—the bridge over the bayou "whose rackety rhythm Laura remembered," the old stories of the whirlpool, Laura's trip to Marmion with Roy when in a kind of baptismal ceremony she is pushed into the Yazoo and loses Ellen's garnet pin.

And any one of dozens of incidents, observations, unspoken perceptions, can become the "central" nexus in the whole complexity of interconnection. One need not start with the trestle episode or with any of the more obviously prominent incidents. One such observation as Shelley's at the reception—of the contrast between the darkened car of the newlyweds and the lighted car bringing the mayor, that "had come up alight like a *boat* in the night" (italics mine)—is enough. The simile has associations—we might assume at this level even somewhat consciously felt by Shelley—as remote as the comparison, early in the story, of a certain lamp in the living room at Shellmound to "a lighted shoe-box toy, a 'choo-choo boat' with its colored paper windows." Here, with the recollection of the dear and familiar object of their childhood play, the lamp itself having the radiance of its associations too already mingled with the light of the toy, is much of the pathos of Shelley's ironic realization that the public gaiety of the wedding party, the extraneous and trivial display of the "occasion" which the visit of so inconsequential and alien a personage as the mayor epitomizes, is a mockery of that darkness of marriage which has closed between her and Dabney. (The darkness which is the inevitable privacy of any marriage, the darkness which for Shelley is especially associated with Troy Flavin, of his hateful "overseer's soul," of the blood of Negroes on the floor of the office.) But beyond any possibility of Shelley's consciousness of the significance of her thought, the *boat* suggests all boats—the boat in which Laura rode with Roy when *she* saw Marmion, the house which is to be hers eventually, not Dabney's, and when she was admitted to the mystery of the Yazoo, the river that measures the time or the timelessness of the Fairchild world. (The prophesy of Shelley's fear for her sister's marriage is not, perhaps, altogether dark.) Or, reinforcing the first effect, the light, the lamp, is all the lamps—the heirloom night-light which Dabney broke.

One can follow a single object through the significance of its reappearances. The garnet pin—first as Battle's gift, and then through Ellen's use of her dream about it as a lullaby-story to Bluet, associated with her motherhood, the symbol both of loss and of gain; figuring in a re-statement of the same theme in her meeting with the girl in the wood; in her effort to get Partheny's assistance in finding it, becoming the symbol of the old Negress's second sight; appearing finally as the central symbol in an incident which embraces all these themes, the womb-return descent of Laura into the waters of the Yazoo. "As though Aunt Studney's sack had opened after all, like a whale's mouth, Laura opening her eyes head down saw its insides all around her—dark water and fearful fishes." And the pin, lost in the water, becomes the image of a relationship between Laura and her new mother Ellen, between her and the Fairchilds a union in the untold *secret* of the loss, which is more enduring even than what she had hoped for as a reward for her finding and returning the jewel.

One could, and would, go on. Devious ways are open from any point. But perhaps with this much of detail, we can hazard a few conclusive generalizations.

To return to the question of Miss Welty's attitude toward the society which she depicts, it should be apparent by now that in terms of approval or disapproval the evidence is mixed. In Ellen's vision of the hero, George, what appears to be a devastating criticism is implicit—the Fairchilds' "myth of happiness" would seem to be myth clearly in the worst sense, a childish retreat from reality. And it is possible to infer that the "wedding" of Dabney and Troy is a mockery of the failure of true marriage everywhere—even the marriage of Battle and Ellen; the marriage of the Fairchilds with the past, or with the future, whichever way one wants to approach it; the marriage of minds among all the characters.

But perhaps the crucial point of the problem is the status of the Negroes. If it must be admitted that Miss Welty does, as we have already suggested, "accept" the Fairchilds' typical attitude here—I think that acceptance is finally, though not perhaps quite so clearly, like her acceptance of the women's attitude toward the men. It is an acceptance as a technical principle only, and one which comes in at a deeper level for some very heavy qualification. For the purposes of that double attitude of pastoral which William Empson has defined, as well as in a more practical sense for people like the Fairchilds, the Negroes are a great convenience. It is at the expense of these "*rude* swains" that the Fairchilds can be the "*gentle* swains" (to use Milton's phrases for it) that they are—so that we can at once look down upon the narrow complacency, and envy the imaginative and moral richness, of their country simplicity. But Miss Welty implicitly recognizes the "convenience" for what it is. And the recognition is, in fact, very closely tied in with that problem of the women's attitude toward the men.

Dabney's preparations for her marriage are, significantly, associated with her riding forth into the fields. Troy Flavin emerges partially as a kind of "field god," similar to Floyd in *At The Landing,* or Cash in *Livvie.* And the mystery of his virility is in the present situation very closely connected, of course, with his intimate knowledge of the Negroes. It is this of which Shelley is at once so afraid and so contemptuous when she finds Troy settling a fight among the Negroes in the overseer's office. And the phrase of her reflection on her way back to the house, her wondering if "all *men*" are like him, makes the connection with George's role. George too, about whom Dabney is thinking on her ride to visit her aunts, is marked with the *blood* of the Negroes—he with the blood of compassion when he caught the knife and bound up the wounds of the little Negro boy, Troy with the blood of his knowledge of the Negroes in their labor. But, the significance of such distinctions as the latter aside, they are *men*—George coming naked from the water to catch the knife, Troy the dark figure on a horse that Dabney catches sight of on her way to her aunts' house; and their tolerance for the blood of Negroes is an essential part of their maleness. And Dabney senses something of this, the part that a new knowledge of the lives of the Negroes, of their intimacy with the earth, must play in the rebellion from her family which her marriage represents.

But this is the crucial point also in the sense that Dabney's discovery of the male mystery is clearly hopeful for the society as well as critical of it. Troy *is* the field god, and as such he is a principle of rejuvenation. The marriage promises ultimately, perhaps, not disruption but renewal, or renewal out of the disruption. And while Troy's is in a sense an influence from outside, it is defined, as we have seen, and complemented, partially by the role of George—and that, paradoxically, as an essential part of his status as the family hero. It can hardly be denied that Miss Welty does see the strength for rejuvenation as in part the family's own strength, the strength of their own myth as they themselves understand it, though she sees with equal clarity the limitations of that understanding.

Or, if the argument requires further elaboration, one must not forget that central to the old aunts' family sense is the *reverence* for disaster. Primrose insisted that people keep "their kinfolks and their tragedies straight." And there is reason to believe that they can accommodate Dabney's breaking the lamp too, that her breaking it is one with her keeping it ultimately, the "present" is given and must be kept whether she will or no, whether the "little old piece of glass" is kept intact or not. The themes of protection and disaster are inextricably bound up together from the first, in the family legend as in the design of the lamp and its shade, and their unity is unbreakable. Accepting the implicit pun on *present*—perhaps the marriage of past and present is not broken; perhaps that quality of the Fairchilds which is at first so baffling to Laura, their being so intensely "of the moment," is simply the result of their feeling supremely confident of their footing in the past. And, finally, Laura herself—who comes closer than anyone else to being Miss Welty's stand-in in the novel—remains to live with the family on terms which are, though again qualifiedly, both sympathetic and hopeful.

And yet I would insist that the question of approval or disapproval, of a prophesy of hope or disaster, is still not the key to Miss Welty's final attitude. Her principal interest in the society, her sympathy with it, is for the *vision* which it supports. We need not trouble ourselves ultimately over the fate of the society as such, or its worth in itself, or even the problem of whether it ever existed or could exist, actually, quite as it is pictured. The picture is *right* enough, in every sense, to provide the vision. And that is unquestionable—the novel itself, its living form, the constant order and quickness of its sensibility, is the essential proof of the vision. In fact, the novel *is* the vision. And I do not see, from the evidence of the novel itself, that Miss Welty is especially either disturbed or elated by the prospects of the actual Fairchild world. She is simply, like Laura with George, for the all-important moment "matter-of-factly intimate" with the dual paradox of the pastoral outlook—that all human society being ultimately suspect, the vision *must* to some extent condemn the society which produces it, and yet that the particular society which makes this truth most apparent is the "best" society.

This is the essential *realism* of Miss Welty's art. This is how her intensely narrow view—the concentration of her narrative which requires more than two hundred pages for the treatment of the events of a few days in the life of a hopelessly provincial family—becomes precisely at its most restricted a world-view.

But the last scene of the novel sums up the situation. We come back to the mind with which we began—Laura McRaven's mind. And Laura achieves her sense of "belonging" at last. She has been told that she is to stay, that Marmion is to be hers some day. The picnic, for her, is a celebration of her reception as a member of the family. But she accepts the decisions from the first with the secret thought that sometime she may go back to Jackson, to her father. The reservation does not diminish her present joy. But it is there. And the moment at which she feels most overwhelmingly at one with the family is when she can hardly see any of them, but sees *with* them the falling star. The "star" *is* a star—single, remote and inaccessibly, indifferent. And if it is not quite indifferent, if it does belong to the family in their common seeing, then it is *falling*. And yet, for the moment of its falling, it brings them together. Laura, and the Fairchilds, and the star, are one in the light of the star— and turning again with a gesture of embracing them, she embraces the firmament, "both arms held out to the radiant night." That one moment of pure vision, the people themselves in darkness, unseen, the star unseeing, becomes the sufficient thing in itself—the one thing.

Meeting the World in
Delta Wedding
Albert J. Devlin°

On 22 September 1986 Peggy Prenshaw and I spent the better part of the afternoon talking with Eudora Welty at her home in Jackson.[1] Interviews—even the most relaxed and affable, as this one was—are never without intent, and in some cases both the writer and his importuning visitor have fish to fry. My fish were real enough, but they were not the murky creatures of curiosity, deplored recently by John Updike, that probe for "the 'real' person" behind the writer's "constructed" persona.[2] No doubt the same genie of confusion is at work here as in the well-known story of the clubwoman who asked Eudora Welty to "just come and tell us one of your stories in your own words."[3] My interests were stirred instead by several of Welty's own statements, of fairly recent vintage, that shift the ground of discussion from story as story—still Welty's preferred locale, of course—to the collective, the corporate achievement, the career.

In 1979 Welty looked back nearly fifty years at her first important publication, "Death of a Traveling Salesman" in 1936, and in seeing the story "afresh," recognized it to be "a member of the general family" of her work. The basis of kinship, Welty remarked, is that the "origin" of the story, "its generative force, comes out of real life."[4] Two years earlier, in talking with Jean Todd Freeman, Welty confessed astonishment at the Pulitzer Prize for *The Optimist's Daughter*, but she showed a deeper regard for the Gold Medal for Fiction, awarded her in 1972. This recognition by the National Institute of Arts and Letters, by artists who were her peers and contemporaries, made Welty feel "very proud" because "it was for a body of work instead of for . . . some one effort."[5] Welty's preparation of *The Eye of the Story: Selected Essays and Reviews*, and *The Collected Stories*, in 1978 and 1980, respectively, and her publication of *One Writer's Beginnings* in 1984 may supply further evidence of Eudora Welty in a canonical frame of mind—admittedly, a term that runs the risk of sounding highfalutin. Nonetheless it was this apparent state of mind that guided my preparation for the interview and, more specifically, pointed my thoughts to *Delta Wedding*. I have stated elsewhere that in choosing the plantation as scene and mythos for her first novel, published in 1946, Welty attempted, again for the first time, to fuse her narrative interests with a distinctively Southern institution.[6] This fusion is not my topic, but it does portend the closely related issues of artistic maturity and the internal dynamics of a

° This essay was written specifically for this volume and is published here by permission of the author.

distinguished literary career. These twin concerns, framed by the superlative achievement of *Delta Wedding*, form my present topic. The interest they hold for me—more importantly, their use as vehicles of literary study—will be clarified if we can turn briefly to the interview itself.

Conversation had turned to the Anglo-Irish writer Elizabeth Bowen whose practice of fiction and criticism remains formative for Welty. I reminded her of the fine preface that Bowen wrote for the Vintage edition of Katherine Mansfield's stories in 1956, and quoted briefly:

> It is with maturity that the really searching ordeal of the writer begins. Maturity, remember, must last a long time. And it must not be confused with single perfections, such as [Katherine Mansfield] had accomplished without yet having solved her abiding problems.[7]

Welty's response was swift and intuitive and seemed to grant maturity a kind of dramatic presence. "That's marvelous. No escaping it once you've got it. . . . It's just the very seed of things, isn't it? The very core." I next stated my enthusiasm for *Delta Wedding* as her "most valuable book," and in responding to Welty's query—"I wonder why, I mean in my case, if that's true"—I speculated that she too had addressed the same "abiding problems," whatever they may be, in framing this fictional world. At first she demurred, modestly, but in following conversation she added new perspectives on the composition of *Delta Wedding* and agreed that with Ellen Fairchild, the self-effacing matriarch of Shellmound Plantation, she had "discovered . . . someone who [was] unlike any character"[8] in the earlier stories. I would like to think that these selections from the interview have succeeded in giving some preliminary definition to a complex literary problem.

Artistic maturity, in Welty's view, appears to be more than a convenient abstraction; it powerfully grips the writer's life and in her phrasing seems to have something of the caustic quality of Flannery O'Connor's grace. "No escaping it once you've got it." This endowment is not spelled by "single perfections," Bowen and Welty agree, but by the writer's cumulative engagement of his "abiding problems" of form and vision. In Eudora Welty's case I take *Delta Wedding* to be a critical site of this engagement. This term does not, however, suggest anything like a deliberate campaign to stare down old foes of the imagination. Nor do I mean to attach special importance to the *fact* itself of Welty's first novel. *Delta Wedding* does not find Welty yielding to pressure that she write a novel, steady and at times intense since the publication of her first story in 1936[9]; nor does it represent any self-questioning of her gift as a "natural" short story writer. I mean to identify instead a process of artistic self-expression and discovery that is at once unbound and inevitable, and in no small degree companionable with the excitement that readers take away from the text. Focused in this way, *Delta Wedding* becomes an object of study both in its internal order and in its harmonies with works that surround it.

We all know the story of *Delta Wedding*. Eudora Welty's much-awaited first novel takes place in September 1923 in the Yazoo-Mississippi Delta and traces the frantic preparations of Battle and Ellen Fairchild to marry off their daughter Dabney, the unpredictable belle of Shellmound Plantation. The whole tribe of Fairchilds, including aunts and great-aunts, regrets Dabney's "wildness for Troy [Flavin],"[10] the laconic overseer from Tishomingo County, but their dismay at this unlikely pairing remains an undertone of gibe and innuendo rather than confrontation with the deliberate hill man. The novel takes a little more than a week's time and ends with the return of Dabney and Troy Flavin from their honeymoon in New Orleans. The outward focus of *Delta Wedding* upon marriage is typical of the large body of plantation romance to which it belongs, beginning with *The Valley of Shenandoah* in 1824 and culminating, one supposes, in *Gone with the Wind*—a book that Welty has always meant to read. But the inner focus of *Delta Wedding*—its subtle expression of sensibility, its lyrical way of seeing—is far removed from the sentimentality and partisanship that historically define the literary plantation. Indeed, Welty's measurement of this distance is one of the more important ways in which the sureness of *Delta Wedding* is achieved. Not every reviewer in 1946 recognized this quality, but over the years Elizabeth Bowen's prediction has been borne out: "I should like to think that *Delta Wedding* may, in time, come to be recognized as a classic."[11]

For Virginia Woolf, much of the early work of D. H. Lawrence and other innovative Georgian writers—Eliot, Forster, Joyce—was spoiled by the sound of demolition, the "breaking and falling" of old forms and the trying out of the new. Writing in 1924, with the new novel as her subject, Woolf may have had in mind the sharp divide between parts 1 and 2 of *Sons and Lovers,* where Lawrence abruptly discards the tools of realism to take up poetic and symbolic means of representation. The "effort and strain" of such writing was all too prevalent during the advent of the modern lyrical novel, Woolf concludes in her famous essay "Mr. Bennett and Mrs. Brown": "We must reflect that where so much strength is spent on finding a way of telling the truth, the truth itself is bound to reach us in rather an exhausted and chaotic condition."[12]

In part at least, the formal sureness and integration of *Delta Wedding* may reflect the quite different literary situation of Eudora Welty. In the late 1930s and early 1940s, for her a surpassing time of productivity, Welty is removed by a generation from the founding and testing of the canons of lyrical narrative. Indeed, as unfriendly reviews note, in 1946 Welty is writing against the grain of a postwar fiction infused with resurgent realism. Perhaps Welty's literary situation can be fleshed out a bit more fully by recalling one of her own reviews of the period—her admiring notice of Virginia Woolf's posthumous collection of stories, *A Haunted House.* Printed in the *New York Times* on 16 April 1944, this review discloses, without very much surprise, Welty's deep understanding of the ways and means of lyrical narrative. The stories, Welty notes, "seem as perfect, and as functional for all their beauty, as spider webs":

> Indeed they were made for a like purpose: to trap and dissect living morsels in the form of palpitating moments of time, instantaneous perceptions, those brief visions of others, which give us when captured—breathing, even struggling and so betraying themselves—an illusion of life.[13]

In *Delta Wedding* Eudora Welty traps the same "illusion of life" within the sensuous web of the Delta itself and the Fairchild myth of bounty and happiness. In the immediate background, of course, is Welty's own subtle narrative practice in *A Curtain of Green* (1941) and *The Wide Net* (1943)—books that I shall turn to later. At a further remove are the conventions, and the models too, of an indirect, oblique art of modern fiction that Welty understands critically and brilliantly adapts to her own special needs. In a sense, her literary situation helps to ensure that there will be no sound of "breaking and falling," no sharp divides of presentation, in *Delta Wedding.* The "truth" of Welty's first novel does not reach us in "an exhausted and chaotic condition," but with the serenity of mature treatment.

In a brief sentence Welty marries Dabney and Troy at Shellmound Plantation. This is not to flout the minister, Mr. Rondo, who knows too well his modest stature in the Delta, but to clear the way for the most important moment in the book. The dancers cover "the downstairs" and then move "outdoors" to begin "a performance of glory" whose deepest effect is reserved for Ellen and her brother-in-law George Fairchild. George, the Memphis uncle, the lawyer, only recently reconciled to Robbie Reid, his runaway wife, approaches Ellen through a field of dancers. "As he looked in her direction, all at once she saw into his mind as if he had come dancing out of it leaving it unlocked, laughingly inviting her to the unexpected intimacy." Ellen possesses George in this moment in a way that grants him perfect freedom. She knows the uniqueness of his acts, "springing" as they do "from long, dark, previous, abstract thought . . . instead of explainable, Fairchild impulse." She knows that it was "inevitable" that George "should stand on the trestle" with his niece Maureen, not resisting his fate; and it followed too "that he was capable of the same kind of love" for the "ordinary" little Robbie Reid. As George makes his way, "smiling," through the dancers, he appears to Ellen as "infinitely simple and infinitely complex," "wholly singular and dear." In his wide sympathy, "he had, and he gave, the golden acquiescence."[14] This moment has a long fuse that extends beyond *Delta Wedding,* but its truth, serene and unruffled, is a formal property of the novel itself and as such reveals Welty's superb control. How, though, has she succeeded in trapping this "illusion of life"?

In "Notes on Writing a Novel"—Elizabeth Bowen's brilliant little catechism published in 1945 and much admired by Welty—plot is defined as "the knowing of destination" rather than a mere account of manipulations. The plot of *Delta Wedding* is not, of course, without its attempted manipulation, as the Fairchilds approach George, the "best loved" uncle, with one or another of their "shimmering" designs—that he be the lover, protector, scapegoat, and conscience of the family; or at the very least that he add to its store of comic reminiscing. As a knowing instrument, Welty's plot refutes these designs without necessarily denying the underlying truth of their characterizations. It succeeds by reticence. George Fairchild is typically seen in "half-light" or "blurred profile," has few speeches, and is only cast in retrospective action by family memory and storytelling—principally his dalliance with fate on Dry Creek trestle. Laura McRaven, the nine-year-old cousin visiting from Jackson, knows from immediate experience "that it was right" for George "to stand apart."[15] Welty knows this on formal grounds and agrees, in effect, with Bowen that "certain characters gain in importance and magnetism by being only *seen.*" Bowen goes on to conclude in the superb "Notes" that such reserve makes a character seem "more romantic, fatal-seeming, sinister. In fact, no character in which these qualities are, for the plot, essential should be allowed to enter the *seeing* class."[16] George's magnetism is essential to the plot, especially as it crests in the wedding celebration, but Ellen's intense consciousness redirects and complicates the lines of force in *Delta Wedding.* Their interplay—George, portentous and vaunting; Ellen, modest, practical, rooted in the family—directs the plot to its "destination" and reveals an author who has recognized all the possibilities of her subject.

In 1946 Welty dedicated the novel—as she had the story "The Wide Net"—to her friend John Robinson, who had lived near Greenwood in the Delta and "introduced" her to this singular land. Welty recalled, in our conversation, visiting his family while he was stationed overseas in the Air Force and reading "lots of old [family] diaries" that gave her "a feeling of the background of the Delta."[17] In November 1943 Welty mailed a carbon copy of the story "The Delta Cousins" to this "good friend" with a fearful, and prescient, notation of its unsuitability for the marketplace: "—it's mighty long."[18] Welty's agent, Diarmuid Russell, agreed and advised her to think of the story as chapter 2 of a novel.[19] We know the happy outcome of this sage and in some ways adroit advice, but the unpublished story is the necessary starting point for study of Ellen Fairchild's evolution and her creative relation to George, the sweetest man ever born in the Delta.

In "The Delta Cousins" Uncle Raymond is a clear antecedent for George Fairchild. He is on a three-day visit from Memphis, and he has recently lost his wife, a runaway. He receives adoring glances from Laura Kimball, his precocious niece, who thinks him "a prince," and from the Sheltons, who place this "best loved" kin "above all." Only in a later holograph addition to the original typescript—very probably Welty's first approach to *Delta Wedding*—does she time Uncle Raymond's visit to coincide with a family marriage, not Dabney's but Dip's.[20] Ellen Fairchild's antecedence is more remote. Aunt Mim is mother to the large family and husband to Uncle Tatum, a boisterous prototype for Battle Fairchild. She is pregnant again, wearily, and seems miscast among the fair-skinned, exuberant Sheltons. Still she is remote in sensibility from Ellen Fairchild, the "town-loving" and "book-loving"[21] Virginian whose displacement is a kind of narrative privilege. Aunt Mim by contrast is dull, opaque, and usually overwhelmed by her large household. To Laura she seems "the least measurable" of all, "for she grew duller instead of brighter."[22] Mim does not join the family for the closing picnic on the Sunflower River, and she is entrusted with virtually none of the story's heavy burden of sensibility, which the child Laura bears well beyond her years. But one can sense in a brief shining of Aunt Mim hints of Ellen's intenser consciousness and her special address to George Fairchild. This moment, more than any other, confirms "The Delta Cousins" as a kind of seedbed for the later novel.

Quite unaccountably, "her eyes grow wide" and she looks afresh at her family as she passes through the dining room. Pausing to rest, Aunt Mim "was astonished at the spectacle she could watch," the Sheltons revealed momentarily in all of their "absorbed, intent" postures. Raymond jumps to his feet and offers Mim his chair, "like a prince offering his seat at blackjack to a princess." Welty does not retain this curious figure in *Delta Wedding*, but in any event Raymond's gallantry cannot prolong the quickening of his sister-in-law. "Aunt Mim's brown eyes blinked, opened and tried to see again, but the curtain had come together and all went on without her once more. The merriment faded, and quite all the astonishment." The "close-watching" Laura observes this encounter and realizes that Raymond "would not tell Aunt Mim such a cruel thing as that she ought to have expected to be loved in this world."[23] Here, I think, is the germ of *Delta Wedding:* Ellen will look enduringly through "the curtain" that opens only briefly for Aunt Mim; George in turn will not be refused or warded off, as Raymond is; and love will be exchanged. "The Delta Cousins" primarily taught Welty, I suspect, that the arduous construction of Ellen Fairchild had scarcely commenced.

I do not know that there are any extant working notes or intermediate drafts of *Delta Wedding*. The final typescript is, however, revealing and shows Welty to have a clear sight of Ellen Fairchild's destination. This control is evident in the broad strokes of her characterization, and it is reflected too in Welty's shrewd revision. In chapter 3, for example, Ellen crosses the bayou on a domestic errand but soon comes upon a loitering girl, "fair and nourished," who "*shed* beauty." Welty's intention is to expose Ellen to a radiance that she often "hoped for" in the familiar world, but when her discourse dulls this encounter—she tells the mysterious girl, for example, "You can come live at Sue Ellen's. . . . You can help her look after her—all her children are boys"[24]—Welty cancels the offending passage that sounds suspiciously like a trace element of Aunt Mim. Later in chapter 4 Welty omits a second passage that apparently does not ring true. George has shouted "That's enough!" to end an impromptu dance in the hallway, and Aunt Tempe, peeved, complains to Ellen that the legendary Denis Fairchild would have begged her pardon "half an hour ago." Ellen too speaks in peevish complaint: "It does look like what we women wish our lives away on, here at Shellmound, is always just the very thing that's impossible! Just the four that two and two won't make."[25] Neither passage, Welty must have felt, served to advance the pace of the narrative or to deepen Ellen Fairchild's sensitivity. Welty made the most important revisions, including these brief examples, after the typescript had been copyedited. Still later changes affecting Troy Flavin were made in the galley stage.[26] But Welty was not discovering at such advanced date very many new things about her plot or characters. More often she revised to bring tone and texture into conformity with the main lines of *Delta Wedding*—lines of sensibility that converge to form Ellen's quietly accruing authority.

The Fairchilds consider the legendary "sweetness" of George— and of his brother Denis before him—to be a home-bound or at least a Delta-bound sympathy. Tempe, the Memphis aunt who "had never put on her grown-up mind," perfectly renders the family innocence. Vaguely dreaming, she imagines "a paradise, in which men, sweating under their hats like field hands, chopped out difficulties . . . and made room for the ladies to . . . flourish."[27] Ellen's geography is quite different. "Not her young life with her serene mother, with Battle, but her middle life . . . had shown her how deep were the complexities of the everyday, of the family, what caves were in the mountains, what blocked chambers, and what crystal rivers that had not yet seen light."[28] Welty has said of Virginia Woolf that her "undeviating purpose" was to penetrate "the abstract world of the spirit."[29] It is not likely that Ellen's attraction to George Fairchild would have occurred to her in anything like these terms, but her empathy and detachment, and her propitious moment in time, superbly equip her to broach the "caves" of her portentous kin. She goes to encounter the only man who "left the world she knew as pure—in spite of his fierce energies, even heresies—as he found it."[30]

At first Robbie's hurting of George leads Ellen to realize his peculiar liability. How "importunate" he was. "How much that man hoped for! . . . They should all fairly shield their eyes against that hope." "A feeling of uncontrollable melancholy" ensues and prods Ellen to ask a potentially despairing question: "What on earth would ever be worth that intensity with which he held it, the hurting intensity that was reflected back on him, from all passing things?"[31] The glimmer of an answer appears when Ellen, "timidly," sees in George "a kind of ascetic streak," and speculates that "left to himself, he might not ask for anything of any of them—not necessarily."[32] Ellen's fainting in chapter 5, amid the flurry of a bird in the house, marks her detachment and final liberation from heroic family portraiture that tempts her to see George impurely. Before fainting, she whispers to him, "Don't let them forgive you, for anything, good or bad."[33]

Ellen takes up again her suspicion that the Yellow Dog episode "was nearer than she had realized to the heart of much that had happened in her family lately."[34] The rehearsal supper is the present occasion of Battle's teasing Robbie—"He didn't do it for you, eh"— and of Ellen's discovery that George "regarded them, and regarded things—just things, in the outside world—with a passion which held him so still that it resembled indifference." On second thought, though, Ellen realizes that she "had always felt this in George and now there was something of surprising kinship in the feeling; perhaps she had fainted in the way he was driven to detachment." Leaning back "against Battle's long bulk," Ellen regards her family and knows that they will never understand the "miracle" of the Yellow Dog stopping in time. George, in his "wild detachment," had seen "death on its way," and was "roused" to "immense contemplation, motionless pity, indifference. . . ."[35] His attention to the world in all its phases— creative and destructive, personal and impersonal, nearby and far away—is a vision of wholeness that Robbie recoils against, sensing in "wifely ferocity" only the "danger" it holds for George. But Ellen sees further and knows that George's indifference to the Yellow Dog is a vital expression of his sympathy, his sweetness, and that its danger cannot be separated from his passion for Robbie, which leaves her "helpless," or, for that matter, from his absorption in all passing things—"Little Ranny, a flower, a horse running, a color, a terrible story listened to . . . in Fairchilds."

The poky Yellow Dog train is a wonderful piece of homemade philosophy. It catches both the accent of a glimmering, floundering, mysterious universe and the act of vision that makes it habitable. *Delta Wedding* more than hints at the nature of this perspective. In their mutual address—their *"confluence,"* to use that "wonderful word" of *The Optimist's Daughter*—George and Ellen Fairchild reconcile the claims of vision and feeling, of the contemplative and social, to form an image of psychic wholeness. It is an image too, as would become clearer in *The Golden Apples* (1949), of the artist striving to integrate vision, and passion, with the uses of common life. This is the ambition that Welty put into the mind and heart of Miss Eckhart, with whom she continues to feel deeply "in touch."[36]

On 23 February 1945 Welty wrote to Diarmuid Russell to say that she had just returned from a visit to the Delta—specifically to the home of John Robinson where she enjoyed access to family diaries—and that she was inspired to work on "The Delta Cousins." Some two weeks later, on 9 March, she would report in another letter to Russell that she was about to marry off Dabney, as the narrative continued.[37] At approximately the same time, Welty was reviewing for the *New York Times,* and in one case we can see, perhaps, an allusion to her own adventure with the Fairchilds. Welty could point to "no vivid after-impression," "no image of a character to cherish," in reviewing *Three Who Loved,* by Edita Morris, in February 1945. One of these "fine-spun" stories, Welty notes, "is seventy-six pages, perilously long to spin out the lyric form." In another story Welty finds a child character who appears to be "some symbol of universal love," but she fears that "he has no root in nature." "Somewhere in these fables," Welty concludes, "there is nobility and tenderness, but not enough vitality to support their thesis."[38]

We do a disservice to Welty if we deprive her of her critical object by treating this review as covert self-address. But Welty's review of Morris is nonetheless a timely restatement of basic critical-aesthetic values—especially her deep understanding of the perils, and the resources too, of the "lyric form"—and it does cast a searching beam on the formal achievement of *Delta Wedding*. Its maturity comes with the sureness of Welty's conception as reflected in the vital interplay of George and Ellen Fairchild. The present critical climate would grant this judgment and it would have no trouble finding characters "to cherish." But at the same time, I think that we have paid too little attention to the "long fuse" of *Delta Wedding*.

As a consequence we do not have a very firm idea of the special mark that it makes, the "abiding problems" that it may address, in Welty's long career. Perhaps it is for this reason too that the recognition scene in chapter 6 seems generally overlooked by readers— or at best strikes a glancing, nostalgic note. I should like to hold out again as destination this important moment, for I take it to be something that *is coming* in a great deal of Welty's earlier work. If a special authority is needed for this kind of study, then perhaps Welty herself can serve: novels "especially," she observed in 1978, "have long fuses that run way back."[39]

The greatest clarity comes from watching Welty's final revision of the *Delta Wedding* manuscript. As Welty rereads, she is attuned to the truth of each character; she listens for the false note, the misplaced accent, and is seldom fooled. Troy Flavin, a heavily revised character, is not allowed to fall from his natural dignity; and Ellen, we know, has succeeded to refinement through her inauspicious origins in "The Delta Cousins" and later manuscript revision. At the same time, however, I want to suggest that *Delta Wedding* incorporates still more subtle kinds of rereading and self-borrowing, and that this may be an educational process of special pertinence to the novel form itself.

Certain self-borrowings in *Delta Wedding* are not especially revealing. In chapter 5 Welty reassembles her familiar trio of censorious ladies. They attend Robbie Reid at the store in Fairchilds with little if any change in function from "Lily Daw and the Three Ladies" (1937), "Asphodel" (1942), or "At The Landing" (1943). They still plague the searching or vaunting or merely vulnerable character with discouraging words. "Why, hello, Robbie, are you back at the store?" asks Miss Thracia Leeds. The former clerk, who has married above herself, and who knows by now that George will not search for her, answers abruptly from the heart: "I thought he might drag the river, even." Troy, nearby, unlettered, asks, "Drag which river?,"[40] but we hear an unmistakable echo of "The Wide Net," the title story of Welty's second collection (1943). Its reuse in *Delta Wedding*—for this is what I take it to be—has more profound importance for Welty's novelistic practice.

Each of the love stories turns on the same marital pivot: the rash deed of a husband—William Wallace carousing all night; George on the trestle with "the look of having been on a debauch"[41]—provokes a sensitive wife to "get back at her husband" by running away. Hazel and Robbie leave notes, and while the former threatens to drown herself in the Pearl River, both expect to raise alarms and to be searched for. Most importantly, each story is set in a "changing-time," as Doc says in "The Wide Net," when human and natural cycles undergo mysterious transformation. Hazel Jamieson is going to have a baby in six months; Robbie wonders if she too has "a child inside her"[42] as she watches George face down the Yellow Dog train.

These materials, perfectly cast in "The Wide Net," are remodeled in *Delta Wedding* to fit the more spacious design of the novel. Robbie Reid, the runaway, unexpectedly replaces William Wallace as searcher; and several of his perceptions of Hazel are redirected, nearly verbatim, to George Fairchild. These substitutions have the important effect of allowing Welty to refocus William Wallace's halting grasp of his wife's trouble.

> Had he suspected down there [in "the dark water"] . . . the real, the true trouble that Hazel had fallen into, about which words in a letter could not speak . . . how (who knew?) she had been filled to the brim with that elation that . . . comes of great hopes and changes. . . . It could be nothing but the old trouble that William Wallace was finding out, reaching and turning in the gloom of such depths.[43]

This dim intuition is refocused more discursively in *Delta Wedding* and becomes the subject matter of Robbie's fiercely directed inquiry and Ellen's more discerning judgment. What, asks Robbie, was the "eventuality" of love and marriage, aside, that is, from "the old bugaboo of pregnancy?" What "unnerving change or beautiful transformation"[44] might one expect after all? Ellen can only answer Robbie that "the old trouble" is well named: our obstinacies and longings have always drawn up hard against our finite nature; and lovers have always suffered "the separateness" in moments that would seem better shared.

Elizabeth Bowen is especially well-equipped to make the distinction that seems warranted by Welty's rereading of herself.

> . . . a writer of short stories is at his or her best sometimes, and sometimes not; and this is true equally at any age . . . at which he or she happens to be writing. "Development" may appear in any one writer's successive novels; in successive stories I hold it to be a myth. The short story is a matter of vision, rather than of feeling. Feeling (which is important in the novel) does or should mature as one grows older. Of vision, one asks only that it should not lose its intensity—and I would say that if vision is there at all that wish is usually granted.[45]

Vision and feeling cannot be reserved strictly for one genre or another, as Elizabeth Bowen knows all too well. But as emphases, tendencies, markings, her distinction between short story and novel is reliable, and it describes rather precisely the nature of Welty's rereading of herself.

The visionary intensity of "The Wide Net" inheres principally in William Wallace's "mythical thinking." In Cassirer's terms, he is "enthralled" by "immediate experience" and "everything else dwindles before it . . . , as though the whole world were simply annihilated." This is William Wallace's extreme concentration as he dives "away from the pale world"[46] to know his wife's "elation." Robbie would also annihilate the world to possess her husband. Accusatory words are spoken in the parlor, but "as though no one else but George were in the room." Robbie, Aunt Tempe realizes, "was leaving out every other thing in the world with the thing she said."[47] But genre here is a greater "putter-inner," as Thomas Wolfe would say. In the refocusing of *Delta Wedding*, the marital theme is given social and economic weightiness, and in discussion with Ellen Fairchild, Robbie's concentration finds "words"[48] and moral context through exposure to a mature and deeply feeling sensibility. The "fight," Ellen explains, is "*in* people on this earth, not between us"; it is "over things, not over people"—"Things like the truth, and what you owe people."[49] In Ellen Fairchild, Robbie meets the world, and although this encounter may in large part be lost upon her, its ethical force resounds throughout the novel.

I shall not defend, either categorically or in reference to Welty, Elizabeth Bowen's claim that "development" in short stories is "a myth." Still her distinction between novel and story points accurately to a moment of transition in Welty's writing when the visionary is comprehended by the dialectical and is caught up in a sensibility that possesses feeling and the "words" too. If this is a self-educational process, it does not efface, correct, or deepen the past performance, for "The Wide Net" can scarcely be improved. But the interplay of Robbie Reid and Ellen Fairchild is only a limited test case, and Welty's reuse of "The Wide Net," while illuminating, points beyond to more subtle and widely scattered rereading. I want to follow this fuse, briefly, in relation to George and Ellen Fairchild, and with greater attention now to the "abiding problems" they may represent.

As a *seen* character, of magnetic properties, with visionary sympathy, George Fairchild has a number of fairly clear antecedents in *A Curtain of Green* and *The Wide Net*. Such "overlays" are never exact, and in a sense their refusal to match up precisely is more interesting and revealing than any congruency can be. Still, with figures such as Powerhouse, the unnamed young man of the story "The Key," the fictive Aaron Burr of "First Love," and even Billy Floyd in "At The Landing," George Fairchild breathes more avidly "in the vague free air of the everyday."[50] How "importunate" they all are, "how much" they hope for, Ellen might say of this uncommon family of characters, as she does of George Fairchild. Their presentation is similar in that Welty usually restricts access to their portentous inner life. In "First Love" Aaron Burr's compromising dream of empire is hidden from "eavesdroppers"[51] by the deaf boy Joel

Mayes. A like impairment in Albert and Ellie Morgan obscures the "interest"[52] of the young man in "The Key" in this traveling couple. Powerhouse and Billy Floyd are more the agents of their own mystery. They wrap themselves in a mystique of energy to confound the disbelievers and censorious. The "brightness" of these performing figures—for they all are that—momentarily arouses the constricted or complacent "audiences" of Natchez, Yellow Leaf, Alligator, and The Landing, before they revert to a more comfortable skepticism or condescension. They meet mystery only with "obstinately blank faces."[53]

The more receptive feel the pull of "genius"[54] and of a "secret . . . endlessly complex"[55]; it is what Joel Mayes suspects of Burr, Albert of the restless young man, the privileged narrative voice of Powerhouse, and, of course, Jenny of Billy Floyd. In each case, suspicion succeeds to a "moment of hope,"[56] and whether the means of vision is a "lifted arm," a dropped key, musical improvisation, or rape, the effect is the same—to restore the world to vividness. For Joel Mayes, the raised arm and parted cloak of Aaron Burr "was like the first movement he had ever seen, as if the world had been up to that night inanimate."[57] Jenny knows from Billy Floyd "that what people ate in the world was earth, river, wildness and litheness, fire and ashes. . . . She ate greedily."[58] The list could be extended to say that Ellen has received from George "the unexpected intimacy"— that now she is "loved in this world," as Laura Kimball put it in "The Delta Cousins"—but just as soon as we do, we recognize a considerable change in the lines of force. They are now reciprocal. George Fairchild's antecedents remain as fugitive as King MacLain in Morgan's Woods. Burr, for example, is oblivious to Joel's touch, preoccupied even in sleep with the enormity of his dream of empire. In "The Key" the young man's fear is borne out that "he would never express whatever might be the desire of his life . . . in standing apart in compassion. . . ."[59] Jenny Lockhart knows finally that "there was a need in all dreams for something to stay far, far away,"[60] which is precisely the distance that Floyd measures after the waters recede. Powerhouse is watched closely by the privileged narrative voice that strains to learn his secret "language."[61] But Powerhouse is elusive too in his perennial creativity: "inspired remarks . . . roll out of his mouth like smoke."[62]

George Fairchild is no less the "genius," and in making Ellen feel "lucky—cherished, and somehow *pretty*," he becomes one of the company that relieves "the heart's overflow."[63] But in dancing with Ellen, he too is known intimately, and not only in his mystic aloofness. He is "very finite," "wholly singular and dear," a "late-tired, beard-showing being."[64] The mutual attraction of George and Ellen—she receiving "the golden acquiescence," he unlocking his mind to Ellen's sensitive understanding—I take to be the consequence of Welty's rereading of the mysterious core of *A Curtain of Green* and *The Wide Net*. Welty has spoken directly to this process in the brief essay "Words into Fiction." The "mystery" of using "language to express human life" is not something that the writer tries "to solve." "No, I think we take hold of the other end of the stick. In very practical ways, we rediscover the mystery. We even . . . take advantage of it."[65] As one who *attends* mystery, Ellen Fairchild is not a radically new character for Welty—she too has her antecedents—her "words," however, are new and as such constitute a rediscovery of mystery in the novelistic terms of *Delta Wedding*.

Elizabeth Bowen put her finger precisely on this spot in reviewing *Delta Wedding*. This "perfectly simple story has drawn into itself the whole of Miss Welty's both human and visionary imagination." Here Bowen expressed some relief as well, for a number of the earlier stories had resembled "flying particles of genius" that threatened to leave this "affectionate reader . . . far behind."[66] The problem that Bowen pointed to is familiar to Welty's readers: the charge of fine writing, tiptoeing, "esoteric incomprehensibility" (Bowen's term), in short, Virginia Woolf's fear that she herself had not "that 'reality' gift." This is the gist of the very unfriendly reviews of *The Wide Net*, and it remained for Katherine Anne Porter in Welty's third collection, *The Golden Apples* of 1949, which she thought to be "a personal showing off as shameless as a slackwire dancer with pinwheels."[67] Be this as it may, the more pressing issue is the apparent "development" that Bowen finds in *Delta Wedding*, where "the whole of Miss Welty's both human and visionary imagination" now resides. Three questions occur to me, and I can treat them only suggestively. Can we speculate intelligently upon the dynamics of such apparent development? As an aesthetic term, is "development" more nearly evaluative or descriptive in Welty's case? And, finally, does Welty's first novel find the author in the clutch of maturity?

Welty's "rediscovery" of mystery, "in very practical ways," may reveal the presence of two subjectivities. Each text bears the unique imprint of the writer. Welty herself has explained that the work gives fundamental knowledge of his distinguishing sympathies: "how he sees life and death, how much he thinks people matter to each other and to themselves, how much he would like you to know what he finds beautiful or strange or awful or absurd."[68] And recently a critic has argued persuasively that Welty's narrative style—indirect, misleading, purposefully delaying—is designed to lead the reader to precise knowledge of this "essential self."[69] At the same time, we may wish to think of a second subjectivity, existing within this writerly presence, but expressing itself in the dynamic relation of stories as they accrue and give shape to a career. Two different, although

related, casualties are involved here—one final, the other proximate—
as well as different levels of the writer's autonomy. The second
subjectivity, which need not be hidden in the dense jargon of struc-
turalist poetics, emerges, in the present case, from Welty's arduous,
repeated, and varied confrontations with mystery in each of her first
two collections. In no way are these stories incomplete, but they do
contain voices that lament both a personal impasse and, by extension,
the very constraints of this visionary medium of expression. Joel
Mayes can serve as illustrative case. "Burr was silent" on his last
night. In sleep "he demanded nothing, nothing. . . ." "Why," Joel
asks, "would the heart break so at absence? Joel knew that it was
because nothing had been told. The heart is secret even when the
moment it dreamed of has come, a moment when there might have
been revelation. . . ."[70] I would submit that this lament—at once
personal and generic—gathers authority as it is struck in first one
key and then another, exerts a kind of cumulative, systemic pressure
that is always recognizably human in its urgency and the further
knowledge it seeks. Again, the writer does not set out "to solve"
the "secret" heart, but if voices of his own creation ratify the deepest
impulses of his personal and aesthetic nature, then shall he not
respond?

In 1972 Welty was asked to comment upon her evasion of "the
novel-first requirement" that publishers still impose upon young writers. In answering she paid tribute to the support and understanding
of her first editor John Woodburn and her agent Diarmuid Russell,
and to her own resolute "nature" as well: "I never wrote anything
that didn't spring naturally to mind and engage my imagination."[71]
This view of the writer's unbounded freedom can readily accommodate the dynamic sense of career that I have proposed. A reflexive
entity, which is sensitive to the promptings of past performance,
Welty's literary career is nothing other than a matrix for the most
intimate communing with the self.

The interplay of subjectivities that relates *Delta Wedding* to
earlier work does bear upon the nature of literary development and
maturity. It is, I think, accurate to say that whatever development
we find in *Delta Wedding* is linked first to genre—to the capacious,
deliberative, ethically prone conventions of the novel. These conventions give pointedness to a composition whose lyrical accent requires that it convey an impression of life meandering, unrationalized,
and the sense that "nothing really, nothing really so very much, [has]
happened!"[72] I am reminded here of Lily Briscoe's hope for her
painting of Mrs. Ramsay in *To the Lighthouse*—a book that "opened
the door" for Welty.[73] Its surface, Lily thinks, must be "feathery and
evanescent . . . but beneath the fabric must be clamped together
with bolts of iron." The pointedness, or clamping, of *Delta Wedding*

is achieved in the merging of George and Ellen Fairchild. She is a domestic poet, rooted in the circumstantiality of the family and the everydayness of human life. Like Mrs. Ramsay, who I suspect was formative in Welty's conception of Ellen, this shy, and rather unwilling, plantation mistress knows in a way that reflects her calling. "She knew then," Woolf says of Mrs. Ramsay, "she knew without having learnt. Her simplicity fathomed what clever people falsified." This unlabored way of knowing is the historic voice of the novel, and it brings the mysterious George Fairchild into "beard-showing" focus.

Again Welty herself can help to define the nature of this development. In her estimation old and new works do not compete for preeminence, nor is one form of literary expression—short story or novel—inherently superior to another. Terms such as "progressing or regressing," in fact, do not describe for Welty either the uniqueness of each literary performance or the imaginative freedom that it implies. Welty prefers to think that she has "just reached something different" as she experiments with form, voice, perspective.[74] Her varying attention to the world, her "great resourcefulness, sensitivity, and intelligence,"[75] as Robert Penn Warren put it in 1944, the inner promptings of her texts—these are the elements of a dynamic system that occasions the special unity of *Delta Wedding* and in turn defines the nature of moral obligation. But for Welty this development is difference, sheer creativity, as precarious a formulation as the "smoke" of Powerhouse.

This sense of development as a descriptive rather than qualitative term of judgment requires that maturity be something other than a solution—for all time—of "abiding problems." Welty has explained that each of her full-length novels began mistakenly as a story. She was so enthralled with Jack Renfro that he forced her "to go on" and include most of the world in *Losing Battles*.[76] Welty also felt "challenged," we know, when Diarmuid Russell read "The Delta Cousins" in November 1943 and opined that it was chapter 2 of a novel. Welty added in our conversation, with no little amusement and satisfaction, too, that *Delta Wedding* "was the most ill-planned or unplanned of books"[77]—confirmation indeed that what a writer knows about his novel is, in Welty's words, "flexible till the end."[78] Flexibility, which is here an openness to narrative possibilities, comes close to defining maturity. It is something as simple and complex as not being short on aesthetic sense when the gravitation of one's subject is unmistakable.

Between 1936 and 1945, Welty opened more than a few letters from New York City that either implored her to begin a novel, or, once undertaken, applauded her for the fine progress. This was the congratulatory mood of John Woodburn when he wrote to Welty during the "sirloin summer" of 1945. With some amazement at his own euphoria, for neither he nor anyone else at Harcourt had seen "a page" of *Delta Wedding*, Welty's editor confessed that we bat "our enthusiasm back and forth badminton fashion as though it were already a best-seller. . . ."[79] Because we live on the other side of *Delta Wedding*, we can look back through these importunings and enthusiasms, and through Welty's own periodic resistance to the novel as well, to see more clearly that her sending schedule was wholly intimate, mysterious, and inevitable, too. When "The Delta Cousins" drifted, or was pulled, into the orbit of the novel, it entered a much larger world that Welty's imagination rushed to fill quite as eagerly as it had the smaller space of the short story. The result in *Delta Wedding* was "the beauty of order imposed."[80] But maturity knows as well that order, unities, gives way to change as the artistic project continues, and so it is content to be drowned again in the contingencies of the world. George, in effect, must drift away from Ellen's arms so that he can look across another gathering, on still another family occasion, and make "a hideous face" at Virgie Rainey. That she, like Ellen Fairchild, "knew another moment of alliance"[81] is curiously, and blessedly, still surprising to the reader. Perhaps this surprise is what Elizabeth Bowen meant when she concluded that only with maturity does "the really searching ordeal of the writer begin."

Notes

1. Albert J. Devlin and Peggy W. Prenshaw, "A Conversation with Eudora Welty, Jackson, 1986," *Mississippi Quarterly* 39 (1986):431–54; Reprinted in *Welty: A Life in Literature*, ed. Albert J. Devlin (Jackson: University Press of Mississippi, 1987).

2. John Updike, "Writers on Themselves: Magic, Working Secrets," *New York Times Book Review*, 17 August 1987, 28.

3. Tom Royals and John Little, "A Conversation with Eudora Welty" (1978), in *Conversations with Eudora Welty*, ed. Peggy W. Prenshaw (Jackson: University Press of Mississippi, 1984), 256.

4. Eudora Welty, "Looking Back at the First Story," *Georgia Review* 33 (1979): 751–52.

5. Jean Todd Freeman, *Conversations*, 191.

6. Albert J. Devlin, *Eudora Welty's Chronicle: A Story of Mississippi Life* (Jackson: University Press of Mississippi, 1983), 80–123.

7. Elizabeth Bowen, Introduction, *Stories by Katherine Mansfield* (New York: Vintage, 1956), vi.

8. Devlin and Prenshaw, "A Conversation," 435–37.

9. The Eudora Welty Collection, at the State Department of Archives and History, Jackson, contains correspondence from editors and publishers urging Welty to undertake a novel. Harold Strauss's letter of 27 May 1936 is representative: ". . . it is quite impossible to publish a volume of stories by a relatively unknown author . . . tackle a full-length novel," he advises (Z 301.1 Folder #1).

10. Eudora Welty, *Delta Wedding* (New York: Harcourt, Brace, 1946), 33.

11. Elizabeth Bowen, review of *Delta Wedding*, by Eudora Welty, *The Tatler and Bystander*, 6 August 1947, 183.

12. Virginia Woolf, "Mr. Bennett and Mrs. Brown," in *Collected Essays*, vol. 1 (New York: Harcourt, Brace, 1967), 335.

13. Eudora Welty, "Mirrors for Reality," review of *A Haunted House, and Other Short Stories*, by Virginia Woolf, *New York Times Book Review*, 16 April 1944, 3.

14. Welty, *Delta Wedding*, 221–22.

15. Ibid., 75.

16. Elizabeth Bowen, "Notes on Writing a Novel," in *Pictures and Conversations* (New York: Alfred A. Knopf, 1975), 169, 183. "Notes" was first published in *Orion* II, 1945. See Devlin and Prenshaw, "A Conversation," 435.

17. Devlin and Prenshaw, "A Conversation," 438.

18. The ribbon and carbon typescripts of "The Delta Cousins" are in the Welty Collection at the State Department of Archives and History, Jackson. The carbon has a covering page dated "Nov. 5" (1943), which is addressed "Dear John" (Robinson) with the inscription "—Here's the story—I hope it gets there—it's mighty long— Still pretty here—" (82.025). Subsequent citation of "The Delta Cousins" follows the ribbon copy, which shows the author's latest revisions and is noted parenthetically in the text (Series 4 Z 301).

19. See Devlin and Prenshaw, "A Conversation," 436–37. Welty recalls the same advice of Russell in *Conversations*, 47, 180.

20. In revising the ribbon typescript of "The Delta Cousins," Welty made an interlinear notation on page 12 that dates Uncle Raymond's return to Memphis and alludes for the first time to his niece Dip's marriage: "as soon as the wedding was over." See Michael Kreyling, *Eudora Welty's Achievement of Order* (Baton Rouge: Louisiana State University Press, 1980), 52–76, for a comprehensive description of Welty's revision of "The Delta Cousins."

21. *Delta Wedding*, 217.

22. Ibid., 31.

23. Ibid., 11–12.

24. Ibid., 64. The typesetting copy of *Delta Wedding*, dated 1945, is in the Welty Collection at the State Department of Archives and History, Jackson. Citation noted parenthetically in the text (Series 4 Z 301).

25. *Delta Wedding*, 101.

26. John Woodburn's letter of 21 March 1946 refers to Welty's "reworking of Troy's character." Apparently, there was some miscommunication regarding this revision, which probably explains Welty's instructions in the manuscript to proofread substituted pages against galley pages 45, 46, and 49 (Welty Collection Z 301.01 Folder #2).

27. *Delta Wedding*, 188.

28. Ibid., 157.

29. "Mirrors for Reality," 3.

30. *Delta Wedding*, 80.

31. Ibid.

32. Ibid., 126.

33. Ibid., 166.

34. Ibid., 157.

35. Ibid., 186–89.

36. Eudora Welty, *One Writer's Beginnings* (Cambridge: Harvard University Press, 1984), 100.

37. I am indebted to Michael Kreyling for supplying this information on the composition of *Delta Wedding.*

38. Eudora Welty, "Fine-Spun Fantasies," review of *Three Who Loved,* by Edita Morris, *New York Times Book Review,* 18 February 1945, 4–5.

39. Royals and Little, *Conversations,* 256.

40. *Delta Wedding,* 140–41.

41. Ibid., 191.

42. Ibid., 146.

43. "The Wide Net" (1942), in *The Collected Stories of Eudora Welty* (New York: Harcourt Brace Jovanovich, 1980), 180.

44. *Delta Wedding,* 144.

45. Elizabeth Bowen, preface, *A Day in the Dark and Other Stories* (London: Jonathan Cape, 1965), 7.

46. *Delta Wedding,* 180.

47. Ibid., 186–87.

48. Ibid., 158.

49. Ibid., 163.

50. Welty, "Words into Fiction" (1965), in *The Eye of the Story: Selected Essays and Reviews* (New York: Random House, 1978), 138.

51. *Collected Stories,* 165.

52. Ibid., 31.

53. Ibid.

54. Ibid., 160.

55. Ibid., 158.

56. Ibid., 33.

57. Ibid., 157.

58. Ibid., 252.

59. Ibid., 33.

60. Ibid., 252.

61. Ibid., 132.

62. Ibid., 141.

63. *Delta Wedding,* 223.

64. Ibid., 222.

65. Welty, "Words into Fiction," 137.

66. Bowen, review of *Delta Wedding,* 182.

67. Katherine Anne Porter, letter to Paul Porter, 2 August 1949; quoted by Joan Givner in *Katherine Anne Porter: A Life* (New York: Simon and Schuster, 1982), 371.

68. Welty, "Words into Fiction," 142.

69. Harriet Pollack, "Words Between Strangers: On Welty, Her Style, and Her Audience," *Mississippi Quarterly* 39 (1986):501. Reprinted in *Welty: A Life in Literature,* ed. Albert J. Devlin (Jackson: University Press of Mississippi, 1987).

70. *Collected Stories,* 165.

71. Linda Kuehl, *Conversations,* 86.

72. *Delta Wedding,* 190.

73. Kuehl, *Conversations,* 75.

74. Freeman, *Conversations,* 197.

75. Robert Penn Warren, "The Love and the Separateness in Miss Welty," *Kenyon Review* 6 (1944): 259.

76. Scot Haller, *Conversations,* 309.

77. Devlin and Prenshaw, "A Conversation," 437.

78. Welty, "Words into Fiction," 138.

79. John Woodburn, letter to Eudora Welty, 22 August 1945, the Eudora Welty Collection, State Department of Archives and History, Jackson (Z 301.01 Folder #2).

80. Welty, "Words into Fiction," 144.

81. *Collected Stories,* 446.

The Golden Apples

Notes by the Way
Margaret Marshall°

The device of "our town" and the tone of reminiscence are almost sure to enlist the reader's sympathy in advance. The American reader is particularly susceptible to this approach, for no one can be more sentimental about the old home town than the rootless American who, for better or worse, wouldn't go back where he came from for anything in the world but enjoys his daydream about going home.

This device and this tone are a great temptation to the writer of fiction: they not only serve to establish an immediate bond with the reader but also seem to save him the labor of creating characters and a world—since these are already given, to a point, once he has conjured up "our town." But the advantages of this artistic short cut, as of any other, are more apparent than real, while the disadvantage can be fatal. The disadvantage is that the writer, relying on the device and the tone, neglects to animate his characters except as "characters" in "our town" and tends to luxuriate in evocations for their own sake of atmosphere and landscape.

At least these are the two great flaws in Eudora Welty's latest book, "The Golden Apples" (Harcourt, Brace, $3), which is composed of a series of sketches having to do with life in a small Mississippi town called Morgana and a group of characters who are ordinary folk but who comprise the town's "main families."

Miss Welty is a talented writer, and she has shown her capacity, in her earlier stories, for creating character and for involving the reader in the fate of even so unlikely a character as a "petrified man." The persons and events in this book are likely enough, but its impact on the reader is not that of participating in the experience of more or less autonomous human beings related to us all but of watching forms of life as through glass—which is transparent but not a very good conductor of primary emotions. Meanwhile, our sense of the reality of Morgana and its inhabitants is diminished, not increased, by the piling up of details of observation and sensibility which are often good in themselves but serve no dynamic function.

° Reprinted with permission from the *Nation*, 10 September 1949, 256. Copyright 1949 by The Nation Company, Inc.

The reviewers have spoken in praise of the trance-like atmosphere of the book, and of the exquisite writing to be found in its pages. I should say that the atmosphere is that of a daydream, which soon becomes claustrophobic, and that Miss Welty, caught in her own spell, has indulged herself in finespun writing that becomes wearing.

In the piece called "Moon Lake" she does come very close to breaking through the spell, and this story comes nearer by far to actuality than anything else in the book. It deals with the relations between the daughters of Morgana's main families and a group of orphans who are thrown together for a week's camping on Moon Lake. Miss Welty sets the scene with humor and perception. She also creates suspense and seems to be building toward a climax that will resolve or at least dramatize the situation she has posed. There is a climax, to be sure, when the orphan Easter is tipped into the water by a small colored boy and is resuscitated only after the prolonged life-saving ministrations of the boy, Loch Morrison, who has been dragooned into acting as the lifeguard for the party. But the meaning of this climax in relation to the rest of the story escapes me, and I must assume that it is just another reminiscence.

The basic trouble, I suspect, is that Miss Welty was somehow led to write, on this occasion, of characters and situations that did not really engage her own primary emotions or her creative energy. As a result they never seem quite real to the reader—and the convention of "our town" combined with the reminiscent tone makes them seem all the more like figures in a remote landscape.

The book does, I suppose, convey the quality of life among the main families of Morgana, but this is its only accomplishment, and the quality of life among the main families of Morgana is, to speak rudely, not worth 244 pages. Even so, one is left wondering if this is really the way it is. Morgana is a small town in the deep South. Yet, reading "The Golden Apples," one is scarcely ever made aware of the mixed racial background which must surely affect the quality of life even of the main families of small towns in the deep South. I don't mean at all to suggest that Miss Welty should have given us stories of race conflict. I only find it curious that a basic and dramatic circumstance of life in the South should count for so little in her picture of Morgana.

Eudora Welty and the
Multitudinous Golden Apples   Thomas L. McHaney°

Eudora Welty's chronicle of human longing, *The Golden Apples* (1949), as the author has affirmed, is not a novel,[1] but it nevertheless manages to create a complex unified impression in the manner of the novel. Its formal elements are well balanced: the first story finds a counterweight in the last, each of the three major movements is separated by related shorter pieces, and there is progression, counterpoint, and a careful interweaving of character, image and theme throughout. The ending is a clear resolution. One way Miss Welty has achieved this effect of completeness is by using themes and variations based on Celtic and Graeco-Roman mythology. Rural Mississippi comes alive with a full pantheon of gods, goddesses, demigods and mortals who play out the timeless legends of love, wandering, struggle, defeat, and success again and again under different conditions and bearing different names. The town in which the stories mostly transpire is a single, complete world, and it is world enough; the diversion in the West of "Music from Spain" only proves that there is no real difference between life in the "whole world" of Morgana, Mississippi, and what is repeated outside. And as the gods themselves are a kind of variously knit family, the people of Miss Welty's Morgana are a family, too, related by the ties of blood and place that also bind the gods and demi-gods. Content and structure make it possible, thus, to speak of *The Golden Apples,* if not as a full-fledged novel, as a "cycle" of stories in the sense that one speaks of related cycles of song or cycles of myth; and in the musical sense it is, as we shall see, thoroughly composed.

Part of the important mythological layer, Miss Welty would surely say,[2] is not program or plan (as in Joyce's dependence on Homer), but discovery, the natural and unplanned perception of a writer who was steeped in mythic tales as a child and who, as a mature artist, now discerns in the lives of her characters patterns that correspond to the old stories she remembers. The people of Morgana would not find such discoveries strange, for they are surrounded by myth in a natural way: the familiar storybook pictures of Perseus and the Gorgon, the Sibyl, and Circe hang framed on their walls; the poetry that also sometimes transmits the myth passes easily through their heads; the names of gods and heroes appear in several forms in the town annals; there is even a statue of "the goddess" in Jinny Love Stark's yard. Nevertheless, an important part of Miss Welty's allusion is also surely intentional, a deliberate effort to display one or two prime

° Reprinted with permission from *Mississippi Quarterly* 26 (Fall 1973):589–624.

myths within the general mythological context in order to underscore the principal concerns of the book. Taken together, these two levels of myth give the book an overriding form. The main lines are laid out for all to see and have not lacked some commentary,[3] but a large amount of myth still remains to be pointed out and discussed. This essay suggests that there is more allusion than hitherto noted, and it aims to show how the form of the book, which is an almost symphonic orchestration of closely related parallels between old myth and modern reality, structures, and thus properly reveals, the several meanings of the golden apples.

The first emanation of the title of the book, as is by now well known, is William Butler Yeats's poem "The Song of the Wandering Aengus" (from *The Wind Among the Reeds, 1899,* and reprinted in the *Collected Poems, 1933*). Because phrases from the poem recur in *The Golden Apples* somewhat more often than has been indicated, it bears quoting in full:

> I went out to the hazel wood,
> Because a fire was in my head,
> And cut and peeled a hazel wand,
> And hooked a berry to a thread;
> And when white moths were on the wing,
> And moth-like stars were flickering out,
> I dropped the berry in a stream
> And caught a little silver trout.
>
> When I had laid it on the floor
> I went to blow the fire aflame,
> But something rustled on the floor,
> And someone called me by my name:
>
> It had become a glimmering girl
> With apple blossom in her hair
> Who called me by my name and ran
> And faded through the brightening air.
>
> Though I am old with wandering
> Through hollow lands and hilly lands,
> I will find out where she has gone,
> And kiss her lips and take her hands;
> And walk among long dappled grass,
> And pluck till time and times are done
> The silver apples of the moon,
> The golden apples of the sun.[4]

Aengus is the Celtic "Master of Love." In notes to another part of the *Collected Poems,* Yeats recalls that in an old Gaelic poem about the wanderings of Oisin, Oisin sees a figure with a hazel wand, whom Yeats identifies with Aengus, and also sees "a young man following a girl who has a golden apple," and afterwards he sees a hound chasing a hornless deer. These images, taken together, Yeats explains, are "plain images of the desire of the man 'which is for the woman,' and the 'desire of the woman which is for the desire of the man,' and of all desires that are as these."[5] Whether or not Miss Welty has read Yeats's brief section of notes in the *Collected Poems*, the desires that trouble and move the characters of *The Golden Apples* are "desires that are as these," and their visions, like Oisin's, are poetic and symbolic representations of their desires, evoked in many ways, not least through Yeats's poetry.

With Yeats, there is also reference to the legends of the Celts, to the whole mythological cycle in Ireland; allusion to the historical Irish background that is an apparent heritage for many of the citizens of Morgana (their surnames alone exhibit the Irish ancestry, but there is also "Loch" Morrison and "Parnell" Moody); and perhaps some use of Yeats's concept of a gyring, repetitive historical process— there are parallel or recurrent events in the forty years of Morgana life depicted here, even when a Morgana person dwells elsewhere. Yeats is also a means to confirm the presence of Graeco-Roman mythology in the book. His version of "Leda and the Swan" has been identified before as underlying King MacLain's seduction of Mattie Will Sojourner Holifield in "Sir Rabbit." His "No Second Troy" seems to be echoed in Ran MacLain's monologue about his unfaithful wife, Jinny Love, in "The Whole World Knows," where the Trojan War is refought in the context of bridge and croquet and imaginary slayings. The "golden apples of the sun" in Yeats's Aengus poem become the multitudinous golden apples that figure in the stories of Perseus, Hercules, and Atalanta, and in the quarrel among goddesses that indirectly caused the Trojan War.

Greek myth is introduced before we are conscious of Yeats, however. Katie Rainey, whose funeral will provide the central occasion of the last story, tells "Shower of Gold," the first movement of the book, and the title is an obvious reference to Zeus's appearance to the maiden Danaë. When she knows she is pregnant, Katie tells us, King MacLain's wife Snowdie looks "like a shower of something had struck her, like she'd been caught out in something bright" (p. 6).[6] The allusion is mixed, including more than the story of Danaë, because if King MacLain in his startling white suit and his brilliant Panama hat is the Zeus or Jupiter of this pocket Olympus, then Snowdie, his long-suffering consort, is Hera or Juno. Like King, she is also "bright," an albino.[7] The progeny of the encounter to which Katie refers is the twins, Randall and Eugene, a casual mingling of the Danaë story with the story of Leda, who bore the twins Castor and Pollux as well as Helen and Clytemnestra after Zeus deceived her in the form of a swan. (Leda's seduction, as noted, comes up in "Sir Rabbit.") Fooled by the shower of golden coin, Danaë later gave birth to Perseus, the hero whose adventures play a very prominent role in *The Golden Apples*. Children of both mythic seductions, Perseus and Helen, figure in stories that concern golden apples. Thus one event in the first section of the book mingles a great amount of mythology, all of it to be built upon significantly as the related stories progress.

Katie tells her story to a "passer-by, that will never see her [Snowdie MacLain] again, or me either" (p. 3). Accepting the device, the reader is doubly involved, not only as listener, for he becomes the stranger hearing Katie's tale, and in the course of the book he will learn what it means to be identified as a wanderer. Among her many roles, Katie is one of the watchers in the novel, seeing life "like something was put to my eye" (p. 7). Loch Morrison will be another, viewing events through his father's telescope, "all eyes like Argus, on guard everywhere" (p. 25); so will his father (p. 240); and the Holifields—Mr. Booney the night watchman, and Junior, and one, perhaps one of these, unnamed—will be like Argus, too, asleep when they should be on guard (pp. 19, 94, 107). Katie recounts one of the returns of King MacLain, the prime wanderer who peoples Morgana and environs with children, known and unknown, evading the various Arguses set to watch him and escaping the scrutiny of his wife, Snowdie, even when she hires the "Jupiter Detective Agency" to check his whereabouts (p. 229). Katie's story is ostensibly about one of King's recent returns, at Halloween, but before she can tell this incident she must reveal what she knows about an earlier return, the time King begot the twins and then departed by way of the bank of the Big Black River, leaving his distinctive hat to suggest falsely that he had drowned.

The present Halloween is not only the anniversary of when King and Snowdie "took up" (p. 5), it is also the traditional beginning of the Celtic year and the time when the souls of the departed return to warm themselves at their old family fires.[8] As a returning "ghost" (p. 16), however, King has the tables turned on him when his twin sons scare him away. They are on roller skates and wear Halloween masks, and their garb may be appropriate and significant, for Halloween, we are told, was also a time when the Celts practiced divination for the purpose of ascertaining their destinies.[9] The skates are among many devices and images of speed and "wandering" that appear throughout (the twins are nicknamed "Ran" and "Scooter"), and the masks they wear suggest something about their futures. Eugene is disguised as a Chinaman, a choice that may be an augury of his later sojourn in San Francisco. Randall is masked as a lady with a "scary-sweet smile" (p. 11)—"the girl's face and the big white cotton gloves falling off" (pp. 13–14), a possible foreshadowing of the terrors of the Gorgon, of his wife Jinny Love (see pp. 142–43), of his own smile in "The Wanderers" (p. 238), which is an expression of all that has happened to him by then, or of the special fate that overtakes him in connection with Maideen Sumrall, the country girl with "new white cotton gloves" (p. 140) whose death he causes. Another possible augury—an event that is apparently taken as significant or portentous by Snowdie—is that coincident with King's abrupt arrival and departure, Katie's baby Virgie swallows a button. "I think she kind of holds it against me," Katie says, "because I was there that day when he come; and she don't like my baby any more" (p. 18). The last story of the book is chiefly about this Virgie, who, however, admits that she is no prophet (p. 243), though there are others in Morgana who are. She will need to wait until she is past forty to put together all she has learned from observing, hearing about and living among the other characters of the book. Then she will arrive at a mature view of life. It is perhaps as if the button she swallows in the opening story is a magical seed of wisdom which slowly, but surely, grows.

Among the things that Katie tells in "Shower of Gold" is that King "might have started something" the time he left his hat by the Big Black and disappeared. She may be right, for Kewpie Moffitt, the sailor, takes the same path in "June Recital" when his sexual romp with Virgie is interrupted, and Virgie herself goes to the river to bathe and think on the eve of her mother's funeral, while Mr. Sissum, the cellist so much admired by Miss Eckhart, drowns in the Big Black sure enough. King starts more than that, however. He is the progenitor, the life force, even though in his wandering he has, he will say at last, "ended up at the wrong end" (p. 223). To Mattie Will, he looks like "the preternatural month of June" (p. 94), and Virgie realizes that all his life he has butted "like a goat against the wall he wouldn't agree to . . . a rush and a stampede of the pure wish to live" (p. 233), a trait of his shared, perhaps unwittingly at the time, by the young Virgie who, as a schoolgirl, "on a rainy day . . . said she was going to butt her brains out against the wall" (p. 38) and "had really tried." (The conjunction of the willful act and rain seems not to be an accident, as subsequent events in *The Golden Apples* will show.)

Before her seduction by King, Mattie Will Holifield has a rhyme running through her head (like Cassie later):

> In the night time,
> At the right time,
> So I've understood,
> 'Tis the habit of Sir Rabbit
> To dance in the wood—(p. 97).

It is King as "Sir Rabbit" who had told Snowdie to meet him in the woods in the "night time" (p. 4) when he fathered the twins, who is "in the habit" (p. 89) of doing as he pleases. Another expression of his fecundity, the title Sir Rabbit will have a number of reverberations elsewhere in the book, but in the first story it is already suggested that he, who has been "Willful and outrageous, to some several" in the area (p. 3), has children "growing up in the County Orphan's, so say several, and children known and unknown, scattered-like" (p. 4). Such statements lead to the suspicion that many of the children in *The Golden Apples* could be King's, if the point were pushed, including Katie's own. If they are not his real progeny, they are, at least, figuratively his, for if he is Jupiter, they are Jupiter's offspring: Virgie is Venus and her brother Victor, to be killed in the war, is Mars. Further suspicion is aroused when we learn that King has promised to bring Loch Morrison a bird that can say "Rabbits" (p. 71) and when Loch, like Eugene, plays the Perseus role. He is connected, likewise obliquely, with a specific child from County Orphan's, Easter. After she is nearly drowned, she lies on the picnic table with her side "slack as a dead rabbit's" (p. 128), and there are other signs of kinship to be introduced later.

Zeus / Jupiter, Aengus the Master of Love, and Sir Rabbit all seem to have in common their association with fecundity, and they all can be thought of as wanderers, too. Katie says she sees "King in the West, out where it's gold and all that" (p. 10), a statement that foreshadows his son Eugene's westward wanderings, which in turn parallel the travels of Perseus, son of Jupiter, who went to the western limit of the earth and wrestled with King Atlas over some golden apples. As the foregoing summary shows, "Shower of Gold" in some respects is less a story than a framing device which introduces most of the characters of the book, establishes the theme of the wanderer, with many of its ramifications, and clearly warns the reader to be aware of the mythological layer.

It is followed by the first major movement in the book, "June Recital," a story that is large in scale, complex in subject and design, and skillfully made to advance the reader's perceptions of what is important in the microcosm that is Morgana. "June Recital" is a mixed rite of spring seen through the eyes of the two Morrison children, Loch and Cassie. It is Cassie who makes the association with Yeats's "Song of the Wandering Aengus" by recalling the poem, but it is Loch, home in bed with malaria, who has Aengus' "fire . . . in my head." Feverish, he watches through the window of his room, and later from the forbidden tree outside, while a grown-up Virgie Rainey (actually no older than Cassie) and her sailor boyfriend make love in the upper room of the supposedly vacant MacLain house next door. Mr. Booney Holifield, the town night watchman, sleeps in another room of the old house while downstairs a mysterious old woman, who also seems to have a "fire" in her head ("She kept putting her hand to her head" [p. 29]), fits up the old music room for a ritual conflagration. The woman is Miss Eckhart, Cassie and Virgie's former music teacher. Virgie had been her prize pupil, but now Virgie plays the musical background at the picture show and acts the part of the thoroughly modern young woman of the 1920s, smoking, drinking Cokes for her meals, carrying on with the sailor in the old MacLain house, and generally flaunting Morgana. As Loch watches, she and the sailor make love. They chase each other around the room, leaping an old mattress propped there, repeating in miniature Aengus' wanderings over hollow lands and hilly lands—the mattress has "hills and hollows" (p. 19)—and making like figures on a Grecian urn: "Who chased whom had nothing to do with it because they kept the same distance between them" (p. 27). Outside, the fig tree in the MacLain yard is "many times a magic tree with golden fruit" (p. 22), and the young innocent Loch is "waiting for the day when the sailor took the figs" (p. 21), not knowing that in a sense the sailor is plucking his golden apples now.

A few notes from the familiar recital piece by Beethoven, *Für Elise,* attract Cassie's attention, too, and while Loch views the present scene, Cassie's memories come flooding and reveal the past. Miss Eckhart—among the associations between her and *Für Elise* must be counted not only her German background, her love for the music of Beethoven, and Virgie Rainey's playing, but also her given name, Lotte *Elisabeth* (p. 61)—is another wanderer and another Perseus. Her life has deeply touched both Virgie and Cassie, though Virgie is apparently still unaware of how deeply she has been affected. But in fact Virgie has been the agent whereby Miss Eckhart has crucially informed Cassie Morrison. Like Katie Rainey going back to recount King's earlier return before she can tell of the more recent one, Cassie hears the piano piece she associates with Virgie's lessons and returns in memory to the yearly recitals at Miss Eckhart's and what they meant. Miss Eckhart and her invalid mother had come from Germany, though no one in provincial Morgana had really known that or understood what it meant until World War I. The two women rented rooms in the MacLain house (King was gone, and Snowdie needed the money). There Miss Eckhart gave piano lessons to the town girls and boys and presented her annual June recital, a local rite of spring. The music room would be decorated with Maypole garlands and the traditional green boughs;[10] "dread and delight were to come down on little girls that special night"; it was a ceremony that "celebrated June" (p. 62).

As with other characters in *The Golden Apples,* a number of mythological references apply to Miss Eckhart. Her hair is "low on her forehead as Circe's, on the fourth grade wall feeding her swine"

(p. 66). She gives Virgie some illustrated music books, but Fate Rainey feeds the "Venusberg pictures" (scenes from *Tannhäuser?*)[11] to his pigs (p. 57). Cassie remembers Miss Eckhart's apparent infatuation with Mr. Sissum, the shoe salesman who played cello at political gatherings and, before Virgie and the piano, at the movie house. The brief story of Miss Eckhart and Mr. Sissum is a little like that of Orpheus and Eurydice, except the roles are slightly reversed. Cassie remembers Miss Eckhart sitting enchanted on the grass, draped in garlands of flowers by Virgie, while Mr. Sissum "shone in a palm beach coat" and "plucked the strings up above her" (p. 46). After he accidentally drowns in the Big Black (Orpheus was thrown into the Styx), Miss Eckhart attends the funeral and seems about to throw herself into his grave (though it was Orpheus who followed Eurydice to the underworld). After her mother has died and she herself has disappeared from town, it is as if she "had gone down out of sight" (p. 58).

Miss Eckhart signifies a "terrible fate" to the townspeople of Morgana because she is attacked one night by a "crazy nigger," and they wish she would move away because they do not like what her presence recalls. Yet the piano teacher can face the hideous act and go on with her life. Through her, Cassie realizes that such acts of fatality exist, terrible contingencies that rise and cross human existence like the planets or constellations crossing the sky: "like Perseus and Orion and Cassiopeia in her Chair," she thinks; "it was not just the sun and moon that traveled" (p. 51). A great deal is linked together in the thoughts of the sixteen-year-old girl: her own name attaches her to Cassiopeia, who in turn is part of the Perseus story, and the Yeats poem runs through her head. She remembers that on recital nights Miss Eckhart would be hot and damp, "as though she had run a long way" (p. 67). Once Miss Eckhart's mother, "with her shepherdess curls she bobbed herself" (p. 54), pushed her wheelchair into the music room and mocked the daughter; waiting until Virgie finished playing, Miss Eckhart slapped her old mother across the face. The gesture repeats Perseus' striking off the head of the Gorgon. In her turn, Virgie defies Miss Eckhart, disappoints her, lays her open to the insight of the other children, so that Cassie experiences the effect of tragedy, the catharsis, learning, in her words, to feel "terror and pain in an outsider" (p. 46). One rainy day—one of only a few in the book, all of them auspicious—Miss Eckhart had played for the girls, erratically and unevenly but with passion and art nonetheless, something that "had an origin in a place . . . where Virgie, even, had never been and was not likely ever to go" (p. 49). Cassie reacts to the music by averting her body "as if to ward off blows from Miss Eckhart's strong left hand" (p. 50). "What Miss Eckhart might have told them a long time ago," Cassie realizes, "was that there was more than the ear could bear to hear or the eye to see, even in her" (p. 50). Like the Spanish guitarist of "Music from Spain," Miss Eckhart, the artist, is "formidable" (p. 35; cf. p. 177).

Virgie's last recital for Miss Eckhart occurs when she is thirteen. She plays *Fantasia on Beethoven's Ruins of Athens,* an appropriately classical reference (especially in view of the role of Minerva, patron of Athens, in the book). When the piece is finished, her white dress is stained bright red; she has sweated through the red sash that circles her chest, but it looks "as if she had been stabbed in the heart" (p. 65). Figuratively and literally, Virgie has come of age. She does not take lessons any more and Miss Eckhart's luck, if she had had any, fails (pp. 55–56). Virgie is soon translated to the "world of power and emotion" (p. 52) of the movies, having skipped the girl-world in between childhood and maturity which is inhabited by her contemporaries.

Miss Eckhart goes down out of sight, but on the day of the story, demented or distracted or both, she has apparently walked in from the county poor farm to decorate the old recital room as before and to set it on fire. It is unlikely, contrary to one critic[12] that she knows Virgie is upstairs with the sailor. It is coincidence, and also coincidental is another return by King MacLain, who comes to the old house thinking his family still lives there. Old Man Moody and Mr. Fatty Bowles also come to wake Mr. Holifield, the night watchman; they have been fishing in Moon Lake, but they have caught no silver fish, and they will put out Miss Eckhart's fire, including the one she sets in the hair of her head, and carry her away. Loch, watching all this transpire, reports what he sees without understanding much of it, not the sex in the upstairs room or the fire ritual or the return of King MacLain. He thinks Miss Eckhart is the "sailor's mother." (He has worn a sailor suit himself, in the past (p. 47), and his name, Gaelic for lake, as well as his later occupation as life guard, all go to associate him with that other traveler, Odysseus.) He confuses King with a Mr. Voight, an exhibitionist who once roomed with the MacLains. He identifies Miss Eckhart's metronome as a bomb. After Mr. Moody, thinking the same thing, throws the metronome out the window, Loch captures it and brings it to his room. Virgie had disdained the metronome and refused to play to its regular beat. Loch puts it in his shirt, caches it later in his room, still expecting it to blow up, but embracing it nevertheless. Time is the subject here: how one views it and whether one can, or should, resist or embrace its relentless pace. In the last story, one of the MacLain grandchildren, little King specifically, also sees time as volatile: "Granddaddy's almost a hundred. . . . When you get to be a hundred, you pop" (p. 229). Time is not volatile, as it turns out, though it is relentless. As Katie Rainey says, "Time goes like a dream no matter how hard you run" (p. 9). Time is perhaps most like the river where Virgie bathes in "The Wanderers." Shortly after her reflective immersion in the waters of the Big Black, Virgie will begin to put together what is, for her, a new and more realistic conception of time.

The scene at the MacLain house ends all at once. As the two old men lead Miss Eckhart away, Virgie and the sailor burst out the door. The sailor takes the short-cut to the river, "where he would just about meet with Mr. King MacLain" (p. 78), and Virgie comes on slowly, like Aphrodite or Venus, moving through a cloud: "A haze of the old smoke lifted unhurryingly over her, brushed and hid her for a moment like a gauzy cloud" (p. 79). She passes Miss Eckhart without a word, and all these wanderers meet the returning members of the Rook party held that afternoon, including Mrs. Morrison. Cassie puts her mother in the role of the Sibyl: "When she told bad news, she wore a perfectly blank face and her voice was helpless and automatic" (p. 43). Cassie accuses her, "You knew it would be this way" (p. 81). The Sibyl is another mythological character familiar to Morgana; along with the picture of Perseus, there is a "framed Sibyl" in the music room at the MacLains'. The Sibyl requested and received the gift of long life, but she forgot to ask for enduring youth, and so she grew ugly and wanted to die; her prophecies were figured in leaves which often blew away when the subject opened the entrance to her cave. Mrs. Morrison, we learn later, is an eventual suicide; after "being so gay and flighty always, Cassie's mother went out of the room one morning and killed herself" (p. 230). Perhaps she, too, despaired without everlasting youth. Cassie commemorates her by spelling her name in the yard with hyacinth and narcissus bulbs, using leafy violets to mark the spot during the summer months (p. 239). The Sibyl helped another wanderer, Aeneas, advising him to seek and pluck the "golden bough" in order to gain admission to the infernal regions, and she accompanied him into the cave which gave access there. In association with Mrs. Morrison's role, on this particular day Fate Rainey (from Lafayette), Virgie's father, is heard selling his buttermilk and berries in the streets, crying the "call of somebody seeking about in a deep cave" (p. 22).[13]

It may be, as one critic argues,[14] that Cassie gains what many of the wanderers seek, even though she remains at home. If so, her knowledge is associated with the meaning of tragedy that Virgie has taught her. It is, perhaps, as Yeats says in his *Autobiography*, "We begin to live when we have conceived life as tragedy."[15] For all Virgie's power and her moving in a world remote from Cassie's, she has not got that knowledge yet. "June Recital" ends with a series of almost mystical images that become clearer as the book goes on. Louella, the Morrison cook, catches sight of Loch and Cassie, both of them running around outside half-dressed, and says, "What orphan-lookin' children is these here? . . . Where yawl orphan come from? Yawl don't live here, yawl live at County Orphan. Gawn back" (p. 81). Thus are they identified, although faintly, with King MacLain and his County Orphan offspring. Their mother and father enter the house, sharing a laugh that signifies something else which Loch doesn't understand, "something that might be seizable and holdable as well as findable, as ridiculous and forbidden to children, as alive, as a stray kitten or a rabbit" (p. 82). The specific words are not spoken, but this seizable, findable mystery—so simple in the desires of a pre-pubescent boy—is the golden apples, too. The connection with human love and longing and with the image of the rabbit forges another link between the elements of the book. The "kitten" will come back again and again, too (pp. 7, 73, 112, 120, 185, 189), finally Sphinx-like, with "womanly eyebrows," and, perhaps, implicit in its demeanor, suggesting the riddle of man.

His fever subsiding into a chill, Loch sleeps and dreams. Cassie has come home from a hayride (that afternoon she had thought of her favorite song, "The Light of the Silvery Moon," and tie-dyed a rainbow-colored scarf[16]); she lies in her "moonlit" bed, thinks of "Moon Lake brimming and the boat on it," and reviews the day. Virgie's sailor is a "mer-man from the lake"—akin to Poseidon or Neptune—and he is also Ulysses, the wanderer, for Cassie thinks that he, who had taken King's old route, is only starting a journey that both Miss Eckhart and Virgie had already made: "she was certain of . . . the distance those two had gone" (pp. 84–85). Both are "terrible" to each other, but they "did not even horrify each other" (p. 85). Cassie realizes that "there were others of them—human beings, roaming, like lost beasts" (p. 85). Two paragraphs before, the dreaming Loch had fallen into space, had "heard his growling voice and the gnashing of his teeth" (p. 84), himself like some lost beast in his unconscious longings. Cassie now sleeps, and in place of Loch's colorful and furious dreams, her mind fills with Yeats's "The Song of the Wandering Aengus." Still sleeping, she sits up in bed and repeats the line that has fitted Loch and Miss Eckhart, "Because a fire was in my head." "Then she fell back unresisting. She did not see except in dreams that a face looked in; that it was the grave, unappeased, and radiant face, once more and always, the face that was in the poem" (p. 85). This visitation from the Master of Love will occur again, and to others, in *The Golden Apples*. A figurative expression of longing and desire, on the literal level it could be anyone: Cassie's mother looking in before going to bed, her father, Loch, King MacLain, or, as in a mirror, herself, for all of them, in some way and at some time, wear the face in the poem. In other sections, the face will take the form of a constellation or of the night or of the Spanish guitarist (who has "little bearded animal faces on the buckles" of his suspenders [p. 188]). As with Miss Eckhart, there is more than the ear or eye can bear in young Cassie Morrison. When we understand how that can be, we know ourselves and our own longings a little better.

With the story which follows "June Recital," "Sir Rabbit," a pattern of alternating major and minor movements begins to emerge. Like "Shower of Gold," "Sir Rabbit" is a short tale and a tale of seduction involving King MacLain; once again an earlier incident must be recounted before the current story is told. The first part is Mattie Will Sojourner's memory of a day when she had let the MacLain twins pin her down and have their way on the wet spring ground (pp. 86–88). Now she is older and married to Junior Holifield; with a little Negro boy, they are in the forbidden Stark woods, firing off some old ammunition, where they meet King MacLain, who is hunting. "Thought I'd see if the birds around here still tasted as sweet as they used to," he says (p. 89), with a little hidden meaning. After a few words, King fires his gun over Junior's head, the hapless husband passes out, and King has his will with Mattie. The rape is described in the language of Yeats's poem "Leda and the Swan." Mattie is staggered by King's grandeur; he comes to her roughly, brings her down as with a "shillelagh" (a Celtic addition by Miss Welty), and like Zeus to Leda he imparts to her his knowledge with his flesh (p. 95). This story functions as a counterpoint, a kind of entr'acte, between the two more extensive and more important sections which flank it. It reiterates one of the multiple figurative meanings of the golden apples, their sexual connotation, and it weaves another figure into the mythological tapestry of the book. It also adds a thread to a peculiar skein of imagery. In "June Recital," Cassie had come home from the hayride remembering "Moon Lake brimming and the boat on it" (p. 84), a recollection that seems normal enough. But as Mattie Will watches the MacLain twins approach, she yawns "strangely, for she felt at that moment as though somewhere a little boat was going out on a lake, never to come back" (p. 87). For now, the image provides a simple link between segments of the book, like images of the rabbit, the cat, the golden fruit, and the hummingbird which are also reiterated. It begins to suggest an awareness of change, perhaps sexual, but little else. In one form or another, however, it will recur in most of the remaining stories, while in "Moon Lake," with which it will be discussed, it is elaborated in a way that makes its meanings more plain.

"Moon Lake" is about Loch Morrison, grown a little older, during his ordeal as life saver at a summer camp for girls outside Morgana. It is also about three of the girls. Loch hates girls; he stays apart, living in a remote tent, eating with his back turned, diving and swimming in Moon Lake only when no girls are around. There are many girls at the camp, half of them from the county orphanage which has been mentioned in the two preceding stories. Three girls are principally involved in "Moon Lake": Nina Carmichael and Jinny Love Stark from Morgana, and Easter, or Esther from County Orphan's. Nina's point of view provides much of the focus of the story, and if there is an apple of discord[17] thrown between these three budding goddesses, it is perhaps Nina's coveted silver drinking cup, one of the collapsible kind that used to come (perhaps still do) in travelling kits. Thus, subtly, is the theme of wandering also evoked. Jinny Love is the willful character she remains in the rest of the book, where she reappears as Ran MacLain's young wife (she must be a good deal younger, since she is pre-pubescent here, while Ran is already twenty-three [p. 132]). Easter is enigmatic, not only by virtue of her strange name. Her eyes resemble coins from ancient Greece or Rome, the pupils like "women's heads, ancient" (p. 106). She may be—and certainly symbolically is—another of King MacLain's children. Like the "crazy nigger in the hedge" that assaulted Miss Eckhart, Easter is Loch Morrison's fate. One day when she has climbed on a high diving perch above the lake, little Exum, a twelve-year-old black boy who wears one of King MacLain's cast-off hats— "brilliant as a snowflake" (pp. 109, 124)—touches her heel with a willow switch and she plummets into the lake.[18] Exum howls and clings to the ladder "as though a fire had been lighted under it" (p. 125). Loch leaps into the lake, searches for Easter, drags her out, puts her on one of the picnic tables, and begins resuscitation, an act seen in crudely sexual terms by more than one of the awestruck onlookers. "If *he* was brutal, her self, her body, the withheld life, was brutal too" (p. 129). Time seems to stop (p. 134). The other children momentarily fear that Easter is dead and will speak to them from "the other side," but Loch triumphs over her apparent death. She recovers.

Loch is the hero now, not the boy scout, and later that night Jinny Love and Nina spy him in his tent, naked, vaunting, posed with one arm up, leaning on his tentpole, a bit like Poseidon with his trident or, when he looks into the "Kress mirror" (p. 137), like Perseus viewing the decapitated Gorgon's head. The girls see his "little tickling thing hung on him like the last drop on the pitcher's lip. . . . Minnowy thing that matched his candle flame . . . he thought he shone forth too" (pp. 137–38). Appropriately it is Jinny Love who derides Loch's coming of age; she had confessed to being "ticklish" earlier (p. 122), and she will become Ran's wife and prove unfaithful. She erroneously and ironically predicts to Nina that they "will always be old maids" (p. 138). The two girls have felt the stir of their own longings and self-consciousness and the statement by

Jinny Love is already whistling in the dark. As she is for Loch, Easter is the agent of their embryonic rite of passage.

Easter is ahead of the town girls; she has budding breasts. She had led Jinny and Nina to an old gray boat on the margin of the lake, as if she had known it was there all the time. They try to push off in it, with Easter as their "figurehead" (p. 117), but the boat is chained; their adventure flounders and they march away from "their little boat" (p. 120). The image has been thoroughly compounded by now, coming from Cassie and Mattie Will and evoked in the song the campers sing about "When all the little ships come sailing home" (p. 100). It clearly signifies a "passage"—the awakening of desire, the discovery of a beckoning lure, the beginning of the wanderer's quest; it suggests analogues to Odysseus' voyaging as well as Aeneas', and to Yeats's poems about sailing to the land of the young, to Byzantium, or in the boat of death.[19] For Nina, it specifically relates to Aengus' catch in the crucial title poem: she thinks that night that the Negroes are fishing and that the boat is "full of silver fish" (p. 121). She associates her feelings in the boat with golden fruit, not the figs that appear in "June Recital" or in Jinny Love's complaint that "All I can concentrate on out here is missing the figs at home" (p. 118), but fine pears "sold on trains and at high prices." "To all fruits, and especially to those fine pears, something happened—the process was so swift, you were never in time for them. It's not the flowers that are fleeting, Nina thought, it's the fruits" (p. 116). Like a leitmotif, the song of the wandering Aengus has played again, sounded, as by different instruments, in the reference to the train, to the golden fruit, and to the evanescence of rare pleasures. Like the Morrison children at the end of "June Recital," Nina drops off to sleep in her reveries. On Moon Lake, which sometimes runs like a river, there is the sound of a moored boat, "its vague, clumsy reaching at the shore" (p. 122), and the night, personified for her as it was for Cassie, comes to the opening of her tent. It is another of the beasts that roam, a giant: "She felt the forehead, the beaded stars, look in thoughtfully at her" (p. 123). Though Nina does not know Cassie's poem, she is watched by the face in it, and she feels in herself what it represents: "compassion and a kind of competing that were all one, a single ecstasy, a single longing" (pp. 123–24). "Moon Lake" is another "recital," another turn of the cycle, for "girlhood" is an "infinity" (p. 122) and Moon Lakes, their appropriately named leader Mrs. Gruenwald tells them, are all over the world. "And into each fell a girl, they dared, now, to think" (p. 137).

"Moon Lake" does not merely repeat the patterns and meanings of "June Recital," it amplifies and advances them, bringing the reader closer to full enlightenment. In the same sense, "The Whole World Knows," though a short entr'acte like "Sir Rabbit," a minor movement like "Shower of Gold," is not merely another tale of seduction, though like them it is about seduction and like them concerns the MacLain men again, though only one directly. The piece is a long *cri de coeur* from Randall MacLain to his father and, briefly at the end, his brother. His wife, Jinny Love, née Stark, has been unfaithful to him with Woodrow Spights. Ran has left her and lives as a roomer in the old MacLain house which figured in "June Recital" (and which was the setting for "Shower of Gold"). The "whole world" is Morgana, or at most MacLain County, a neat reminder, like Katie Rainey's hope that the "rest of the world" (p. 10), that is, of the town and county, will not say anything to Snowdie about King's abrupt arrival and departure on Halloween, that as far as anyone here is concerned this rural Olympus is all existence. Ran lays seige to the Stark household, driving his car back and forth along Morgana's main street like the Greek warriors charging and retreating before the walls of Troy. But, as Yeats asserted in his poem, "No Second Troy," modern men do not have courage equal to their desire. Ran is no exception. The summer of his discontent is very hot, and his room in the old MacLain house is like fire, driving him out to take the air in his car. He revenges himself on Jinny by picking up Maideen Sumrall, an unsophisticated young country girl who has come to town to work. He carries her to the Stark house, flaunting the unconcerned Jinny. If this is his Trojan horse, it does not work. He imagines shooting Jinny full of holes or hacking his rival, Woody Spights, to bits with a croquet mallet. But he is no hero. The endless croquet game proceeds in the yard (it is the yard with the statue of the goddess). The only creature he kills is a sick and dying dog which he puts out of its misery, and still he cannot escape his own. In fact he will compound it. He takes Maideen Sumrall to Vicksburg one night, mostly out of belligerence and despair; they go to a nightclub that is built on a barge in the river, riding there and back in a little boat. Earlier Ran had seen the Starks' porch as "like a boat on the river . . . an excursion boat I wasn't going on" (p. 148). As before, the boat imagery signals a change, and in this case it may be the death boat. Ran carries Maideen to a cheap motel; he pulls his pistol, threatening to blow out his brains, but the pistol misfires, and in the aftermath Maideen relieves him of the weapon and they make love.

Randall asks three questions (the magic number often granted in fairy tales): "How was I to know she would go and hurt herself?" (p. 160). In the last story we learn that Maideen has taken this affair seriously; she has killed herself. Her mother's family name, it turns out, is Sojourner, and perhaps she is even akin to the willing Mattie Will of "Sir Rabbit" whom Ran, his brother, and his father seduced. At any rate, Ran knows, "God help me, the name Sojourner was laid on my head like the top teetering crown of a pile of things to remember. Not to forget, never to forget the name of Sojourner" (p. 153). His second question is "Father, Eugene! What you went and found, was it better than this?" (p. 160). The answer, apparently, is No, not necessarily, but the last two sections of *The Golden Apples* will tell it better than that. The third question is "And where's Jinny?" (p. 160). She's at home. Eventually she and Ran will reunite and have children; the town will elect him Mayor, as much because of his well-known sin as anything (a recognition of, and hence a way of controlling, the fate, like the rapist and the girl falling in Moon Lake, which comes on men unpredictably but regularly). Ran stays in Morgana and grows fat.

The details of "The Whole World Knows" indicate that, for all its timelessness, Morgana has come into the post-war era of the twentieth century. Rook—played with number cards and thus different from games played with decks containing face cards, called "sin cards" in the not-so-remote Mississippi past—has given way to bridge played for money. Infidelity and divorce and suicide, not exactly new in the world but newfangled in Morgana, are more possible. Victor Rainey has been killed in World War I. The automobile has given the wanderers an illusory mobility (up and down the principal street; as the phrase used to go, "dragging Main"); it has made it easier to leave, though not for long and not, as in Ran's case, without terrible consequences. By the "present" time of the last story, the vines and berry bushes from which Katie Rainey took her wares are dried; and the road by which she sold them is full of logging trucks and the "wrong people" who do not "stop to pass words on the season and what grew" (pp. 213–14). It may not have come as far as in one of the unreal cities, but the wasteland has encroached seriously in Morgana.

The third major movement, and next-to-last section of *The Golden Apples*, "Music from Spain," is balanced against "June Recital" not only by position but also by virtue of its musical subject. The musical analogy has a number of applications in the book, as a matter of fact. The connected stories do correspond to the sequences of a mythological cycle, but they may as aptly be regarded as movements like those in a piece of cyclic music, a sonata or a symphony. There is exposition, development, recapitulation, and coda; the shorter pieces which divide the major stories have in common the subject of seduction, as well as other themes and subjects important to the whole conception. They seem to constitute a kind of counterpoint or perhaps a key variation like the alternation from tonic to dominant in the sonata form. Given all the references to Beethoven in "June Recital"—and Miss Eckhart's sonata—it might even be that we should think of that great composer's powerful symphonies which, like *The Golden Apples*, hold the individual movements together with a strong

textural consistency that comes from the reiteration of themes and
figures and tonal material. If we accept the musical context, then
"Music from Spain," with its alien setting, may be regarded as
something played in a slightly different key before the return to
home key (Morgana) in the last story, "The Wanderers," which itself
can be seen as coda and ending.

"Music from Spain" is set in San Francisco, where the protagonist,
the other MacLain twin, Eugene, replays the Perseus story. His
adventure begins on the morning he reaches across the breakfast
table and, like Miss Eckhart slapping her mother, slaps his wife's
face. He leaves her, seeing "his face go past the mirror with a smile
on it" (p. 161). He carries a folded newspaper under his arm, like
a sword; he wears what amounts to a magical hat (one of a number
of important hats in the book, by the way). His raincoat becomes a
cloak of invisibility—he is later able to slip past the jeweler's where
he works without being spotted by his boss, even though the boss
is standing in the front and "on the lookout for what he might miss"
(p. 167). When Perseus slew Medusa, the blood sinking into the
ground produced Pegasus, the winged horse; as Eugene passes his
shop, he sees their own brand of "rhinestone Pegasus" in the window
(p. 167). In his forties, Eugene seems to have passed the age for
heroics; "it was doubtful that he would ever see the Seven Wonders
of the World" (p. 168). Because he suggested it on the anniversary
of their little daughter's death, his wife, Emma, will not even take
a trip down the California peninsula with him. Emma is turned to
stone by her unappeasable grief over their lost daughter, "her eye
was quite marble-like" (p. 168). Unlike Miss Eckhart or Loch or
Cassie or even Ran MacLain, she has not found a way to face and
control and defeat the Gorgon in her life, the horror that fate introduces into all lives. She will not even go with Eugene to "Half Moon
Bay" (p. 170)—a faint reminiscence, perhaps, of Mrs. Gruenwald's
pronouncement about the ubiquity of Moon Lakes. But the night
before the story opens, she had accompanied him to Aeolian Hall to
hear a Spanish guitarist perform. The musical performance has affected
Eugene. Now, unaccountably having slapped his wife and resolved
to skip work, he leaves the house and fortuitously meets the giant
Spanish guitarist on a downtown street, saves the artist from walking
into the path of an automobile, and the two of them, neither speaking
the other's language, spend the day wandering the city together.

The story is told that after the slaughter of the Gorgon, Perseus
flew to the western limit of the earth. There he encountered King
Atlas, a giant who had gardens filled with fruit of gold. Remembering
an ancient prophecy that warned of a son of Jove who should one
day rob him of his golden apples, Atlas fought with Perseus. He was
too strong for the youth, but, using the slain Gorgon's head, Perseus

froze his adversary into the mountain that supports the earth. Perseus' further adventures took him to the rescue of Andromeda, the daughter of Cassiopeia. Comparable feats were performed by Hercules, whose most difficult task among the twelve labors was getting the golden apples of the Hesperides, identified, so Bulfinch tells us, with the oranges of Spain. In the tale of Hercules, the West is identified as a region of "brightness and glory,"[20] like Katie Rainey's vision in "Shower of Gold" of a land "out West where it's gold and all" (p. 10). Like Perseus, Hercules also struggles with a giant, Antaeus, who was invincible as long as he remained in contact with Mother Earth. All these stories seem to be paralleled in "Music from Spain," where they are fittingly compounded with other references to the golden apples of Celtic and classical mythology.

Eugene remembers the Spaniard's face during the preceding night's performance. It seems to be "the face in the poem" that Cassie Morrison and Nina Carmichael see in their bedtime reveries. The face "had the enchanted presence of a smile on the face of a beast" (p. 173). Like Miss Eckhart's playing for Cassie and Virgie on that rainy afternoon, the Spaniard's music is "most unexpected" (p. 173). In the guitarist's presence in daylight, the old "Scooter" MacLain feels "fleet of foot"—like Perseus with the winged shoes he received from Mercury—and wonders at the way life throws up things which retard or distract us, "like the apples of Atalanta perhaps" (p. 174). He sees a tattooed mulatto whose strange beauty emanates a palpable aura of disgrace and sadness and a side-show fat woman whose name is the same as his wife's. These grotesques remind him that he had once paid his Sunday school money to see an "optical illusion," a woman's head on top of a stepladder, "golden-haired, and young" and smiling invitingly (p. 175). Much that attracts us, perhaps including Aengus' glimmering maiden, is illusion, and we should be reminded that Morgana derives its name from the watery illusion of the desert, the *fata morgana,* the mirage.[21]

In the face of life's glittering illusions, how does one know reality and master life? In "Moon Lake" Nina Carmichael had realized, "You couldn't learn anything through the head" (p. 119). But there may be another, non-rationalistic way to learn; art and the artist provide an answer. Just as Miss Eckhart has taught Virgie and Cassie, though Virgie does not yet realize what she knows, the guitarist will instruct Eugene. Such communications are, however, indirect, and, like all knowledge, are not necessarily lasting. As the men dine—on a meal Eugene will buy because the Spaniard seems unconcerned about such necessities—Eugene realizes that "the formidable artist was free" (p. 177). He begins to think about his present life. He has wondered if hearing the Spaniard has somehow prepared him to slap his wife and discover "something new, something entirely different about life" (p.

177). He tries to imagine "he were still . . . leaving Mississippi" (p. 178) and not settled in San Francisco but only visiting; in other words, still a wanderer instead of a sojourner. What would he do? Perhaps he would go out "looking: not for anyone in particular; on the track, say, of his old man? . . . an old goat, a black name *he* had" (p. 178). Thus King is identified again with the Dionysiac. His thoughts return to a piece *he* used to play at Miss Eckhart's recitals, "The Stubborn Rocking Horse" (p. 180)—again, no true Pegasus— and a green hummingbird darts in front of him and vanishes, "like a little fish" (p. 180), compounding the hot day in San Francisco with summers in Mississippi and his whole past.[22] His vision includes the picture of the Sibyl on the wall of Miss Eckhart's studio and an illustration in one of his father's geography books (King *would* like geography): "the kneeling Man in the Wilderness . . . who hacked once at the Traveler's Tree, opened his mouth, and the water came pouring in" (p. 180). But somewhat unexpectedly Eugene dismisses any extraordinary meaning to be distilled from these memories— though surely the picture of the wanderer slaking his thirst is sig- nificant—and he thinks, "What did Eugene MacLain really care about the life of an artist, or a foreigner, or a wanderer, all the same thing?" (p. 180). The joining of the three names, whether Eugene wants to admit its importance for him or not, makes it plain that the major characters of the book are, in some respects, "the same thing," and that they are all images of the artist, or, more aptly, the truth may be that the artist in his struggle to create is an intensified image of all human longing and desire. Ironically, Eugene is himself all three: artist (a watchmaker, a jeweler), foreigner (a Mississippian unsuccessfully transplanted to San Francisco), and a wanderer. Truly, he does care. He is searching for the satisfaction of his long-suppressed longings, whether it be in the form of a Traveler's Tree or a new love (p. 164). His encounter with the Spanish guitarist will provide the opportunity for acts of heroic proportions that are, in terms of the myths they reflect, emblematic of self-discovery and the mastery of life.

As Eugene and the Spaniard continue through the streets, they see a woman killed, struck down by a streetcar, victim of the sudden fate from which Eugene has saved the Spaniard. The witnesses to the accident "seemed to consider themselves gently floating like the passengers on a raft" (p. 182), another association of the boat with death. The two men are bound. It is as if Eugene has found his lost half, a possibility reinforced by general references to twins (in the restaurant, p. 177, and on the street, p. 184) and by Eugene's quick wave of "overwhelming, secret tenderness toward his twin, Ran MacLain, whom he had not seen for half his life" (p. 187). They go to "Land's End" (p. 191), the western limit to which Perseus goes after slaying the Medusa.[23] Impulsively, Eugene tries to throw the Spaniard off the cliff; it is playful, but in earnest, a deliberate grasping of the other's life and putting it into the balance. They struggle, but Eugene is no match (he weighs even less than his wife) for the giant. He is Perseus against Atlas, and later, when they wrestle again, he cannot move the Spaniard, like Hercules with Antaeus. He is also Theseus confronting the Minotaur, for the Spaniard, who had seemed to have "horns on his head" and be "waiting—or advancing!" (p. 179), gives a "bullish roar" (p. 195). He repeats a "terrible recital" which Eugene cannot understand. When his hat blows away, Eugene clambers for it, puts it on, and feels elation run "all through his body, like the first runner that ever knew the way to it" (p. 196). After more wrestling, in which the Spaniard holds Eugene in the air, they return in the dark, looking "together for the thread of the way back," like some Theseus returning *with* the monster (p. 199), an important distinction which puts the story closer to Perseus' capture of the Gorgon's head and to the meanings that may be derived from that act.

Eugene leaves the Spaniard at an all-night restaurant and comes home alone, back to Emma, an ending he had begun to expect and to dread, but it is more deflating than he anticipated. Emma has forgotten his dreadful act of the morning.[24] She is not interested in his wanderings or his bout with the Spaniard. A neighbor visiting in the house puts a vulgar tone on the anti-climactic closing scene of the story. In "The Wanderers" we learn that Eugene MacLain returns to Morgana without his wife, without ever revealing anything about his wife, his life in San Francisco, or his lovely dead child. He dies of tuberculosis and like Miss Eckhart and Mrs. Morrison and other dissatisfied wanderers and sojourners, he is buried near Morgana.

We see the graves of these people in the last story, which brings *The Golden Apples* to resolution and end. Katie Rainey dies, is mourned and buried. With the skill typical of her handling of all country rites, Miss Welty portrays the ritual before, during and after her funeral. The story concerns Virgie, chiefly, who is back in Morgana, too, after a short sojourn in Memphis when she was much younger (it isn't far, a few hundred miles; Morgana is located between Jackson and Vicksburg, Mississippi). She is fortyish, unmarried, host to a succession of unworthy lovers. But the love goddess who as a child had run beneath the linked arms of lovers and garlanded the infatuated Miss Eckhart (pp. 45–46), still has a walk that people have to watch: "head, breasts, and hips in their helpless agitation" (p. 210). Like the day she and Kewpie Moffitt came out of the MacLain house, she still moves in a cloud of smoke or vapor. She wakes to see the morning star, Venus, and feel its presence. After she has bathed in the Big Black River, she rises out of the waters into the view of two silent, motionless naked boys a distance away in a scene like the birth of Venus (pp. 219–20).[25] With her mother dead, Virgie thinks at last that she will really go away, as Loch Morrison has done, to find the life she desires. Loch is in New York; that is all we know, although what we know of Eugene MacLain in San Francisco may color our speculations about Loch's possible success. King MacLain, the far wanderer, has come back, stopped at the wrong end of his travels, as he says. He is under the control of his wife Snowdie, now, and an old man, but the life force is still strong in him, strong enough for him to make an ugly face and yell silently at Virgie the day of her mother's funeral: "It was a yell at everything—including death" (p. 227). Snowdie lures him away from the ham at the Raineys' house with "that nice Moody fish from Moon Lake" they have at home (p. 229), so he doesn't go to the cemetery where Virgie sees the graves.

There is Mr. Sissum's grave, into which Miss Eckhart—"her old piano teacher whom she had hated" (p. 230)—had tried to throw herself; the grave of Victor, her brother, if he is in the "box that came back from the other war" (p. 232); and the grave of Maideen Sumrall, the country girl whom Ran MacLain had ruined, buried with the Sojourners, her mother's clan: "I hate her, Virgie thought calmly. . . . Hate her grave" (p. 231). It is doubtful that Virgie's words mean exactly what she says. Her "hate" is more like an expression of doubt or fear, since what happened to Miss Eckhart and Maideen Sumrall figuratively represents Virgie's own possible fate. Later on she drives the seven miles to MacLain Courthouse, the county seat hamlet, and sees another cemetery. There Eugene MacLain is buried, having "lived in another part of the world, learning while he was away that people don't have to be answered just because they want to know" (p. 241). There too are buried King's grandfather, who had killed someone—"what would be the long story behind it," Virgie thinks, "the vaunting and the wandering from it?" (p. 241)— and Miss Eckhart. Virgie's lovers pass in review: Bucky Moffitt the sailor; Simon Sojourner; Mr. Mabry; Mr. Nesbitt, who waited hopefully as Mr. Mabry waited for her to return. But she may not be going back to the one or forward to the other. "Could she ever be, would she be, where she was going?" she thinks (p. 242). In her reverie, the picture of Perseus that had hung on Miss Eckhart's wall reappears, threatening, the "same thing as Siegfried and the Dragon," Miss Eckhart had said, referring to the story of the Rhinegold. Suddenly, Virgie can explicate the myth:

> Cutting off the Medusa's head was the heroic act, perhaps, that made visible a horror in life, that was at once the horror in love, Virgie thought—the separateness. She might have seen heroism prophetically when she was young and afraid of Miss Eckhart . . .

but she was never a prophet. Because Virgie saw things in their time, like hearing them—and perhaps because she must believe in the Medusa equally with Perseus—she saw the stroke of the sword in three moments, not one. In the three was the damnation—no, only the secret . . . beyond the beauty and the sword's stroke and the terror lay their existence in time—far out and endless, a constellation which the heart could read over many a night. (p. 243)

The passage brings together much of what has gone before in the book. Past forty, Virgie arrives at the stage Cassie Morrison had reached when they were sixteen.[26] Cassie had seen obscure things emerge and turn like the constellations in the night sky, and she had understood that these mysteries, these uncertainties one read in the stars, could be borne. That was for Virgie, by contrast, the year of Kewpie Moffitt, and the next year she had gone off to Memphis, and after she had returned there had been the succession of older Kewpie Moffitts, other lovers. Virgie's surprising statement a few pages earlier about hating Miss Eckhart is negated; she had not hated her, she "had come near to loving" the woman (p. 243). She realizes that Miss Eckhart had hung the picture of Perseus on the wall for herself. "She had absorbed the hero and the victim and then, stoutly, could sit down to the piano with all Beethoven ahead of her." Then, with mingled hate and love and life, she "offered Virgie her Beethoven. . . . offered, offered, offered—and when Virgie was young, in the strange wisdom of youth that is accepting of more than is given, she had accepted *the* Beethoven, as with the dragon's blood" (p. 243). This is a wisdom that has lain hidden in Virgie since that time. The melody—*the* Beethoven, the essence of Beethoven, of art, the mystery—lifts: "Every time Perseus struck off the Medusa's head, there was the beat of time, and the melody. Endless the Medusa, and Perseus endless" (p. 243).

Long before, Virgie had spurned the metronome which stood for Time, Process, the perpetual repeated joys and sorrows, loves and hates of existence. There had been that illusory other world of "power and emotion" to which she had aspired. She is reconciled to time now, and to a more mature vision of existence. Some pages earlier, she had stated her realization that "all the opposites on earth were close together, love close to hate, living to dying; but of them all, hope and despair were the closest blood" (p. 234). Like a character in a fairy tale, she had resolved to "sell the cows to the first white man I meet in the road" (p. 236), and then she had driven the seven magical miles to MacLain Courthouse, where the rest of her thoughts fall into place. It is raining, as it was on the day she had resolved to butt her brains out on the schoolhouse basement wall and on the day Miss Eckhart played for her and Cassie. The rain sets up a contrast between the real world where people must live and the world of their desires—a perfect world which must remain an illusion for mortals, though it be a reality for the gods. Using Bulfinch's quotation from Cowper's *Odyssey* will suffice to prove the difference:

> . . . Minerva, goddess azure-eyed,
> Rose to Olympus, the reputed seat
> Eternal of the gods, which never storms
> Disturb, rains drench, or snow invades, but calm
> The expanse and cloudless shines with purest day.
> There the inhabitants divine rejoice
> For ever.
>
> (Bulfinch, p. 9)

Virgie *Rainey*—the name must not be an accident—has come down to earth.[27] She has a companion, an "old wrapped-up Negro woman with a red hen under her arm," and "she and the old beggar woman, the old black thief, were there alone and together in the shelter of the big public tree, listening to the magical percussion, the world beating in their ears" (p. 244). The "old black thief" is the woman about whom Virgie had spoken to Juba, the servant sent to help her pack. "I saw Minerva," she had said, and she had listed the things Minerva had stolen from the house (p. 238). In mythology, the old woman was one of Minerva's disguises. Virgie is at peace, now, and Minerva, the goddess of wisdom, is a fitting companion.[28] The percussion of the rain is like the beat of time. The public tree under which they sit reminds us of the world ash, the rowan oak, the axle-tree, the center of things, and we may see that Virgie has reached the point also described so well by T. S. Eliot in the *Four Quartets,* "the still point of the turning world," "the moment which is not of action or inaction," where knowledge comes.[29] She and Minerva hear the wheeling constellations which, like the myths of the ancients, depict universal and timeless human actions and human desires. They are almost all there—Perseus, Cassiopeia, Hercules, Castor and Pollux, Pegasus and Equuleus, Ursa Major and Minor, Lynx and the Leos, Draco (the dragon who guarded the golden apples of the Hesperides), and Cygnus—the figures whose tales have played major and minor roles in *The Golden Apples.* But Virgie mentions only a few: "the running of the horse and bear, the stroke of the leopard, the dragon's crusty slither, and the glimmer and the trumpet of the swan" (p. 244).

The stories of Aengus and Perseus, which are two of the chief analogues of the very real human experiences dramatized in Miss Welty's book, may at first seem to be polar opposites. Aengus catches a fleeting glimpse of unexpected beauty, the ungraspable and lovely phantom of human desire, and spends his life seeking to recapture it. Perseus faces and overcomes, by his artfulness, the kind of horror that can turn men to stone. The legend and the myth unite, however, in the sense that they present the full and common experience of life. We search for love and beauty in a world where we also must face terror, death, and the threat of meaninglessness. All the opposites, as Virgie says, are close together, but hope and despair are the closest. The Gorgon was herself once a beautiful woman, but she defied Minerva and paid the penalty. Virgie can say she "hates" Miss Eckhart and Maideen Sumrall because she can see them, in one way, as the unsatisfied wanderer and the person unprepared to strike off the Gorgon's head. The stories of Aengus and Perseus are also united by the simple presence of the golden apples. Between the apparent poles of these experiences lie the many other stories and characters which run the gamut of human possibility. There are multitudinous golden apples, and they represent not merely objects of longing and desire or the goals in a quest filled with jeopardy; they are discord, illusion, distraction, and all that is precious and rare. Taken together they are the fruits of life, the golden fruit of existence, not forbidden but sometimes foreboding; not unattainable, but always difficult to seize; perpetually worthy and capable of celebration.

In a connection unrelated to Miss Welty, the novelist Reynolds Price has written that the Perseus myth is a far better myth of the artist than the often-used Narcissus story. The artist, he writes, is Perseus, the mirror, and the Gorgon, and though Price does not elaborate, he apparently means that the artist is one who faces the terrors of existence, he is also the device by which they are rendered impotent and visible, and he is finally the demons themselves. The artist, that is, uses the mirror of his art to display and conquer the creations of human consciousness or unconsciousness. In the same essay where he offers this analogy, he imagines the effect the primitive artist must have had on his companions when he limned "a likeness of the awful world . . . reduced to visible size, held, even yoked."[30] Without making any claims for the ultimate truth of Price's interpretation of either Perseus or the artist, we can still see that it is a conception that applies usefully to a reading of *The Golden Apples*. It even parallels Virgie Rainey's explication of Perseus, her believing in Medusa equally with Perseus, and her seeing the stroke of the sword in three moments. *The Golden Apples* is by no means a book solely about art, though it is both an artistic book and a book which mentions art quite frequently; but it is a book in which the difficulties of human understanding are shown to be closely akin to the efforts of the artist. It is not even so much that all ordinary men and women are lesser beings than the artist as that the artist has the interest and the gift to put his discoveries into a pleasing form. The artist's goals are our goals: to discern ultimate reality, to face and to achieve control over experience, to be conscious of the deep roots of the past, to enrich the fleeting present, and to face the uncertain future with courage and purpose. It is not a program everyone will agree with, but it has been accredited by generations of men and women, artists and not, and it seems to be validated by both Virgie Rainey and Eudora Welty in the book at hand.

Ultimately, of course, we must reject any simple statement of what *The Golden Apples* is "about," what it does, or how it does it, since the richness, the humanity, the intricate orchestration of its varied subjects and themes defies mere summary. MacLain and Morgana, as Miss Welty has depicted them, represent a palpably human world that supports a complex but typical human life. It is not pure reality, but fiction, and what makes it remarkable and moving is the shapely form and language with which it has been depicted by its creator. With her customary skill, Miss Welty evokes her place in all its moods, and, as we know, place is more than just location for her. It is a meaning in itself.[31] Eugene MacLain is not carried away by the Spaniard's music until he plays "very softly some unbearably rapid or subtle songs of his own country, so soft as to be almost without sound, only a beating on the air like a fast wing—then was Eugene moved" (p. 183). The reader is likewise moved, and by similar means, possibly even when he does not have a past that can be suddenly brought to life by the glimpse of the hummingbird's flight. Like the greatest art, which this underrated book clearly represents, *The Golden Apples* exists for us on its own terms as its own best expression. Even the broadest discussion of the apparent method and effects of the book does not quite express the kind of mutation which has occurred. As indicated in the second paragraph of this essay, it would be wrong to insist too strongly that Miss Welty has programmed her fine book with myth or analogies to musical form, or any single scheme of allusion and structural underpinning; we can credit many of the patterns and much of the allusion no doubt to her deft improvisations as she went about the process of discovery and analysis and creation. At the same time, we must not deny her all the credit we can give, for art is not merely a mystery, but also a discipline; *The Golden Apples* is conscious art. Like *Moby-Dick* or *Huckleberry Finn* or *Absalom, Absalom!* and however it is composed, *The Golden Apples* is also something new, something that did not exist before: a unique glimpse of life, a new myth fashioned out of the old. Though we can only do so with comparative naivete, we should be as pleased by it and proud of it as Miss Welty herself, who has said that it "in a way is closest to my heart of all my books."[32]

Notes

1. In a 1972 interview by Charles T. Bunting, " 'The Interior World': An Interview with Eudora Welty," *Southern Review,* N. S. 8 (Autumn 1972), 715.

2. In a question and answer session during the 1965 Southern Literary Festival at the University of Mississippi, 23 April 1965, Miss Welty responded to a question about the use of mythology in her work by saying that she did not deliberately put in mythology. Because she was steeped in mythological stories as a child, however, she said, she often discovered patterns in the lives of her characters that corresponded to the stories she knew. More recently, and somewhat more candidly, she has said, "I have used not only Mississippi folklore but Greek and Roman myths or anything else, Irish stories, anything else that happens to come in handy . . . [though] I don't start out just to write something and use folklore. It is just there to be plucked" (Television interview with Eudora Welty and Walker Percy on William Buckley's *Firing Line* program, produced in Jackson (Miss.) 12 December 1972, and broadcast over the Public Broadcasting Service network 24 and 27 December 1972. The quotation is taken from the unedited transcript of the program. A version of the interview is printed elsewhere in this volume).

3. The most well-balanced discussion of *The Golden Apples,* as of all Miss Welty's work up through about 1961, is Ruth M. Vande Kieft's *Eudora Welty* (New York: Twayne, 1962). Vande Kieft discusses some, but by no means all the mythological allusions, and though she has an excellent section on the repeated fruit and hummingbird images reiterated in the book, she omits consideration of several important repeated images. Harry C. Morris' "Eudora Welty's Use of Mythology," *Shenandoah,* 6, ii (Spring 1955), 34–40, is a good brief introduction to myth in *The Golden Apples,* as far as it goes, but he has not seen the unifying force of the mythology or the patterns and development in the book, concluding erroneously that Miss Welty's work "breaks down most seriously" in its attempts to "fuse previously separate myths into an artistic whole," and that *TGA* is an unsuccessful experiment. Robert W. Daniel discusses *TGA* and mythology in two versions of a single essay on Miss Welty; his work, which lacks any depth, appears as "The World of Eudora Welty" in *Southern Renascence,* ed. Louis D. Rubin and Robert D. Jacobs (Baltimore: Johns Hopkins, 1953) and, slightly revised, as "Eudora Welty: The Sense of Place," in *South: Modern Southern Literature in Its Setting,* ed. Rubin and Jacobs (Garden City, N. Y.: Doubleday, 1961). Louis D. Rubin, in "The Golden Apples of the Sun," in his collection *The Faraway Country: Writers of the Modern South* (Seattle: University of Washington Press, 1963), writes an admiring account of *Delta Wedding* and *TGA* which includes consideration of mythology in the second book. J. A. Bryant, Jr., *Eudora Welty* (Minneapolis: University of Minnesota Press, 1968), a pamphlet in the Minnesota series, discerns a limited amount of mythology; for instance, he calls Loch Morrison the single Perseus figure. Like Rubin's essay, as a general discussion, however, his work is sympathetic and helpful. Alfred Appel's book, *A Season of Dreams: The Fiction of Eudora Welty* (Baton Rouge: Louisiana State University Press, 1965) is blatantly dependent on the Vande Kieft book and does not deserve serious consideration. F. D. Carson, " 'The Song of the Wandering Aengus': Allusion in *TGA,*" *Notes on Miss. Writers,* 6, No. 1 (Spring 1973), 14–17, suggests that more should be done with Yeats's poem.

4. William Butler Yeats, *The Variorum Edition of the Poems of W. B. Yeats,* ed. Peter Allt and Russell K. Alspach (New York: Macmillan, 1957), pp. 149–50. The poem was available in more than a dozen collections prior to the time of Miss Welty's *TGA.*

5. Yeats, p. 807. These Notes were in most of the editions noted in fn. 4.

6. Eudora Welty, *The Golden Apples* (New York: Harcourt Brace, 1949). All references are to the first edition.

7. The association of the godhead with brightness is common enough not to require a source, but the way the "god" and his consort are linked here invites some speculation about a possible use of James G. Frazer's *The Golden Bough* in its one-volume abridgement. Frazer notes that "the two pairs of deities, Jupiter and Juno on the one side, and Dianus and Diana, or Janus and Jana, on the other side, are merely duplicates of each other, their names and their functions being in substance and origin identical. With regard to their names, all four of them come from the same Aryan root DI, meaning 'bright,' which occurs in the names of the corresponding Greek deities, Zeus and his old female consort Dione" (*The Golden Bough*, one volume, abridged [New York: Macmillan, 1951], pp. 190–91). The passage is of course also in the twelve-volume original, but the abridgement, first published in 1922, is a more convenient and more readily available source for most writers. For other possible borrowings from Frazer in *TGA*, see notes 8, 9, and 10 below.

8. Frazer writes of the Celtic peoples "who inhabited the Land's End of Europe"; compare Miss Welty's use of the real San Francisco site, also called Land's End, in connection with allusions to the Perseus myth in "Music from Spain." The Celts, according to Frazer, did not organize their festivals around the solstices but "without any reference to the position of the sun in the heaven. They were two in number, and fell at an interval of six months, one being celebrated on the eve of May Day and the other on Allhallow Even or Hallowe'en" (Frazer, p. 733). Both these festivals seem to be used in the Celtic-haunted world of Morgana. Action begins on Halloween, which is an anniversary for King and Snowdie, and the book will also end in October. "June Recital," for all that it takes place in the month of the solstice, is celebrated like the eve of May Day, with garlands and green boughs and, as with the Celts, a "fire festival." See Frazer, pp. 715–20, 732–37.

Sitting in her chair by the road as by the portals to Morgana, Katie Rainey is like one of the goddesses of the seasons. In the last story it will be lamented that no one stops any more to "pass words on the season and what grew" with her (pp. 213–14). The day she recounts, when King returns, has a "two-way look, like a day will at change of the year," she observes (p. 16). It is King who claims to have given Katie the chair she sits in, saying that her husband "never got her the thing she wanted. I set her on a throne!" (p. 224). These passages, plus later ones which suggest that King could possibly be the father of Katie's children, Virgie (Venus) and Victor (Mars), though they may not be meant literally, do find further meaning in the context of Frazer's discussion of like-named deities, explicitly Janus and Jana (see note 7). Janus' two-way look, as well as the etymology of the name, according to Frazer, identifies him as a watcher of portals and a divine watchman in general.

Except where *The Golden Bough* is specified, Bulfinch's *Age of Fable*, also widely known and readily available, is the source for mythological references in this essay. It is worth noting that long before Joyce and Eliot, Bulfinch's discussion of mythology identified its use and its usefulness in "modern" literature—that is, poetry up through the 19th century. For the goddesses of the seasons, see *Bulfinch's Mythology: The Age of Fable, The Age of Chivalry, Legends of Charlemagne* (New York: Modern Library, [1934]), p. 9.

9. Frazer, pp. 734, 735.

10. Another feature of the Beltane celebration on the even of May Day was the passing round of a special cake. At the recitals, Miss Eckhart supplied "Punch and *kuchen,*"—"little cakes that . . . were sweet, light, and warm, their tops sprinkled with colored 'shot' " (pp. 65–66); and on the day Miss Eckhart decorates the MacLain house with "Maypole ribbons of newspaper" and a green bough and attempts to set

it afire, Mrs. Morrison returns from the Rook party and tells her children about the delicacies served there (p. 83).

11. Wagner's opera *Tannhäuser*, which uses the legend of the minstrel who sought admission to the court of Venus and then found life there boring, is a fitting allusion in a book where so many characters search for love. The musical and Germanic associations are also in an appropriate context.

12. Vande Kieft, p. 119. All the arrivals at the MacLain house may parallel Bulfinch's report that all the gods came to Jupiter's; almost everyone in *TGA* visits the house at one time or another. See Bulfinch, p. 9.

13. Bulfinch, pp. 212-13. There may be faint resemblance, also, to Hercules, who was the consort of Hebe. Like Katie selling her ice cream and cakes at Morgana political gatherings, Hebe, the cupbearer of the gods, handed round food at gatherings on Olympus. Fate never performs the famous twelve labors, but like Aeneas, Hercules descended into the underworld; his companions were Mercury and Minerva, the god and goddess who also aid Perseus. Elsewhere in *TGA*, Perseus and Hercules figure prominently; both, by the way, had to wrestle powerful giants and both sought the golden apples.

14. Rubin, *The Faraway Country*, p. 154.

15. The *Autobiography of William Butler Yeats* (New York: Macmillan, 1938), p. 165.

16. Perhaps associating her with Iris, goddess of the rainbow and attendant to Juno. See also the reference Cassie makes to the rainbow colors of the recital dresses (p. 59).

17. See Bulfinch, p. 171.

18. Easter is identified with the Delphic oracle when she smokes a dried vine: "Easter once more looked the same as asleep in the dancing shadows, except for what came out of her mouth, more mysterious, almost, than words" (p. 119). See Bulfinch, p. 237. Her fate at Moon Lake reminds us of many mortal maidens who perished, or were metamorphosed, rather than submit to would-be seducers, while little Exum, wearing King's old hat and carrying a willow switch very much like Aengus' hazel wand, appropriately suggests one of the disguises of the amorous god.

19. With so much dependence on the Perseus story in the book, possibly the boat imagery also reflects Bulfinch's speculation that the Gorgons were personifications of the terrors of the sea (Bulfinch, p. 96).

20. Bulfinch, p. 120.

21. See Linda Kuehl, "The Art of Fiction XLVII: Eudora Welty," *Paris Review*, No. 55 (1972), 93: "I was drawn to the name [Morgana] because I always loved the conception of *Fata Morgana*—the illusory shape, the mirage that comes over the sea. . . . My population might not have known there was such a thing as *Fata Morgana*, but illusions weren't unknown to them, all the same—coming in over the cottonfields."

22. In working papers for *TGA* now at the University of Texas, the last story of the book carried the title "The Hummingbirds," and it also appeared under that title in *Harper's Bazaar*, March 1949. I am indebted to Professor Noel E. Polk of the University of Texas at Arlington for information on the Welty papers at Austin. See Ruth Vande Kieft's illuminating discussion of the repetitive hummingbird imagery in *Eudora Welty*, pp. 145-47.

23. "Land's End," it has been noted, is a real attraction in San Francisco, just as the Big Black River near Morgana is a real river running through Miss Welty's Mississippi, but in both cases the artist has found names that serve more than simple geographical functions. Big Black is suggestive of the rivers of the classical underworld,

and Land's End comes up figuratively, and literally, in the tales of Hercules and Perseus as well as in the Celtic material she may have drawn from.

24. Somewhat ironic in the context of the references to Yeats's poetry is that Emma MacLain apparently looks like "Madame Blavatsky," whose picture Eugene sees in "the flyblown window" of a San Francisco bookstore. For a brief history of Yeats and the theosophist, see the *Autobiography*, pp. 151–59.

25. The passage descriptive of Virgie's bathing is very close to the account of Arethusa's encounter with the river god in Bulfinch, pp. 49–50. The "burns and scars on Virgie's hands" (p. 225) resemble the wounds suffered by Aphrodite when she intervened in the Trojan War.

26. When the townspeople who have come to Katie's funeral leave, to Virgie "they seemed to drag some mythical gates and barriers away from her view" (p. 218). Eugene MacLain may never be quite so lucky, and the popular song of the time, "Open the Door, Richard," recurs in "Music from Spain" perhaps to signify his need (pp. 169, 186).

27. The "same old Rainey from Louisiana" who had come to Fate's funeral explains that the family has mostly died out, and he "told what had happened to the French name with all the years" (p. 222). Miss Welty may have invented her own etymology. If the Louisiana Rainey thinks the name comes from Old French *reigne*, then then that in turn derives from Latin *regnum*, from *rex*, a king, and we are back with King MacLain, where we started. "King" appropriately derives from a root meaning, among other things, to beget. Source: *The American Heritage Dictionary*, 1969 edition. C. L'Estrange Ewen says English names beginning in "Rain-", etc., derive from Old English *regen*, "mighty" (*History of Surnames of the British Isles* [London: Kegan Paul, Tench, & Trubner, 1931], p. 370).

28. Minerva appears as an old woman in her encounter with Arachne; in the weaving contest between the two, the contrasting dyes of the wool were like "the bow, whose long arch tinges the heavens"—that is, the rainbow. Arachne weaves her tapestry with subjects representing the failings of the gods: Leda and the Swan, Danaë and the Shower of Gold, and the story of the rape of Europa. This last story may be represented in *TGA* by Easter's plunge into Moon Lake; Europa was carried off into the sea. In connection with the annual recital, Miss Eckhart is "tireless as a spider" (p. 33), recalling Arachne, while Cassie's tie-dyed scarf in rainbow colors is supposed to have "a design like a spiderweb" (p. 32). See Bulfinch, pp. 90–92.

29. T. S. Eliot, *Four Quartets* (New York: Harcourt, Brace & World, 1943), p. 5 ("Burnt Norton") and p. 25 ("Dry Salvages"). This is not to suggest borrowing from Eliot, only an explanatory parallel.

30. Reynolds Price, *Things Themselves* (New York: Atheneum, 1972), p. 8. The point that Price's occasion was not the discussion of Miss Welty's work is made because he has written about her on other occasions so thoughtfully and appreciatively. Since he knows and likes her work so well, it may be, nevertheless, that her use of the Perseus myth was in the back of his mind when he devised this explanation.

31. When Linda Kuehl asked her, "Is place your source of inspiration?" Miss Welty replied, "Not only that, it's my source of knowledge. It tells me the important things. It steers me and keeps me going straight, because place is a definer and a confiner of what I'm doing. It helps me to identify, to recognize and explain. It does so much for you of itself. It saves me" (Kuehl, p. 92).

32. *Southern Review*, 8 (Autumn 1972), 714.

Seeing Double in
The Golden Apples J. A. Bryant, Jr.°

Eudora Welty's *The Golden Apples* came out in 1949, seven years after *The Robber Bridegroom* and three years after her phenomenally successful *Delta Wedding*. The chapters of Miss Welty's new work had all been published previously as short stories; and that fact, in the eyes of readers who preferred their literary taxonomy unambiguous, kept it from being a proper novel. Since then a number of responsible critics have insisted on the unity of *The Golden Apples* (especially Louis D. Rubin, Jr., and Alfred Appel); and readers generally, having had an opportunity to read the book carefully and reflectively, seem to have recognized in it the presence of an elusive principle that makes what might have been simply an interesting chronicle of Morgana, Mississippi, into a single aesthetically coherent work. It would be presumptuous in a short essay like this to attempt to pluck the heart out of such a mystery or to lay bare the intricate concatenation of nerve and sinew that gives *The Golden Apples* its integrity. Of such larger matters let it suffice here to record agreement with all those who have been able to disregard shifts in place, leaps in time, and the absence of any single character who can be said to dominate the whole and declare *The Golden Apples* a unified work rather than a collection. My more limited purpose will be to focus upon one part of the mystery and to call attention to a detail which not only characterizes all those persons in the novel who embody its life and action but also constitutes the link between it and much of the rest of Miss Welty's fiction, early and late. A good place to study this or any other aspect of *The Golden Apples* is the second chapter of the work, the justly admired "June Recital"; for that selection is the crossroads of the book, the place where most of the themes, devices, and important characters intersect and make themselves known. With "June Recital" in our eye we can deal more economically with several of the other parts, notably the remarkable final chapter with its startling conclusion.

The detail to be considered here can best be described as a special way of seeing, or perceiving, which conditions in some degree the total vision of most of the principal characters and which, if they persist in it, may drive them to go on strange quests or otherwise wander from the patterns of normal behavior. Perception of this special kind is not unknown in other fiction, but all too often commentators and even authors sentimentalize it as a visionary dream of

° From *Sewanee Review* 82 (Spring 1974):300–15. Copyright 1974 by the University of the South. Reprinted with permission of the editor.

some sort, the possessor of which is expected to seek and find appropriate fulfillment—in love, adventure, self-realization or some other accomplishment. The characters of *The Golden Apples* do not reach goals or attain prizes or even seem to know what such things are. For them, or so the book would have us believe, seeing is its own fulfillment, a reward that carries with it a rare kind of vitality which more than compensates for the restlessness and anguish it sometimes causes. "June Recital" helps us to understand that unusual gift by presenting several examples of it in action and by invoking an instructive illustration from outside the novel. That illustration is a quotation from Yeats's familiar poem "The Song of Wandering Aengus," which provides a convenient place to begin.

Readers will recall that one of the most interesting characters in "June Recital"—not herself a seer or a seeker—is an adolescent girl named Cassie Morrison, who on the day of the story has been tie-dyeing a scarf to wear on a hayride and who recalls as she fritters away her afternoon the poem by Yeats, which she probably read in school. Only four lines of the poem get through to us in this final version of "June Recital," but the rest is there for any reader halfway familiar with it; and in the whole poem we find both an explanation for the title of the novel and a clue to the unifying action. To understand fully how the poem gives us the second of these we must keep in mind that Aengus is not initially "wandering Aengus." He has begun his quest presumably where all of us must begin—where many of the lesser characters in the story end as well as begin—with only a fire in the head. For Aengus, however, the fire precipitates an activity (fishing), and the activity produces a fish, which turns momentarily (or so he thinks) into a glimmering girl who calls him by name. Thereafter he does indeed wander, seeking the substance of that vision which, wanderers believe, is somehow contained within or behind the simple appearances that day after day present themselves to all beholders; and like all wanderers he continues until he is "old with wandering." As far as Yeats's poem tells us, Aengus never reaches his goal which, in his own compelling terms, is to

> . . . kiss her lips and take her hands;
> And walk among long dappled grass,
> And pluck till time and times are done
> The silver apples of the moon,
> The golden apples of the sun.

As has been noted, however, reaching goals is of minor importance. The goal that Aengus has already achieved is that elusive vision of the doubleness of things which tantalizes forever all beings lucky enough to be possessed even once by it; and that vision, though

Aengus may not know it, is its own reward, in itself the silver apples of the moon and the golden apples of the sun.

Miss Welty's fiction at all periods abounds in characters who are unwittingly lucky in this way. One thinks immediately of the characters in stories like "A Memory," "Old Mr. Marblehall," and "A Curtain of Green"; or of Ruby Fisher and her piece of newspaper, or Powerhouse and his keyboard. Some see, some hear, some perform; but all perceive in the special way that is the prerequisite to poetry and the mythic consciousness. *The Robber Bridegroom* provides several examples of such characters, and it also contains at least one striking statement of the principle. Near the middle of the book Clement Musgrove is speaking to his daughter, Rosamond, about her husband:

> "If being a bandit were his breadth and scope, I should find him and kill him for sure," said he. "But since in addition he loves my daughter, he must be not the one man, but two, and I should be afraid of killing the second. For all things are double, and this should keep us from taking liberties with the outside world, and acting too quickly to finish things off."

In short, in *The Robber Bridegroom,* as in *The Golden Apples,* the commonplace and even the repulsive must be respected; for nothing we see is merely what it seems to be, and the familiar may, and often does, conceal a miracle. This is what William Wallace in "The Wide Net" discovers when he dives in the river in search of a presumably drowned wife only to find in "the dark clear world of deepness" a suggestion of the source of his being. Afterward he relaxes with his friends on the sandbar in relative peace, eats catfish, sleeps, and ends up marvelling like a child at the King of Snakes and enjoying the mystery of a thunderstorm. This is similar to what happens in the miraculous transformation of the Venetian mirror in "The Burning" and in the epiphany that comes on Easter morning to the true bride of the *Innisfallen.* Again and again we find in Eudora Welty's world, as in the world of Lewis Carroll's Alice—that all things are double, at least double—and that the fortunate person among us is the one who habitually, occasionally, or even once in his lifetime has the necessary fire in his head to see the golden possibility of that doubleness in some fragment or detail of the world about him.

The character in *The Golden Apples* who sums much of this up for us and thus becomes the nearest thing we have to a Mississippi version of Wandering Aengus is a travelling tea-and-spice salesman named King MacLain, who drifts in and out of the story in several guises until at last his wife manages to pin him down at home and put an end to his wandering. MacLain's dream is never explicitly presented, but it is probably a glimmering girl of some sort; for in addition to the two legitimate sons (twins) whom he fathers on his albino wife, Miss Snowdie Hudson, town gossip credits him with several children in the county home and still others, "known and unknown, scattered like." Appel thinks he is very likely the father of the orphan named Easter, who appears in "Moon Lake," and perhaps even of Loch Morrison in "June Recital." In any case, like Jove, his classical counterpart, King MacLain has many favorites and delights in encountering them in extraordinary ways. In the episode appropriately called "Shower of Gold" we hear how he returned home after a long absence and met his wife, not in their lawful bed, but in Morgan's Woods. Afterward (or so her friend Katie Rainey reports) "it was like a shower of something had struck her, like she'd been caught out in something bright." On this cue we are expected to supply the comparison and see a Mississippi Danaë, bleached skin and all. In the episode called "Sir Rabbit" the wandering MacLain is more clearly like the Celtic Aengus, but then we come to that story with the promptings of "June Recital" fresh in our minds, and we are ready for the author's report that "when she [Mattie Will Sojourner Hollifield] laid eyes on Mr. MacLain close, she staggered, he had such grandeur, and then she was caught by the hair and brought down as suddenly to earth as if whacked by an unseen shillelagh." We see King MacLain again at the end of the novel, caught but not tamed, still lusting after his own version of golden apples, a wanderer to the finish.

King MacLain appears also in "June Recital," the episode to which we now return; but the wanderer King's role there is even more mysterious than it is elsewhere, and it is by no means the central role. For "June Recital" is dominated by three other wanderers whose presence makes it seem likely that wandering and the double vision that prompts it are endemic in Morgana, Mississippi. To show who these are and how they are related a more detailed review of the story is now in order.

"June Recital" tells of two houses on a June afternoon—one lived in by Mr. and Mrs. Wilbur Morrison and their children, Loch and Cassie; the other, next door to it, empty save for old Mr. Hollifield, the night watchman down at the cotton gin, who sleeps there in an upstairs room during the day. This house next door was for a long time the home of the MacLains—King, Miss Snowdie, and the rambunctious twins. For a shorter period of time it was also the home of a Miss Eckhart, who lived there in rooms rented from the MacLains, taught piano to the children of Morgana, and gave her June recitals; and of a wild and mysterious Mr. Voight, who disliked the piano playing and expressed his displeasure by exposing himself to teacher and pupils on the staircase. But these times are past. On the June day of the story Loch Morrison is confined to his room with an attack of malaria, and Cassie Morrison is in her room tie-dyeing a scarf. Loch's room has the better view of the house next door, and from his window he sees Virgie Rainey, a former pupil of Miss Eckhart's and now piano player at the local movie, enter from the back with a young sailor friend and go upstairs to eat pickles and make love naked on an abandoned mattress. He also sees a dirty and distracted Miss Eckhart, temporarily escaped from the county farm, enter from the front, decorate her old quarters with newspapers, magnolia leaves and blossoms, and her metronome (which she rescues from long neglect in the corner cupboard), and set the whole festive parody of a June recital afire with a lighted candle. Fortunately two local characters, Old Man Moody and Mr. Fatty Bowles, who are on their way home from fishing at Moon Lake, choose this moment to turn in at the house and wake up their friend Mr. Hollifield, and they stop Miss Eckhart and her fire before she can do damage of more permanent kind. So much for the outline of the story.

We see all this activity from two different perspectives, which alternate, then merge into one, and finally separate again as the story advances. One perspective is provided by Loch Morrison, who at first watches from his window and then leaves his room by way of a large hackberry tree which stands between the houses. Loch is thus physically at the scene for the finish, which involves not only the capture of Miss Eckhart but the unceremonious departure of Virgie Rainey and her sailor friend and the unexpected appearance of a man in a golden Panama hat, whom Loch takes to be the strange Mr. Voight but whom Cassie identifies as King MacLain, returned briefly from his wanderings. Cassie, of course, provides the other perspective for this narrative; and between those two, Loch and Cassie, we come close to seeing the whole episode from an ideal perspective that combines the perception of the so-called normal senses—heightened, however, by youthful attention to detail and enhanced by a vigorous memory—with that extraordinary doubleness of vision that characterizes the wanderer. Loch, who is clearly a wanderer for all his tender years, sees easily through and beyond the appearances that confront him; but for that very reason he is susceptible to making mistakes about things that are immediately apparent to the senses. Cassie, who sees only what her physical senses make available to her but sees that much without metaphysical distraction, is able to provide the corrective ground for what some might call Loch's fantasying. She also provides the memory which makes available to us the illuminating lines from Yeats's poem and the three-dimensional image of a Miss Eckhart of real June-recital days. Without Cassie's help "June Recital" would have no center, and Miss Eckhart would be for us only the unhappy little woman who escaped from the county farm and tried to set fire to a piano.

Miss Eckhart is a wanderer, too; but she is a trapped wanderer. Like the hummingbird that symbolizes all the wanderers in this novel, she is touched with exotic ways and eventually does manage to wander to what is for most of Morgana's citizens a far country—the county farm—and after that to the alien burial plot of the MacLains, with whom she has lived for a time. What most marks her as a wanderer, however, is the fire in her head and that telltale vision which permits her to see gold in the commonplace. Caught in Morgana and compelled to teach music to Morgana's indifferent children, she succeeds in creating out of the dreary round of music lessons and whatever spring bounty the community can be made to provide an annual June recital that becomes Morgana's initiation of summer; and occasionally, as on one memorable morning during a thunderstorm when she gives an impromptu performance for an uncomprehending trio of little girls, she reaches through the music she possesses to make audible for a moment the real treasure that is there. Unfortunately for Miss Eckhart, fit auditors for such penetrations are rare; but she does find in Morgana one pupil, a greater wanderer than herself, who will eventually, though not in her lifetime, come to understand her promptings and take heed. We see that finally at the end of *The Golden Apples*. On the morning of the story "June Recital," however, when she appears demented and much diminished and all but ready for the resting place in MacLain's burial plot, it is enough that she manages to strike on the keys of the decayed piano a brief phrase from Beethoven's "Für Elise," that ancient and honorable ornament of June recitals everywhere, which sounds the piper's call to three young people who hear it, Loch and Cassie Morrison and Virgie Rainey upstairs with her sailor on the mattress, and brings them all together for one furious moment in reluctant sympathy.

Loch Morrison, the youngest of these, has never been one of Miss Eckhart's pupils, but he has heard his sister practicing and the sounds of lessons next door; and he is sensitive to the mysterious phrase from "Für Elise" when it comes drifting in:

> The tune came again, like a touch from a small hand that he had unwittingly pushed away. Loch lay back and let it persist. All at once tears rolled out of his eyes. He opened his mouth in astonishment. Then the little tune seemed the only thing in the whole day, the whole summer, the whole season of his fevers and chills, that was accountable; it was personal. But he could not tell why it was so.
>
> It came like a signal, or a greeting—the kind of thing a horn would play out in the woods. . . . It took him back to when his sister was so sweet, to a long time ago. To when they loved each other in a different world, a boundless, trustful country all its own, where no mother or father came.

And Loch's sensitivity to such a summons is indicative of his kinship with the hummingbirds.

So is his choice of playthings. Imprisoned in his room with an attack of malaria, he takes to bed not a nigger-shooter or a cap pistol but his father's telescope, "smelling of brass and the drawer of the library table where it came from." Through its liberating lens he sees magnolias in bloom, a thrush's nest, Woodrow Spights's old ball on the roof, the half of a china plate deep in the weeds, and a sailor and his girl friend making love on a mattress in the upstairs room. What he looks at repeatedly, however, is not any of these but the fruit of a fig tree at the corner of that house next door: "like marbles yesterday, wine-balls today. Getting these would not be the same as stealing. They were rusty old fig trees but the figs were the little sweet blue. When they cracked open their pink and golden flesh would show, their inside flowers, and golden bubbles of juice would hang to touch your tongue to first." Falling into his drowsy malarial sleep, he sees that "the big fig tree was many times a magic tree with golden fruit that shone in and among its branches like a cloud of lightning bugs—a tree twinkling all over, burning, on and off, off and on. The sweet golden juice to come—in his dream he put his tongue out." In brief, for us as readers of the story, and perhaps for Loch Morrison himself, the distant untouchable fruit has become symbolic of the golden apples of the sun or their equivalent, and he makes a tentative implementation of his commitment to go in quest of them when he slides out along the branch of the large hackberry tree separating the two houses and silently invades the world that his telescope has opened to him.

When in the course of the events that follow he encounters King MacLain, briefly returned home to find his house on fire, Loch immediately recognizes a fellow wanderer but, not knowing MacLain as MacLain, imagines that he is the mysterious Mr. Voight, also a wanderer, who once promised him a talking bird. Voight vanishes from his mind, of course, as MacLain's identity becomes clearer; but mystery remains, for the rest of the day and far into his malarial dreams of the night. When black Louella brings him supper, her chicken broth sparkles like diamonds in the evening light; and later as she sits with him in the dark while he tries to go to sleep, he hears the bullfrog in the swamp, confuses him with the wanderer briefly encountered in the afternoon, "felt the pressure of his frown and heard his growling voice and the gnashing of his teeth." "He dreamed close to the surface," Miss Welty tells us, as she turns out the light on Loch Morrison and moves to Cassie, "and his dreams were filled with a color and a fury that the daytime that summer never held."

Cassie Morrison's sensibility is of a different order almost entirely, though it is not necessarily of an inferior order. She has no telescope. She is, as we said, no wanderer. She responds, however, to all inhabitants of the world around her, including the wanderers, with a charity that is rarer than the wanderers' double vision. Appropriately she is the one in the story who sees and appreciates the hummingbird, but she has no impulse to catch the creature or to fathom his mystery: "Metallic and misty together, tangible and intangible, splendid and fairylike, the haze of his invisible wings mysterious, like the ring around the moon—had anyone ever tried to catch him? Not she. Let him be suspended there for a moment each year for a hundred years—incredibly thirsty, greedy for every drop in every four-o'clock trumpet in the yard, as though he had them numbered—then dart."

This is the way Cassie observes most things; and because she observes with an attentiveness born of love, she also recalls with more precision than most. Thus when Miss Eckhart's fumbling quotation from Beethoven taps the springs of her memory, the days of her music lessons and June recitals come flooding back with a richness of detail that makes Cassie's reverie something that we find intrinsically appealing even as we see it providing a credible base for the rest of the episode to anchor in. One may imagine that Cassie herself, could she read "June Recital," would see nothing of this. She would not even see Miss Eckhart's spiritual kinship with the hummingbird and the poor woman's tragedy in not being able to suspend a moment and then dart. Cassie remembers but does not sense the irony of her own success in winning a coveted music scholarship given annually by the Presbyterian church (when Miss Eckhart had hoped that Virgie Rainey might get it), and she fails to recognize that the music she dutifully tries to play can never be golden apples for her but only a succession of yellow Schirmer books stretching ahead for the rest of her life. Nevertheless the stir across the way that prompts Cassie to look out and see Old Man Moody and Mr. Fatty Bowles forcibly escorting Miss Eckhart out of the house does cause her to race out in her petticoat and loudly protest the indignity. By contrast Virgie Rainey, who admittedly suffers a minor indignity of her own when she escapes from the house with her half-dressed sailor friend, walks insolently down the street and passes her old teacher with scarcely a glimpse of recognition.

One might say that Cassie loves Morgana and hence feels no desperate urge to escape, but the "hence" would be wrong. There is no fire in Cassie's head and no wanderer's vision; hence wandering simply never crosses her mind. For her the pleasure of a tie-dyed scarf is enough—that and a June hayride to wear it on. She does risk her father's displeasure to venture out on the June night, but she returns home pleased that she has behaved with decorum on the forbidden excursion and let no one touch her. Afterwards she lies in bed thinking of creatures like Virgie and Miss Eckhart and comparing them to lonely lost beasts. The poem that unlocks the entire novel for us races through her head but does not enlighten her: "Into her head flowed the whole of the poem she had found in that book. It ran perfectly through her head, vanishing as it went. . . . She slept, but sat up in bed once and said aloud, 'Because a fire was in my head.' Then she fell back unresisting. She did not see except in dreams that a face looked in, that it was the grave, unappeased, and radiant face, once more and always, the face that was in the poem." Virgie and Miss Eckhart are indeed lost beasts, doomed in one way or another to wander for the rest of their lives; but they have the power to see clearly and persistently the face in the poem, and they are not entirely to be pitied.

Virgie Rainey, the third young person of consequence in "June Recital," is a wanderer like Loch, Miss Eckhart, and King MacLain, but she also has a touch of Cassie's charity; and that touch makes her superior to all the others—to Cassie with her limitations and to the other wanderers, Loch with his telescope, Miss Eckhart, and even King MacLain. In fact The Golden Apples comes eventually to focus on the experience of Virgie Rainey, who has a story of her own at the end. Miss Eckhart is at last dead and buried, Loch Morrison has gone to New York, and Cassie has remained in Morgana to be what Morgana would call an old maid. Virgie is past forty now and past playing at the Bijou. She too has stayed in Morgana, working for a lumber company and taking care of her mother; but she is hardly an old maid. The point of the episode, once called "The Hummingbirds" and now "The Wanderers," is the liberation of Virgie that comes with the death of her mother. Much of this episode (or chapter) is a detailed account of old Mrs. Rainey's funeral and the mores that the inhabitants of Morgana dutifully display for that occasion. For them it is one of several rituals by which they periodically assert their continuity, and they all know the roles they are expected to fill and fill them graciously—all, that is, except Virgie and King MacLain. These two have always had more compelling roles to fill, as MacLain knows only too well and as Virgie comes to see clearly in this remarkable conclusion to the whole affair.

The climax comes as the funeral is in progress when King MacLain sneaks down the hall to pick at the ham and looks up to see that Virgie is seated where she can observe his defection. Then "he made a hideous face at [her], like a silent yell. It was a yell at everything— including death, not leaving it out—and he did not mind taking his present animosity out on Virgie Rainey; indeed, he chose her." King MacLain's anger here calls to mind the anger that in the earlier episode drove an aged and frustrated Miss Eckhart to attempt de- struction of that world which she believed had entrapped and destroyed her. Now himself entrapped, the aged MacLain silently howls his frustration at a newly liberated Virgie, who in awaking to her freedom is suddenly beginning to sense her kinship with all those who go on quests: "Was it . . . King himself with whom she really felt it? . . . She knew the kinship for what it was, whomever it settled upon, an indelible thing which may come without friendship or even too early an identity, may come even despisingly, in rudeness, intruding in the middle of sorrow. Except in a form too rarefied for her, it lacked future as well as past; but she knew when even a rarefied thing had become a matter of loyalty and alliance."

The novel has other wanderers besides those whom we have already named—Ran and Eugene MacLain (King's twin sons by Snowdie), Bucky Moffitt, the orphan named Easter, and an old black woman without any name—and Virgie Rainey is kin to them all. Like all of them she comes in her time to see past the surface of things to that other aspect of reality whereby all things are related. Unlike all the others except Miss Eckhart, she makes her penetration by means of her hearing; and she understands—far better than Miss Eckhart, we believe—what she has penetrated to.

Virgie's time for understanding comes shortly after her mother's funeral, when just before leaving Morgana for good she drives seven miles to the village where the MacLains lie buried and where Miss Eckhart shares the MacLain burial plot. There, as a gentle rain begins to fall, she recalls her encounters with that person whose gifts more than any other have stirred her into awareness, unfortunately before she was ready to act on it—the gift of Beethoven, offered again and again, a picture of Perseus with the Medusa's head that hung on the studio wall, and the myth of Siegfried and the dragon. All these gifts and more are there in her newly awakened consciousness as she sits in the rain with only a nameless black beggar woman to keep her company: "she and the old beggar woman, the old black thief, were there alone and together in the shelter of the big public tree, listening to the magical percussion, the world beating in their ears. They heard through falling rain the running of the horse and bear, the stroke of the leopard, the dragon's crusty slither, and the glimmer and the trumpet of the swan." Thus the novel ends; and with these concluding words, which surely constitute one of the genuinely moving experiences in modern fiction, we bring into focus the insight that unites all the wandering characters in this novel about wanderers. For Virgie this incident is neither the beginning nor the end of wandering; its importance is that it brings her to a recognition that wandering itself is fulfillment. She now knows that like the hummingbird she must forever be sipping and darting, living from one rare moment of epiphany to another—her consolation, to be sustained by the knowledge and expectation of those elusive golden apples that most inhabitants of Morgana have long since ceased even to despair of attaining.

Moments of this kind are as rare in literature as they are in the lives of most wanderers. There is something like it at the end of the eighth book of the *Iliad,* when the campfires of the Greeks seen through Homer's Jovian eye become for an instant indistinguishable from the multitude of fiery stars in the heavens; and there are similar moments in the whirling choruses of Sophocles and in the songs and set speeches of Shakespeare's *The Tempest,* when we catch our breath and briefly feel ourselves suspended between zenith and the abyss. Richard Eberhart has given us such a moment at the end of his familiar poem "The Groundhog"; and Faulkner has had the audacity (or perhaps it was only a careless lapse) to use a single breath-catching device twice—once to articulate for us Ike Snopes's vision of the earth that his beloved cow walks on as "that frail inextricable canopy of the subterrene slumber—Helen and the bishops, the kings and the graceless seraphim"; and again much later to help us comprehend the epiphany that Mink Snopes achieves when he finally sees himself as "inextricable from" and "anonymous with . . . the beautiful, the splendid, the proud and the brave, right on up to the very top itself among the shining phantoms and dreams which are the milestones of the long human recording—Helen and the bishops, the kings and the unhomed angels, the scornful and graceless seraphim." In moments like these the eternal hostility of our atoms halts briefly, and time seems to stand still. We may believe in them or not, as we will or as we ourselves are wanderers; but whether fact or fancy, they redeem the chaos we are all heirs to.

The remarkable things about Eudora Welty's re-creations of such moments, aside from the frequency of those moments in her work, are, first, their credibility and, second, their lack of that self-conscious sentimentality which characterizes most such re-creations in our own time. In this late twentieth-century post-Christian and technological age we reach as readily as in any other for the transcendent; but all too often in our eagerness we grasp at the occult, cast horoscopes, attempt to raise spirits, or glorify seagulls. It is reassuring to have among us one writer who begins with life as it appears in all its richness and undeniable immediacy (Cassie's way of seeing) and finds in the tangible stuff of our day-to-day existence the ground for a kind of miracle that can redeem life from the dullness that rationalism and common sense have often reduced it to. For that reassurance *The Golden Apples* with its collection of gifted wanderers is of central importance. Even without *The Golden Apples,* however, Miss Welty's work would give us our miracles; for the miraculous lurks just beneath the surface of all that she has written, establishing thereby that her relationship with the wanderers she has created is one of kissing kin and not mere acquaintance. If some readers prefer to call her craft fantasy or magic, we should allow their terms and remember that even Shakespeare's skeptical Leontes refused to quibble over such trivialities when what appeared to be his wife's statue suddenly came to life. "If this be magic," he exclaimed, "let it be an art lawful as eating." Apply Leontes's exclamation to the art of Eudora Welty— which like the statue in *The Winter's Tale* derives its special life from being first and finally a part of this credible world—and we can only say amen.

Eudora Welty's
"I" of Memory
Merrill Maguire Skaggs°

In the public television program "The Eye of Memory,"[1] Eudora Welty—along with Robert Penn Warren, Eleanor Clark, Peter Taylor, Joan Givner, and Paul Porter—shares her memories of Katherine Anne Porter. In fact, some have felt that Welty steals the show, or at least that she emerges as the most important character in the production. While her charm and apparently easy candor always win her audiences during her public appearances, Welty's shrewd literary and psychological insights carry great weight during this particular fifty-five-minute session. Welty puts her finger deftly on several key traits of Porter and her work: Porter's vivacity, her gaiety, her deep (if ambivalent) attachment to her grandmother, her use of childhood incidents to convey a worldview, and her pervasive sense of betrayal. Shrewd as these insights are, however, it is what Welty reveals about herself and her own work that makes her remarks most interesting.

Because zooming in on a master work can teach as much about a creator as a wide lens shot of her entire oeuvre, illustrative matter will be limited to the several magnificent short stories that comprise *The Golden Apples.* The favorite of many critics,[2] this work seems to be Welty's favorite as well, for she comments, "Not in Miss Eckhart as she stands solidly and almost opaquely in the surround of her story, but in the making of her character out of my most inward and most deeply feeling self, I would say I have found my voice in my fiction."[3] She explains further, "What I have put into her is my passion for my own life work, my own art."[4] Many believe that Welty's passion for fiction is most completely realized in *The Golden*

° This essay was written specifically for this volume and is published here by permission of the author.

Apples, and that the book therefore serves perfectly to illustrate Welty's strengths and the practice of her own artistic ideals.

"The Eye of Memory," of course, is edited and arranged to tell a story about Katherine Anne Porter. As it presents Welty's comments, her first admiring remarks concern Porter's insouciance and eager participation in the life around her—her "spring-heel walk, just so anticipating—no telling what." Welty's loyalty to a former mentor is unmistakable. But perhaps Welty's most significant comment on Porter as "foremother" or literary model arrives when she says, "[She was] . . . the first person I ever met or knew who very consciously was aware that she was an artist and that she was practicing an art, and who respected it above all things that anyone could do. . . . She always knew what she was doing."

Eudora Welty is now recognized as a worthy and equal literary peer of Porter's and is herself considered among the most self-consciously controlled and controlling of artists. The Porter standard is nowhere more apparent than in the intricate stories of *The Golden Apples.* As Katherine Anne Porter did, Welty always knows what she is doing. But her self-conscious awareness of her own techniques is especially evident when she analyzes the primary difference between her own practices and Porter's:

> It was hard for me at first to think that I completely understood her stories because I have a visual mind and like things translated into what the eye sees. And then I learned through her work that what she was seeing was not just what is in front of your eyes. In fact she *doesn't* see that! She's talking about the inner vision—what is looking; the mind that's looking at it, and what she perceives of things that are from memory or her life or so on. It's a different vocabulary from any I have been used to.

Here Welty, in identifying a primary characteristic of Porter's, also identifies one of her own. For Porter, the changes occurring in the mind on which the story focuses are of paramount concern. Remembering, for example, that "The Jilting of Granny Weatherall" is primarily the stream-of-consciousness sketch of a dying woman illustrates this difference. Of course one learns of Granny's life, family, triumphs, defeats, and character from Porter's brilliant sketch. And one learns the same from Welty's sketch of dying Katie Rainey. The difference is in the materials from which one gleans this information. In Miss Katie's dying seconds she communicates how highly she values herself (though she has always been among the poorest in town), how she regards herself as rich, having led a rich life, how she loves and approves of the world in which she has lived, and how she confuses herself with both her mother and her daughter, for all have shared the same human experiences. The point, however, is that this

information is conveyed by objects and external acts that the eye
can see:

> Dying, Miss Katie went rapidly over the list in it [the *Market Bulletin*,
> with which her daughter Virgie is fanning her], her list. As though
> her impatient foot would stamp at each item, she counted it, corrected
> it, and yet she was about to forget the seasons, and the places things
> grew. Purple althea cuttings, true box, four colors of cannas for
> fifteen cents, moonvine seed by teaspoonful, green and purple jew.
> . . .
>
> Faster and faster, Mrs. Rainey thought: Red salvia, four-o'clock,
> pink Jacob's ladder. . . .
>
> "Fan me. If you stop fanning, it's worse than if you never
> started."
>
> And when Mama is gone, almost gone now, she meditated, I
> can tack on to my ad: the quilts! For sale, Double Muscadine Hulls,
> Road to Dublin, Starry Sky. . . . Mama's rich in quilts, child.
>
> Miss Katie lay there, carelessly on the counterpane, thinking,
> Crochet tablecloth, Sunburst design, very lacy. She knew Virgie
> stood over her, fanning her in rhythmic sweeps. Presently Miss Katie's
> lips shut tight.
>
> She was thinking, Mistake. Never Virgie at all. It was me, the
> bride—with more than they guessed. Why, Virgie, go away, it was
> me.
>
> She put her hand up and never knew what happened to it, her
> protest.[5]

Both old ladies—Porter's and Welty's—die confusing past and present
or live and dead relatives, and both die with a gesture of protest.
Behind Granny Weatherall's protest, however, is outrage, while behind Katie Rainey's is concern for her daughter. Though the predicament is the same, the characters of the two are radically different,
and the key to the difference is Katie Rainey's sense of continuity
with the past and future. Granny Weatherall dies breaking off connections.

That sense of continuity which permeates each page of *The
Golden Apples* illuminates another difference to which Welty's television appearance draws attention: the different attitudes toward home
apparent in the work of the two writers. For Porter, home is the
place you escape from physically, although you return to it in memory
for the rest of your writing life. The embodiment of home, for Porter,
was the figure of her grandmother Aunt Cat, Catherine Anne Skaggs
Porter, who suggested, as Welty phrases it, "the forms of etiquette
and the *strict, rigid* ways that Granny imposed."[6] Welty amplifies
later, "In a Southern sense, the grandmother embodied the old order.
I mean that was the real, *genuine* old order that was in the old lady."

To have such a figure in her past, however, did not create in Porter a maximal affirmation. As Welty explains it,

> . . . everything that came after her, that depended on her, that hung around her and so on—and the dispersal of the children and all that, weren't the true old order, and everything got distorted and proved to be not really so. And I suppose Miranda [acknowledged here as Porter's alter ego] was really the only one of the grandmother's descendants who was clear-eyed enough to see the difference, which was borne in upon her after she got old enough to see. And then she saw the travesties that happened, the travesties that the lives of some of the people became.

Welty's old order, exemplified in the microcosm of Morgana, is simply more benign than Porter's. With all exceptions in this cycle tale noted—desertion, death, murder, rape, suicide, madness, unabashed egotism, and rampant injustice—the impression remains that on a given representative and symbolic day, "That rainless, windless June the bright air and the town of Morgana, life itself, sunlit and moonlit, were composed and still and china-like."[7] In a repeated and visual image, people hang together in Morgana like strings of paperdolls, cut from the newspaper.[8] They exist, even if just alike, to amuse and entertain. They sustain each other as well, as Lizzie Stark sustains the preparations for Katie Rainey's funeral, after Katie's death, flatly rejecting the suggestion that her dues are paid too late.

Welty's point is not that nothing happens in Morgana (because in fact everything that can happen in the world *does* happen in the town). Rather, the point is that Morgana exists as an emotionally safe place in which to assimilate all that can possibly happen: " 'Virgie brings me good luck!' Miss Eckhart used to say, with a round smile on her face. Luck that might not be good was something else that was a new thought to them all."[9] People in Morgana expect good luck and accept (or deny) whatever happens in order to sustain this expectation. Lives here, as well as in Porter's fiction, sometimes become travesties. But most of the absurdities are forgiven or dismissed as an inconsequential "thing of the flesh."[10] Morgana is safe enough even to assimilate wildness or danger: Virgie "was full of the airs of wildness, she swayed and gave way to joys and tempers, her own and other people's with equal freedom."[11] Virgie remains important, even to a stranger from the country who brings her a night-blooming cereus after her mother's death because "I thought you's the prettiest little thing ever was."[12]

Morgana is every reader's wistful dream of home. Life here revolves around generations of the same families, who stay in place. Welty has written, "I've been writing about the structure of the family in stories and novels ever since [my first story]."[13] Her writing is especially sensitive to the variety and change within homes and family life.[14] In the beginning of "June Recital," for example, Loch Morrison hears a tune played on a neighboring piano that "took him back to when his sister was so sweet, to a long time ago. To when they loved each other in a different world, a boundless, trustful country all its own, where no mother or father came, either through sweetness or impatience—different altogether from his solitary world now, where he looked out all eyes like Argus, on guard everywhere."[15] Interestingly, within the Morrison family Loch retreats from Morgana to New York, Mrs. Morrison commits suicide, Mr. Morrison grows senile, and Cassie keeps the home fires burning by giving piano lessons that replace Miss Eckhart's and by planting grotesque flower beds that spell out *Catherine,* her dead mother's name, in three kinds of flowers. The later facts, however, do not change the strong impression of early stability and security. In its tragedy, heartbreak, dispersal, and defeat, the Morrison family still suggests its valuable record of occasional sweetness and shared concern for each other.

Perhaps the way in which stable things dissolve and orders inevitably change is always experienced on some level as a betrayal. Welty comments on Porter,

It's the grotesqueries that life throws in the face of children, or anyone else, in "The Circus," because she believes that the clown really was about to slide to his death in front of these people who were laughing and cheering . . . and indeed people *do* those things. The behavior of the masses of people in the face of life and death was what horrified her. She could face the reality of it but not the witnessing of it in a false way, or in a cruel and heartless way— that's what she couldn't face. *Life* betrays you, I think, in Katherine Anne's stories. . . . Life betrays you.

Life betrays in Welty's stories, too, but the fact creates a different effect. Loch Morrison of "June Recital," for example, who remembers so longingly the sweetness of his earlier childhood, is betrayed by his senses—he mistakes King MacLain for the former boarder and next door exhibitionist Mr. Voight; by his body, which has developed the malaria that in turn incarcerates him; by his sister who has emotionally deserted him for her friends; by his parents who fail to take him seriously. Later, in "Moon Lake," he is betrayed by his mother who forces him into the odious job of serving as lifeguard to a camp of girls; by his duties that force him to risk his life for uncooperative and ungrateful charges; by his ignored acts of heroism, for which he is kicked off a table; and by his private nakedness, for which he will be reported in town.

The point, of course, is that characters like Loch are betrayed as systematically in Welty's stories as they are in Porter's. The difference between the two bodies of fiction resides not in the *type* of events reported but in the *attitude* toward those events created by the stories. Considering the relationship between Miss Eckhart and Virgie Rainey, for example, townsfolk conclude, "And sooner or later, after taming her teacher, Virgie was going to mistreat her. Most of them expected some great scene."[16] Morganans know as much about betrayal as any in Porter's Old Order. They simply take their facts a bit more philosophically, expecting at least to get some drama from them (The children pray for freight train wrecks, to get the bananas).

Welty summarizes, "What Katherine Anne saw was where somebody failed someone. There is always a sense of betrayal, I think, in her stories, of one kind or another. . . . Most of her stories are about the lurking dangers of betrayal." In Welty's stories the betrayals furnish events, often ironic, but not necessarily moods. In Welty's stories, after the hurt gasp, the injured feelings, the violent explosion, life goes on—not only with chagrin, but also with smiles and moments of fulfillment.[17]

In any case, betrayals seem especially poignant in childhood, and Porter and Welty both capitalize on those wounding childhood moments. As Welty remarks appropriately for both of them, the betrayals occur especially to "children in reference to adults who can be the go-between between the childhood world and the world of adults. That is its danger to the trusting and loving heart. . . . And not just [within] unadulterated childhood. It's adulterated childhood [presented in these stories]."

Childhood is a subject of intense and special interest to both writers. Welty speculates that a life story or individual destiny "all begins in childhood. You know, the expectations, and the hope, and the wish or the will and what befalls it. That's what the tension of her stories is." The most interesting child with whom to trace a fictional destiny unrolling inexorably from childhood traits is the beautiful brat of *The Golden Apples,* Jinny Love Stark. Because Jinny is described in enough detail for readers to track her from her childish recital days to her preadolescent camp experiences, to her nearly broken early marriage, to her child-rearing as a matron, she is an exceptionally appropriate figure with which to test Welty's generalization.

Jinny Love Stark, like a jinny or genie in a bottle, provides that magic ingredient all desire, only to find that once it is uncorked, it always brings chaos. As a child, Jinny is remembered as the only performer in Miss Eckhart's recitals who refused to give up her congratulatory bouquet in order to complete a crescent moon design on the floor. From her earliest years she is selfish, malicious, narcissistic, aggressive, and rude. Her verbal assaults, however, are often very funny, and so she is always accepted and forgiven.

When introduced to mumbletypeg at Moon Lake Camp, Jinny assets accurately, "I may not know how to play, but I bet I win."[18] Jinny respects winning, with or without cheating, and loves making trouble. Forced to socialize in camp with orphans, she comments bluntly on one name: "Easter—tacky name, as Jinny Love Stark was the first to say."[19] As swimming period arrives, Jinny suggests, "Let's let the orphans go in the water first and get the snakes stirred up. . . . Then they'll be chased away by the time *we* go in."[20] Reminded of the MacLain twins, one of whom she will eventually marry, she remarks prophetically, "Who cares about them?"[21] Jinny dreams of telling on people,[22] loves to worry her elders,[23] and walks thoughtlessly over other bodies.

Self-love is Jinny's only strong emotion: "I was named for my maternal grandmother, so my name's Jinny Love. It couldn't be anything else. Or anything better."[24] She cries at night when other campers are trying to go to sleep, but her reasons are obscure: "Jinny Love cried into her pillow for her mother, or perhaps for the figs."[25] Jinny exhibits tenacity and endurance only when the gestures assure her a central spot in the drama of resuscitating half-drowned Easter. In fact, the fanning she provides is the first clue others have that Easter will be revived again—"Jinny Love's always being on the right side."[26]

Others tolerate Jinny because in all circumstances "she looked the most beautiful of all."[27] What her childhood patterns simply suggest is that she must seek negative attention because she has no resources with which to command positive admiration. Jinny has no courage, and no real adventure. Sighting a boat, she immediately declares, "I don't choose to sit myself in a leaky boat. . . . I choose land."[28] On the lip of a spring, "Jinny Love was down drinking like a chicken, kissing the water only."[29] When Jinny enters the woods, she alone comes back with poison ivy. Jinny declares she is ticklish, to discourage being touched.

Her fate is clearly sealed and signalled in her childhood. Jinny captures Ran MacLain's heart because of her beauty and punishes him for his demands by having an affair with Woody Spights. She eventually wins their emotional struggle, of course, but only after breaking his and her mothers' hearts and hastening the suicide of Maideen Sumrall, who is in love with Ran. In all, she is so centrally the focus of town interest and gossip and advice that it seems "The Whole World Knows" of her faithlessness, which causes her no apparent concern: "Her look always made contamination plain. Or plainer."[30]

In "The Wanderers," the final story of the volume, Jinny arrives at the Rainey house after Miss Katie's death, only to enter the crowd demanding, "Look at my diamond."[31] She explains, "I deserved me a diamond." The marriage now stabilized, Ran has become a fat mayor, elected for the glamorous past he has clearly put behind him. He stands back to back with Virgie Rainey, another exceptional one who never got away, and is recognized by his wife as the only man around with enough passion to match or mate Virgie appropriately. For in her prosperous and settled middle years, with a husband at the political apex of Morgana life and happy children playing in the yard, "Jinny, who in childhood had seemed more knowing than her years, was in her thirties strangely childlike; was it old perversity or further tactics?"[32] Jinny seems to feel that if she drives everyone else to marriage, "only then could she resume as Jinny Love Stark, her true self."[33] We learn at the end that "all opposites on earth were close together," but that "hope and despair were the closest blood."[34] The statement seems especially applicable to Jinny and Ran MacLain.

Whether the writer is Welty or Porter, the elements woven into the intricate tapestry of a story or sequence of stories come from details observed and absorbed in the sensitive heart. From such experiences, visual or emotional, the writer produces her fictions. The reservoir of such experience is memory.[35] Welty is especially shrewd when she assesses the uses to which Katherine Anne Porter put memory. As she explains, "The stories she wrote of Miranda's childhood are something else, when *memory* sees back. And that's again what life does to you, to your hopes and your original equipment of innocence and clear-sightedness and trust. *Memory* is the *correcter* of a life."

When Welty considers Katherine Anne Porter's attitude toward memory, she explains,

> I think she trusts her memory. I think she sees it also as a tragic instrument. It [memory] often sees the tragedy in life as the looking back at something. . . . She uses this, though, as part of an eminence from which she can look back and see a whole story in its dramatic shape and form. And she sees her whole life in a story regardless of the segment she writes about. Birth and death are implied all the way through and death is a very dramatic part of the drama of a story and of life. The whole story was made for Miranda. Miranda was on the spot with the eyes to see and the heart to feel and the imagination to surmise. That's what makes the story.

Both writers appear to trust their memories. The difference between Welty and Porter, however, would seem to be a difference in the kinds of memories they retained, and the uses to which they put their remembered material. Welty speculates about Porter's Texas memories,

> In the stories in Texas, memory is often used in an ironic sense, because the things that people remember and tell of the old stories,

Miranda comes to see were not really the truth but were the romantic compulsions they had had to see things in a certain way, and that they were not to be trusted. And that she would have none of it from then on, she would "live her own life," as she said, "in her hope . . . and her ignorance."

Finally, the persona Eudora Welty displays in her fiction chooses not to punish her characters who are judged, as Porter judged them, "full of romantic compulsions." Welty's characters are no more to be trusted than Porter's are. But the "I" who speaks for Welty seems to prefer delight over dismay when considering memories—even the most ironic or distorted. If memory, as Welty has suggested, is the great *correcter* of a life, Welty chooses corrections, apparent memories, which suggest wholeness, completion, laughter, and resolution. Porter chooses anguish, irony, dismay, and sometimes derision. It is finally, then, the reader's choice to decide which moods match best her own memories, which patterns complete or explain his own dreams.

"The Eye of Memory": A Transcript of Eudora Welty's Comments on Katherine Anne Porter

"I like to think of her spring-heel walk when we were at Yaddo. In those days on those summer evenings, we were expected to wear long dresses into dinner. And she and I walked together from the farmhouse we were both staying in, and how she would walk lifting her long skirts through the long grass in the evening—that spring-heel walk, just so anticipating—no telling what."

"[She was] . . . the first person I ever met or knew who very consciously was aware that she was an artist and that she was practicing an art, and who respected it above all things that anyone could do. It was all out in the open—it was there; it was just as much in the world as a tree, or something like that. She always knew what she was doing."

"She was wonderful at singing an old ballad—"Bury me beneath the willers, beneath the weeping willer tree"—you know, with her voice quavering and rising and falling."

"It was hard for me at first to think that I completely understood her stories because I have a visual mind and like things translated into what the eye sees. And then I learned through her work that what she was seeing was not just what is in front of your eyes. In fact she *doesn't* see that! She's talking about the inner vision—what is looking; the mind that's looking at it, and what she perceives of things that are from memory or her life or so on. It's a different vocabulary from any I have been used to."

"There's a great deal about clothes and fashion and the forms of etiquette and the *strict, rigid* ways that Granny imposed. But I think it was just another manifestation of what Katherine Anne's Miranda, or her—the spirit of herself—was trying to get out of. I think that was just something in life that could be seen on the outside, that stood for something inside, that helped flesh it out. . . . I don't mean it wasn't real. It was real. She *had* to get away."

"No conversation I ever had with Katherine Anne had any deceit in it whatever, or any wish to deceive. I think that would have bored the devil out of her, to have tried to fabricate some kind of fancy. . . . She had more to think about than *that* sort of. . . ."

"In a Southern sense, the grandmother embodied the old order. I mean that was the real, *genuine* old order that was in the old lady."

"But everything that came after her [i.e., the grandmother], that depended on her, that hung around her and so on—and the dispersal of the children and all that, weren't the true old order, and everything got distorted and proved to be not really so. And I suppose Miranda was really the only one of the grandmother's descendants who was clear-eyed enough to see the difference, which was borne in upon her after she got old enough to see. And then she saw the travesties that happened, the travesties that the lives of some of the people became."

"What Katherine Anne saw was where somebody failed someone. There is always a sense of betrayal, I think, in her stories, of one kind or another. They're [i.e., betrayals the children see] there in the stories as children in reference to adults who can be the go-between between the childhood world and the world of adults. That is its danger to the trusting and loving heart. Most of her stories are about the lurking dangers of betrayal. And not just unadulterated childhood. It's adulterated childhood."

"It all begins in childhood. You know, the expectations, and the hope, and the wish or the will and what befalls it. That's what the tension of her stories is."

"It's the grotesqueries that life throws in the face of children, or anyone else, in "The Circus," because she believes that the clown really was about to slide to his death in front of these people who were laughing and cheering . . . and indeed, people *do* those things. The behavior of the masses of people in the face of life and death was what horrified her. She could face the reality of it but not the witnessing of it in a false way, or in a cruel and heartless way—that's what she couldn't face. *Life* betrays you, I think, in Katherine Anne's stories. It's all about the whole world of how life betrayed. . . . Life betrays you."

"She kept trying to establish herself bases everywhere she went. She kept buying houses and fixing them up as somewhere to be the center of where she wanted to be. But it never worked."

"What it [i.e., KAP's attitude toward her grandmother] started out as, of course, was reverence. And I think she always had love and respect and tremendous admiration for the grandmother. She was a kind of heroine to her."

"She liked to generate it, gaiety, and she believed in it—an expression of the lyrical in her nature. . . . It also, she saw it as a woman's—something a woman could be very usefully. I mean, it's a woman's part to make life around her go well. I think she felt that social persuasion at all times. It had nothing to do with not facing what was down there. . . . That severe, implacable look she had. It would be nice if life could have been like that. It has nothing to do with hope for the future."

"I think she trusts her memory. I think she sees it also as a tragic instrument. It [memory] often sees the tragedy in life as the looking back at something. . . . She uses this, though, as part of an eminence from which she can look back and see a whole story in its dramatic shape and form. And she sees her whole life in a story regardless of the segment she writes about. Birth and death are implied all the way through and death is a very dramatic part of the drama of a story and of life. The whole story was made for Miranda. Miranda was on the spot with the eyes to see and the heart to feel and the imagination to surmise. That's what makes the story."

[In "The Grave"] "What she sees is the great whole of life and death, the way one is in the other. Literally placed within the capsule of the other. It's the whole thing. The *wonder* of the whole thing."

"The stories she wrote of Miranda's childhood are something else, when *memory* sees back. And that's again what life does to you, to your hopes and your original equipment of innocence and clear-sightedness and trust. *Memory* is the *correcter* of a life."

"In the stories in Texas, memory is often used in an ironic sense, because the things that people remember and tell of the old stories, Miranda comes to see were not really the truth but were the romantic compulsions they had had to see things in a certain way, and that they were not to be trusted. And that she would have none of it from then on, she would 'live her own life', as she said, 'in her hope . . . and her ignorance.' "

"Well, all those things I remember, mostly the *pleasure* she took in life. She could show her pleasure, as I used to hear said as a great compliment to someone—'She knows how to show her pleasure!'— . . . and she did. And her displeasure." [And with a final chuckling aside, "That was good!"]

Notes

1. "The Eye of Memory," produced by Lumiere Productions and KERA-TV in Dallas, first aired on public television in spring, 1987, on "American Playhouse." Its producer, Calvin Skaggs, supplied the videotape on which this study was based and checked the transcript taken from that video and following this essay.

2. See, for example, Ruth M. Vande Kieft, "Eudora Welty: The Question of Meaning," *The Southern Quarterly* 20 (Summer 1982):38–39: *"The Golden Apples,* flawed as it is, remains my favorite among her works, an inexhaustible source of delight and truth." *The Golden Apples* is also my own personal favorite.

3. Eudora Welty, *One Writer's Beginnings* (Cambridge, Mass.: Harvard University Press, 1984), 101.

4. *One Writer's Beginnings,* 101.

5. Eudora Welty, *The Golden Apples* (New York: Harcourt, Brace & World, 1949), 235–36. In *One Writer's Beginnings,* Welty chronicles her own understanding of the importance of the external: "But it was not until I began to write, as I seriously did only when I reached my twenties, that I found the world out there revealing, because . . . *memory* had become attached to seeing, love had added itself to discovery, and because I recognized in my own continuing longing to keep going, the need I carried in myself to know—The apprehension, first, and then the passion, to connect myself to it. . . . This is, of course, simply saying that the outside world is a vital component of my inner life" (76).

6. For a brief discussion of Aunt Cat's influence on Porter, see Joan Givner, *Katherine Anne Porter: A Life* (New York: Simon & Schuster, 1982), 52–56, passim.

7. *Golden Apples,* 35.

8. Ibid., 28–30, 51.

9. Ibid., 42–43.

10. Ibid., 165.

11. Ibid., 43.

12. Ibid., 267.

13. *One Writer's Beginnings*, 86.

14. For a broader view of the use of family, see Sara McAlpin, "Family in Eudora Welty's Fiction," *Southern Review* 18 (Summer 1982):480–94; Jane L. Hinton, "The Role of Family in *Delta Wedding, Losing Battles,* and *The Optimist's Daughter* in *Eudora Welty: Critical Essays,* ed. Peggy W. Prenshaw (Jackson: University Press of Mississippi, 1979), 120–31.

15. *Golden Apples*, 27–28.

16. Ibid., 47.

17. Indeed, in contrasting the philosophical attitudes of her father and mother in *One Writer's Beginnings*, Welty notes that "he the optimist was the one who was prepared for the worst" (45).

18. *Golden Apples*, 120.

19. Ibid., 118.

20. Ibid., 115.

21. Ibid., 122.

22. Ibid., 134.

23. Ibid., 135.

24. Ibid., 133.

25. Ibid., 138.

26. Ibid., 148.

27. Ibid., 134.

28. Ibid., 129.

29. Ibid., 118.

30. Ibid., 163.

31. Ibid., 243.

32. Ibid., 254.

33. Ibid., 255.

34. Ibid., 265. The classic discussion of such contrast in Welty's fiction is Robert Penn Warren, "The Love and the Separateness in Miss Welty," *Kenyon Review* 6(Spring 1944):246–59.

35. Welty's comments on memory at the end of *One Writer's Beginnings* are especially instructive: "Of course the greatest confluence of all is that which makes up the human memory—the individual human memory. My own is the treasure most dearly regarded by me, in my life and in my work as a writer. Here time, also, is subject to confluence. The memory is a living thing—it too is in transit. But during its moment, all that is remembered joins, and lives—the old and the young, the past and the present, the living and the dead" (104).

The Ponder Heart

A Trial with No Verdict
William Peden*

Did good-natured Uncle Daniel Ponder knowingly murder his young wife, Bonnie Dee Peacock, or had he just been playing "creep-mousie" with her, as his niece Edna Earle Ponder testified in court? (Anyone who was *anybody* in Clay, Mississippi, knew for a fact that Uncle Daniel had always been a great tickler and squeezer.) Or had Bonnie Dee dropped dead of a heart attack in the parlor of the old Ponder place, where she had been living alone after sending Uncle Daniel off to stay at the Beulah Hotel with Miss Edna?

Around such questions and these characters Eudora Welty's new novel, "The Ponder Heart," is centered. Miss Welty, as almost everyone knows, is a very cunning writer who is an old hand at the skillful exploitation of paradox, ambiguity, and subtlety. "The Ponder Heart" is a masterly *tour de force;* it is as successfully contrived as is the mouth-melting peach pie with which Miss Edna regales Old Judge Waite during a recess of Uncle Daniel's trial.

Some of the incidents of "The Ponder Heart" are as clear as is Miss Edna's account, to the judge, of the last minutes in Bonnie Dee's life. There was handsome, white-haired Uncle Daniel, "rich as Croesus," splendid in his white suit and pretty red bow tie. Then there was Bonnie Dee, no-account little white trash whom Uncle Daniel (who was as crazy as a hoot-owl) had picked up in the five-and-dime store, and married. There they were, in the parlor of the old Ponder Place, that fateful afternoon when the ball of fire rolled across the floor.

From here matters are less clear. They become, in fact, increasingly opaque, as meaningful and as misleading as is most of the testimony at the trial. Miss Welty revels in working in terms of conscious ambiguity; she leaves the last word unsaid, the ultimate action unconsummated. Writing with swift, sure, and often devastating understanding of her characters, and indulging a humor which is at times like the despairing cry of a child being swallowed up by

* Reprinted with permission from *Newsweek,* 11 January 1954, 83. Copyright 1954 by Newsweek, Inc. All rights reserved.

quicksand, she has created out of artifice and artistry a world unmistakably her own and authentically real.

It might be said that the town of Clay is in effect the main character of this unforgettable short novel. Clay, dozing in the white summer sun while Uncle Daniel peeps benevolently (or could it be malevolently?) from behind the blinds of the Beulah Hotel, or buys a mess of banana ice cream cones for the burlesque queens at the fair; Clay, where the coroner is blind and the presiding judge recesses court when Miss Edna is like to be embarrassed; Clay, where someone like Bonnie Dee might cross the Ponder barrier in life but could never, least of all in death, conquer the Ponder heart.

"The Ponder Heart" is, in my opinion, the best thing Miss Welty has done since "Delta Wedding," published seven or eight years ago. Whether its recent appearance as a single-issue instalment in *The New Yorker* and the present book-form publication will win Miss Welty many new readers remains to be demonstrated. Meanwhile her admirers (who in recent years have had some cause for alarm) can relax. "The Ponder Heart" represents Eudora Welty at her best, which is another way of saying that here is a distinguished, individualistic, memorable work of fiction.

Dialogue as a Reflection of Place in *The Ponder Heart*   Robert B. Holland*

"I am . . . touched off by place," writes Eudora Welty.[1] And although place "is one of the lesser angels that watch over the racing hand of fiction,"[2] Miss Welty's regional stories are written out of sure knowledge of her region.[3] This region is the small town middleclass South of China Grove, Victory, Morgana, or Clay, Mississippi, the small town with the square across which Grandpa Ponder goes "fording" his way with his walking cane "through farmers and children and Negroes and dogs and the countryside in general."[4] Its people view progress with skepticism, as when Edna Earle Ponder says that Clay has "gone down so," with "the wrong element going spang through the middle of it at ninety miles an hour on that new highway . . ." (p. 13).

This place is one in which, above all else, people talk, in which talk is the verbalization of place, and in which speech structure and

* From *American Literature* 35, no. 3 (November 1963):352–58. Copyright 1963 by Duke University Press. Reprinted with permission of the author and Duke University Press.

culture structure are in constant interaction. Korzybski said that "As words *are not* the objects which they represent, *structure, and structure alone* becomes the only link which connects our verbal processes with the empirical data"[5] (meaning the world and what goes on in it). Speech structure (syntax, rhythm, image, idiom) with Miss Welty's characters is more than a connection with "empirical data." The word is, in fact, life; and these regional characters would be quite sure, since words are their joy and salvation, that words, *spoken* words, are one with things, or at least that things are nothing civilized without words. Edna Earle Ponder says to her auditor, as naturally as breathing (both the semantic and the structural patterns carrying her meaning): "And listen: if you read, you'll put your eyes out. Let's just talk" (p. 11). The author's handling of the structure of this talk is among her better achievements in fiction. Her ear is surer than a mirror, for in her rendition of speech forms she becomes, as she said of Faulkner, "twice as true as life."[6] Using *The Ponder Heart* as evidence, I shall attempt to show how the structure of the dialogue of her characters is a vocalization of the design of the culture in which they move.

1

The people of Clay, Mississippi, inheriting a uniform tradition, live in a closed society of intimate relationships. Their integrity is the integrity of knowing and being known. As members of two families, the blood family and the regional family, they are rarely out of hearing of fellow members of either. There is no lonely crowd in Miss Welty's South, for everybody is quite at home with everybody else. It is not surprising that the Judge interrupts the trial of Uncle Daniel Ponder when Edna Earle's "girl" comes to see how many will come to the hotel to dinner: " 'Just a minute,' says the Judge. 'Miss Edna Earle's girl is standing in the door to find out how many for dinner. I'll ask for a show of hands,' and puts up his the first" (p. 94).

The lineaments of these people have been shaped by long cultural involvement. Their idiosyncrasies are themselves long-lived, and even their crudities and enormities are understandable only in the context of tradition. The progressive world cares little for "context" in the sense of perpetuation of environmental forms, and more and more for the present moment and constant change. Miss Welty's people live in a context of enduring human relationships, in which one act and word are colored by all other acts and words, and in which time past is present in time future.[7] They cannot separate a fact from a feeling or one feeling from another, and their basic feelings are responses to a total involvement in a stable and shared tradition. All good stories seem new, says Eudora Welty, but "there will always be some characteristics and some functions about them as old as time, as human nature itself. . . ."[8]

One of the most common patterns in the dialogue of Miss Welty's characters is a three-stress structure, which occurs so frequently as to be a most obvious mannerism (italics are mine):

> He's been a general favorite *all these years.* (p. 8)
> Now just a minute. *Not so fast.* (p. 10)
> He dresses fit to kill, you know, in a *snow-white suit.* (p. 11)
> His nature was impatient, as *time went by.* (p. 12)
> He loved happiness like *I love tea.* (p. 14)
> There's a white man sitting at the crossroads store with a telephone and nothing to do all day but *feed those birds.* (p. 61)
> see what a *large head size* he wears? (p. 7)

Highly metered speech is the rule:

> You could hear her day and night in the remotest parts of this hotel and with the sheet over your head. . . . (p. 22)
> The bank sent a freezer of peach ice cream from their own peaches, beautifully turned and packed. (p. 85)
> oh, it was Edna Earle this, and Edna Earle that, every minute of my day and time. This is like the grave compared. (p. 10)
> She was away out yonder on Ponder Hill and nothing to do and nothing to play with in sight but the Negroes' dogs and the Peppers' cats and one little frizzly hen. (pp. 48–49)[9]

These structures are a counterpart to the conservative order of what Hoffman (p. 66) calls a coherent and "predictable" culture in which the "formal, even ceremonial, values are treasured." They reflect a social structure with its levels and classes, interlinked and stable family arrangements, and continuity of habits through generations.

Rhythm in structure is paralleled by rhythm in substance—in short, by the platitude. Richard M. Weaver says that the stability of Southern institutions "makes possible a vocabulary. . . . whose acceptance does not have to be called into question. . . ."[10] The speech forms of the people of Clay are uttered as much for the taste of the words and the intimacy of the idiom as for any literal relationship with the "empirical data." Speech is a torch which is handed down, particular forms being like heirlooms, old china, worn rugs; it is full of little nameless unremembered but always remembered forms of greeting and farewell, and of words to fill voids and reinforce the sense of community. The people of Clay have no love for originality, either in words or in ideas. They are, rather, at home with the well-worn, the old-fashioned, the platitude ennobled and made legal tender for a culture.

I hope I'm not speaking of kin of present company. (p. 16)
We were all running and flying to do his bidding, everything under
the sun he said. (p. 24)
Grandpa Ponder (in his grave now). . . . (p. 8)[11]

Edna Earle Ponder naturally assumes that her worn counters, with
all their comfortable connotations, are universally used. It would not
occur to her that her listener could need any explanation of the
allusions which fill her monologue, since it would be astonishing to
her that anyone either would not know or would not fill the gaps,
as a matter of course. She takes in whoever comes along and establishes
intimacy. She speaks to her listener of "that old slow poke postman"
(p. 9). "I size people up," she says; "I'm sizing you up right now"
(p. 11). She does not hesitate to speak of her private affairs. "Mama
never did hold up—she just had me and quit; she was the last of
the Bells . . ." (p. 13). Gossip is for everybody: "*You're* only here
because your car broke down, and I'm afraid you're allowing a Bodkin
to fix it" (p. 11).

Verbal symmetry and platitude are not only a positive reflection
of a culture, but also the particular Southern expression of what Cash
calls an "excessive nicety" and a "denial of the ugly."[12] Miss Welty's
characters color the "empirical data" with a layer of words which is
a comforting dike against "realism":

> The Peacocks are the kind of people keep the mirror outside on
> the front porch, and go out and pick railroad lilies to bring inside
> the house, and wave at trains till the day they die. (p. 29)
>
> Around his hat is a bunch of full-blown roses, five or six Etoiles in
> a row, with little short stems stuck down in the hatband—they're
> still growing in Grandma's garden, in spite of everything. (p. 90)

This view of an illiterate old Negro man is precisely the view that
most white people in Clay would take. To them, the monotonous,
the dirty, and the miserable are, more often than not, quaint and
picturesque, partly in rationalization, partly because of a reliance on
feeling rather than reason, partly because of a sense of humor created
by adversity. The surface realism of daily life is not necessarily the
truth. Expression becomes an improvement on the "real." As a result,
the euphemism is commonplace. "'Njoyed it!" is the usual farewell
of the Southern girl to the Southern boy, whether she enjoyed it or
not. Though "false" in a literal sense, the expression is restful, and
serves a different truth. The most unlikely situations receive this
gilded treatment. Edna Earle relates, for example, the instance of the
lightning which strikes the house: "Careened around the parlor a
minute, and out through the hall. And if you've never seen a ball of
fire go out through bead curtains, it goes as light as a butterfly with
wings" (p. 119). Bonnie Dee Peacock (the name itself illustrates much

of what has been said so far) lies dead: "She was dead as a doornail. And she'd died laughing. I could have shaken her for it" (p. 141). And as described by Narciss: "And dere her, stretched out, all dem little pleats to do over, feets pointin' de other way round, and Dr. Lubanks snappin' down her eyes" (p. 98).

Since Miss Welty's people find words so essential and savory, they have grown expert at their use. In this flood of words, exaggeration becomes unavoidable. Lawyer Gladney speaks to Narciss on the witness stand: "Mr. Daniel Ponder, like Othello of old, Narciss, he entered yonder and went to his lady's couch and he suffocated to death that beautiful, young, innocent, ninety-eight-pound bride of his, out of a fit of pure-D jealousy from the well-springs of his aging heart" (p. 98). Since the speech patterns, like the corresponding culture patterns, are artificially ordered, lapses from the design are frequent and inevitable. The result is a sort of bathos or falling off from the formal to the informal, from the important to the trivial, from logical sequence to the *non sequitur*. Judge Waite shouts at the unruly courtroom:

"Si-lence! . . . Let the public please to remember where they are at. I have never, in all my jurisprudence, seen more disrespectful behavior and greater commotion and goings-on at a trial. Put that right in the record, Birdie Nell" (p. 150).

The trivial is often verbalized into a formal and precise structure:

Divinity travels perfectly, if you ever need to know. (p. 16)

And I couldn't get off the Ferris wheel till I'd been around my nine times, no matter how often I told them who I was. (p. 23)

2

When Miss Welty says that she is "touched off by place," she suggests a journey beyond the region of the touching off. And indeed her imagination molds her material into beautifully symmetrical essences and shapes. She participates in the life around her with such perception and fidelity that she catches it exact, and then she colors it and carves it into an entity beyond the realism of daily life, which is just what the people of her region have done with the often shallow and monotonous basic material of their lives. The result is an ironical tension between form and content, in which prosaic experience is enveloped in a mist of rhetoric, and irrational action is reported in the most attractive of verbal forms. The eccentric and farcical behavior of the characters in *The Ponder Heart* belies the harmony of its verbal rendition as it belies the metaphysical order of the "Southern design," and as the symmetry of this design is belied by the injustices committed in its name. From inelegance of action the characters escape into a symmetry of utterance. They live with the mock heroic: "And my other grandma was the second-to-longest-living Sunday School teacher they've ever had, very highly regarded" (p. 21).

If verbal order is a reflection of the "design" of Southern culture, it is also an assuagement for defeat. As the only defeated man in the nation, the Southerner is historically on the defensive; his verbal posturing is an assertion of ego in compensation. Because words have had to suffice, deeds have become secondary. The autonomy of the word, and the departure of the word from a one-to-one realism of the average is not a lie, or even necessarily a conscious distortion; it is merely, as Edna Earle would see it, another kind of truth. The exaggeration, the euphemism, the assuagement which are the function of words are not to the people of Clay the untruth which they might seem. Looked at in the best light, these people are no more indefensible than one who says of an ugly hat, "Just lovely." Edna Earle would say "Just lovely," at least to the wearer, and in saying it would serve the spirit of neighborliness, which would take precedence in her mind over any form of literal fact. Words are an essential nourishment to Miss Welty's people who have learned to remain noble in spite of humiliation and proud in spite of debasements inflicted upon them and monstrosities which they themselves have created.

What Eunice Glenn says of Eudora Welty's fiction is therefore true only in a limited sense. While conceding that there is no sensationalism in it, and that Miss Welty does not see life as hopeless, Miss Glenn nevertheless says that Miss Welty writes of "individuals pitted against modern society—a diseased society, which finds its reflection in disordered minds and lives." Miss Welty "writes of those whose lives are circumscribed by corruption, bitterness, power mania, and human cruelty that cuts deep."[13] While this judgment may be true of some of Miss Welty's fiction, what it seems to overlook is the persistent tenderness and sense of humor which pervades it, a tenderness native to one who feels sympathetically, and a sense of humor which makes the Southerner pleasantly at home with certain kinds of ugliness and violence. It fails to give proper attention to the sympathy with which Miss Welty views her world, a sympathy which excludes the furious indignation of Faulkner and which supersedes exact judgment and rigid justice. It especially seems to overlook the fact that Eudora Welty's people, amid all the cruelty and bitterness and power mania in the world, can, and do, find comfort and a sort of hypnotized delight in verbalizations which, since they are one's own, can be interposed between one and any kind of unpleasant "empirical data."

Notes

1. "How I Write," *Virginia Quarterly Review,* XXXI, 242 (Spring, 1955).

2. "Place in Fiction," *South Atlantic Quarterly,* LV, 57 (Jan., 1956).

3. Miss Welty is a "proud partisan" of regionalism. Like other good regional writers, she is of course an author of universal vision. "Since her first published story she has been working toward a fusion of the universal mythic elements embodied in the various culture-heroes with the regional world that she knows first-hand" (William M. Jones, "Name and Symbol in the Prose of Eudora Welty," *Southern Folklore Quarterly,* XXII, 174, Dec., 1958).

4. *The Ponder Heart* (New York, 1954), p. 12. Page numbers in the text, unless otherwise indicated, refer to this book.

5. Quoted in *Language, Meaning and Maturity,* ed. S. I. Hayakawa (New York, 1954), p. 215.

6. "Place in Fiction," p. 66.

7. "She orders her view of the present by constantly manipulating the parallel between past and present" (William M. Jones, "Eudora Welty's Use of Myth in 'Death of a Traveling Salesman,' " *Journal of American Folklore,* LXXIII, 18–19 (Jan., 1960). This judgment holds good not only in regard to Miss Welty's uses of ancient myth, but also in regard to her uses of the myth and the traditions of the South.

8. "The Reading and Writing of Short Stories," *Atlantic Monthly,* CLXXXIII, 54 (Feb., 1949). Frederick J. Hoffman notes that "Much is made in Southern literature of the ceremony of living and of the fact that living acquires certain habitudes if it persists evenly in time. . . . The forms are derived from habits of family living through predictable generations, and from the symbolic values implicit in inherited and inheritable particulars" ("The Sense of Place," *South: Modern Southern Literature in Its Cultural Setting,* ed. Louis D. Rubin, Jr. and Robert D. Jacobs [New York, 1961], p. 65). According to Louis D. Rubin, Jr., the writers of the South produce art which is characterized by "historical and tribal memory" and by a sense of "tradition and continuity . . ." ("Thomas Wolfe in Time and Place," *Southern Renascence,* ed. Rubin and Jacobs [Baltimore, 1953], p. 292).

9. These metrical forms are frequently found in other stories also.

10. "Aspects of Southern Philosophy," *Southern Renascence,* p. 18.

11. "We might have had a little run on doing that in Morgana, if it had been so willed" ("Shower of Gold").

12. W. J. Cash, *The Mind of the South* (New York, 1941), p. 82.

13. "Fantasy in the Fiction of Eudora Welty," *A Southern Vanguard,* ed. Allen Tate (New York, 1947), p. 80.

The Bride of the Innisfallen and Other Stories

Two Ladies of the South
Louis D. Rubin, Jr.°

Katherine Anne Porter, Elizabeth Madox Roberts, Caroline Gordon, Carson McCullers, Eudora Welty, more recently Flannery O'-Connor, Elizabeth Spencer—the list of women writers who have helped to make the Southern renascence of the past several decades so remarkable a literary flowering is a distinguished one. Miss Porter has written little of late, and Miss Roberts is dead now, but Miss Gordon continues to produce a new novel every few years, while Miss Welty, who is somewhat younger than several of the others, seems only to be gaining momentum. This array of writers has produced an imposing fiction, and the end is not yet. This year, within two months' time, we have been given a new collection of Eudora Welty's short stories [*The Bride of the Innisfallen*], and a first collection by Flannery O'Connor [*A Good Man is Hard to Find*]. To read the first is to be assured that a sensitive, discerning artist is steadily extending her range; to read Miss O'Connor's volume is to watch the emergence of a clear-sighted and sure talent.

The adjective "elusive" is one of the more overworked words used to describe Miss Welty's work. "Elusive" is just the word, however, because though she seldom lacks for praise, what Miss Welty is really doing in her fiction often eludes even the most perceptive of critics. In all her work, a great deal goes on, much of it humorous, piquant, graceful; and beneath the surface there is another and deeper dimension entirely. We see it in the story "Kin" of her present collection, if we read carefully, and since it is a dimension that is necessary to the proper appreciation of Miss Welty's extraordinary art, I should like to devote particular attention to the one story.

"Kin" has to do with a young woman, Miss Dicey Hastings, who was born in Mississippi but who now lives in the North. It describes Dicey's reactions to a visit home. She and her cousin Kate ride out

° Excerpted from *Sewanee Review* 63 (Autumn 1955):671–77. Copyright 1955 by The University of the South. Reprinted with permission of the editor.

into the country to visit their ailing great Uncle Felix at Mingo, the family homestead. An old maid relative, Sister Anne, is presiding over the home, and when they arrive it is to find Mingo filled with visitors. Their immediate thought is that Uncle Felix has died, but quickly they learn that Sister Anne has merely loaned out the parlor of Mingo to an itinerant photographer to use as a studio for the day. Uncle Felix has been removed to a back room, apart from the rest of the house, for safekeeping. As Dicey enters the house, she glances about:

> I looked and saw the corner clock was wrong. I was deeply aware that all clocks worked in this house, as if they had been keeping time just for me all this while, and I remembered that the bell in the yard was rung every day at straight-up noon, to bring them in out of the fields at picking time. And I had once supposed they rang it at midnight too.
>
> Around us, voices sounded as they always did everywhere, in a house of death, soft and inconsequential, and tidily assertive.

When they find Uncle Felix, he is lying in an old, nondescript bed in the back room. Dicey holds her handkerchief, scented with mag-nolia-fuscata flowers, under Uncle Felix's heavy brown nose. "Hide," Uncle Felix says with difficulty, and again, "Hide . . . Hide, and I'll go in. Kill 'em all. I'm old enough I swear you *Bob*. Told you. Will for sure if you don't hold me, hold me." Sister Anne winks at Dicey. The old man speaks again. "Surrounded . . . They're inside."

Uncle Felix then grasps Dicey's arm and pulls her down to the edge of the bed. He gropes for a pencil, writes some words on the page of a hymnal, then tears it out. While he is doing so, Dicey sees lying on a barrel nearby an old stereopticon, which long ago had reposed in the parlor. "It belonged to Sunday and to summertime . . . My held hand pained me through the wish to use it and lift that old, beloved, once mysterious contraption to my eyes, and dis-solve my sight, all our sights, in that. In that delaying, blinding pain, I remembered Uncle Felix. That is, I remembered the real Uncle Felix, and could hear his voice, respectful again, asking the blessing at the table."

The sight of the stereopticon momentarily recalls to Dicey the image of her childhood, of family dinners at Mingo on Sunday with her dead parents and all the others present. Afterwards she would run to the front porch steps, and sit with Uncle Felix to look through the stereopticon, handing him the cards as he signaled for them, while he peered intently through the lens and she watched him at it.

> It's strange to think that since then I've gone to live in one of those picture cities. If I asked him something about what was in there, he never told me more than a name, never saw fit. (I couldn't

read then.) We passed each other those sand-pink cities and passionate fountains, the waterfall that rocks snuffed out like a light,
islands in the sea, red Pyramids, sleeping towers, checkered pave-
ments on which strollers had come out, with shadows that seemed
to steal, further each time, as if the strollers had moved, and where
the statues had rainbow edges; volcanoes; the Sphinx, and Constan-
tinople; and again the Lakes, like starry fields—brought forward
each time so close that it seemed to me the tracings from the beautiful
face of a strange coin were being laid against my brain. Yet there
were things too that I couldn't see, which could make Uncle Felix
pucker his lips as for a kiss.

The three-dimensional image of the stereopticon used to transport
the child Dicey to fabulous, faraway lands; now the vision of the old
device there (actually a sterescope rather than a true stereopticon)
on the barrel serves to take the adult Dicey back into the past, to
the "real Uncle Felix"—to the real world of her childhood, as it
was, "cypressy and sweet, cool, reflecting, dustless." For the moment
Mingo, just as the house in St. Louis does in Thomas Wolfe's "The
Lost Boy," has ceased to be a curio, an old museum of a homestead
where an old man is dying and strangers are being photographed,
and has become a moment of Dicey's life. She has, swiftly, momentarily, reached back through decades of time to what she was as a
child.

The girls bid Uncle Felix goodbye, Dicey taking the message
written on the hymn-book page. They go outside, watching the
photographer preparing to take Sister Anne's picture in the parlor
against an artificial backdrop:

> What would show in the picture was none of Mingo at all, but the
> itinerant backdrop—the same old thing, a scene that never was, a
> black and white and gray blur of unrolled, yanked-down moonlight,
> weighted at the bottom with the cast-iron parlor rabbit doorstep,
> just behind Sister Anne's heel.

Dicey tells Kate what Uncle Felix has written on the paper:
"What he wrote was, 'River—Daisy—Midnight—Please.' " The lit-
eral-minded Kate cannot understand; Uncle Felix's wife was named
Beck, not Daisy. They leave the house, and Dicey thinks:

> I took so for granted once, and when I had left for ever, I
> wondered at the moment, the old soft airs of Mingo as I knew
> them—the interior airs that were always kitchen-like, of oil lamps,
> wood ashes, and that golden scrapement off cake-papers—and out-
> side, beyond the just-watered ferns lining the broad strong railing,
> the fragrances winding up through the luster of the fields and the
> dim, gold screen of trees and the river beyond, fragrances so rich
> I once could almost see them, un-transparent and Oriental. In those

days, fresh as I was from Sunday School in town, I could imagine the Magi riding through, laden.

Her reverie over the so near, so far away world of her childhood is broken by Kate, who cannot understand Uncle Felix's note. It is a kind of shorthand, Dicey explains. "Yet it had seemed a very long letter—," she thinks; "didn't it take Uncle Felix a long time to write it?" Kate still cannot understand why Daisy, and not Beck, is the recipient. "I expect by now Uncle Felix has got his names mixed up and Daisy was a mistake," she says. This exasperates Dicey: "She could always make the kind of literal remark, like this, that could alienate me, even when we were children—much as I love her. I don't know why, yet, but some things are too important for a mistake even to be considered."

Meanwhile the country people who have been the photographer's clientele have come out onto the porch, and Dicey and Kate climb into the car and drive away. Kate, the literal minded, is leaving an old farmhouse where a great uncle is dying and a foolish relative holds forth. Dicey, however, knows much more is taking place. She is leaving a moment of her childhood, of herself, never again to be recaptured. Nor does the old homestead remain, either, because Mingo has gone, too. Mingo is the sound and smell and feel and weather of that long ago Sunday of childhood, gone forever. (We remember that the clocks in Mingo no longer kept time.) The real Uncle Felix has gone forever, too. The old man who is in the house, gradually dying, has traveled far from that past day, though not the way Dicey has. Rather, he has gone backward toward his own youth, talking confusedly of joining the Confederate army (Miss Welty is careful to point out that there is a Civil War musket in the corner of his room), arranging a tryst with a long-forgotten girl—Dicey, Daisy—at midnight by the river. From the moment in time and space that was Mingo, with the cool cypressy smell, the old, kitchen-like soft airs, the fragrances winding through the fields, the stereopticon with its views of sand-pink cities, fountains, waterfalls—childhood— from that moment time and mortality have sent the participants spinning far away like an exploding galaxy. It is this knowledge of time, of loss, of the weather of a childhood remembered and gone again that assails Dicey's consciousness then.

> But the grouping on the porch still held, that last we looked back, posed there along the rail, quiet and obscure and never-known as passengers on a ship already embarked to sea. Their country faces were drawing in even more alike in the dusk, I thought. Their faces were like dark boxes of secrets and desires to me, but locked safely, like old-fashioned caskets for the safe conduct of jewels on a voyage.

Dicey and Kate drive away in silence. They are going back into the present world again, into now:

> All around, something went on and on. It was hard without thinking to tell whether it was a throbbing, a dance, a rattle, or a ringing—all louder as we neared the bridge. It was everything in the grass and trees. Presently Mingo church, where Uncle Felix had been turned down on "knick-knack," revolved slowly by, with its faint churchyard. Then all was April night. I thought of my sweetheart, riding, and wondered if he were writing to me.

Thus the story "Kin" ends. They have come back into everyday life. The noise of that past world of Mingo, outside of time and preserved in it by memory, has ceased. For the first time in the long narrative, Dicey thinks of present concerns, of the man to whom she is engaged in the North. She is "in time" again.

So we see that, beneath the humor of Sister Anne's rendezvous with the photographer, beneath the assiduous and delightful description of place and the acute delineation of personality, Miss Welty has all along been exploring, with penetrating insight, the nature of memory, the meaning of time and the past. "Kin" is the story of a moment recaptured from past time: "when I had left for ever, I wondered at the moment." Achieved, it liberated as well the place where it occurred, and the child who had experienced it.

In a sense, each of the stories in *The Bride of the Innisfallen* is about time—a moment, an afternoon, a day. The search for the meaning of the moment of time provides the structure of the story, and each has this for its progression. Each is a development toward inactivity, to the reality of self freed of the distractions of elapsing events. In "No Place For You, My Love," two strangers, a man and a woman, go for a long drive southward from New Orleans, only to return eventually to the city. It is a silent, passive, inactive liaison. They say little; they do not even discuss their lives and families back home, for that is in time. Time seems to have stopped, while they have been suspended outside of it for a day. When they leave each other, the man "remembered for the first time in years when he was young and brash, a student in New York, and the shriek and horror and unholy smother of the subway has its original meaning for him as the lilt and expectation of love."

In a bizarre story, "The Burning," an idiotic Negro slave girl undergoes a harrowing day during the Civil War in Mississippi. Here the reverse of the usual situation occurs: the idiocy of the girl can permit no meaning, no knowledge to become real. Events are not "lost" for her; they do not even exist. She cannot understand that her two mistresses are dead; nothing but the most trivial can make any impression on her consciousness. She wades into a river: "she had forgotten how or when she knew, and she did not know what day this was, but she knew—it would not rain, the river would not rise, until Saturday."

The title story of Miss Welty's collection, "The Bride of the Innisfallen," concerns an American girl in England who leaves her husband to board a train that will travel to a seaport, where she will journey by boat to Cork. Beautifully written, it records the delightfully inane conversations of her fellow travelers, with all Miss Welty's gift for that sort of thing. Through it all, the American girl is inactive, impersonal; merely a listener to talk. Finally, in Cork, she hears the speech of the Irish, sees the trees and sights, drinks in the weather of spring in Ireland. This is all, and this is everything: "it was the window herself that could tell her all she had come here to know— or all she could bear this evening to know, and that was light and rain, light and rain, dark, light and rain." She tries to write out a telegraph message to her husband. But she pauses. To do it, to do anything, she realizes, would interfere with the sudden access of life, of complete stasis. Nothing else matters but the moment; she is by herself, among strangers in a strange land, and in the very anonymity of her status she finds herself closer to her real self, furthest removed from the conditionings of her life in time, than for many months. Upon the precious moment of now, the "evening of extraordinary splendour and beauty," nothing else must be allowed to impinge: "The girl let her message go into the stream of the street, and opening the door walked into the lovely room full of strangers."

So with each of her stories, the moment, the realized experience, is the goal, the key. In a fine story of a Southern youngster who plays hookey to join his father at fishing, it will be years before the true significance of the day's events are to be understood, until the youngster will realize that his father had intended a liaison with a girl that day when he had interrupted. One of Miss Welty's funniest stories is "Going To Naples," in which she describes the activities aboard ship of a group of Italian-Americans going home again. A half-dozen characters are delightfully realized, and at the end it is to the awkward, good-natured, reluctant Gabriella that it all "happens":

> all seemed caught up and held in something: the golden moment of touch, just given, just taken, in saying good-by. The moment—bright and effortless of making, in the end, as a bubble—seemed to go ahead of them as they walked, to tap without sound across the dust of the emptying courtyard, and alight in the grandmother's homely buggy, filling it.

That is the "meaning" of the long and pleasant sea voyage, the discovery: it was a time, a sequence, and now it is over. For each of the tales in *The Bride of the Innisfallen,* the plot is the character's discovery of himself, and events all occur for that final purpose. The progress of Miss Welty's art is in time, directed toward the movement outside of it, the matchlessly revealed moment of knowledge and feeling in a perfect inutility of place.

A Frail Travelling Coincidence: Three Later Stories of Eudora Welty
Alun R. Jones[*]

For a foreigner, the most dramatically obvious feature of American life is the violent collision between the past and the future. Change seems to be accelerating at such a rate that someone adjusted to the obstinate conservatism of a different culture, might, perhaps, be forgiven for seeing change on this scale as a threat to those values that, after all, need time to take root and mature.

American cities seem to be in a constant state of demolition and reconstruction: there is little sense of completion but instead a dynamic sense of movement towards some undefined objective. Yet the cry of "Tear it down" is loudest in New York, a city of staggering contrasts, a town that sometimes seems to have been built by machines to house machines.

I remember once, when Miss Welty was staying there: opposite her hotel one of those thin high buildings was being welded together and suddenly to her pleasure she saw a workman with a hammer and nails; in that landscape he seemed like some figure emerging from the dim past insisting, in his primitive way, on the idea that cities were once built by human hands for human needs: as if one of Hardy's peasants had inadvertently wandered into Cape Kennedy with horses and plough ready for the spring sowing.

Certainly change brings its own excitements though it seldom brings any sense of completion or fulfilment. Moreover, it always presents itself in mechanical terms that seem to demand some appropriate human response, a psychedelic or electronic man perhaps would be happier than old-fashioned human beings in this kind of landscape. Certainly if Miss Welty could be said to be a committed writer of any kind, and I feel sure she would reject the very idea of such a thing, then she is committed to the idea of the writer as shaper and creator of the individual imagination. In her early stories,

[*] From *Shenandoah* 20 (Spring 1969):40–53. Copyright 1969 by Washington and Lee University. Reprinted with permission of the editor.

particularly in *A Curtain of Green,* she cast a baleful, caustic eye on the social world around her and for the most part she was content to define her characters by their social roles. The commercial travellers, the drifters, came up against those who had settled, however precariously, and put down roots, however shallow. The settlers took their time from the seasons and in their unhurried way they were one with the landscape in which they lived and the community to which they belonged. The travellers, always hurrying from here to there, identified themselves with the cars in which they travelled and if they were representative of anything, it was of the mechanical world of business for which they acted as representatives. In the same way as Faulkner's Snopeses with their sewing machines, Miss Welty represented the present in mechanical terms and saw that present as threatening to destroy the old-fashioned human virtues, to demolish the sense of community and especially that feeling of a way of life which man and nature had established after centuries of living familiarly together. To her a sense of place is also a sense of the past, a sense of belonging to a community and being related to the world of nature. She seizes the paradox of human fulfilment instinctively: only by recognizing the claims of the past, of belonging to an established network of relationships can the individual fulfil his individualism. While the world is rushing forward into the future looking for purpose and meaning, those who stay still have meaning and purpose conferred on them, an inheritance from a living past.

Perhaps it is easier to arrive at such conclusions living in the South, firmly identified with a particular place and a specific past and established within the easy commerce of accepted family and social relationships. Yet, seen in this way, the South represents what is, after all, the traditional way of life, conserving and conservative; a settled order of living in which the past and present interpenetrate with the minimum of conflict. Those who write off such feelings as "regional" are more than merely condescending for they fail to see the centrality of this tradition. However far the urban writers are willing to go to mechanise their art in order to relate to the electronic landscape in which they live—and the last decade, particularly, has seen them go at least as far as sociology—each step they take seems to bring them nearer to the world of the computer and farther than ever from the vital tradition.

Miss Welty has been applauded for the sharpness of her eye and of her tongue; her fidelity to observed detail of landscape and human behavior, and the uncanny precision with which she reproduces the authentic accents of colloquial speech. In this world of social satire she is as indigenous as Ring Lardner. Yet she is so much more than that. The comedy of her early fiction is as contemporary as eye and ear can make it but its roots are deep in the living traditions of imaginative fiction. Her subject has always been, not the comedy of manners, but the comedy of the human condition which is much the same at all times in all places. She takes upon herself the traditional role of myth-maker, disciplining her vision in order to gain deeper penetration into the dark and lovely realities of the lonely human spirit and shaping her fiction so that each story should be something achieved, an aesthetic form salvaged and preserved from the wreck of time. As her art matured so she moved farther away from the idea of fiction as anecdote; plot and character became less important. Dialogue, in which earlier she excelled, often becomes a means of evading contact and communication. The intensity of felt experience is established obliquely, through natural images for the most part, as she attempts to give substance to the unseen world of feeling. Not what happens and why but what is felt to be happening and how are the subjects of her later fiction. The dramatic realization of the surface of life is as confidently seized as in her earlier work but her interest lies below and beyond the world of sight and sound. She shows only a perfunctory interest in the narrative of cause and effect and focuses interest on that silent landscape of human consciousness where the lonely and elusive spirit of man wanders in search of its own identity which is to be found, if at all, in moments of love. Yet these moments have little or nothing to do with the act of love, but are more like what in Welsh is called *hiraeth,* the home-sickness of those in exile. Behind this notion is the larger one that suggests that life is itself an exile, an Odyssean wandering in search of lost happiness and innocence, a conviction that home is that state of mind, instantly recognised, when we are momentarily flooded with a sense of meaningful peace, of knowing that we are, if only momentarily, at home. When two people find that elusive sense of peaceful belonging together then we can say that they have found love.

The three stories that pursue this theme in the boldest and most original way are the title story of Miss Welty's collection, *The Bride of the Innisfallen* and two other stories in that collection, *No Place for You, My Love* and *Going to Naples.* These three stories are undoubtedly experimental and in all these Miss Welty is breaking free of those categories within which her critics and commentators have tried to confine her. In her earlier stories, the outsiders— descendants of the carpet-baggers—draw down on themselves the full weight of human resentment of those who insist upon the inviolable dignity of the individual's right to order his own affairs in his own way. In these three stories, Miss Welty sees life from the point of view of the outsider though hers is a very different kind of outsider than either the carpet-bagger or the culture-hero created by Camus. Her outsiders are certainly travellers, or at least wanderers, but they are not casualties of society or in any popular sense alienated.

Moreover, although she regards them with something more than interest she, nonetheless, maintains her distance. She never treats her characters with anything less than respect or anything more damaging than irony. All three of these stories are concerned with travelling; *The Bride of the Innisfallen* tells of a journey from London to Cork, *No Place for You, My Love* is concerned with a car ride into the delta country south of New Orleans, and *Going to Naples* describes the ship's passengers travelling tourist class between New York and Naples. Each of the stories defines its own particular mood and creates the world it contemplates. Each is more concerned with the texture of that mood and world than with character and plot which are subdued elements in the overall pattern of each story. As a group the three stories are attempts to define what Philip Larkin, the English poet, calls a "frail travelling coincidence"; the accident of being at the same place at the same time and sharing intensely for a brief period the lives of others. There is a strong feeling also that travelling exists between places in a kind of nowhere; that travelling is something that happens outside of time somewhere between departure and arrival. At best travelling is a disembodied kind of existence somewhere between time and space. Miss Welty is quick to take advantage of the ambiguities of travel. The first paragraph of *No Place for You, My Love* tells us that,

> This time was a Sunday in summer—those hours of afternoon that seem Time Out in New Orleans.

Each of these stories deals with "Time Out," each of them is concerned with those occasions when travelling for a while we share a common destiny with the world of strangers. Gabriella, in *Going to Naples,* comes to recognize this clearly when she realizes her sudden intimacy with Aldo is ending as the ship nears Naples,

> Was now the time to look forward to the doom of parting, and stop looking back at the doom of meeting? The thought of either made sorrow go leaping and diving, like those dolphins in the water. Gabriella would only have to say "Good-by, Aldo," and while she was saying the words, the time would be flying by; parting would be over with almost before it began, no matter what Aldo had in store for an answer. "Hello, Aldo!" had been just the other way.

For Gabriella, "Time Out" is that period of intense feeling that spanned the gap in time between "Hello, Aldo!" and "Good-by, Aldo," for however meaningful the experience, ordinary life must be picked up and continued at the end of the journey. Miss Welty does not insist upon the connection between destiny and destination but she does firmly though unobtrusively assert the symbolism of these "frail travelling coincidences." Travelling, after all, reenacts the jour-

ney from birth to death and therefore is always a representation of
life, if only in miniature, but in these stories the most significant
voyage is the voyage within the self and the most precious find is
the rediscovery of some meaningful territory of feeling, some otherwise irrecoverable state of mind. Thus the man in *No Place for You,
My Love*

> remembered for the first time in years when he was young and
> brash, a student in New York, and the shriek and horror and unholy
> smother of the subway had its original meaning for him as the lilt
> and expectation of love.

The American girl in *The Bride of the Innisfallen* recovers the joy
of innocence and the sense that life will endure—"light and rain,
light and rain, dark, light, and rain." Gabriella's Mama in Naples
recovers the memory of the nightingale,

> "And the nightingale," Mama's voice just ahead was beseeching,
> "is the nightingale with us yet?"

Yet Gabriella herself experiences a sense of loss. In each of these
stories there is also a sense of something lost, of having participated
in some intense experience but of having missed the meaning.

In these stories Miss Welty's attitude is deliberately casual and
detached. Her attention does not seem to be fixed on anything or
anyone in particular but seemingly wanders from one thing to another.
In point of fact she identifies completely not with the travellers but
with their travelling. For instance, not until very near the end of her
story, *The Bride of the Innisfallen,* does the bride appear at all,

> "There's a bride on board!" called somebody. "Look at her,
> look!" Sure enough, a girl who had not yet showed herself in public
> now appeared by the rail. . . .

Moreover, only at the very end of this story does she fix her attention
on the American girl.

In *No Place for You, My Love* the Eastern business man and the
girl from the Middle West are thrown together because they are
"strangers to each other, and both fairly well strangers to the place."
Miss Welty emphasises their shared sense of exile and their feeling
of the hostility of New Orleans. The girl's "naive face" seemed to
say "Show me," in contrast to the "Southern look—Southern mask—
of life-is-a-dream irony, which could turn to pure challenge at the
drop of a hat." Yet the author does not identify with her characters
who have surprisingly little to say to each other but with the landscape
through which they drive. This landscape itself takes on the atmosphere of a dream as if all roads going South from New Orleans led
to the edge of the world, to the very borders of consciousness.

Existence in this elemental world is dominated by light so intense that it is felt as weight and heat so stifling and claustrophobic that it seems to imprison all who enter. The roads themselves are paved with seashells and the inhabitants wait for the Shrimp Dance to begin as if they lived in that unchartered, amphibious region when life first emerged from the sea on to the shores of consciousness. They return to the world with a sense of some profound mysterious experience they have shared like mythical voyagers returned from the underworld,

> A thing is incredible, if ever, only after it is told—returned to the world it came out of. For their different reasons, he thought, neither of them would tell this (unless something was dropped out of them): that, strangers, they had ridden down into a strange land together and were setting safely back—by a slight margin, perhaps, but margin enough. . . .
> Something that must have been with them all along suddenly, then, was not. In a moment, tall as panic, it rose, cried like a human, and dropped back.

This "something" embodied that elemental relationship that grows up between these two strangers, who together visited the very borders of consciousness, and who came to know and accepted an order of being utterly remote from their everyday life, falls away like some shade from out of Hades as they return to the known world and a different order of reality. Thus although the man, at least, recovers a memory of innocence as keen as love, he also relinquishes his knowledge of a profound order of being that exists below and beyond the world in which people have names, occupations and families.

The journey of these two is like the journey of Conrad's hero into the heart of darkness, a voyage into the interior world where the trappings of social life fall away and leave the individual naked in an elemental landscape confronting the deeper realities of self and of the heart of the mystery we call life. Yet at the level of ordinary life this deeper reality is, she says, "incredible"—perhaps another way of saying mystery—and more important it cannot be directly articulated. The telling of the story makes "incredible" the experience that can only be confronted. So much that is vital to the experience itself is beyond words and to relate the experience would be like translating from one language to another; the body of the experience would be conveyed but its meaning would be lost for ever like that "something" that cried and "dropped back." Miss Welty's achievement is, for this reason, all the more startling for she has created and shaped in language an experience that she recognizes as being beyond articulation.

Nothing could be further from naturalism. Her characters, who are never even named, live only in the present of the story, their past only hinted at, their future unknown. The art of the story is to re-enact and convey, as precisely as such experiences can be conveyed, that strange order of reality that exists on the edge of being; those profound and significant moments when we meet at a level more profound than social and domestic interchange can ever take into account. A way of meeting and knowing older than words themselves. These significant experiences may or may not radically alter the course of our everyday lives but after such moments our lives can never be quite the same again and we never cease to remember that these experiences were charged with mysterious significance. We have lived, however briefly, on another plane of reality and have gained a glimpse of another dimension. Ultimately in such a story as this Miss Welty's achievement is not only to hand over bodily, so to speak, the nature of the felt experience but to confirm her readers in the belief that such experiences, however strange, are indeed charged with significance.

Although *The Bride of the Innisfallen* and *Going to Naples* are less concentrated in their effects, mainly because they concern themselves with larger groups of people, nonetheless in both stories the travellers take a similar voyage to that taken by the man and the woman in *No Place for You, My Love.* That is to say they journey into strange and unknown areas of being and bring back knowledge about themselves and about the world in which they live. In the train between London and Fishguard a random collection of passengers are joined by the fabulous Irishman from Connemara exiled, like all true Irishmen, from the Hills of Tara, home of the high kings of ancient Ireland. They are joined also by the loquacious and inquisitive Welshman who pounds the travellers with questions both direct and oblique (I wish for my part he had been a little more sympathetic and that all the Celtic and legendary past had not been reserved for the Irish). Each of the passengers is tightly wrapped within himself rather like the middle-aged lady wrapped tightly in her extravagantly colored raincoat. "What she had on under her raincoat" Miss Welty remarks, "was her own business and remained so." She does, it is true, undo the top button of the raincoat but this is as much as she is prepared to reveal of herself. Similarly, the other passengers in the carriage are prepared to talk, or at least, to exchange pleasantries and observations but this is as much as they also are prepared to reveal of themselves. The American girl gives less of herself than anyone in the compartment. Each passenger withdraws farther and farther into himself as the journey proceeds until they reach the complete stillness of total isolation on the ferry boat between Fishguard and Cork.

In the deeps of night that bright room reached some vortex of quiet, like a room where all brains are at work and great decisions are on the brink. Occasionally there was a tapping, as of drumming fingernails—that meant to closed or hypnotized eyes that dogs were being sped through. The random, gentle old men who were walking the corridors in their tweeds and seemed lost as Jesus's lambs, were waiting perhaps for the bar to open. The young wife, as desperate as she'd feared, saw nothing, forgot everything, and even abandoned Victor, as if there could never be any time or place in the world but this of her suffering. She spoke to the child as if she had never seen him before and would never see him again.

The contraction of the world into "some vortex of quiet" is a gradual process of turning more and more inwards towards the center of self. It is a claustrophobic and diminishing process towards a greater degree of separateness. Starting on a fairly broad base of common humanity the perspectives of the story narrow to this point. As the *Innisfallen* docks and the passengers disembark and disperse the perspectives of the story open to embrace the town, the landscape and the morning. Only the American girl is left alone shut within herself but she too in a sudden vision of light and joy is drawn back into the world of life and people. Suddenly the darkness of her inner self becomes a light streaming through a window onto the world; she reaches out from loneliness to love and the world rushes to meet her,

> a glad cry went up at her entrance, as if she were the heresy herself, and when they all called out something fresh it was like the signal for a song.
> The girl let her message go into the stream of the street, and opening the door walked into the lonely room full of strangers.

She is one of those who expect too much of life and when life fails to live up to her expectations—as it always will—she blames life itself. Meanwhile, she is unable to accept what life has to offer, unable to give to life what she can offer. Once she learns to give, life breaks back into her loneliness and disappointment and carries her forward into the world of love, that "lonely room full of strangers." Yet the most obvious feature of the story is not the character of the people who enter or leave at particular points of the journey but the journey itself. Somehow the narrative sharply captures the sense of travelling itself as if the author had focussed single-minded attention on the flux and rhythms of travelling. She is interested in those who step into the movement of travelling the moment they become part of that flux and rhythm and loses interest the moment they step outside. They exist not as characters but as characters travelling who share a sense of common destination and little else. At the end of the story, the journey over, she re-establishes a different rhythm, a personal

sense of the way life is changed and the way life is always, in spite
of the change, caught up in an enduring rhythm of "light and rain,
light and rain, dark, light, and rain." We travel through life, she
seems to suggest, to find what we have always known but to know
it for the first time.

Going to Naples is a very much more sociable affair than either
the drive to the delta country or the journey from London to Cork.
Moreover, it is very much more a family journey. The interest centers
on the eighteen-year-old girl, Gabriella Certo, and her relationship
with Aldo Scampo. The relationship is awkward, inarticulate and
tender; a feeling of love that starts but never blossoms; an awareness
of self that is as yet unrealized and only half-recognized for what it
is. Again, as in *The Bride of the Innisfallen,* the story establishes its
own rhythm although in this journey it is a slower and more definite
one. There are broad alternations between those scenes in which
Gabriella the girl is stifled by her mother and the sense of family
relations and those scenes in which Gabriella senses the freedom of
being a woman. The story sets up a steady rhythm of contraction
and family set against expansion and love. Gabriella who is no longer
a child but not yet a woman herself expresses this alternation. By
the end of the voyage she has a more precise realization of herself
and has anticipated some of the pains and joys of growing up. For
the most part this touching and gauche story of young love is set in
the context of a comedy of manners played out by a group of Italian-
Americans travelling tourist class to Naples. Miss Welty never cari-
catures her characters, although there must have been a temptation
to do so, but places them with uncanny accuracy. She also reproduces
perfectly the broken patterns of their speech; in fact her ear for
conversation is as exact with the tones of the Italian-Americans as it
is with idioms of her native Mississippians. Her eye is also just as
sharp and wicked. Mr. Ugone, for instance, is beautifully placed as
he describes the beauty of Genoese cemeteries;

> "For one thing, is in Genoa most beautiful cemetery in world,"
> said Mr. Ugone—and did well to speak in English; otherwise who
> could have understood this voice from the north tonight? "You have
> never seen? No one? Ah the statues—you could find nowhere in
> *Italia* more beautiful, more sad, more real. Envision with me now,
> I will take you there gladly. Ah! See here—a mama, how she hold
> high the little daughter to kiss picture of Papa—all lifesize. See
> here! You see angel flying out the tomb—lifesize! See here! You see
> family of ten, eleven, twelve, all kneeling lifesize at deathbed. You
> would marvel how splendid is Genoa with the physical . . . . you
> will see this and more. Oh, I guarantee, you will find it sad! You
> want to see tear on little child's cheek? Solid tear?"

Certainly as described by Mr. Ugone Genoa seems a place hardly to be missed. Yet as he is, in his dramatic grand-opera style, bringing the cemetery to life so Miss Welty through his words and attitude is bringing Mr. Ugone to life, even if a little more than life-size. Her sense of the comic, of the incongruous and the irrelevant never deserts her. On board the *Pomona* are six young men, three of whom she characterizes. The others are lumped together throughout the voyage as "three for the priesthood." Gabriella's Papa spends the voyage blowing a whistle and is steadily ignored by his wife and daughter. Yet at the center of the story is the feeling that exists briefly and intensely between Gabriella and Aldo and in spite of everything else this awakening bears the weight of significant interest,

> Aldo buried his face in Gabriella's blouse, and she looked out over his head and presently smiled—not into any face in particular. Her smile was as rare as her silence, and as vulnerable—it was meant for everybody. A gap where a tooth was gone showed childishly.
>
> And it lifted the soul—for a thing like crossing the ocean could depress it—to sit in the sun and contemplate among companions the weakness and the mystery of the flesh. Looking, dreaming, down at Gabriella, they felt something of an old, pure loneliness come back to them—like a bird sent out over the waters long ago, when they were young, perhaps from their same company. Only the long of memory, the brave and experienced of heart, could bear such a stirring, an awakening—

This "awakening" informs every part of the story; it is the "vortex of quiet" into which all else is drawn. Below the human comedy being enacted on the voyage, lie the deeper realities of love and loneliness, youth and age, innocence and experience. The essential human predicament binds all men together as intimately as the passengers in the tourist class of the *Pomona*. Theirs is a "frail, travelling coincidence" but as the passengers disperse on the quay-side in Naples they take from the experience of the voyage a sense of something lost balanced precariously against what was found. These travellers, having arrived at their destinations, have also gained some insight into the meaning of human destiny.

All three of these stories are set outside Miss Welty's home patch; she is the outsider looking in, a reversal of her earlier attitude. Yet being outside also confers on her a certain detachment, a lack of direct involvement which is also an increase in freedom. She does not impose any pattern on the stories, for instance, but allows each journey to set its own pace and to establish its own rhythm. She sees the journey in all its various aspects without needing to adopt any one particular attitude. The world of love that she defines so precisely in her earlier stories is now the world of man; in America or in Europe, she finds that love and loneliness are basic to the human condition. Each story creates its own authenticity. She maintains with all the dexterity of her seemingly casual art the exact appearances of life, though in each of the stories she is more concerned with the profounder levels of experience that lie beneath the surface. Whether she is probing deeply and narrowly, as in *No Place for You, My Love,* in which she explores the elemental world at the back of beyond or whether, as in *Going to Naples,* she proceeds from a broader social and domestic base, she follows the implications of her story to the limit of artistic understanding. Each story is itself both literally and metaphorically an exploration, a voyage into hitherto unknown and uncharted territory of consciousness. Each is achieved with such apparent simplicity that it is all too easy to overlook the way in which she deploys all the skills and arts learnt painfully from that intolerable wrestle with words and meanings that is the writer's lot. She never resorts to the mechanical aids of allegory or symbolism as so many contemporary writers have. She has chosen the harder course of insisting that if there is any symbolic or allegorical meaning to be gathered from her stories then these meanings must be inseparable from the total vision of the story.

She is firmly and completely committed to the traditional role of the artist. Indeed it is, in some ironic way that I feel sure she herself would appreciate, because she has pursued the traditions of her art with such singleminded dedication that the critics trained in the contemporary schools of hunt the symbol have been completely baffled by her later work. She takes for granted the traditional assumption that each story written, each work carefully achieved, is necessarily a raid on those areas of felt experience that are essentially inarticulate. Looking at her last collection of stories, *The Bride of the Innisfallen,* it is, perhaps, easier for someone brought up within the tradition to recognize the sheer virtuosity of her achievement. In a more fluid cultural situation that confronts the American reader, the meretricious, the novel and the shocking can often be mistaken for originality. But originality is the true marriage of the traditional and the individual talent. There is no doubt that Miss Welty has recognized this and accepted it and that her individual talent has extended and enlarged the tradition in a way that authenticates the originality of her talents. With a firm and undeniable ability to seize and recreate the contemporary world, she has recognized that the past and the present interpenetrate at a personal, historical and traditional level and that nothing short of the total resources of her art will satisfy the demand that the artist's vision must comprehend the glory, jest and riddle of the human predicament while at the same time creating in language a vision of human experience which will endow life with beauty and meaning. The vision of each of these stories is something achieved in the face of time and enhances the life of each of us.

The quality of Miss Welty's prose in these stories is such that it seems to ebb and flow in rhythm with the events each describes so that the prose itself appears to embody the stream of time through which each voyager passes. The point of view moves in and out of the consciousness of her characters as if the narrator were nowhere and everywhere simultaneously. Each story carries forward a sense of something of great significance pending but never fully realized. Her vision of reality moves confidently in that narrow area poised precariously between comedy and tragedy. If anarchy and chaos are the lot of man, the artist attempts with all the gifts at her command to control and define the fluidity of time itself; to record those fleeting events and emotions in such a way as to confer order, shape and meaning upon them. In the modern world—and particularly in America where past and future conflict so violently—to create significant form from that flux we call the present, Miss Welty stands with all those traditional artists represented by the heroic Yeatsian archetype Cuchulain fighting the indomitable seas. Art is something of beauty and value snatched from the wreck of time; it is in this respect that Miss Welty shows herself to be so much the classicist aware of the human need to confront the destructive fluidity of the modern world and to give to time, if only for a time, a local habitation and a name.

Losing Battles

Eudora Welty's New Novel:
The Comedy of Loss
Louise Y. Gossett[°]

One of the most reassuring events in recent American literary history is the reappearance of Eudora Welty. When a voice so disciplined and flexible as hers has not been heard in a large work for fifteen years, its sounding again is an occasion meriting special attention. Miss Welty was last heard in a collection of short stories *The Bride of The Innisfallen* (1955) in which for the first time she used to any extent settings and characters from outside her native Mississippi. Now, in *Losing Battles,* she returns to her state with a novel almost twice as long as any other book she has published, and in it we listen to the tumble of talk among northeastern Mississippi farmers, their lives and dialect colored by isolation, poverty, and humor in the red-clay hills. What we hear is an impressive addition to the scale of human existence and literary achievement which Miss Welty has already ranged.

Not for a moment in her career—a career which among contemporary Southern writers has for its magnitude of invention and sustained excellence been exceeded only by that of William Faulkner—has Miss Welty doubted the inexhaustibility of literature. Her certainty that the combinations of emotion and thought, movement and rest, success and frustration in human life are infinite and that only portions of these complexities can be brought up in any one narrative net underlies the freedom with which she has tried fictive modes and themes. These have not been experimental in the manner of writers like Joyce or Beckett, but they have been suitably varied to relate with precision the awareness of life which Miss Welty at any one instant desires to express. For her purposes she trusts, respects, and loves language, so that it does for her what pre-McLuhanites cherish: it enkindles and illuminates reality in coherent relationships of images, symbols, rhythms, and tones.

The substance of these relationships appears increasingly impor-

° From *The Southern Literary Journal* 3 (Fall 1970):122–37. Copyright 1970 by Department of English, University of North Carolina. Reprinted with permission of the University of North Carolina Press.

tant as one thinks even briefly over the books that make up the core of Miss Welty's work and pauses again to be moved by the penetration with which Miss Welty cuts through the teeming surface of life to the universals of love and longing in her first two collections of short stories, *The Curtain of Green* (1941) and *The Wide Net* (1943); the imaginative control that interrelates stories about human distress in microcosmic Morgana, Mississippi, in *The Golden Apples* (1949) and groups together stories of searchers for truth in *The Bride of The Innisfallen;* the clarity and verve with which she reconstitutes history and fairy lore in the novella *The Robber Bridegroom* (1942); the jubilant intervention that carries Edna Earle and Uncle Daniel through the improbable in the short novel *The Ponder Heart* (1954); the wisdom that measures the demands of love—private and familial— in the full-length novel *Delta Wedding* (1946). In addition Miss Welty has generously shared with us her theories about writing and reading in critical essays that are an invaluable record of a writer's views.

The vitality of Miss Welty's literary thought and practice is abundantly exhibited in *Losing Battles.* Tempo in the novel, the pacing of event and revelation which keeps us alert and looking forward while allowing us to contemplate and digest, is one of Miss Welty's triumphs of management. *Losing Battles* has more breathing space than does *Delta Wedding,* even though there are a few more main characters (thirty-five are named in the cast) to be deployed in a larger number of episodes. In *Delta Wedding* the headlong pitch of the Fairchilds toward the wedding of Dabney and Troy jams the plantation with preparations: voices never stop planning and directing; bodies never repose; irons and ovens never cool. The house crowded with eight Fairchild children, their cousins and friends, running, playing, dancing, and with parents, uncles, aunts, and servants about their chores makes the reader fell claustrophobic. Their behavior, the visiting cousin Laura feels, is *"compelled."*

The Fairchilds on the surface are driven by the demands of events, but inwardly they are driven by consciousness, striving for a private identity and competing with other consciousnesses to preserve the identity. The Renfro house in *Losing Battles,* on the other hand, is merely a receiving station for food and gifts for Granny Vaughn's ninetieth birthday. Preparations are over and the celebration has begun. Children, kept on the periphery, play ball in fields, coming in only for food and goodbyes. Adults sit on the gallery, relaxed and reminiscent, secure in their identities as Renfros or Beechams. Their narratives of past action intersperse the activity occurring in the present.

With the assured sense of timing of a stage comedian who knows exactly when to release the punch line, Miss Welty withholds the resolution of the comic catastrophe in *Losing Battles.* For three-fourths of the novel, Judge Moody's Buick dangles over the edge of Banner Top or Lover's Leap while the reunion of Renfros and Beechams continues. With uproarious gusto Miss Welty draws out the story of the predicament of the car and its ignominious return to the crossroads community of Banner, hauled by two mules, a school bus, and a truck. In the humor, however, one also senses that the car hangs suspended like an extravagant and preposterous image of man and his subjection to the strains of life. Jack Renfro, the favored son, had first encountered the recalcitrance of life in a comic courtroom tangle out of which Judge Moody sentenced him to the state penitentiary for two years for "aggravated battery." Nearing home on his return from Parchman, Jack helps Judge Moody, whom he does not recognize, to extricate his car from a ditch. When Jack learns that it is Judge Moody who is in the neighborhood, he—in accordance with the code of his family—sets out from the reunion with his wife Gloria and child to avenge himself against the Judge. Jack quickly loses control of his plans to accident and chance, which in Miss Welty's view are the essence of life. Contingency eventually humbles his pride before two enemies.

The "accident" planned to force the Judge's Buick into the ditch at the Renfro mailbox becomes a sudden rescue when the Judge veers uphill to avoid striking Gloria and the baby Lady May. The Moodys are brought to the reunion to wait out the recovery of their car. The Judge, formerly the enemy, is now the benefactor, a complication which only the young people like Jack and Gloria are capable of accepting. The rubric hospitality which the parents, aunts, and uncles offer insulates them against any genuine exchange with their guests. The real possibility for growth toward a wisdom which will be more genuine than the superficial heroism imposed on Jack by the family lies in the young man's capacity for moral discrimination. When the family in an outburst of sentimental piety "forgive" the Judge for everything from living to sending Jack to Parchman, Jack draws distinctions. He can be grateful for the rescue of Lady May and Gloria, but he cannot forgive the sentence. Surrounded by the babbling family, Jack and Judge Moody affirm Jack's view by shaking hands. Earlier, Jack has endured being humbled by his original antagonist Curly Stovall, whose charges had brought Jack to trial. Now possessed of Jack's beloved truck, Curly says he feels sorry enough for Jack to help him remove the Buick. This pitying condescension, like Gloria's being laughed at by her teacher and mentor Miss Julia Mortimer for wanting to marry Jack, makes the young husband and wife feel united against the world: "That's being married," Gloria declares.

From the beginning of her career, Miss Welty has explored the intricacies of human relationships, sensitively articulating the rhythms of the inner emotional life, the alternations between love and hate, calm and anger, security and fear, communication and isolation, closeness and distance that torment and entertain man. The pairing of alternatives, the oscillations between opposites or obverse has been the structural symbol for her thought. She has never adopted any single social, material, or metaphysical map for her world. It is as if she has refused to number the routes into human experience for fear of implying that any one must be followed instead of another. Her mind has thus in the Jamesian sense remained unviolated by ideas. Like Virginia Woolf, she records the emergence of experience; the relationship of persons generates the fabric of life. Her treatment of behavior accords with the theories of existential psychologists as they insist that behavior takes meaning from the relation between human beings, not from clinical fragmentation of consciousness. Miss Welty's sense of wonder before what relation discovers or destroys is one with the impulse from which she notes that stories take shape, "the impulse to praise, to love, to call up, to prophesy."[1]

In *Losing Battles* the focusing of the drifts and pulls in the mind of a woman like Gloria as she enacts her multiple roles of wife, mother, and daughter-in-law, of practical problem-solver and romantic idealist, is typical of Eudora Welty's vision of behavior and relation. The craving for perfection and the acceptance of limitations, the sustained desire for the ideal and the awareness of its inevitable defeat, characterize stories in most of her volumes. In "The Whistle" *(A Curtain of Green)*, Sara and Jason Morton can only momentarily warm their emotions as well as their bodies by the fire built from the last of their furniture. In "At The Landing" *(The Wide Net)*, Jenny, the young initiate into passion, must seek and suffer without assurance that she will again find the dazzling male Billy Floyd. Defiance of frustration and death or creative cooperation with the inevitable typifies the reaction of most of Miss Welty's women characters. Appropriately both rebellion and resolution are the center of the title story in the first collection. In the youthful Mrs. Larkin, her vitality chilled by the death of her husband, the protest of life reasserts itself. It is manifest in the jungle growth of her flower garden and in the pairing of life and death at the climax when, at the moment that Mrs. Larkin raises her hoe to kill her Negro gardener in compensation for her husband's death, rain falls, and she drops to the earth reconciled to her impotence against fate and reunited with nature and her own sexual vitality. In Miss Welty's second collection of stories, *The Wide Net*, again the woman's experience is imaged by the ambiguous life-death pairing. Livvie, surrounded by the symbolic growth of spring, is freed by the death of Solomon from the security of her elderly husband's respectability to take the risk of love with the young field hand Cash. The motif recurs in the title story of *The Bride of The Innisfallen* when the young American wife feels compelled to abandon her husband in order to live the secret she holds like a prophetic figure from Blake: "You must never betray pure joy—the kind you were born and began with—either by hiding it or by parading it in front of people's eyes; they didn't want to be shown it." Like Virgie Rainey in the stories in *The Golden Apples,* she would rather risk promiscuity than loss of passion.

In the two full-length novels this defiance crystallizes in the young wives who assert their individuality against the expectations of the families into which they must marry. They fight not only for themselves but also for the identity of their husbands as husbands, not as the idolized brother, uncle, or son their families claim them to be. Much has been made of the indignation of Robbie when her husband George Fairchild chances being killed by the oncoming train when he stays on the trestle to free the caught foot of his half-witted niece Maureen. Robbie interprets the act as an insulting absence of consideration for her, as a flagrant lack of commonsense judgment, as part of the flamboyant heroics of a Fairchild. Although the narrator's sympathies are with Robbie, the incident is also a curious implied criticism of Robbie or an instance in which Miss Welty has called on an incident to mean more than in fact it could. The fact is that George simply by his nature as a human being would have stayed on the trestle to rescue any endangered person, a Fairchild or not. Robbie is as affected by the insularity of the Fairchilds and as unaware of the true nature of George as are the blooded Fairchilds if she takes the action for a demonstration of Fairchild high drama. The more serious threat—and the one which Gloria in *Losing Battles* constantly defies—is the intention of the family to exploit George or Jack for the group. George as an educated self-aware person has far more defenses than Jack. Robbie acknowledges George's strength when toward the end of *Delta Wedding* she suggests they come home to the Grove. Gloria, on the other hand, sees Jack poised between late adolescence and manhood: he may become a provincial, self-satisfied Renfro stuck forever on the decaying farm at Banner or he may move away and grow up to fuller responsibilities as an independent adult. To his astonished family, Gloria declares, "We'll live to ourselves one day yet, and do wonders. And raise all our children to be both good and smart—." But Eudora Welty doesn't promise escape, for as Gloria looks away from the house to the future "beyond the bright porch she couldn't see anything."

Gloria's resistance to the Renfros and Beechams is carried beyond humor and the conventional struggle of a young wife to wean her husband from his family. More directly than heretofore Eudora Welty criticizes the limitations of her characters. Gloria attacks their domestic complacency and selfishness. The chief critic, however, is Miss

Julia, who for all her caricatured schoolmarmism, is the presence of
thought, learning, and organized intelligence, which the Renfros and
Beechams have unequivocally rejected. A joke to them for being an
old maid, for keeping school despite cyclone, flood, bad boys, planting
and plowing, she has nevertheless been responsible for "a Superior
Court judge, the best eye, ear, nose, and throat specialist in Kansas
City, and a history professor. . . ." Some pupils like Dr. Carruthers
and Judge Moody she convinced to return to their home county in
hopes of improving it.

Though she never appears in person, Miss Julia is the nerve
center of the novel. She is a persistent rebuke to the backcountry
folk. However amusing and proverbial they are, they choose to be
victims of ignorance, prejudice, and pettiness. Their attachment to
the land has no rationale except Uncle Dolphus' declaration that they
are "Farmers still and evermore will be." Families have moved away,
the well has run dry, the river is low, but the Renfros intend to stay
on, Jack being expected to save them by the same methods of farming
which have already exhausted the land and the people. There are
no Faulknerian meditations on the moral complexity of the relationship
between man and the land, but the obtuseness of unthinking, un-
cultivated minds is revealed: "It's the fault of the land going back
on us, treating us the wrong way." They can remember when the
country ran with squirrels, quail, and deer, and they complain about
Dearman who followed the railroad into the woods and cut the largest
trees, but they are incapable of implicating themselves. No Ike McCaslin
arises to judge and attempt to atone. Uncle Nathan's confession that
he killed Dearman and let a "sawmill nigger" hang for it only
momentarily silences the family; his act is not taken as a protest
against exploitation and waste. It is quickly absorbed by the family
as a private act done for the younger brother Sam Dale, Granny
cryptically says. Its significance is lost as the family turns away from
any larger moral view to savor again its own feelings and intuitions.
Their poverty ultimately is intellectual and spiritual; their boast that
they can survive is an empty sentimentality cutting them off from
the truth of their condition.

The power of mind, of knowledge, of experience meditated upon,
which the backcountry folk fear, is symbolized by their scorn for
Miss Julia's habit of reading. That she kept a shelf of books at Banner
School might be tolerated; that she read at home during the day was
beyond acceptance, "a thing," Mr. Renfro remarks, "surpassing strange
for a well woman to do." Books, her former pupils are sure, were
to blame for Miss Julia's considering—against all local loyalty—that
Mississippi was the state most in need of improvement. The intran-
sigence she had battled in her school was with her at the end in the
tart stubbornness of her house-companion Miss Lexie, Mr. Renfro's

sister. In a cruel triumph of ignorance and cantankerousness, Miss Lexie would refuse to bring the aged, bedfast teacher a book because the old woman did not name a title. Reading as a sign of the incompatibility of reasoned thought with Mississippi habits of life has been touched upon offhandedly by Miss Welty at other times. In *The Ponder Heart*, Edna Earle, who interrupted the reading of her hotel guest in order to talk—"if you read, you'll put your eyes out"— describes herself as "a great reader that never has time to read." What she really likes to read is sets of directions. The busyness of life at Shellmound makes reading all but impossible. Laura hides her books under her pinafore and steals away to the seldom-used library. Shelley cannot bring a reading lamp into her bedroom. Although the tradition of action and talk in the South fosters the art of narration, saluted by such writers as Faulkner and Flannery O'Connor as well as Miss Welty, the absence of intellectual life shows in *Losing Battles* as a serious deprivation.

The ultimate charge against Miss Julia, more damaging than her reading or her remaining unmarried, emerges from deep in the Southern ethos: "She never did learn how to please." Aunt Beck has the charity to suggest that Miss Julia had other goals, but the family will not be drawn away from castigating someone unable or unwilling to smooth her way with appropriate social oils. They boast that "she didn't damage our spirits much." The undercurrent of bitterness, however, suggests that they clumsily sense how blindly they walked by every door she tried to open. Their pride in clan and state is defensive whistling. The family is ignorant and incompetent; the state is at the bottom of the ladder. The family takes no option except to resist receiving government commodities as long as possible. The desirability of change, such as George Fairchild foresees in planting crops other than cotton, is beyond them. The adumbration of a new order in the plans of George and in the marriage of the plantation daughter to the overseer are backed by the energy of the young and the trained. In *Losing Battles* Gloria's reiterated hope that "some day yet, we'll move to ourselves" seems largely a dream to be dissipated by Jack's optimism that he can bring in the sheaves right where he is.

If sociological and economic motifs run stronger in this novel than in Miss Welty's previous fiction, they accompany the familiar— but always freshly-treated—motif of lostness, linked again with the journey and the search. The routes are broader this time and less introspective. Instead of the intricate symbolic tracings which bring together and then separate characters like Lorenzo Dow, James Murrell, and Audubon in "A Still Moment," for example, or the precise nuances of the relation between the deaf boy Joel Mayes and the heroic Aaron Burr in "First Love," there is a more self-evident delineation. Instead of the dream-journey into death of the salesman R. J. Bowman in "Death of a Traveling Salesman," there is the Sunday drive of Judge Moody over Mississippi back roads and into the human tangle of the Renfro-Beecham reunion. "He's where he is now because he's lost," Mrs. Moody announces, although she doubts her husband's courage to admit his condition. The spiritual destination of both the judge and the salesman, however, is similar. Each comes up against his emptiness, his unawareness, his carelessness. Bowman has a vision of love and a fruitful marriage, richnesses of communication from which he is forever cut off. Judge Moody undergoes an ethical revelation in which he admits his cowardice in failing to respond to Miss Julia. Against the background of the Beecham reminiscences, he now understands Miss Julia as the same compound of character and chance as himself and all mankind, not knowing "what would *happen* to what she was." What happened seemed nothing but a series of defeats, and yet she fought on out of the drive she calls inspiration. Careless about the significance of her letter summoning him to her bedside, the Judge has waited too long. Now he is left with the shock of his own failure, of his being part of the mortification of her life, of his complicity in neglecting, denying, rejecting another's suffering. Beyond the fact of having lost his way in the Mississippi countryside, the Judge had wandered from his humanity. During the Sunday of the novel he has journeyed to contrition and confession and now assumes his burden of shame and humiliation: "I don't care quite the same about living as I did this morning."

The image of a journey is the dying word of Miss Julia herself. Of Willy Trimble, who finds her lying in the road before her house, she asks "What was the trip for?" More significant than the conventional question is Willy's sententious observation that "she picked the wrong one to ask. It's the chance you are always taking as you journey through life." The difference between Miss Julia and the others is that she risked giving the answer to them before they knew the question was there to be asked. Characteristic of her honesty about the mixed nature of human existence, Miss Welty near the end of the novel lets Gloria enter a gentle caveat. Gloria recognizes Miss Julia's desire to enlighten, to bring everything "out in the wide open, to see and be known," but she also recognizes that people cherish their own mystery: "they don't want to be read like books."

The novel is bounded by two ritual journeys, culminating in arrival and departure. It opens with the triumphant return of Jack, who with the divine independence of a hero, has escaped from Parchman a day before his parole in order to attend Granny Vaughn's birthday. His progress home has been a comic sequence of hitching rides with garrulous preachers and finally stealing a ride on the back tire of a car driven by Judge Moody, whom he fails to recognize.

Like a feudal lord he has been accompanied by a faithful retainer, Aycock Comfort, sentenced along with Jack. The Renfro house has been topped with a brilliant blue roof for the hero's homecoming. The folk have gathered. The feast has been prepared. Jack arrives as breathless and sweating as if he had been killing giants. He jousts briefly with his younger brother with cornstalks, he is cleaned and dressed in a shirt armored by starch, his seignorial rights are acknowledged by the welcoming company. The return of the lord has been accomplished in Fieldingesque parody. The energizing male principle and the revenge motif have been introduced into the festival. Later the reunion's celebration of life (in which the dead are kept unchanged in memory) has to open up to include news of the death of Miss Julia and her demand that all Banner people be her mourners. The competition of life and death is humorously pointed up by Miss Beulah, Jack's mother, who doubts that the food and crowd at Miss Julia's could equal the supply at the reunion. At the end of the novel Miss Julia's funeral procession journeys across Banner bridge, one of the many crossings related in the story on a bridge as chancy as life. Through the funeral Miss Julia delivers her *memento mori* like a final wisdom to the people she had struggled to enlighten.

In addition to the accounts of those who travel specific journeys, other references suggest the pervasive lostness of man. The symbolic extensions of this image are not so developed in *Losing Battles* as they are in a work like *The Golden Apples*. The wanderers in these stories of the gains and losses of the heart in a small Mississippi town move like figures in myth to destinies in varying degrees comic or pathetic. The wanderers in *Losing Battles* enact their fates less portentously. In the novel the family name of Mattie Will Sojourner, one of the women taken by the Jovian King MacLain in *The Golden Apples*, reappears when Granny declares that fox-headed Rachel Sojourner was the mother of fox-headed Gloria. Rachel (echoing perhaps Melville's lost *Rachel*), evidently rejected by her family for her "secret," had been found sick and wandering on Banner bridge by Miss Julia. Brother Bethune wanders through the country, his old mind and memory too wavering to give directions. Uncle Nathan does penance by wandering for the Lord. On his cornet Uncle Nathan plays the theme "Poor Wayfaring Stranger." The historical wandering of a nation moving West is recalled by the Wayfarer's bell. It still hangs at the Renfro farm, where it used to be rung once an hour to signal direction along the faint trail that ran through the then-thick woods. Although technology and national progress have now set the traveler on his way, the bell remains as if to ring should these fail.

The search for self, for identity, for a being relatable to others which draws many of Eudora Welty's characters through resistant psychological undergrowth, is comically reversed in *Losing Battles*.

Gloria, the orphan, is the voice of the present disclaiming the past. Without known parents, she has been free to create herself, especially to count herself superior to her environment. She doesn't want parents now, nor does she want "family." Most vociferously she rejects a possible Beecham father out of the very family from which she is trying to save Jack. Instead of an epic reunion of child and father, we are given a comic tribal initiation, a watermelon fight to make Gloria swallow the juice as though partaking of a blood ritual that stains her forever a Beecham. The furor over the possibility that Jack has violated Mississippi law by marrying a first cousin and thus subjecting himself to imprisonment and the nullification of his marriage is resolved by Judge Moody on grounds which he would never admit in court. Like a classic figure of authority tilted over in a Greek comedy, the Judge takes the law into his own hands and rules that no crime has been committed.

Through it all, Gloria continues to reject the identity searched out for her. She resolutely insists: "That I'm one to myself, and nobody's kin, and my own boss, and nobody knows the one I am or where I came from. . . . And all that counts in life is up ahead." The confusion has about it much of the joyous inconsequence of the action in "The Wide Net" when William Wallace Jamieson and his retinue drag the Pearl River for his moody pregnant wife, and like "The Wide Net" it has a center of consequence at which Gloria and the Judge define themselves more exactly, especially in regard to their vocations—marriage and law. In the compactness of the short story the ritualistic elements figure more obviously than they do in the novel's sprawling episodes.

The pilgrimage theme finally is emphasized by a question studiedly ambiguous. Out of the mouth of a baby it falls into an unanswering cosmos. The reunion guests have left; Vaughn, Jack's young brother, has stumbled through the house like an embodiment of all wanderers looking in vain for a place to sleep; a thunderstorm breaks. Lady May awakens and speaks her first sentence, a prophetic, "What you huntin', man?"

Miss Welty has never answered that question with metaphysics, but always with narrative. This literary purity is both the power and the limit of her work. With consistent excellence she has told what tone, characters, narrators, dialogue, metaphors, symbols, and rhythms can discover about human experience. There is no argument or justification; there is the telling. And it seems likely that from the caves of our human past to the recesses of our future expanding consciousness we can bear reality best when it comes personalized as time, place, and person. It is not by chance that most of Miss Welty's stories open, as does "A Curtain of Green," with localizing details: "Every day one summer in Larkin's Hill, it rained a little."

The texture of place and anticipation comes immediately in the opening paragraph of *Losing Battles:*

> When the rooster crowed, the moon had still not left the world but was going down on flushed cheek, one day short of the full. A long thin cloud crossed it slowly, drawing itself out like a name being called. The air changed, as if a mile or so away a wooden door had swung open, and a smell, more of warmth than wet, from a river at low stage, moved upward into the clay hills that stood in darkness.

In her essays Miss Welty has repeatedly emphasized the principle which she eloquently practices as the ground of her fiction: "Fiction depends for its life on place. Location is the crossroads of circumstance, the proving ground of 'What happened? Who's here? Who's coming?'—and that is the heart's field."[2]

Over and over again the specificity of the vision lures us to accept it. When shaped by the logic of actuality, the vision gives us details that we believe in as "life in Mississippi," or at least the Mississippi of Miss Welty's characters. When shaped by the logic of fantasy—and like J. R. R. Tolkien, Miss Welty knows that fantasy is more relocation than dislocation—the vision turns inside experience outside: Eugene MacLain in *The Golden Apples,* for example, grieved by the death of his daughter and the maudlin triviality of his wife, revolts against the ordinariness of his routine to wander for a day with a Spanish guitarist whose strange sympathy enlarges and exhilarates Eugene. In the colloquial, idiomatic fiction like *The Ponder Heart* and *Losing Battles,* fantasy is converted into the tall tale— Uncle Daniel's loony generosity or the story of the car-that-climbed-the-sky.

The authenticity of the spoken idiom in *Losing Battles* is unshakable in structure, diction, intonation, and rhythm. Miss Welty makes us hear the breathless, alternately exasperated and proud voice of Miss Beulah, the twittering of the telephone operator Miss Pet Hanks and her school bus load of teachers, the ministerial swing of Brother Bethune launched into Beecham history as if into Biblical begats, the imperatives of Miss Julia, the backslapping heartiness of Uncle Noah Webster's exclamations. When the characters are not speaking, the omniscient narrator supplements and moves ahead with descriptions, summarized narrative, and infrequently, explicit interpretations. Descriptions may be an exact account, such as that of the logs, limestone and clay, low roof, and hewn posts showing heart-grain which details the Renfro house, or it may be a lyrical response to moonlight "the thickness of china" and shadows of trees "stretched downhill, lengthened as if for flight." The shifts in mode create part of the action of the story, much of which takes place in anecdotes.

In these the language conveys the impervious practicality and skepticism of the people involved in incongruous and outlandish situations.
To Mrs. Moody staring at her improbably perched car, Jack says
matter-of-factly, "Go a step further and you're going to be in badder
trouble." Miss Beulah interrupts the orgy of forgiving to observe,
"That coconut cake's so tender I advise you to eat it with a spoon."
Something of the exultant hyperbole throughout the novel is suggested
by the narrator's description of Curly's truck running berserk:

> The empty truck was jolting headlong toward the road, skating
> in and out of the tracks it had made backing up. It was held back
> only a little by its laboring engine and by the brief fingering of plum
> bushes. It banged into Banner Road, a puddle walling up in front
> of it, then through its shower limped on across the road as if
> pretending something was broken, and threw itself into the ditch,
> ushering a part of the syrup stand with it and still dragging a long
> clay tail behind, which was its end of the rope.

Losing Battles as one of the colloquial fictions is more explicit
and less cryptic than are the lyrical *The Robber Bridegroom, The
Golden Apples,* or *The Bride of The Innisfallen. Mystery* and *secret,*
almost cabalistic words with Miss Welty, seldom appear in it. The
similes and metaphors which call obtrusive attention to themselves
at times, for example, in *The Golden Apples* are abundant but functional. A snake crawls over the edge of a hill "like a long black
stocking being rolled out through the wringer," stocking and wringer
both appurtenances of backcountry life. Mr. Renfro steps along "like
a pigeon stepping down a barn roof." To Gloria the faces of the
Moodys in the reunion crowd stick out "like four-leafs in a clover
patch." The length of the novel gives leisure, as if Miss Welty had
had time to come to terms with the world and to invent exuberantly
out of her ability to be delighted by the absurdity of life. She follows
more narrative lines than in *Delta Wedding* and with greater relaxation
and ease. Parallels between these two novels, however, crowd in: the
hero-brothers to the families—Jack and George—who have wived
outsiders, Gloria and Robbie; the observing mothers—Miss Beulah
and Ellen; the helpless children—Lady May and Maureen—to be
rescued from the power of the machine—the car and the train; the
family festivals—reunion and wedding; the choric commentators—
aunts and sisters; the feminine foci of judgment—Gloria and Miss
Julia, and Ellen, Robbie, and Laura.
    The tour de force of creating Miss Julia entirely from the mem-
ories of others is brilliant. She emerges from the facets as a person
idealistic, honorable, wise, defiant, irascible, intolerant, ridiculous—
the fighter and the loser, missing achievement by the ironies and
mortification that Judge Moody says "could make a stone cry." In

contrast, Granny Vaughn, although her birthday occasions the gathering and she sits in the midst of the grandchildren she has reared, is a peripheral figure. She naps, confuses past and present, and straightens out or entangles facts according to the whim of her memory. She is teased and loved by the family, but unlike Miss Julia, she makes very little happen. Because Miss Julia without being a tragic figure comes close to revealing the depth at which human beings can suffer, we are reminded that in the comic perspective of Miss Welty's fiction the emotions are wonder, willfulness, spite, not pity, anguish, despair. The ambiguous title of this novel reminds us that *losing* describes both the essence of the nature of battles and the process by which man lives, for battles may be life-giving. The rain following Granny Vaughn's birthday, for example, falls in images of fire and conflicts: lightning like kindled wood, Miss Beulah up as if alerted by a fire alarm, the tin roof making battle noises. Miss Welty does not consider defeat tragic, and while her reader may miss the doom note of irrevocable act and fatality, he must respect and—it is to be hoped—rejoice in her commitment to seeing life as it is lived. Miss Welty's people will see fecund godmen like Billy Floyd and King MacLain, but they will see no burning bushes. The women like Virgie Rainey and Gloria will be touched with the knowledge of love and left frustrated and dreaming the rest of their lives by the incompleteness of their knowing. The men like the MacLains, George Fairchild, and Jack Renfro will be touched by the possibility of heroism but will adventure no farther than their stores and banks, barns and front yards. No farther than most human lives go. Miss Welty keeps us company—both tender and robustious—as we edge along avoiding doom.

Notes

1. "How I Write," *Virginia Quarterly Review*, XXXI (1955), 241.
2. "Place in Fiction," *South Atlantic Quarterly*, LV (1956), 59.

Conflict and Resolution in Welty's *Losing Battles*
William E. McMillen°

The conclusion of Eudora Welty's *Losing Battles* (1970) is far from ambiguous. Jack Renfro and his young wife Gloria are reunited

° From *Critique* 15, no. 1 (1973):110–24. Reprinted with permission of the Helen Dwight Reid Educational Foundation. Published by Heldref Publications, Washington, D.C. Copyright 1973.

after a year-long separation. They settle their debts both old and new and decide on a new life. A scene in a cemetery closes the novel, symbolizing the dead past and the dead people who are no longer able to exert their paralyzing influence on the couple. However, not only have the shadows fallen away from around Jack and Gloria, the shadows have also fallen away from between the couple. The two day reunion—the celebration of a birthday which ends in the celebration of a death, events significantly difficult to distinguish—has seen many partings of curtains.[1] No parting is so important as the delicate opening through which Jack and Gloria meet and step into a new and hopeful life.

Before discussing *Losing Battles* and the concept of the parting of the curtain as it is used twice—in the conflict between the life styles of Granny Vaughn and the schoolteacher Julia Mortimer and in the struggle of Gloria to exist on her own terms with her husband—one should describe Welty's approach to writing and delineate two of her most important motifs. In her review of *Losing Battles* Joyce Carol Oates notes: "Everything is brought back to its most humble origins; there is a wonderful gravitation backward, downward, inward, to the deepest and most simple and most soothing area of the imagination."[2] The novel is quiet, too quiet for some reviewers: one saw Welty's vision so benign that she "removed from the battle of her title any real sense that people get hurt."[3] Another entitled his review "Too Slow and Not Terrific Enough."[4]

Surely neither the fury and passion of Faulkner nor the apocalyptic vision of O'Connor is found in Welty's writing, since she wishes "but to part a curtain." To achieve that goal, she uses subtle movements which do not always leave the reader with a definite conclusion. Jack and Gloria Renfro are still in Banner and only the suggestion has been made that they will leave someday. The important concept is that the door has been opened both physically and psychologically. The proper terms for the physical and psychological as applied to her fiction are the concept of place for the physical and the conflict between those characters who stay and those who are forced to wander from the place for the psychological. In a sense, place is always subordinate to character since it is the backdrop against which the human drama must be played. Yet place is not simply a scene. All of Welty's best fiction is deeply rooted in Mississippi, its delta, backwoods, and small towns. As she has stated, "It seems plain that the art that speaks most clearly, explicitly, directly, and passionately from its place of origin will remain the longest understood."[5] The whole of *Losing Battles* grows directly out of the small patch of northeast Mississippi called Banner. The very opening of the novel telescopes from the moon to the clouds to the ridge and finally to the house, as if this little backwoods dwelling is the center of the universe—and it is for the characters who populate Banner.

Against the background of place, a small universe, some of Welty's characters play roles in which they systematically perform their designated functions in life. Others constantly struggle to exceed their roles, to obtain a destiny greater than the one laid out for them by society, and have been identified as "wanderers who are expressive in action, wild, rebellious, free, over-flowing, self-determining."[6] In Welty's more complex writing, the main characters almost always make some movement away from a potentially stifling center, yet the external "escape" is obviously not all that happens. What is more important is a central character's coming to grips with his own being. The character must reach a psychological understanding and peace; he becomes whole because he admits to a private reconciliation which includes other characters, the dead past, the concept of place, and, finally, an unknown but generally optimistic future.

Such reconciliation certainly allows the curtain to part and the shadows to fall away. Welty's stories and novels end just as her characters step through the parted curtain. They are never shown arriving at a destination for where they are going is not important. What is essential is that the characters arrive at a state of mind in which they can depart. The ending of *Losing Battles* is not ambiguous because it clearly shows that Jack and Gloria are beginning their wanderings. More difficult to interpret are the forces which brought about their decision and their psychological reactions to these forces.

The word *battle* provides a controlling metaphor for the entire novel. On the surface, the setting of Banner seems to be almost an idyllic retreat. It is gentle and quiet and has seemingly escaped the awful effects of the 1930's Depression. Banner does not appear to be a battleground. Even the one obvious physical battle which is recounted—Jack and Curly's fight which ends with Jack at the prison farm in Parchman—is told by the members of the reunion so that it becomes more humorous than serious. The real battles, fought beyond the surface reality of flying fists, are primarily the battles of wills and the battles of life styles.

Miss Julia Mortimer, the Banner schoolteacher who dies on the day of the reunion, has been the chief combatant in these battles. Her last letter-will which one of her most prominent pupils, Judge Moody, reads at the reunion admits defeat after a life-time of struggling:

> All my life I've fought a hard war with ignorance. Except in those cases that you can count off on your fingers, I lost every battle. Year in, year out, my children at Banner School took up the cause of the other side and held the fort against me.[7]

The children at Banner School for two generations have been, to a great extent, the very family now gathered for Granny Vaughn's birthday, and their attitudes are most accurately personified by the matriarchal head of the family, Granny Vaughn.

Julia Mortimer and Granny Vaughn are inexorably connected in *Losing Battles*. They are, in a sense, mirror images of one another, both strong-bodied and strong-willed women who have struggled all their lives against what at times have been overwhelming odds in order to maintain their own views of the world. Granny's world is fruitful and prolific, and she has been able to create an entire, loyal, and loving family. Her world is the physical: the children, the earth, the new tin roof, and the reunion feast. Her world is also incestuous, to the point that everyone is continually drawn back into the family circle. An irrational confidence is displayed that Jack will return to the reunion from the prison farm only because it is Granny's birthday and he should be present. Members of the family who stay away too long either die (Sam Dale Beecham in World War I) or are thought to be dead (when Uncle Nathan shows up after a long absence from Banner, Granny remarks "defensively," "What are you doing here. . . . Thought they told me you was dead").

Julia's schoolteaching world, in contrast, is one of enlightenment. She has led a noble crusade throughout her life to educate the children and show them much more of the world than they could see in Banner. She has produced a few doctors, judges, and politicians who have escaped into the world and have led productive lives. Her world has been that of the intellectual, surrounded by piles and piles of books, started as a one shelf library underneath the window on her first day of teaching. Julia's world has also been barren, spotted by lost chances at love, and tragically ended without finding a successor to carry on her teaching.

The battle between Julia and Granny throughout the years has been an attempt to hold one's own view of life without effort to integrate or really understand another's viewpoint. Uncle Percy as he tells the story of how Jack ended up in Parchman begins: "Well, crops was laid by one more year. Time for the children to all be swallowed up in school" (22). The emphasis is on the physical; the crops are in, and the children do not just go to school but are literally "swallowed up." The school is a monster because it is one more threat to the family unity. Granny and the family must fight a falling away, such as happened to Uncle Curtis whose nine sons have scattered. He now laments, "All nine! And they're never coming home" (67). Jack's return home for the reunion is crucial to the family as proof that the family still has a holding power.

Miss Julia is not discussed or even acknowledged by the family until after Jack has returned. His return takes doubt away, and the family feels justified in beginning its attack on the schoolteacher, prompted by her death and the inquisitiveness of the newest member of the family, Uncle Nathan's new wife, Aunt Cleo. The reunion scene is perhaps the most crucial thematic scene in the novel (227–271) and has two significant functions. First, we have the direct and mostly bitter retelling of the various family members' experiences with Julia. Second, we have the surfacing of the conflict between Gloria and the family, culminating in the "rape," to which we will return, and from which Jack is significantly absent since he is taking supper to Aycock stuck up in Judge Moody's car on the crest of Banner Top. Jack, throughout the novel, is an innocent who is either saved from exposure to evil or refuses to acknowledge it. Even at the end when he comes to some sort of understanding and agreement with Gloria, he has not gone through the emotional struggle his wife has.

The family makes the usual recounting of Julia Mortimer's switch and school attendance, Uncle Percy claiming that "She put an end to good fishing" (235). The true hatred for Julia is not displayed by the ordinary complaints. Instead we come to understand a gradual realization by the family that Miss Julia was after something more than a spelling bee champion. "She had designs on everybody," Uncle Percy claims. "She wanted a doctor and a lawyer and all else we might have to holler for some day, to come right out of Banner" (235). Uncle Noah Webster echoes the sentiment: "She thought if she mortified you long enough, you might have hope of turning out something you wasn't" (236). Miss Beulah replies that Julia wanted to take the credit when it really belonged to the mothers. If Julia had stuck to the surface expression of ambition, she would perhaps not have developed quite the hatred that the reunion members expressed. However, we discover she forced the issue one step farther which proved to be the breaking point: " 'She told us a time or two what her aim was! She wanted us to quit worshipping ourselves quite so wholehearted!' cried Miss Beulah, and set her hands on her hips. . . . 'Maybe just about then is when we quit worshipping her,' Uncle Curtis said" (236). The schoolteacher had struck on the final truth, the real core of the family. They worship their family, the ground they control and walk on, and their loyalty to one another. But Julia realized that self-love meant the children could progress neither materially nor intellectually.

An overriding concern in Julia's struggle was not simply to have her students escape Banner. She placed a map of the world on the schoolroom wall for the purpose of showing what else existed in the world. Yet she stated repeatedly that she wanted to put Banner on that map. Escape was not enough in itself. Her chief spokesman throughout the novel, Judge Moody, sums up her failure: "She's made her a Superior Court judge, the best eye, ear, nose, and throat specialist in Kansas City, and a history professor somewhere—they're all scattered wide, of course. She could get them started, lick 'em into shape, but she couldn't get 'em to stay" (305). No one would return to Banner. Even her very last carefully planned campaign to perpetuate her school fails when Gloria gives up teaching to marry. The final blow to the schoolteacher comes when she discovers Gloria's husband is a member of the family which has resisted her the most over the years.

Judge Moody is one of Julia's early successes when she first taught in Ludlow. He arrives at the Vaughn reunion by chance after a freak accident on Banner Top leaves his car tottering on the brink of the highest spot in the county. At the reunion he functions as the schoolteacher's spokesman and defender. He is more, however, than just a lawyer defending his client against the rabble. Indeed, he is suffering from a deficiency, ultimately very similar to Miss Julia's, for he has embraced the intellectual at the expense of the physical.

Judge Moody's lack of physical control is best seen in direct contact with the Vaughn family. At the beginning, he is merely attempting to drive through Banner to answer an urgent letter from Julia. But he loses his way in a maze of backroads and his driving is actually manipulated for sport by some members of the family. After the accident he is helpless and can only suggest calling an "outside" mechanic. The suggestion is heartily mocked by Jack and the family. Finally, he and his wife end up unwelcomed guests at the reunion, eating the family's food.

As Julia's story unfolds, the Judge plays an important part filling in some of her early background, such as the fact that from the very beginning she was ambitious for her students. Also, he admits to a certain affection for her, although he is quick to generalize his comment: "Why, every young blade in Ludlow was wild about Miss Julia Mortimer at one time" (304). Significantly, both Julia and the Judge end childless.

Judge Moody's most important function is to read Julia's letter-will, a bitter final document from an old woman who has spent her last days tied to her bed, denied her books, and denied her writing paper by an old maid member of the family, Miss Lexie Renfro. Julia demands to be buried under the front step of the school and directs all the "fools" to attend her funeral. But then she must admit to her defeat on the battlefield and decides that she has spent her life, and will spend heaven, in ignorance. Her final warning to the Judge is to watch out for innocence: "There's been one thing I never did take into account. Most likely, neither did you. Watch out for innocence. Could *you* be tempted by it, Oscar—to your own mortification—and conspire with the ignorant and the lawless and the foolish and even the wicked, to hold your tongue?" (300). Julia in her final self-admitted near madness hopes to gain back her one greatest loss. She ends the letter by urgently asking the Judge to visit her to hear a story that "leads to a child," another angle on a developing theme throughout the novel: Gloria's place in the family.

In the course of the family reunion, the family becomes convinced that the orphan Gloria is actually the daughter of Sam Dale and a young girl who once lived with the Vaughns, named Rachel Sojourner. Granny supposedly "proves" the parentage by a war-time postcard hidden in the family Bible. Contrary evidence from Miss Beulah that Sam Dale was made sterile by a childhood accident with fire is ignored by the family. If the story is true, however, Jack and Gloria would be first cousins and their marriage would be "null and void" under the state law. (A law, Judge Moody admits, that Julia may once have helped get passed.) Julia apparently has suspected the relation and wanted to consult with the Judge in hopes of annulling the marriage and regaining Gloria as her teacher. Even though Julia dies, Judge Moody comes to hear all the facts in the case. Yet he finally does not respond the way Julia would have wished: "For a moment he stood silenced. 'It's that baby,' he said. 'I think we'll have to leave it that what's done is done. That there was no prior knowledge between the partners. And no crime' " (325). The first of Miss Julia's proteges has passed judgment on the last, and in that judgment Judge Moody has added a bit of wisdom beyond anything he had ever learned from the schoolteacher. The one-year-old baby, Lady May, is a being which all the learning of the schoolteacher and the Judge were not able to achieve. In Lady May the two contrasting worlds which have for so long held the field of battle are joined.

Lady May Renfro can be seen as a symbol of a new generation, a generation which will develop under neither the half-world of the physical nor the half-world of the intellectual. Julia Mortimer is dead, and Granny Vaughn cannot survive much longer. Lady May will grow up knowing neither. Her battles will be of a different sort, whatever they may be. Perhaps Lady May can be considered as one of Welty's wanderers who is able to depart although her destination is unclear. Little can be said about the baby in the context of the struggles of the novel; she will certainly be influenced by the outcome but has not gone through any struggle herself. Instead, that burden falls on her mother who also becomes a wanderer by the end of the novel. Gloria's dilemma is clearly stated by James Boatwright:

> Gloria doesn't want to be read, to add her voice to this babel of voices, and this conflict is at the core of the novel and at the center of Miss Welty's vision. We are all doubles at war in our own minds and hearts, and we are inescapably losers in these battles. Being fully human is being participant and observer, torn between our desires for love, safety, blind acceptance, communion, and equally

strong desires for separateness, danger, clear knowledge and individual and primal joy.[8]

Gloria's decision to be a wanderer is made by conscious choice, a decision that is the central character development in *Losing Battles*.

If the primary battle of the novel is between Julia and Granny, then Gloria is the main prize of that battle. Whoever wins Gloria will assure the perpetuation of their chosen life style. Losing her means for Julia losing the school, for Granny and the family losing not only a bright young grandchild but, more importantly, losing Jack, the oldest son of the family. Louise Gossett states that "Gloria, the orphan, is the voice of the present disclaiming the past."[9] Gloria makes a decision not to care for either the school or the family, not to care for the past in any way, but only to care for the present and the future. When the busload of thirty schoolteachers tells Gloria of Julia's death, Gloria refuses to climb in the bus and join them as they head to the funeral. As she breast feeds Lady May, she looks up at the schoolteachers hanging out of the bus windows: " 'Can't you understand?' Gloria asked the busload. 'I've got my hands so full!' . . . 'Oh. Of the living,' said one of the voices, gone flat" (162). The "gone flat" would seem to indicate that the schoolteachers are unimpressed and perhaps even jealous of Gloria's reason for not coming with them. Their attitude is surely the same as Julia's would have been.

Gloria rejects the schoolteachers and Miss Julia's memory because she knows that she must not allow herself to regress in any manner into the past. In every way, the past has been painful for Gloria. She was an orphan. She was raised under the strict hand of Miss Julia, whom she learned to love but painfully turned from to marry Jack. Almost immediately after the wedding, Jack was sent to prison. However, the family's attitude toward the past is to treat it as transformed, mythologized adventure. The long involved introduction to Jack, which occupies almost the first hundred pages of the novel, is not a realistic picture of Jack, but one of a legendary young hero. All sorts of legendary implications are contained in the simple story of Jack's fight with Curly and the loss of Granny's wedding ring. The fight becomes a battle with a brute enemy, Gloria becomes a maiden singing "Sail On," and Jack performs a tremendous feat of strength for a golden treasure. Gloria disdains the family version as much as possible, sitting on a "polished cedar trunk" with her back to the family.

The end of the first section features Jack's joyous return to the family. Almost immediately Jack, Gloria, and Lady May go off by themselves to Banner Top to be alone and to put Judge Moody back in a ditch. On his way home, Jack had unwittingly helped the Judge push his car out of a ditch. Now Jack wants to even affairs.

We soon realize that Jack's attitude toward his family may be undergoing some change and Gloria intends to pursue any means of breaking with the family. Jack notes how the family members have "all growed old, that's the shock!" (97). As he kneels down to thump a melon in the melon field: " 'Don't crack Lady May one,' said Gloria. 'I'm not anxious for her to start on common ordinary food.' . . . 'What're you trying to tell me, Possum?' he asked, turning his head to look at her" (97). The melons have a dual implication here. A great deal of commotion has already been raised over the family's gathering of the melons and laying them out for the reunion. Gloria is obviously indicating to Jack that she believes Lady May is better than the family. She is also still breast feeding the baby, although Lady May is really quite old. Perhaps Gloria's insistence on breast feeding is her continual attempt to keep her baby away from any of the polluting effects of the family. By maintaining an actual physical attachment, the baby will take on her mother's identity and independence instead of becoming one of the nameless cousins running about the farm.

Gloria's struggle for identity and independence is what she has had to maintain ever since Jack went away to Parchman. Physically, this was difficult since she has been living in a very small home with Granny, Beulah and Ralph Renfro, and their children, three girls and the little brother Vaughn. Mentally, however, there was not much closeness. Gloria could, for three reasons, maintain an independent distance before Jack returned: although she was "family," the absence of Jack meant she was really still a visitor of sorts to the household; she was an orphan who came from a mysterious background; and, she was raised by Julia Mortimer and had a definite schoolteacher air about her which the family, bred by Julia, treated with grudging respect.

Jack's return, the reunion's gossiping, and Julia's death take away all three of these supports. The family begins an all-out campaign to incorporate Gloria fully into their structure. One of their main efforts is to identify and mythologize the past and provide Gloria with a mother, Rachel Sojourner, whom the family piously remembers they went out of the way to help, and a father, Sam Dale Beecham, who is actually a family member. When Gloria angrily rejects such efforts, the family continues to taunt her, bringing up Jack's loyalty to the family and her own desertion of Julia.

The culmination of the conflict between Gloria and the family occurs at the end of the novel's long central scene. The family, in the person of the aunts, actually attempt to rape Gloria of any individuality. They surround her as she screams her defense: "I don't want to be a Beecham! . . . Now it's ten times worse! I won't be a Beecham—go back! Please don't squeeze me!" (268). But the aunts attack to "welcome" Gloria officially into the family with a watermelon fight. All Gloria has to say to indicate defeat is "Beecham." She is wrestled to the ground, and watermelon is stuffed down her throat as she yells to the absent Jack for help. But no help comes as the aunts continue their assault: "Come on, sisters, help feed her! Let's cram it down her little red lane! Let's make her say Beecham! We did!" (269). The aunts, all married into the clan and forced to give up their identities, make a final effort to gain control of Gloria. As the fight breaks up, Gloria is still resolute, "I still don't believe I'm a Beecham . . . I'm standing my ground" (270–1). Miss Lexie Renfro, Julia's final tormentor, now becomes Gloria's last attacker. As Gloria stands defiantly in the dust, Lexie pulls out her scissors and begins to remake the wedding dress Gloria is wearing for the reunion. The dress symbolizes Gloria and Jack's meeting and new start after a year's absence, but Lexie starts cutting and tearing at the dress "so we can stand the sight of her" (271).

When Jack returns from Banner Top, Gloria must convince him that they have to break away from the family. In their few brief previous conversations, Jack has never acknowledged that he sees any problems. In fact, he simply does not reply to such direct questions as "When will we move to ourselves?" (111) or such statements as "If it wasn't for all the other people around us, our life would be different this minute" (112). Now in the gathering twilight, Gloria has obviously gone through quite a shock, and Jack tries to soothe her. Gloria will have none of it. She is defiant to everyone including Judge Moody. The emphasis has shifted from her own freedom and independence to freedom and independence for her small family of Jack and Lady May:

> "I've been trying to save him [Jack] since the day I saw him first. Protecting his poor head!"
> "From what?" Miss Beulah demanded, both hands on hips.
> "This mighty family! And you can't make me give up!" Gloria threw back her hair, and a few dried watermelon seeds flew out from it. "We'll live to ourselves one day yet, and do wonders. And raise all our children to be both good and smart—" (320)

That night, after the reunion has broken up, Jack and Gloria (with the Moodys settled in their bed) prepare to go to sleep on the porch. Gloria's pressure and the family's actions finally make Jack confront how he and his wife and baby are going to face the future. He cannot believe that his family has any ill traits such as vengeance, ignorance, jealousy, or fear. Gloria insists the family is an impingement on their complete love: "Jack, the way I love you, I have to hate everybody else" (361). Still, Jack does not respond to the argument until Gloria illustrates by the physical, the act of making love which unites the couple exclusive of all others:

> She put her mouth quickly on his, and then she slid in her hand and seized hold on him right at the root. And so she convinced him that there is only one way of depriving the ones you love—taking your living presence away from theirs; that no one alive has ever deserved such punishment, although maybe the dead do; and that no one alive can ever in honor forgive that wrong, which outshines shame, and is not to be forgiven until it has been righted. (362)

Thus Gloria and Jack establish a new union. Their separation has been righted after a long struggle to come to understand one another. The physical joining symbolizes their understanding and ends the long day of the reunion with positive expectation.

The last section of *Losing Battles*, Part 6, is less than eighty pages yet it must tie up all the loose ends that were left by the day-long family reunion. Judge Moody's car is still on the crest of Banner Top; Julia Mortimer still has to be buried; Gloria and Jack must discover a way to live with and deal with their new-found freedom. In a sense, all three loose ends are dependent on one another, and each leads to the next's resolution.

The comic action throughout the novel has centered on Judge Moody's Buick and its precarious perch. Jack finally figures out a way of rescuing the car although it ends up toppling over the edge (taking Jack and Gloria on a whiplash ride through an old tree), landing on its nose on a ledge, and landing right side up in an old river bed. Then, in order to get the car down to Curly's store where the only phone is located, Jack organizes a brilliant train headed by the Banner schoolbus. The Buick is tied behind the schoolbus and Curly's truck is tied behind the Buick. Little Vaughn rides two mules at the rear to act as the brake. When the wild-riding caravan (which has also picked up school children all the way down the road) arrives in a cloud of dust at Banner, everyone frantically goes his own way, now free of the isolation of Banner Top. Judge Moody gets on the phone; Ella Fay, one of Jack's younger sisters, threatens to marry Curly; the junkman from Foxtown picks up the truck which Curly has sold for votes in the upcoming election; and the Judge and Jack finally get the Buick running. As the confusion (including a fight between Jack and Curly over the truck) is sorted out, "Judge Moody put out his rope-burned hand, Jack put up his bloody one, and they shook" (421).

Gloria and Jack are then left to walk to the cemetery where Julia is going to be buried. Gloria has just told Jack that "through it all I tried to keep my mind on the future" (421). They stand almost beneath a small bridge as the hearse bearing Julia passes above them. As they walk to the cemetery they discuss the reunion and the dead people who are in the graves and the dying people who will be there soon. Jack leads both discussion of the future and the possibility of becoming wanderers. Perhaps the last straw has been for Jack the losing of the truck. But Gloria knew the truck was only a plaything, "It was never going to carry *us* anywhere. We'd always have to be carrying *it*" (425).

When they arrive at the funeral, Jack leads Gloria to the front of the mourners despite low, nasty comments from the crowd concerning Jack's and Gloria's torn and dirty clothes: " 'I don't think they've got any business at a funeral,' said the voice of a very old man or a very old woman" (429). Indeed, Jack and Gloria do not have any business with the dead; they and Lady May represent the epitome of the living. By the novel's end they have joined both the physical world of Granny Vaughn and the intellectual world of Julia Mortimer. At the end Gloria has survived and has brought her husband and daughter with her without being subdued and compromised by the shadows of the past or the physical effects of the present.

In a sense, innocence is over. The struggles, loneliness, and confusion of Gloria's growing up are in the past. Likewise, Jack's battles, youthful exuberance, and youthful playthings are gone:

> "Between 'em all, they've taken away everything you've got, Jack," said Gloria.
> "There's been just about a clean sweep," he agreed.
> "Everybody's done their worst now—everybody and then some," she said. "They can't do any more now."
> He set his lips on hers. "They can't take away what no human can take away. My family," he said. "My wife and girl baby and all of 'em at home. And I've got my strength. I may not have all the time I used to have—but I can provide. Don't you ever fear." (434)

Here Jack kisses Gloria, where before Gloria initiated the effort to show their physical union and their independence from the rest of the family. The mule Bet now appears symbolic of the physical effort Jack and Gloria will need to start a new and independent life:

> "The surest thing I know is I'll never let you out of my sight again. Never," Gloria swore. "I never will let you escape from me, Jack Renfro. Remember it."
> "It's the first I knew I was trying," he said, with his big smile.
> He lifted her and set her up on Bet's waiting back, and took Bet by the bridle and led her. They started for home.
> "And some day," Gloria said, "some day yet, we'll move to ourselves. And there'll be just you and me and Lady May." (435)

As Jack leads Gloria home singing "Bringing in the sheaves" at the top of his lungs, the shadows have fallen away from between them. Jack and Gloria have stepped through the part in the curtain to meet and will soon step through another part into a new country. Away off one day up in Banner County, Eudora Welty has not pointed a finger of judgment but has simply parted some shadowy curtains.

Notes

1. "But away off one day up in Tishomingo County, I knew this, anyway: that my wish, indeed my continuing passion, would be not to point the finger in judgment but to part a curtain, that invisible shadow that falls between people, the veil of indifference to each other's presence, each other's wonder, each other's human plight." Eudora Welty, Introduction, *One Time, One Place.*

2. Joyce Carol Oates, review of *Losing Battles, Atlantic Monthly,* 225 (April 1970), 118.

3. Christopher Ricks, review of *Losing Battles, New York Review of Books,* 15 (July 1970), 10.

4. Christopher Lehmann Haupt, *New York Times,* 10 April 1970, p. 37.

5. Eudora Welty, "Place in Fiction," *South Atlantic Quarterly,* 55 (January 1956), 57–72, quoted in Ruth M. Vande Kieft, *Eudora Welty* (New Haven: Twayne, 1962), p. 20.

6. Vande Kieft, p. 122.

7. Eudora Welty, *Losing Battles* (New York: Random House, 1970), p. 298. Subsequent references in the text are to this edition.

8. James Boatwright, review of *Losing Battles, NYTBR,* 12 April 1970, p. 32.

9. Louise Y. Gossett, "Eudora Welty's New Novel: The Comedy of Loss," *The Southern Literary Journal,* 3, No. 1 (Fall 1970), 133.

Enlightening Darkness: Theme and Structure in Eudora Welty's *Losing Battles*
Larry J. Reynolds°

The most noticeable qualities of Eudora Welty's *Losing Battles* (1970) are its geniality and humor, and, understandably, a number of critics have stressed these in their discussions of the work. For example, Robert J. Griffin has observed that the novel is "an outrageously comic explosion of naturalistic 'history,' all the better for occasional moments of lyric tenderness or elegiac nostalgia."[1] Similarly, James Boatwright has called the book "a joyous, rich, uproarious comic spectacle, teeming with brilliant characters."[2] With less enthusiasm, Joyce Carol Oates has also focused on the book's enter-

° Reprinted with permission from *Journal of Narrative Technique* 8 (Spring 1978):133–40.

taining qualities, writing that "it does not seem to me as successful a novel as *Delta Wedding*, nor is it as warmly comic and appealing as *The Ponder Heart*. Its serious and psychological concerns are muted, and so it must depend a great deal upon interludes of comedy and charm (there is, perhaps, too much made of the innocent prettiness of starched dresses and the ubiquitous baby, Lady May Renfro, and the casual give-and-take of family life)."[3] In contrast, John W. Aldridge has observed that while the serious concerns of the novel are "muted," they provide a depth and significance to the work.[4] Indeed, as I hope to point out, the true strengths of *Losing Battles* lie beneath its entertaining surface where the story of an intense struggle for survival is subtly and carefully told.

The nature of this struggle is defined most explicitly by Julia Mortimer, the local school teacher, who speaks from beyond the grave in the letter read by Judge Moody late in the novel. Here Julia declares:

> All my life I've fought a hard war with ignorance. Except in those cases that you can count off on your fingers, I lost every battle. . . . Oscar, it's only now, when I've come to lie flat on my back, that I've had it driven in on me—the reason I never could win for good is that both sides were using the same tactics. . . . A teacher teaches and a pupil learns or fights against learning with the same force behind him. It's the survival instinct. It's a mighty power, it's an iron weapon while it lasts. It's the desperation of staying alive against all odds that keeps both sides encouraged. But the side that gets licked gets to the truth first.[5]

These words, I think, provide the key insight for understanding the meaning and shape of the novel. What Julia realized before she died, and what a sensitive reader discovers as he reads, is that the Renfros and Beechams are a desperate people fighting a determined battle for survival and their ignorance is essential to that survival. Their struggle is not just with a dry and eroded land, but also with the unbearable truth about themselves, that is, that they are poor, inept, insignificant, isolated, and on the verge of extinction. They nurture and defend their ignorance because to recognize the truth would bring unbearable loneliness and despair.

Miss Welty carefully selects a situation allowing her to focus on this battle against truth and self-knowledge at its most intense moment. The family reunion being held on Granny Vaughn's birthday allows the family to rely upon the rituals of storytelling, eating, singing, gossiping, and gift-giving to create and sustain their illusion of importance and well-being. On the other hand, the time is the depression thirties. The crops in Banner have failed due to drought. Starvation threatens. Julia Mortimer, the family's teacher and foe, has died on the morning of the reunion, and consequently unwelcome outsiders invade the reunion's midst—all of which bring the truth perilously close at hand.

Miss Welty develops this basic situation by gradually revealing to the reader the nature of the family's struggle, and by conveying the emotions that accompany the temporary success or failure of their efforts. In the first three parts of the novel, as the reunion progresses the family slowly succeeds in creating an illusion of importance and well-being, and feelings of joy and hope are conveyed with increasing intensity; however, in parts four and five, the truth about themselves and their situation is gradually forced upon them and loneliness and despair slowly come to the fore. This five-part development occurs during the day of the reunion with shifts in the time of day corresponding to changes in the emotional texture of the narrative. In the sixth and last part of the novel, a new battle begins and progresses from morning to noon of the next day. Here the previous emotional cycle is half-repeated and the novel thus ends on a hopeful and joyous note that, in turn, is transitory.

Although the above summaries may suggest that the meaning and structure of *Losing Battles* are obvious, critical commentary on the novel indicates that they are elusive. Miss Welty's thematic and structural methods are subtle; she never explicitly reveals what a character thinks or feels nor does she comment directly on the significance of her narrative. Instead, she relies almost solely upon dialogue, dramatic event, and a limited amount of imagery to shape and inform her work. For example, her subtle use of imagery can be seen in the opening poetic description of the Renfro farm during the transitional moments of daybreak. Here Miss Welty writes that

> as if something came sliding out of the sky, the whole tin roof of the house ran with new blue. The posts along the porch softly bloomed downward, as if chalk marks were being drawn, one more time, down a still misty slate. The house was revealed as if standing there from pure memory against a now moonless sky. For the length of a breath, everything stayed shadowless. (10)

This hushed and delicate scene serves as an effective contrasting prelude to the noisy activity that follows, but, more important, it introduces the main controlling images of light and darkness. Throughout the novel, these images fulfill their conventional emotional roles, that is, light or brightness accompanies positive human emotions such as love, joy, and hope, while darkness or shadows accompany negative emotions such as loneliness and sorrow; however, Miss Welty also surprisingly and unconventionally links darkness with reality and truth in this work, and light with illusion and ignorance. In other words, as the day progresses, an enlightening darkness gradually overtakes the reunion. Significantly, the shadowless moment occurring at the beginning of the novel corresponds to a second such moment at the formal mid-point, when the sun and spirit of the reunion are at their height, and to a third at the very end, which is again tentatively joyous and hopeful. In essence then, this apparently sprawling comedy has a skillfully shaped form within which the serious conflict between illusion and reality is explored. A closer look at the individual parts of the novel will, I think, show this.

After the opening description of part one, Miss Welty steps into the background with her own voice, and the Beechams and Renfros rush in to dramatically establish their own apparent situation and mood. Hugs, kisses, greetings, laughter, scampering dogs and children all contribute to the illusion of well-being and to a developing joyful mood, a shadowless mood, if you will. Although Beulah at one point reveals that the new roof has exhausted the family's funds, part one of the novel conveys the impression that all is well and will continue so because Jack Jordan Renfro, the family hero and savior, is on his way home from the penitentiary. Even Gloria, Jack's wife, who considers herself an outsider, does not disturb the lightheartedness of the others; she sits apart on the swing accompanied by the yellow butterflies of August, which according to Miss Welty, are "as wild and bright as people's notions and dreams" (44). Although a ripple of sadness occurs when Jack arrives and learns of the sale of his truck and horse, his reunion with Gloria and their child sustains and augments the hopeful mood, and part one ends with joyful anticipation as he leaves to do battle for the family honor by running Judge Moody into a ditch.

Part two of the novel ostensibly provides a riotous comic interlude and introduces the main element of suspense. Judge Moody's car becomes suspended on the edge of a cliff to remain there until the near-end of the novel; however, in the process some serious truths about the family and their situation are revealed. For example, on the way to Banner Top, Jack and Gloria march through the drought-stricken corn and cotton, and when Jack thumps a melon, Gloria tells him not to crack one for the baby because she does not want her to start on ordinary food. In reply, Jack asks, "What're you trying to tell me, Possum?" (98), and the unspoken answer is that Gloria is protecting the baby from starvation. Yet while Jack perceives this, he feigns ignorance; being a loyal member of the family he refuses to acknowledge their plight.

On Banner Top the antics by Jack, the Moodys, Aycock, Curly Stovall and others are, of course, quite comic; nevertheless, Jack's unsuccessful attempt to run Judge Moody into the ditch reveals that this young family hero is no savior, but instead an inept and rather simple-minded boy. The family, we suspect, knows this, for although they brag about Jack and made a grand offer in part one to help him in his heroics, they do not come to Banner Top even after he sends word that he needs their help. The most assistance he gets occurs when Uncle Homer roars out the drive past them and throws out a piece of chain "a little shorter than the length of Jack's arm" (132).

Although thus faced with undeniable evidence of the family's disregard, Jack maintains his confident air. He clings to the illusion of the strength and importance of the family just as they cling to their illusion concerning him. Whenever the truth is evident, it is ignored. "We've still got the whole reunion solid behind us," (169) he tells Gloria as they head back, yet his words are undercut by previous events and by the description of a flock of birds, having "feathers of that blue seen only in the loneliest of places," which flit across the path that leads home.

By the end of part two then, the tone of the novel has changed slightly, and in the first sentence of part three, we are told that "the shade had circled around to the front yard" (171). This shade serves as a subtle indication that the truth, along with sorrow and loneliness, is forcing its way into the midst of the reunion even as the illusion of well-being is reaching its height. Part three of the novel focuses on the family rituals, and as the Beechams and Renfros eat fried chicken, award prizes to the youngest, the oldest and the fattest, put Judge Moody through the ceremony of forgiveness, retell the family history, and give Granny her birthday presents, one recalls similar rituals described by Miss Welty in *Delta Wedding*. Granny Vaughn's family has little in common with the wealthy and secure Fairchilds, however, and the rituals here are more than mere entertainment; they are also one of the few means the family has to battle against the unbearable truth about themselves and their situation. Throughout part three, their battle is successful and during the uncomfortable moment when Brother Bethune teases them about going on relief, his words are countered by the men's laughter and by Beulah's cries of "Ready for your next plateful? Here's the sausage I saved you from last year's hog! Here's some more home-cured ham, make room for more chicken. Elvie! Buttermilk! This time bring him the whole pitcher!" (188). One critic of the novel, having noted the extreme poverty of Granny Vaughn's family, has said that "one feels strangly enough that these fundamental economic problems really are not important,"[6] yet if one reads carefully, I think he will see their importance and sense the hidden fears and doubts behind the laughter and offers of food.

At the end of part three (the formal mid-point of the novel), the spirit of the reunion reaches its height as Granny receives her presents and the family joins in the singing of "Gathering Home." Miss Welty

subtly suggests the transitory nature of the illusory world the family
has created, however, by relating that

> as they sang, the tree over them . . . with its ever-spinning leaves
> all light-points at this hour, looked bright as a river, and the tables
> might have been a little train of barges it was carrying with it,
> moving slowly downstream. . . . nothing at all was unmovable, or
> empowered to hold the scene still fixed or stake the reunion there.
> (218)

In the next and fourth part of the novel, a series of events occur
that indeed change the nature and mood of the reunion by forcing
unpleasant truths upon the family, truths that eventually overwhelm
them. First Willy Trimble arrives, tells of the funeral activities at
Julia Mortimer's, and declares that the reunion is not the most
important event in the community that day. The family successfully
recovers from Willy's words by collectively recalling their past relations with Julia and making her a subject for scorn, but they soon
face a second challenge when Gloria refuses to accept Granny's
declaration that she is not an orphan but a blood relative. The aunts
respond to Gloria's refusal with the watermelon initiation rite, and
despite their laughter, there is an inherent cruelty in their actions
as Miss Welty's description reveals. She writes that they "rolled her
by the shoulders, pinned her flat, then buried her face under the
flesh of the melon with its blood heat, its smell of evening flowers.
Ribbons of juice crawled on her neck and circled it, as hands robbed
of sex spread her jaws open. 'Can't you say Beecham? What's wrong
with being Beecham?' " (259).

After this revealing playful but inherently violent display of
insecurity, the mood of the reunion continues to darken as Lexie
tells her story of Julia Mortimer's last days. When she relates how
she fought with Julia, tied her in bed, prevented her from writing
letters, intercepted her mail, and told her to die, she remains the
one member of the family not shamed by her story. When she finishes
talking, "the sun is setting" and Granny's and Beulah's faces have
become grief-stricken. Although Uncle Noah and Beulah try to rescue
the mood of the reunion with song, this provides only momentary
relief, for Judge Moody reads Julia's letter, bitterly tells his own
story, and then damns the family by saying: "I could almost believe
I'd been *maneuvered* here. . . . To the root of it all, like the roots
of a bad tooth. The very pocket of ignorance" (293). The family
pretends not to understand Julia's letter and Judge Moody's words,
of course, yet they are obviously affected and the emotional texture
of the reunion has changed since mid-day. Granny's temporary loss
of her mental faculties reflects the anxiety and helplessness of them
all. The family here no longer has the upper hand, for their defenses

of memory, laughter, singing, and all the rest are shown to be giving way; their illusory world is being destroyed and reality is taking its place.

Significantly, part five of the novel opens with Aunt Birdie saying, "Nightfall! When did that happen!" (299). Other images of light and darkness convey the sense of isolation and despair against which they have all been fighting. In a key passage, Miss Welty writes:

> Suddenly the moonlit world was doused; lights hard as pickaxe blows drove down from every ceiling and the roof of the passage, cutting the house and all in it away, leaving them an island now on black earth, afloat in night, and nowhere, with only each other. In that first moment every face, white-lit but with its caves of mouth and eyes opened wide, black with the lonesomeness and hilarity of survival, showed its kinship to Uncle Nathan's. . . . (300)

Part five, which opens with this passage, constitutes the conclusion of the reunion's battle with the truth, and after more painful revelations, the novel progresses further into both literal and figurative darkness. The electric lights go out and Uncle Nathan makes the climactic confession that many years in the past he killed a man and "let 'em hang a sawmill nigger for it" (330).

Although the reunion comes to a close with a few more rituals and then hearty farewells, Miss Welty has made it clear that the battle has been lost. When Beulah and Ralph go to bed for the night, Beulah's voice, coming from the bedroom window, says, "I've got it to stand and I've got to stand it. And you've got to stand it. After they've all gone home, Ralph, and the children's in bed, that's what's left. Standing it" (346). Her words refer specifically to Jack's being sent to prison, but they obviously relate to the truth of their situation in general. Vaughn Renfro's painful and nightmarish vision as he encounters Granny in bed further discloses a reality neither light-hearted, comic, nor charming. We see that when the family stops bragging, singing, and pretending, all that remains is frightening isolation and despair. Granny is ready to ask someone to share her bed, not knowing nor caring who it is, because she does know that that person represents relief from the loneliness she feels.

As part five of the novel comes to a close, the last source of light, the moon, disappears behind a cloud, thus complementing the fact that the truth about Granny Vaughn's family has been completely revealed. Significantly, however, in the darkness it begins to rain, and this life-giving event suggests that a new cycle is about to begin. And indeed, the sixth and final part both resolves the complications on Banner Top and shows that the battle fought on the previous day was not the final one. The new day of part six begins as the novel began, with a sense of activity and anticipation. The events on Banner

Top are again comic, yet within the comedy appears a subtle clue that soon the family may have to face a permanent defeat rather than a temporary one. The very old cedar tree on the Top goes over the cliff, misses the ledge below, and continues falling to the bottom of the valley, and, as this tree hangs by its roots before falling, we are told "Nothing but memory seemed to have propped the tree. Nothing any stronger than memory might be holding it where it was now— some last tag end of root, that was all" (361). Memory is the strongest bond holding the family together, and thus the fate of the cedar undoubtedly anticipates the fate of Granny Vaughn's clan.

Within the pages of the novel, however, the family still struggles and survives, and at the end, it is shadeless noon and Jack Renfro is singing "Bringing in the Sheaves." One critic has called this "an appropriate coda to a beautiful and valuable novel."[7] And indeed it is. Yet, if the reader has been alert to the underlying themes and structure of the novel, he will recognize that few sheaves will be gathered in Banner for some time and that the mood of hope and joy is part of one more battle to ignore reality and to survive with some sense of dignity. In summary then, *Losing Battles* is a superbly shaped work that subtly explores the serious problems of human existence and survival. The novel ultimately has meaning for us all, of course, for whatever our financial state, we are all engaged in creating our own illusions and avoiding painful truths. As Miss Welty writes at one point, the world is "one huge, soul-defying reunion," and thus *Losing Battles* not only entertains the reader, but also tells him something about himself and his world.

Notes

1. "The Ballad of Banner, Miss.," *The Nation,* 1 June 1970, p. 663.

2. *New York Times Book Review,* 12 April 1970, p. 1.

3. "Eudora's Web," *Atlantic,* 225 (April 1970), 120.

4. "Eudora Welty: Metamorphosis of a Southern Lady Writer," *Saturday Review,* 11 April 1970, pp. 21–23, 33–36.

5. *Losing Battles* (Greenwich, Conn.: Fawcett, 1970), pp. 287–88. Page numbers in the text refer to this edition.

6. Oates, "Eudora's Web," p. 119.

7. Boatwright, *New York Times Book Review,* p. 33.

The Optimist's Daughter

The Onlooker, Smiling:
An Early Reading of
The Optimist's Daughter   Reynolds Price*

On March 15, this year *The New Yorker* published an issue half
filled with a story by Eudora Welty called *The Optimist's Daughter*.
The story is some 30,000 words long, 100 pages of a book—much
the longest work published by Miss Welty in fourteen years, since
her fourth collection of stories, *The Bride of the Innisfallen* in 1955.
In those years, in fact, fewer than twenty pages of new fiction by
her have appeared (two extraordinary pieces rising from the early
civil rights movement, "Where Is the Voice Coming From?" and
"The Demonstrators"). Now there is this novella—and, close behind
it, news of a long comic novel, more stories, a collection of essays.

A *return*, in our eyes at least (Miss Welty could well ask "From
where?"); and some eyes (those that haven't raced off after the genius-
of-the-week) have got a little jittery with time. Returns in the arts
are notorious for danger—almost always stiff-jointed, throaty, short-
winded, rattled by nerves and ghosts of the pressures which caused
the absence. There have been rare and triumphant exceptions—among
performers in recent memory, Flagstad and Horowitz, grander than
ever. But who among creators? American arts are uniquely famous
for silent but audibly breathing remains—novelists, poets, playwrights,
composers. The game of naming them is easy and cruel, and the
diagnoses multiply. Yet why must I think back seventy years to Verdi's
return with *Otello* thirteen years after *Aïda* and the *Requiem* for an
ample precedent to Miss Welty's present achievement?

I have known the new story for less than a month and am straining
backward to avoid the sort of instant apotheosis which afflicts the
national book-press; but I don't feel suspended over any fool's pre-
cipice in saying this much—*The Optimist's Daughter* is Eudora Welty's strongest, richest work. For me, that is tantamount to saying that

* From *Shenandoah* 20 (Spring 1969):58–73. Copyright 1969 by Washington and Lee
University. Reprinted with permission of the editor. An updated version of this review
appears in Price's *Things Themselves: Essays and Scenes* (N.Y.: Atheneum, 1972),
114–38.

no one alive in America now has yet shown stronger, richer, more useful fiction. All through my three readings, I've thought of Turgenev, Tolstoy, Chekhov—*First Love, The Cossacks, The Steppe*—and not as masters or originals but as peers for breadth and depth.

—And an effortless power of *summary,* unity (of vision and means). For that is what I have felt most strongly in the story—that Miss Welty has now forged into one instrument strands (themes, stances, voices, genres) all present and mastered in various pieces of earlier work (many of them, invented there) but previously separate and rather rigidly compartmented. I'm thinking especially of "comedy" and "tragedy." In her early work—till 1955—she tended to separate them as firmly as a Greek dramatist. There is some tentative mingling in the larger works, *Delta Wedding* and the linked stories of *The Golden Apples;* but by far the greater number of the early stories divide cleanly—into rural comedy or farce, pathos or tragic lament, romance or lyric celebration, lethal satire. This is not to say that those stories over-select to the point of falsification (fear and hate lurk in much of the laughter, laughter in the pain); but that the selection of components-for-the-story which her eye quickly or slowly made and the subsequent intensity of scrutiny of those components (place, character, gesture, speech) exhibited a temporary single-mindedness as classical as Horace's, Vermeer's.

But now in *The Optimist's Daughter* all changes. If the early work is classic, this might be medieval—in its fullness of vision, depth of field, range of ear. Jesus *and* goblins, Macbeth *and* the porter. There is no sense however of straining for wholeness, of a will to "ripeness," no visible girding for a major attempt. The richness and new unity of the story—its quality of summary—is the natural image produced by *this action* as it passes before Miss Welty's (literal) vision—look at a room from the perfect point, you can see it all. She has found the point, the place to stand to see this story—and we discover at the end that she's seen far more than that. Or perhaps the point drew her—helpless, willing—towards it, her natural pole?

For it is in this story that she sustains most intensely or has the fullest results extracted from her by the stance and line-of-sight which, since her first story, have been native to her—that of the onlooker (and the onlooker's avatars—the wanderer, the outsider, the traveling salesman, the solitary artist, the bachelor or spinster, the childless bride). Robert Penn Warren in his essay "Love and Separateness in Eudora Welty" defined the stance and theme as it formed her early stories—

> We can observe that the nature of the isolation may be different from case to case, but the fact of isolation, whatever its nature, provides the basic situation of Miss Welty's fiction. The drama which

develops from this basic situation is of either of two kinds: first, the
attempt of the isolated person to escape into the world; or second,
the discovery by the isolated person, or by the reader, of the nature
of the predicament.

And a catalogue of her strongest early work and its characters is a
list of onlookers, from R. J. Bowman in "Death of a Traveling Salesman" (her first story) and Tom Harris in "The Hitch-Hikers" (both
lonely bachelors yearning for the richness which they think they
glimpse in the lives of others—mutual love, willful vulnerability), to
the young girl (a would-be painter) in "A Memory" and Audubon
in "A Still Moment" (the artist who must hole-up from life, even kill
it, to begin his effort at description and comprehension), to the
frightening and hilarious spinsters of "Why I Live at the P.O." and
The Ponder Heart or the more silent but equally excluded Virgie
Rainey of *The Golden Apples,* to the recently orphaned Laura who
visits her Fairchild cousins in *Delta Wedding* as they plunge and
surface gladly in their bath of proximity, dependence, love.

You might say—thousands have—that the onlooker (as outsider)
is the central character of modern fiction, certainly of Southern fiction
for all its obsession with family, and that Miss Welty's early stories
then are hardly news, her theme and vision hardly unique, hardly
"necessary," just lovely over-stock. Dead-wrong, you'd be.

In the first place, her early onlookers are almost never freaks as
they have so famously been in much Southern (and now Jewish)
fiction and drama. (Flannery O'Connor, when questioned on the
prevalence of freaks in Southern fiction, is reported to have said,
"It's because Southerners know a freak when they see one.") They
have mostly been "mainstream" men and women—in appearance,
speech and action at least. Their visions and experiences have been
far more nearly diurnal—experiences comprehensible at least to most
men—than those of the characters of her two strong contemporaries,
Carson McCullers and Flannery O'Connor, whose outsiders (often
physical and psychic freaks) seem wrung, wrenched, from life by a
famished special vision.

In the second place, the conclusions of Miss Welty's early onlookers, their deductions from looking—however individual and shaped
by character, however muted in summary and statement—are unique.
Their cry (with few exceptions, her salesman the most eloquent) is
not the all but universal "O, lost! Make me a *member*" but something
like this—"I am here alone, they are there together; I see them
clearly. I do not know why and I am not happy but I *do* see, and
clearly. I may even understand—why I'm here, they there. Do I
need or want to join them?" Such a response—and it is, in Miss
Welty, always a response to vision, literal eye-sight; she has the

keenest eyesight in American letters—is as strange as it is unique. Are we—onlookers to the onlookers—moved to sympathy, acceptance, consolation? Are we chilled or appalled and, if so, do we retreat into the common position?—"These people and their views are maimed, self-serving, alone because they deserve to be. Why don't they have the grace to writhe?" For our peace of mind (the satisfied reader's), there is disturbingly little writhing, only an occasional moment of solemn panic—

> "She's goin' to have a baby," said Sonny, popping a bite into his mouth.
> Bowman could not speak. He was shocked with knowing what was really in this house. A marriage, a fruitful marriage. That simple thing. Anyone could have had that.
> Somehow he felt unable to be indignant or protest, although some sort of joke had certainly been played upon him. There was nothing remote or mysterious here—only something private. The only secret was the ancient communication between two people. But the memory of the woman's waiting silently by the cold hearth, of the man's stubborn journey a mile away to get fire, and how they finally brought out their food and drink and filled the room proudly with all they had to show, was suddenly too clear and too enormous within him for response. . . .

Or a thrust through the screen, like Lorenzo Dow's in "A Still Moment"—

> He could understand God's giving Separateness first and then giving Love to follow and heal in its wonder; but God had reversed this, and given Love first and then Separateness, as though it did not matter to Him which came first. Perhaps it was that God never counted the moments of Time . . . did He even know of it? How to explain Time and Separateness back to God, Who had never thought of them, Who could let the whole world come to grief in a scattering moment?

But such moments are always followed by calm—Bowman's muffled death or Dow's ride onward, beneath the new moon.

Yet in those early stories the last note is almost invariably rising, a question; the final look in the onlooker's eyes is of puzzlement— "Anyone could have had that. Should I have tried?" Not in *The Optimist's Daughter* however. The end clarifies. Mystery dissolves before patient watching—the unbroken stare of Laurel McKelva Hand, the woman at its center. The story is told in third person, but it is essentially seen and told by Laurel herself. At the end, we have not watched a scene or heard a word more than Laurel; there is not even a comment on Laurel which she, in her native modesty, could not have made aloud. That kind of secret first-person technique is

at least as old as Julius Caesar and has had heavy work in modern
fiction, where it has so often pretended to serve Caesar's own apparent
aim (judicial modesty, "distancing") while in fact becoming chiefly
a bullet-proof shield for tender egos, an excuse for not confronting
personal failure (Joyce's *Portrait* is the grand example), a technical
act of mercy. But Laurel Hand is finally merciless—to her dead
parents, friends, enemies, herself; worst, to us.

This is what I understand to be the story—the action and Laurel's
vision of the action.

Laurel Hand has come on sudden notice (and intuition of crisis)
from Chicago, where she works as a fabric designer, to a New Orleans
clinic where her father Judge McKelva, age 71, is being examined
for eye trouble. (The central metaphor begins at once—vision, the
forms of blindness; the story is as troubled by eyes as *King Lear;*
and our first exposure to Laurel's sensibility suggests youth and
quivering attentiveness.) In a clinic she has time to notice this—

> . . . Dr. Courtland folded his big country hands with the fingers
> that had always looked, to Laurel, as if their simple touch on the
> crystal of a watch would convey through their skin exactly what
> time it was.

Laurel's father is accompanied by his new wife Fay; and at the
diagnosis of detached retina, Fay's colors unfurl—hard, vulgar, self-
absorbed, envious of Laurel and, in Laurel's eyes, beneath the McKelvas
and Laurel's dead mother. The doctor advises immediate surgery,
over Fay's protests that nothing is wrong. The judge declares himself
"an optimist," agrees to eye-repair; the surgery goes well, and Laurel
and Fay take a room in New Orleans to spell one another at the
Judge's bedside—their important duty, to keep him still, absolutely
motionless with both eyes bandaged through days of recovery. Friction
grows between the two women but with no real discharge. Fay shows
herself a kind of pet, baby-doll—her idea of nursing consisting of
descriptions of her new shoes or earrings, her petulance at missing
Mardi Gras whose time approaches loudly through the city. Laurel
watches quietly, reading Dickens to her father, oppressed by his age
and docility—

> He opened his mouth and swallowed what she offered him with the
> obedience of an old man—obedience! She felt ashamed to let him
> act out the part in front of her.

Three weeks pass, the doctor claims encouragement, but the Judge's
deepening silence and submission begin to unnerve Fay and to baffle
Laurel. (It is only now—nearly fifteen pages in—that we learn Laurel's
age. She is older than Fay and perhaps Fay is forty. We are, I think,
surprised. We had felt her to be younger—I'd have said twenty-four

and only now do I notice that she bears a married name; yet no husband has been mentioned and will not be till just before the midpoint of the story. There is no air of caprice or trick about these crucial withholdings, only quiet announcement—"Now's the time for this.") Then on the last night of Carnival, Laurel in her rooming house senses trouble and returns to the hospital by cab through packed, raucous streets. (Inevitably, a great deal of heavy holy weather will be made over Miss Welty's choice of Carnival season for this opening section and the eve of Ash Wednesday for the first climax. So far as I can see, she herself makes almost nothing of it—the revelry is barely mentioned and then only as a ludicrously inappropriate backdrop to death. Even less is made of the city itself, almost no appeal to its famous atmosphere—it is simply the place where a man from the deep South finds the best doctors.) At the hospital, Laurel finds her fore-knowledge confirmed. Fay's patience has collapsed. She shakes the silent Judge, shouts "Enough is enough"; and Laurel enters to watch her father die—

> He made what seemed to her a response at last, yet a mysterious response. His whole pillowless head went dusky, as if he laid it under the surface of dark pouring water and held it there.

While Laurel and Fay await the doctor's confirmation in the hospital lobby, they watch and listen to a Mississippi country family come to oversee their own father's death—the Dalzells, family of the Judge's deranged roommate. (Their sizable appearance is not, as might first seem, a chance for Miss Welty to ease tension and pass necessary clock-time with one of her miraculously observed country groups. Funny and touching as they are—

> "If they don't give your dad no water by next time round, tell you what, we'll go in there all together and pour it down him," promised the old mother. "If he's going to die, I don't want him to die wanting water"—

the Dalzells make a serious contribution towards developing a major concern of the story. They are, for all their coarse jostling proximity, a *family* of finer feeling and natural grace than whatever is constituted here by Fay and Laurel; and they will soon return to mind, in sweet comparison with Fay's Texas kin who swarm for the funeral.) At final news of the Judge's death, Fay lunges again into hateful hysterics; but Laurel tightens—no tears, few words. Only in the ride through revellers toward the hotel does Laurel begin to see, with a new and steelier vision, meanings hung round people, which she does not yet speak—

> Laurel heard a band playing, and another band moving in on top of it. She heard the crowd noise, the unmistakable sound of hundreds, of hundreds of thousands, of people *blundering*.

Part II opens with the train ride home to Mount Salus, Mississippi. (Laurel's view from the train of a single swamp beechtree still keeping dead leaves begins to prepare us for her coming strangeness, her as yet unexpected accessibility to ghosts.) Mount Salus is a small lowland town and is now home only to the dead Judge—Fay will inherit Laurel's childhood home but is Texan forever; Laurel will return to Chicago soon. But two groups of her friends survive in the town— her dead parents' contemporaries and her own schoolmates—and they rally to her, ambivalent hurtful allies, as Fay's kin—the Chisoms—arrive for the funeral. Led by Fay's mother, they cram the Judge's house like a troupe of dwarfs from a Goya etching, scraping rawly together in a dense loveless, shamingly vital, hilarious parody of blood-love and loyalty—"Nothing like kin. Yes, me and my brood believes in clustering just as close as we can get." It is they—Fay's mother—who at last extract from Laurel what we have not yet known, that Laurel is a widow—

> "Six weeks after she married him . . . The war. Body never recovered."
> "*You* was *cheated,*" Mrs. Chisom pronounced . . . "So you ain't got father, mother, brother, sister, husband, chick nor child." Mrs. Chisom dropped Laurel's finger to poke her in the side as if to shame her. "Not a soul to call on, that's you."

So the Chisoms stand at once—or pullulate—in Laurel's sight, as a vision of the family and of love itself as horror, hurtful, willfully vulnerable, parasitic. Yet one of them—Wendell, age seven, viewing the corpse—also provides her with a still point for temporary sanity, for "understanding" Fay and her father's love for Fay—

> He was like a young, undriven, unfalsifying, unvindictive Fay. His face was transparent—he was beautiful. So Fay might have appeared to her aging father, with his slipping eyesight.

That emergency perception and the cushioning care of friends prop Laurel through Fay's last hysterical kiss of the corpse and on through the burial.—Propped but stunned, and open on all sides—especially the eyes—for gathering menace to her saving distance. Above the graveyard, she sees a flight of starlings—

> . . . black wings moved and thudded in perfect unison, and a flock of migrant starlings flew up as they might have from a plowed field, still shaped like the grounds of the cemetery, like its map, and wrinkled in the air.

And afterwards, at the house again, she numbly accepts more insults from Fay and waits out the slow departure of the Chisoms—taking Fay with them for a rest in Texas.

Part III is the longest of the four parts, both the story's journey through the underworld and the messenger of what the story learns there. It has four clear divisions. In the first, Laurel entertains four elderly ladies, friends of her parents, who raise a question so far unasked (among the signs of mastery in the story, one of the surest is the patience, the undefended gravity with which Miss Welty answers—or asks—all the reader's questions in her own time not his, and finally makes him admit her justice). The question is, why did Judge McKelva marry Fay?—"What happened to his judgment?" One of the ladies flatly states that Laurel's to blame; she should never have married but stayed home and tended her widowed father. Laurel makes no defense, barely speaks at all till the same lady weakens and begins "forgiving" Fay—

> "Although I guess when people don't *have* anything . . . Live
> so *poorly*—"
> "That hasn't a thing to do with it," Laurel said . . .

This new ruthlessness (a specific defeat of her own attempt to forgive Fay through the child Wendell) calms in the following scene—Laurel alone in her father's library. Here, because of a photograph, she thinks for the only time in our presence of her own marriage—"Her marriage had been of magical ease, of *ease*—of brevity and conclusion, and all belonging to Chicago and not here." But in the third scene— Laurel's contemporaries, her bridesmaids, at drinks—she bristles again, this time to defend her parents against affectionate joking—"Since when have you all thought my father and mother were just figures to make a good story?" Her friends retreat, claim "We weren't laughing at them. They weren't funny." (Laurel accepts the clarification; only at the end, if faced again with "They weren't funny" might she offer correction, huge amplification.) The fourth scene is longest, strangest, the crisis—from which Laurel, the story, all Miss Welty's earlier onlookers and surely most readers emerge shaken, cleared, altered. On her last night in Mount Salus before returning to Chicago and before Fay's return, Laurel comes home from dinner with friends to find a bird flying loose indoors, a chimney swift. She is seized at once by an old fear of birds (we are not reminded till the following morning that a bird in the house means bad luck ahead), and in panic shuts herself into her parents' bedroom—now Fay's— against its flight. Here, alone and silent except for sounds of wind and rain, among her parents' relics, she endures her vision—of their life, hers, the world's. Her initial step is to calm herself, to examine the sources of her recent angers, her present terror—

> What am I in danger of, she wondered, her heart pounding. Am
> I not safe from *myself*?
> Even if you have kept silent for the sake of the dead, you cannot
> rest in your silence, as the dead rest. She listened to the wind, the

rain, the blundering, frantic bird, and wanted to cry out, as the
nurse cried out to her, "Abuse! Abuse!"

What she first defines as the "facts" are these—that her helpless
father had been assailed and killed by his own senseless, self-absorbed
young wife and that she—his only child—was powerless to save him
but can now at least protect his memory. Protect—and flush her own
bitterness—by exacting justice from Fay, extracting from Fay an
admission of her guilt. Yet Laurel knows at once that Fay, challenged,
would only be baffled, sealed in genuine blind innocence. Balked in
advance then by invincible ignorance, is Laurel to be paralyzed in
permanent bitterness? She can be, she thinks, released and consoled
by at last telling someone—the facts, the names. But tell whom? Her
own mother, long since dead. To tell her mother though—should
that ever be possible—would be an abuse more terrible than Fay's.
Laurel can only go on telling herself and thereby through her perpetual judging become a new culprit, another more knowing Fay.
That is—and can go on being—"the horror." At that moment, desperate with rage and forced silence, she makes the only physical
movement open (the bird still has her trapped in the room). She
retreats into an adjoining small room. It had been her own nursery,
where she'd slept near her parents; then the sewing room; now a
closet where Fay has hidden Laurel's mother's desk. Here, memory
begins—a long monologue (yet always in third person) which bears
Laurel back through her parents' lives, her life with them. (The
structure and method of these fifteen pages at first seem loose, old-
fashioned. No attempt is made through syntax or ellipsis to mimic
the voice or speed of Laurel's mind, to convince us that we literally
overhear her thoughts. Yet the process of memory proceeds with
such ferocious emotional logic to an end so far beyond Laurel's
imagined needs or desires—Laurel's and ours—that we are at last
convinced, as shaken as she.) The memories begin warmly—here are
things they touched, relics of their love, a family desk, a small stone
boat carved with her father's initials, his letters to her mother (which
Laurel will not read, even now), a photograph of them in full un-
threatened youth. In the flood of affection, Laurel begins to move
from her old stance of onlooker to a conviction of having shared her
parents' lives, been a corner of their love. She continues backward
through memories of summers in the West Virginia mountains with
her mother's family. (Both her parents' families were originally Virginian; and it would be possible—therefore someone will do it—to
construct a kind of snob-machine with these genealogies: Virginians
are finer than Mississippians are finer than Texans. The story says no
such thing; only "This is what happened"—Miss Welty's own mother
was from West Virginia, her father from Ohio.) Those summers,

recalled, seem made of two strands—her mother's laughing immersion in family love and her own childish bafflement: tell me how much and why they love you, your mother and brothers. This early bafflement is focused for Laurel in her first sight of her grandmother's pigeons. Without claiming a mechanical connection which Miss Welty clearly does not intend, it is worth noting that this sight is the beginning (so far as we know) of Laurel's present personal distance, her stunned passivity in the face of the Chisoms feeding on one another—

> . . . Laurel had kept the pigeons under eye in their pigeon house and had already seen a pair of them sticking their beaks down each other's throats, gagging each other, eating out of each other's craws, swallowing down all over again what had been swallowed before: They were taking turns . . . They convinced her that they could not escape each other and could not be escaped from. So when the pigeons flew down, she tried to position herself behind her grandmother's stiff dark skirt, but her grandmother said again, "They're just hungry, like we are."

It was a knowledge and revulsion which her mother had seemed to lack—until her long final illness at least. The terms of that illness are not fully explained—Laurel's mother went blind, lay in bed for years, growing slowly more reckless and condemnatory, more keen-sighted in her observation of husband and daughter as they hovered beside her helpless. As the illness had extended through five years (just after Laurel's widowhood) and as Laurel now recalls it, her mother had at last endured the awful knowledge in its simple killing progression—that we feed on others till they fail us, through their understandable inability to spare us pain and death but, worse, through the exhaustion of loyalty, courage, memory. In the pit of her illness, Laurel's mother had said to the Judge standing by her—

> "Why did I marry a coward?" . . . Later still, she began to say— and her voice never weakened, never harshened; it was her spirit speaking in the wrong words—"All you do is hurt me. I wish I might know what it is I've done. Why is it necessary to punish me like this and not tell me why?"

Then she had sunk silent toward her death, with only one last message to Laurel—"You could have saved your mother's life. But you stood by and wouldn't intervene. I despair for you." In the teeth of such judgment, Laurel's father—the optimist—had married Fay; had chosen to submit again to need, and been killed for his weakness. What had been betrayed—what her mother like a drugged prophetess had seen and condemned before the event—was not his first love but his first wife's *knowledge*, the dignity and achievement of her unanswerable vision. Fay's the answer to nothing. Then can love be?—

Answer to what? Death and your own final lack of attention doom you to disloyalty. You're killed for your cowardice. With that news, the scene ends. Laurel sleeps.

> A flood of feeling descended on Laurel. She let the papers slide from her hand and put her head down on the open lid of the desk and wept in grief for love and for the dead.

—Grief surely *that* love had not saved but harrowed her parents, a love she had not shared and now can never.

Part IV is a quick hard but by no means perfunctory coda. Laurel wakes in early light, having slept at her mother's desk. Now unafraid, she leaves her parents' room, sees the exhausted bird perched on a curtain. Mr. Deedy, the blundering handyman, calls by to peddle spring chores. Laurel asks him in to catch the bird. He declares it bad luck and scares it around from room to room but only succeeds in making a nosey tour of the house. Then Missouri, the maid, arrives and she and Laurel gingerly arrange the bird's escape in the only passage of the story where the touch seems to me to press a little heavily, uneasily—

> "It's a perfectly clear way out. Why won't it just fly free of its own accord?"
>
> "They just ain't got no sense like we have . . . All birds got to fly, even them no-count dirty ones. . . ."

Laurel burns her mother's papers, saving only the snapshots and the carved stone boat. She calls herself a thief—the house and contents are Fay's now—but she justifies herself—

> It was one of her ways to live—storing up to remember, putting aside to forget, then to find again—hiding and finding. Laurel thought it a modest game that people could play by themselves, and, of course, when that's too easy, against themselves. It was a game for the bereaved, and there wasn't much end to it.

Her calm seems complete, her departure foregone and unprotested; but in a final look through kitchen cupboards, she finds her mother's breadboard—its worn polished surface inexplicably gouged, scored and grimy. Her numb peace vanishes, her rejection of revenge. She knows that, in some way, this is Fay's work, Fay's ultimate murder of Laurel's mother, the house itself, that she has "conspired with silence" and must finally shout both "Abuse!" and "Love!" And indeed Fay arrives at this moment, her return from Texas timed for Laurel's departure (the bridesmaids by now are waiting at the curb to drive Laurel to Jackson). Laurel challenges Fay with the ruined breadboard—

"It's just an old board, isn't it?" cried Fay.

"She made the best bread in Mount Salus!"

"All right! Who cares? She's not making it now."

"Oh, my mother could see exactly what you were going to do!"

Laurel has judged at last, in rage, and in rage has discovered the order of experience, the mysterious justice of time and understanding, her mother's final accurate desperation—

> Her mother had suffered every symptom of having been betrayed, and it was not until she had died, had been dead long enough to lie in danger of being forgotten and the protests of memory came due, that Fay had ever tripped in. It was not until then, perhaps, that her father himself had ever dreamed of a Fay. For Fay was Becky's own dread . . . Suppose every time her father went on a business trip . . . there had been a Fay.

So memory itself is no longer safe, no "game for the bereaved." The past is never safe because it is never *past,* not while a single mind remembers. Laurel requires revenge. She accuses Fay of desecrating the house, but in vain—as she'd known the night before, Fay does not understand and will not ever, least of all from Laurel (she had used the board for cracking nuts). Fay can only resort to calling Laurel "crazy," to hurtful revelation, an anecdote of Laurel's mother's last wildness—throwing a bedside bell at a visitor. Laurel raises the breadboard to threaten Fay. Fay has the courage of her ignorance, stands and scornfully reminds Laurel that her friends are waiting outside—"You're supposed to be leaving." Then Fay goes on to claim she'd intended reconciliation, had returned in time for that—". . . we all need to make some allowance for the cranks . . ." Laurel abandons the weapon, one more piece of Fay's inheritance, and hurries to leave, escorted away by her own bridesmaids.

I have summarized at such length because it's my experience, both as reviewed writer and teacher, that even a trained reader (especially trained readers) cannot be relied on to follow the action, the linked narrative, of any long story, especially of a story whose action is interior. (Ask ten trained readers what happens in *Heart of Darkness*—not what are the symbols or controlling metaphors but, simply, who does what to whom and why? Who knows what at the end? *Then* you'll see some darkness.) Also because to summarize *The Optimist's Daughter* is to demonstrate how perfectly the meaning inheres in the form and radiates from it. Nothing is applied from outside or wrenched; the natural speed of the radiation—action into meaning—is never accelerated (with the possible exception of the trapped bird's escape); and no voice cries "Help!" at its lethal rays— lethal to illusion, temporary need.

But the length of a summary has left me little space to discuss important details—to mention only two: first, the language (which in its stripped iron efficiency, its avoidance of simile and metaphor, bears almost no resemblance to the slow dissolving impressionism, relativism, of the stories in *The Bride of the Innisfallen;* that was a language for describing what things are *not,* for intensifying mystery; this is a language for stating facts) and, second, the story's apparent lack of concern with Mississippi's major news at the time of the story—the civil rights revolution. Its apparent absence is as complete as that of the Napoleonic wars from Jane Austen. And for the same reason, surely—it is not what this story is about. When Judge McKelva's old law partner says of him at the funeral, "Fairest, most impartial, sweetest man in the whole Mississippi Bar," no irony seems intended nor can honestly be extracted. (I've stressed *apparent* absence because any story which so ruthlessly examines blindness is "about" all the forms of blindness; and if any reader is unprepared to accept the fact that in all societies at all times good and evil coexist in all men and can, under certain conditions of immense complexity, be compartmentalized, quarantined from one another within the same heart, then this story's not for him. So much the worse for him—neither will most art be.)

What I cannot skimp is my prior suggestion that the puzzlement or contented suspension of onlookers in Miss Welty's earlier fiction vanishes in *The Optimist's Daughter,* that the end clarifies. The stance of the onlooker—forced on him and/or chosen—is confirmed as the human stance which can hope for understanding, simple survival. The aims of participation are union, consolation, continuance—doomed. Laurel (who might well be the adult of the girl in "A Memory" or even of Laura in *Delta Wedding*) might so easily have left us with a last word fierce as her mother's. She might have said, "Show me a victor, an *actor* even." Or worse, she might have laughed.

For there is at the end, each time I've reached it, a complicated sense of joy. Simple exhilaration in the courage and skill of the artist, quite separate from the tragic burden of the action. Joy that a piece of credible life has been displayed to us fully and, in the act, fully explained (I take Laurel's understanding to be also the author's and ours; there can be no second meaning, no resort to attempts to discredit Laurel's vision). And then perhaps most troubling and most appeasing, the sense that Laurel's final emotion is joy, that she is now an "optimist" of a sort her father never knew (if not as she drives away from her home, then tomorrow, back at work)—that the onlooker's gifts, the crank's, have proved at last the strongest of human endowments (vision, distance, stamina—the courage of all three); that had there been any ear to listen, Laurel would almost surely have laughed, abandoning her weapon (as Milton's God laughs at the ignorance and ruin of Satan, only God has hearers—the Son and His angels). For Laurel has been both victim and judge—who goes beyond both into pure creation (only she has discovered the pattern of their lives—her parents', Fay's, the Chisoms', her friends', her own) and then comprehension, which is always comic. All patterns are comic—snow crystal or galaxy in Andromeda or family history—because the universe is patterned, therefore ordered and ruled, therefore incapable of ultimate tragedy (interim tragedy is comprised in the order but cannot be the end; and if it should be—universal pain—then that too is comic, by definition, to its only onlooker). God's vision is comic, Alpha and Omega.

Images of Memory in
Eudora Welty's
The Optimist's Daughter   Marilyn Arnold°

Flannery O'Connor once commented on the difference between her way of writing and Eudora Welty's way. She said, "I am not one of the subtle sensitive writers like Eudora Welty. I see only what is outside and what sticks out a mile, such things as the sun that nobody has to uncover or be bright to see."[1] It is precisely those respective qualities identified by O'Connor that render her own meanings so starkly difficult and Eudora Welty's so elusive. It may not have occurred to O'Connor that things sticking out a mile can be harder to see than things hidden behind doors, but she was aware of something in Welty's mental, sidedoor approach to life and fiction that allows her to slip through our fingers. This characteristic of Welty's work is especially apparent in the final section of *The Optimist's Daughter*, published some sixteen years after O'Connor's remark.[2] The book is about the struggle of a widow in her middle forties to make sense out of the past, to understand her mother's and then her father's dying, to comprehend why her father took for a second wife a crass, lowbred woman younger than his daughter, and to interpret her own brief marriage ended suddenly by war and death.

Although the novel's overt action centers around the death of Judge McKelva following eye surgery in New Orleans, and his funeral and burial at home in Mount Salus, Mississippi, its meanings are realized through conflicting motions in the mind of Laurel McKelva Hand, daughter of Judge Clinton McKelva and Becky McKelva. Wel-

° From *The Southern Literary Journal* 14 (Spring 1982):28–38. Copyright 1982 by Department of English, University of North Carolina. Reprinted with permission of the University of North Carolina Press.

ty's several themes are death, human relationship, and the effects of memory on the past, but through the use of image, symbol, ritual, and parable she weaves them together into one thematic whole. Death, Welty says, plunges the dead into the past by snapping the present shut, and what becomes important then is what living memory does with the past. Laurel must now ponder the nature of her parents' love; she must reconsider the brief perfection of the love she and Philip Hand had shared; and she must recognize that it is not the dead but the living who, in their loneliness and uncertainty, are in danger.

Imagery and symbol are especially important in conveying the elusive character of Welty's idea. The book's most pervasive system of symbolic imagery centers around birds, with the first reference coming in the very beginning of the book when the Judge associates his initial awareness of vision problems with the flashing of bright tin reflectors in his fig tree. The reflectors are remnants of Becky's efforts to protect the fruit from the bold appetites of birds. They are ineffectual, of course, as evidenced later when an irreverent band of cardinals is seen zooming playfully at their own reflections in the shiny round tins. The futility of trying to protect anything precious from outside incursions is one of the painful lessons Laurel learns from her father's dying. She grows increasingly disturbed as friends and townspeople invent an heroic past for Judge McKelva while he lies helpless in his coffin. Foiled in her wish to close the coffin lid against the eyes of the townspeople, Laurel feels that her father has "reached at this moment the danger point of his life," for it seems almost "as though he were in the process of being put on trial here instead of being viewed in his casket" (pp. 100–101) and she were being forced to testify in his behalf. Laurel can provide no more protection to her father against this joyous, irresponsible myth-making than the reflectors can provide to the fig tree. Miss Adele Courtland's comment about the undaunted cardinals, and, by implication, about the neighbors' gossip on a day following the funeral, could well apply to the storytelling ritual acted out in the presence of the corpse: "Oh, it's a game, isn't it, nothing but a game" (p. 138)!

Laurel was even less able to provide protection for her father while he lived. She could not save him from Becky's scorn, and she was too far away in Chicago to save him from marrying Fay. In the New Orleans hospital, against the backdrop of the Mardi Gras ritual, his silent, shrouded body prefigures his corpse lying in its garish coffin (Fay chose the colors) against the backdrop of another ritual, the public viewing and funeral of a dead man. Laurel cannot protect him either place. In an unguarded moment in New Orleans, the impatient Fay attacks the helpless man with a flurry of demands that precipitate his death. After the return to Mount Salus and the funeral,

Laurel reflects bitterly that neither she nor her mother could save their fathers, but she holds herself more blamable than her mother because Laurel "did not any longer believe that anyone could be saved, anyone at all. Not from others" (p. 170).

Laurel abandons her efforts to protect the dead from the living and to preserve the past intact only after a long night of wrestling with her own version of the past, confronting it, examining it, reinterpreting it, and finally freeing it from the chains of her sheltering need. Welty represents Laurel's struggle to evade and then finally to free the past by portraying it symbolically as a chimney swift trapped inside the family home the night before Laurel is to leave for Chicago.[3] The past is caught in Laurel's inflexible idea of it just as the bird is caught in the house. But the bird, like the past, becomes the pursuer, and Laurel becomes the pursued. In running frantically from the bird, Laurel flees into what was her parents' bedroom and shuts the door against the bird. Its insistent drumming, however, drives her further into the recesses of the house, into the little sewing room off the bedroom. Here she feels momentarily safe, having outrun the figurative past; but here she unexpectedly confronts the peril of the empirical past, her mother's desk and all its memorabilia.

The next morning the bird is caught and released, but not before "it had left the dust of itself all over everything" (p. 192). The release of the bird confirms that Laurel must also release the past from the shackles of her unyielding view of it. Her night in the sewing room under the seige of mementos and remembrances predicts the saving change in her, but the final test comes when Fay returns unexpectedly early (she had gone home to Texas with her family after the funeral) and finds Laurel in possession of one last relic from the past, the breadboard which Phil had lovingly made for Becky McKelva. In Fay's careless hands it had become gouged and filthy, and in her anger Laurel determines to take it with her to Chicago. She even seems poised at one point to strike Fay with it. When Fay scornfully asks, "What do you see in that thing?" Laurel replies, "The whole story, Fay. The whole solid past" (p. 206). In the moment of Fay's reflexive bragging that she belongs to the future, that the past means nothing to her, Laurel is granted a culminating, redeeming revelation: she acknowledges first that Fay is nothing to the past and can do nothing to the past; and then she wonderingly confesses, "And neither am I; and neither can I, . . . although it has been everything and done everything to me, everything for me" (p. 207). She realizes that she had been foolish in trying to protect her father, her mother, and the past. She had been wrong to resent the town's chatter, wrong to suppose that the keepsakes of the past contain it. The past is a fact, Laurel realizes, "no more open to help or hurt than was Father in his coffin. The past is like him, impervious, and can never be awakened" (p. 207).

In that moment, Laurel relinquishes the past to memory, knowing at last that it is memory, not the past, that can "never be impervious," that "can be hurt, time and time again—but in that may lie its final mercy." The past is static, invulnerable; but memory is fluid, dynamic, "vulnerable to the living moment," and takes its life from the living.[4] If the dead are to have any continuing life, they must be subject to the shifting, reinterpreting memory of the living. The dead are not saved by being shut off from the vicissitudes of memory; they are saved by being released into memory, freed by it and its capacity for pardon. In the process the living are also freed from awkward notions of what constitutes allegiance to the past. Thus, Laurel needs no breadboard, no house, no stack of her father's letters to her mother.[5] She can exchange those lifeless tokens for the continuous promise of memory which, she realizes, "lives not in initial possession but in the freed hands, pardoned and freed, and in the heart that can empty but fill again, in the patterns restored by dreams" (pp. 207–208).

Laurel's revelation about the freeing effects of allowing memory its due has particular application to her interpretations of the human relationships she had protectively sealed up in the past. Before her apocalyptic night with the chimney swift, Laurel had locked her parents inside a rather idyllic notion of their relationship. And she had done the same thing with her own marriage. When she thought of the Judge and Becky, she thought of "two beloved reading voices . . . rising in turn up the stairs every night to reach her. She could hardly fall asleep, she tried to keep awake, for pleasure." Laurel interpreted the uninterrupted flow of their reading as a verification of their complete conjugal harmony. They never let "a silence divide or interrupt them" as their two voices "combined into one unceasing voice and wrapped her around as she listened" (p. 71). She had also "sealed away into its perfection" her love for Phil and "had gone on living with the old perfection undisturbed and undisturbing" (p. 181).

Laurel learns on that crucial night that she had wronged both her parents and Phil by trapping them in the stagnation of a manufactured ideal. She had refused to imagine a desperation in Phil's death just as her father had refused to recognize the desperation in her mother's fitful, angry dying. Again, Welty uses bird imagery and symbolism, this time to represent the static perfection of Laurel's reconstruction of her marriage to Phil. Phil had tried to teach her that love was not a shelter, and that she must forgo the urge to both "protection" and "self-protection" that she had "foolishly saved from childhood" (p. 188). But since she had grown up "in the kind of shyness that takes its refuge in giving refuge" (p. 187), she slipped back into that pattern when Phil was killed. Her recollections of her marriage to Phil, like her earlier recollections of her parents' marriage, are expressed in images of unity. Laurel remembers that from the train carrying them south for their wedding, she and Phil had seen two great rivers come together, the Ohio and the Mississippi. As they looked down, "all they saw was at the point of coming together, the bare trees marching in from the horizon, the rivers moving into one." And providing heavenly accent to the scene below was "the long, ragged, pencil-faint line of birds within the crystal of the zenith, flying in a V of their own, following the same course down." Laurel reflects, "All they could see was sky, water, birds, light, and confluence." And they were a part of it, "riding as one with it," because of their "joint act of faith" (p. 186). This cherished vision of flawless union, whether applied to Becky and the Judge or Laurel and Phil, could not survive the honest probe of memory.

Subjecting the past to the "somnambulist" memory is a painful process, for memory "will come back in its wounds . . . calling us by our names and demanding its rightful tears" (p. 207). Looking back through the wavy lens of memory during the night she spends in her mother's sewing room, Laurel comes to understand that the interdependencies of love can produce an inner sense of alienation equal to its outward signs of unity. This happened with her mother and father; it might have happened with her and Phil had he lived.

The death of Laurel's father in the wake of his eye surgery, and Laurel's recollection of her perplexing inability to penetrate the wall of his dark suffering with comfort force to the surface thoughts of her mother's dying. Both the Judge and Becky were victims in that dying. Not only did he absorb her angry reproaches and her charges of betrayal, but for the first time, perhaps, he intuited the unsettling truth that her life with him in Mount Salus ran a distant second to her life "up home" in West Virginia. Becky spent every summer in West Virginia until her mother died; she and Laurel "might have stayed there always" and the Judge "had not appeared to realize it" (p. 167). In order to handle his wife's dying, the Judge became a self-proclaimed optimist, and in so doing he made Becky a victim of love as well as illness. He refused to recognize that she was desperate and angry, and he used forgiveness as a shield against all the manifestations of her desperation and anger: "Whatever she did that she couldn't help doing was all right. Whatever she was driven to say was all right." "But," Laurel knows now, "it was *not* all right! Her trouble was that very desperation." The Judge's refusal "to consider that she was desperate" constituted "betrayal on betrayal" (p. 176). After a final crippling stroke, Becky is convinced that she has been "left among strangers, for whom even anger meant nothing, on whom it would only be wasted. She had died without speaking a word, keeping everything to herself, in exile and humiliation" (p. 177). Becky's final humiliation, aside from the fact that the Judge survived her, was his marriage to a woman like Fay. Laurel sees now that "Fay was Becky's own dread" (p. 201), that Becky's sense of betrayal in her life predicted Fay's arrival after her death. The Judge's character had always contained an element that would be drawn to a relationship that made no internal demands of him.

In searching the past with new understanding, Laurel also realizes that she has wronged Phil. By allowing him no voice of protest in her carefully orchestrated mental tableau of his unruffled glide into death, she had failed him just as surely as her father had failed her mother. Now she senses him "here waiting, all the time," looking "at her out of eyes wild with the craving for his unlived life" (p. 181); and she grants him freedom in her memory to cry in anguished protest against his death. She imagines him appealing to her repeatedly and shouting that he wanted life.

Laurel's troubled meditations on the complex claim and protest of love relationships are underscored by still another image of birds. Laurel remembers how, as a little child "up home" with her mother, she was frightened and dismayed over the expectation that she gladly feed her grandmother's fluttering, flapping pigeons. Especially distressing was their behavior in the pigeon house, brazenly "sticking their beaks down each other's craws, swallowing down all over again what had been swallowed before: they were taking turns." Like human beings knotted in the web of loving and being loved, the birds "could not escape each other and could not themselves be escaped from." Her grandmother's explanation that they were "just hungry, like we are" (p. 166) was no comfort to Laurel. And since her mother seemed oblivious to the behavior of the birds, Laurel could not tell her or anyone else about her fears.

The sometimes stark and indelicate realities of human interdependence and intimacy, suggested figuratively through the behavior of the pigeons, are predictably distasteful to Laurel.[6] Facing them openly for the first time the night she spends shut up with the past, she realizes not only her parents' urgent, baffling dependence and their simultaneous and paradoxical inability to meet each other's needs, but also her own longing for her parents and their utter unreachableness: "In her need tonight Laurel would have been willing to wish her mother and father dragged back to any torment of living because that torment was something they had known together, through each other. She wanted them with her to share her grief as she had been the sharer of theirs." In her despair, she fastens her mind on "only one thing, . . . her mother holding and holding onto their hands, her own and her father's holding onto her mother's, long after there was nothing more to be said" (pp. 176–177).

It is finally her discovery of a reference to the pigeons in a long ago letter from her grandmother to her mother that breaks the stubborn wedge of grief in Laurel. The older woman wrote that she wished she could send Laurel one of the pigeons for her birthday, adding, "It would eat from her hand, if she would let it" (p. 180). In those few words, "if she would let it" (p. 180), Laurel's grandmother has given her the key for unlocking her garrisoned heart. In idealizing the relationships of those she loved, in seeking to protect the dead from the scrutiny of memory, and in arming herself against those born, like Fay, "without any powers of passion or imagination" (p. 206), Laurel had denied her loved ones and herself access to memory's freeing powers, the powers that prompt forgiveness and love in the promise of continued renewal and blessing. But now the gates are opened and Laurel weeps "in grief for love and for the dead. She lay there with all that was adamant in her yielding to this night, yielding at last. Now all that she had found had found her" (pp. 180–181).

In still other minor ways bird imagery underscores theme. For example, as Laurel works in the garden prior to returning to Chicago, the gossipy chatter of her visiting neighbors is punctuated by the song of a nearby mockingbird. The bird's song is particularly associated with Adele Courtland, who in a voice that contains "the faint note of mockery" (p. 127), makes verbal jabs at both her neighbors and the object of their scorn, Fay. But since the cardinals are seen flying at their own reflections as this scene ends, Welty could be suggesting that the neighbors, in attacking Fay and chuckling over the Judge and Becky, are in fact only revealing and flying at themselves. Laurel's protective urge makes her vulnerable to this prattle, but her parents are entirely safe.

It is partly through bird imagery also that Welty describes Judge McKelva as a man who evaded the past because the past was too painful a reminder of his own mortality. He kept records of his public activities, for the results of those works are still in evidence and constitute a kind of immortality for him. His personal letters from Becky, however, were not saved because they could only testify to change and the passing of time. It was perhaps the Judge's long helplessness against Becky's absorption in her past "up home" that led him to take for a second wife a woman for whom the past meant nothing, a woman, in fact, who virtually erased her past by killing her family in a lie to Laurel. As the Judge's mourners approach the grave site Fay had selected in the new section of the cemetery, near the buzzing freeway (Becky is, of course, buried in the old section), "black wings thud in sudden unison, and a flock of birds flies up."

In rising, these starlings retain the shape of the ploughed field they might have just left, looking "like an old map that still served new territory" (p. 110). There is in this image just the suggestion that in marrying Fay, the Judge willfully became "an old map" that tried to serve "new territory." Significantly, as the mourners leave the grave, the starlings return and settle on the ground, "pushing with the yellow bills of spring" (p. 111). The Judge's final release seems assured.

The efforts of Judge McKelva to stay a step ahead of the past, to claim eternal title to the present, are represented by numerous references to time. In the hospital, forced to remain motionless to allow his repaired retina to heal, the Judge silently, motionlessly concentrates all his energies on the fact of time passing, as if through his solitary effort he can keep it and his pulse going.[7] But after Fay has "laid hands on him" (p. 43) in an effort to jar him out of his dark study into life and action, he stops counting and lets time go by him. It is as if this violent encounter with his present and future, embodied in Fay, opens his inner eye to reality. He makes a deliberate, if regretful, decision to die and slip into the shelter of the past. His continuing life now depends solely upon the function of memory among the living; and since Fay has no capacity for memory, he is at least safe from her in death.

Welty fashions an ingenious blend of time and bird imagery as Laurel speeds with her father's body toward Mount Salus. From the train window Laurel sees a "seagull . . . hanging" against a clear sheet of sky with its "wings fixed, like a stopped clock on the wall." Later, coming out of a dream, she imagines the image repeating itself as the seagull becomes "the hands on the clock in the Courthouse dome" (p. 57). And when Laurel arrives at the family home in Mount Salus, she discovers that the parlor clock has (fittingly) stopped.

One vital, but unusual, image is introduced through a parable which serves as a capstone for the entire book, the image of white strawberries. The dying Becky describes them in sermon-like reproach to the minister who had come to offer spiritual comfort, but who was so obviously her inferior in theological dexterity that he had nothing to give her. In its capacity for at least dual interpretation, the strawberry tale brings together two basic thematic strands of the novel: the strand of the past and its relationship to memory, and the strand of human interdependence.[8] Becky says that on the mountain for which she longs "up home," in a wild place that very few can find, there grows a most luscious and delicate white strawberry. Although Becky had called for the minister in desperation over her husband's evasive bewilderment at her dying, it is the minister, not the Judge, that she accuses of being one, who, if he did stumble upon the strawberries, would try to gather them up and carry them out cradled in his hat. "That," she says, would show "how little you know about those berries. Once you've let them so much as touch each other, you've already done enough to finish 'em." Almost accusingly she adds, "Nothing you ever ate in your life was anything like as delicate, as fragrant, as those wild strawberries. You had to know enough to go where they are and stand and eat them on the spot, that's all" (p. 175).

Becky's parable could be suggesting, on the one hand, that one's personal past, like the strawberries, is inestimably precious. As such, it must not be exposed to the common view nor brought into the present. The one who would taste its nectar must find the fruit and partake of it where it dwells. To remove the past from its setting and subject it to the present is to destroy it. Becky could also be saying that human beings, like the wild white strawberries, are very delicate organisms. The very nature of human relationship that brings these delicate beings into intimate association can also damage them irreparably. Becky had craved inviolate privacy, and throughout her married life she had escaped into her past "up home" in an effort to achieve it.

But ultimately, Becky was wrong; her blindness, like the Judge's, was spiritual as well as physical. She thought that she could escape into the safety of solitude and the past indefinitely. The Judge's blindness was that he thought he could escape from the past by warding it off through absorption in the present. In that sense he was using Fay as much as she was using him; she was his reprieve from old age and the past. Laurel's blindness was that she thought that both the past and love could be sealed up into perfection, out of the reach of memory and change.[5] What Laurel learns—Becky and the Judge are past learning, and Fay is immune to it—is that people and the past and love are like Becky's climbing rose. Though Becky had marveled at its ability to be "utterly strong" and "on its own roots," blooming the next year if not this, Laurel knows that it is partly the pruning and the care that produce the blooming. And if the past seems dead like winter, the rose promises that "memory returned like spring." In fact, "Memory had the character of spring. In some cases it was the old wood that did the blooming" (p. 136).

Notes

1. Letter to "A," February 26, 1956, in *The Habit of Being*, letters selected and edited by Sally Fitzgerald (New York: Farrar, Straus, Giroux, 1979), p. 141.

2. The first published version of *The Optimist's Daughter* appeared in *The New Yorker*, March 15, 1969. With some changes it appeared in a Random House edition in 1972 and won the Pulitzer Prize for fiction. Citations in this discussion are from the Fawcett Crest edition, 1973, and will be noted parenthetically.

Reynolds Price would probably disagree with my observation about the mental, elusive character of Welty's prose in *The Optimist's Daughter*. He describes the language of the magazine version as having a "stripped iron efficiency" and bearing "almost no resemblance to the slow dissolving impressionism, relativism" of some earlier stories. He calls it, in fact, "a language for stating facts." See "The Onlooker, Smiling" in his collection of essays, *Things Themselves: Essays and Scenes* (New York: Atheneum, 1972; first publ. in *Shenandoah*, 20, Spring 1969), p. 133. I think that although scattered segments of the first part of the novel have something of the quality Price mentions, most of it is far from "efficient" or factual, and the later (and very long) revelatory section during which Laurel calls up the past is highly cerebral and poetic. The changes Welty made in the later version of the story may partly account for our differing perceptions. In a postscript to his essay, for example, Price notes that in the later version Laurel "has acquired memories and reflections" about her relationship with Phil that were not in the *New Yorker* story.

3. There are a variety of interpretations of the chimney swift in the critical literature on the book. Thomas Daniel Young, for example, says that the swift "suggests her [Laurel's] innermost feelings," the "turbulent state" of her emotions. See "Social Form and Social Order: An Examination of *The Optimist's Daughter*," in Peggy Whitman Prenshaw, ed., *Eudora Welty: Critical Essays* (Jackson: University Press of Mississippi, 1979), p. 382. John F. Desmond, "Pattern and Vision in *The Optimist's Daughter*," in a collection of essays he edited entitled *A Still Moment: Essays on the Art of Eudora Welty* (Metuchen, New Jersey: The Scarecrow Press, Inc., 1978), p. 121, says Laurel "at once associates" the swift "with all the blundering forces of life and particularly with Fay's assult on her dying father." Cleanth Brooks, in "The Past Reexamined: *The Optimist's Daughter*," *Mississippi Quarterly*, 26 (Fall, 1973), 582, makes several suggestions about the bird's possible symbolic meaning. "Does the bird merely represent the vague terrors of the night that beset Laurel?" he asks. "Or does the sooty bird . . . betoken the alien presence of Wanda Fay in the house, troubling its old inhabitants, putting a smudge on everything? Or is the bird . . . Laurel herself, trapped in the past that has suddenly become to her strange and problematical?" Brooks then says that "perhaps all of these suggestions apply," or perhaps the bird has no "symbolic import" at all. At the very least, it conveys Laurel's "sense of a disturbing element in the house on this gusty night of spring."

4. Price, p. 132, like most commentators who mention the book's treatment of the past, does not make the distinction that Welty appears to make between memory and the past. Rather, Price equates the two, suggesting that "memory itself is no longer safe," and that "the past is never safe because it is never past, not while a single mind remembers." Ruth Vande Kieft, however, in "The Vision of Eudora Welty," *Mississippi Quarterly*, 26(Fall 1973), 541, notes in a passing comment that Welty regards the past as beyond harm while memory remains vulnerable.

5. John Edward Hardy, "Marrying Down in Eudora Welty's Novels," in Prenshaw, p. 119, does not see Laurel's leaving the breadboard behind as an act of character. He says with obvious sarcasm that she can pick up another at Marshall Fields, though it will certainly be "no *better* than what she has sacrificed to spite and to dubious principle in Mount Salus."

6. Commentators are generally in agreement as to the symbolic meaning of the pigeons. Michael Kreyling, for example, in *Eudora Welty's Achievement of Order* (Baton Rouge: Louisiana State University Press, 1980), p. 169, believes that "the heart of the novel might be located" in the passage about the pigeons, illustrating as it does the "cost to the individual" in giving up "its individual freedom" that the group might survive. Desmond, p. 132, calls the feeding of the pigeons "Welty's complex symbol for Laurel's fear of life 'up close' and the whole mystery of human relationships—violation and sustenance, protecting and protesting, love and separateness." Noel Polk

"Water, Wanderers, and Weddings: Love in Eudora Welty," in Louis Dollarhide and Ann J. Abadie, eds., *Eudora Welty: A Form of Thanks* (Jackson: University Press of Mississippi, 1979), p. 120, describes the pigeons as "powerfully emblematic of the difficulties and paradoxes of love relationships." Vande Kieft, p. 540, sees the pigeon episode as having particular application to the turn the relationship between Laurel and Philip Hand has taken since his death. Laurel, she says, has behaved "like an exceptionally complacent pigeon," who has for many years now "been chewing and swallowing" Phil's life while she kept him tucked in an idealized corner of the past. Price, p. 128, is wary of making "a mechanical connection" with the pigeons that "Miss Welty clearly does not intend." Nevertheless, he feels that the episode becomes a focus for Laurel's "childish bafflement" at intimate family relationships. It "is the beginning (so far as we know) of Laurel's present personal distance, her stunned passivity in the face of the Chisoms feeding on one another."

7. Kreyling, pp. 164–165, comments on the Judge's "aggressive" efforts at "pushing time forward," and on Laurel's picture of him "losing a futile struggle against an irreversible process. The Judge's strategy against time, Laurel imagines, had been to take control of it, or seem to, making a line of progress out of random moments."

8. The white strawberry parable has received surprisingly little critical attention. Kreyling, p. 164, does mention it, paraphrasing it and then commenting, "Becky's credo is heresy to the 'clusterers'; it is private and secular, but still reverent."

9. For a lengthy discussion of the vision/blindness motif, see Desmond's entire essay. See also Vande Kieft, pp. 517 ff., for a useful exploration of vision in Welty's work, including *The Optimist's Daughter*. Price, p. 120, believes that vision is the book's central metaphor.

A Return to the Source: Eudora Welty's *The Robber Bridegroom* and *The Optimist's Daughter*   Bev Byrne*

Enigmatic Clement Musgrove, "successful man . . . willy-nilly" of *The Robber Bridegroom* (28), is a key character in Eudora Welty's fiction. Perhaps Welty spent thirty years of storytelling trying to unravel *all* that Clement meant when he said "all things are double" (*Bridegroom* 126). From 1942's *The Robber Bridegroom* to 1972's *The Optimist's Daughter*, the currents of "doubleness" have run as surely and deeply through Welty's fiction as the Mississippi River and the Natchez Trace have run.[1] Different as they are, the two stories are doubles of one another as each explores a doubleness that exists within the self and the doubleness perceived outside the self. *The Robber Bridegroom*, written at the outset of Welty's career, is a fairy tale about setting out, growing up and changing, about Rosamond and Jamie's love, their starting a new generation and making

* Reprinted from *The Southern Quarterly* 24 (Spring 1986):74–85.

the circle turn. Like any good fairy tale, it suggests immortality and, despite bloodshed and violence, ends happily in a new beginning. Only the Indians and Clement are "sure of the future growing smaller always" (21). The daughter of the optimist, however, in a story written thirty years later, faces her own future grown smaller, her own mortality and all the turns of life that fairy tales don't take. Clement's mystical insight that all things are double finds experiential verification in the extremely physical, sensory mode and language of *The Optimist's Daughter*.

The method of each story leads to differing discoveries about doubleness. *The Robber Bridegroom*'s hybridizing of fairy tale, captivity narrative, folklore and local history with Welty's perspective on American history yields its own doublings: mistaken identities, transformations, misperceptions, deceptions and historical comment as the other side of burlesque. Overlappings of past with the frontier present of the story provide almost more doublings than a wary reader can handle—Harp brothers, Harpe brothers, Harpies, and so on. The novel's inclusive ebullience is rare contrast to the realistic method of *The Optimist's Daughter*. Laurel McKelva Hand's story avoids allusiveness, avoids nearly all but what her eye takes in during the days of tending her father, coping with his second wife, with her father's wake and funeral and with the truths which the eye of memory seeks. Welty has told Laurel's story in an adventurously limited but insistent vocabulary of *hand* and *eye*, *foot* and *cheek*—of the nouns and verbs that remind us of our bilateral selves and the accompanying limitations of self. *The Optimist's Daughter* is a litany of the names of the physical organs which provide our most concrete sense of duality. Exploitation of this almost deprived language holds its own riches and pulls the reader into a kinesthetic awareness of doubleness that begins with hand and eye but infiltrates the range of perception.

Examination of the revisions Welty made in the novel after its appearance in the *New Yorker* shows that most of the changes involved strengthening, in one way or another, this vocabulary of physical duality as it reverberates in story line and imagery.[2] "In fact, I think I deepened it in some ways," Welty said of the ". . . many small changes that probably no one but me would notice" (Prenshaw 242).

Welty's description of *The Robber Bridegroom* to the members of the Mississippi Historical Society outlined her purposes concerning the doubleness of that story. It was her firm intention, she said, to bind together "local history and the legend and the fairy tale into working equivalents," and though it is not a "historical historical novel," the figures born of fairy tale and legend incorporate the spirit of time and place, Rodney Landing about 1798 (*Eye of Story* 302–5). "The line between history and fairy tale is not always clear, as *The Robber Bridegroom* along the way points out." Her story took its

life, she said, from their interplay (309). Welty's comment that she
had drawn the "horrors as well as the felicities" into plot points to
another way in which the work is double: it is at once a rowdy caper
in frontier times and shrewd comment on the acquisitiveness and
violence of frontier life.

Welty's perception of the southwest frontier as reiteration of past
tales, Grimm and otherwise, gives rise to encompassing doublenesses
in the tale and to a "doubleness in respect to identity that runs in
a strong thread . . . spun . . . out of the times," Welty said. "Life
was so full, so excessively charged with energy in those days, when
nothing seemed impossible in the Natchez country, that leading one
life hardly provided scope enough for it all. In the doubleness there
was narrative truth that I felt the times themselves had justified"
(*Eye of Story* 310–11).

Welty's "narrative truth" is psychological and perceptual as well
as historical and mythical. Jamie Lockhart, with his two faces, is
pulled between dream and reality, between "two" Rosamonds, between desire and duty. His night and day identities stay fluid until
the transforming love of Rosamond settles his identity for him. His
change from robber/woodsman to townsman/merchant is simultaneously the truth of fairy tale, the truth of growing up, and a truth
about the sort of virtue needed for success in America. Jamie was
both dreamer and man of action, and not one to bother unduly with
guilt. Such a man turned loose on the frontier will be double within
himself, no doubt, but will also attract usurpers or those who wish
to stand in his shoes: Goat, lord of misrule in *The Robber Bridegroom*,
is both shadow and would-be double for Jamie as Rosamond's lover,
and Little Harp, the double of the historical Harpe brother, wants
also to double for Jamie as leader of the robber band. Jamie imagines
more doubles than really he has when he supposes that other bandits
are copying his kidnapping of Rosamond. Mike Fink thinks Jamie is
Jamie's ghost, another doubling with narrative truth, for Mike has
been so sure all along of his own identity that he is easily deceived.
In a story with two of everything—Clement's twin babies at the
beginning and Rosamond's twins at the end, with two strangers to
sleep in Clement's bed, two failures by Clement to rescue his daughter, and at least two identities for most of the characters—we can
expect doubleness in sense perception also to give rise to plot. Nature
plays as many tricks as Goat does. Sometimes Nature's tricks are
played on Goat: when he is searching for Rosamond's green dress,
he thinks he sees the dress but it was "only the lily pads" floating
on the creek or "only the old flying cow of Mobile going by"
(*Bridegroom* 57). Bushes turn into Indians in the forest, the sound
of a wildcat sounds like a baby's cry to Rosamond for good reason,
and Clement wages a mighty night-long battle with a giant or spirit

or, as he supposes, with wickedness itself only to discover in the morning he has wrestled with a willow tree (106). Nature's tricks occur as they occur in life: wishing or fearing alters reality and there is instability beyond as well as within.

It is Clement who sets free the most mysterious narrative truths about doubleness in the novel. As the novel's seer, Clement knows evil for what it is and fears it; he withholds judgment, however, hoping for the best but not expecting it. He is not concerned with his own identity as Jamie and Rosamond are, but wonders about "the identity of a man," the time and place, what we are in the universe (141–44). As for himself, Clement knows he has been shaped by chance and circumstance. Past and present have a sameness for him, and experience has shown him that good and evil are not separate, nor ugliness and beauty.

His wife, Salome, becomes more than "wicked stepmother" or "pioneer spirit"—the two identities borrowed from fairy tale and history—when Clement bestows upon her a more remarkable doubleness. He tells Jamie of his past: that he and his first wife, Amalie, with their infant twins, Clement and Rosamond, along with Salome and her husband, Kentucky Thomas, had been captured, tortured and "decreed upon" by Indians. Amalie "fell dead out of the Indians' arms before the sight" of the infant son dropped into boiling oil; Kentucky Thomas had been put to death, then Clement, Salome and Rosamond had been bound together and turned into the wilderness (20–23). Clement knows how greedy, ambitious and wily Salome now is, but he supposes or guesses that she once may have been otherwise.

> From the first, Salome turned her eyes upon me with less question than demand, and that is the most impoverished gaze in the world. *There was no longer anything but ambition left in her destroyed heart* [italics mine]. We scarcely spoke to each other, but each of us spoke to the child. As I grew weaker, she grew stronger, and flourished by the struggle. She could have taken her two hands and broken our bonds apart, but she did not. *I never knew her in any of her days of gentleness, which must have been left behind in Kentucky* [italics mine]. The child cried, and she hushed it in her own way. One morning I said to myself "If we find a river, let that be a sign, and I will marry this woman," but I did not think we would ever find a river. Then almost at once we came upon it— the whole Mississippi. . . . (24–25)

Clement's knowledge that all things are double pertains to Salome's past possibility, but to Rosamond and Jamie's future possibilities, as we see when he is talking to Rosamond about Jamie.

> If being a bandit were his breadth and scope, I should find him and kill him for sure. . . . But since in addition he loves my daughter, he

must be not the one man, but two, and I should be afraid of killing the second. *For all things are double, and this should keep us from taking liberties with the outside world, and acting too quickly to finish things off* [italics mine]. All things are divided in half—night and day, the soul and body, and sorrow and joy and youth and age, *and sometimes I wonder if even my own wife has not been the one person all the time, and I loved her beauty so well at the beginning that it is only now that the ugliness has struck through to beset me like a madness* [italics mine]. And perhaps after the riding and robbing and burning and assault is over with this man you love, he will step out of it all like a beastly skin, and surprise you with his gentleness. For this reason, I will wait and see. . . . (126–27).

Clement has understood Jamie's doubleness because he himself has become a pioneer, planter and husband quite by accident. The "great tug at the whole world, to go down over the edge" had turned him into a pioneer, and "our hearts and our own lonely wills may have had nothing to do with it" (21). He became a planter with as little forethought as he had given to marrying Salome. The flow of time and events is more real to Clement than any decision or plan in his ambitionless heart, but is it only time's flow that makes Amalie and Salome one for Clement? There is a strong psychological component in his philosophical discernment.

Clement intuits the range of the possible. Was Salome once gentle and lovely as Amalie had been? Had Amalie lived, might she have borne a destroyed heart like Salome's? been wily and greedy and wanted always for Clement to do what he did not wish? The Indians had scorned Amalie when she died; they "thought she should have lived on where she stood" (23). Does Clement surmise that Salome has the strength to defy the Indians that Amalie had not? Salome finally dances herself to death, needing no one, submitting to no power, and expecting the sun to stop at her command. She comes to summarize both the courage and the carelessness of the settlers who pushed aside tribes and forests for their prosperity. Clement's attitude toward Salome remains mysterious. The years have taught him that the possession of beauty is as deceptive as the struggle with evil, and that beauty and evil, like Jamie Lockhart, have two faces; so he is willing to grant Salome that other possibility, perhaps a fairy tale's restoration to an original state.

Clement is the key to what Welty called the "validity" of her fantasy as well as the link to her exploration of doubleness in *The Optimist's Daughter*. That validity rests, she said, with "the human motivations apparent alike in the history of a time and in the timeless fairy tale . . . in the end, to find out . . . exactly who we are and

who the other fellow is, and what we are doing here all together"
(*Eye of Story* 311).

Clement is the one who wants to know who we are; he is a seer
in the guise of Salome's Milquetoast. His talk within the circle of
stones within the larger circle of Indians about to capture them all
is an untranslatable lyric which wonders about the existence of man,
the motion of time, and the simultaneity of ugliness and beauty. He
has imaginative access to mysteries: "He stayed and looked at the
place where he was until he knew it by heart, and could even see
the changes of the seasons come over it like four clouds. . ." (141).
A perceiver of doubleness, he is double in his innocence whose other
face is wisdom, and in his trust which transforms evil into good more
often than it betrays him. Jamie, for instance, passed by three chances
to rob Clement, "for the old man had trusted the evil world and
was the kind of man it would break your heart to rob" (102). And
while Clement appears to be only the philosopher poet sitting in his
circle of stones in the forest, he delivers an acute analysis of frontier
history: "Massacre is hard to tell from the performance of other rites,
in the great silence where the wanderer is coming. . ." (143). Because Clement is double and sees doubleness, he is willing to wait
and see. He withholds judgment, does not "act too quickly to finish
things off." This aspect of Clement's vision has a new working out
in *The Optimist's Daughter* when the reader is entrusted with the
task of seeing doubleness and of withholding judgment.

"*A journey is forever lonely and parallel to death*" (*Bridegroom*
143). Clement's meditations are the most important link between the
two novels, though Clement, Rosamond and Salome all have their
counterparts in *The Optimist's Daughter,* as fairy tale metamorphoses
into a pared-down, realistic version of the forever lonely journey.
Where the earlier novel is a magical story of starting out in life, *The
Optimist's Daughter* is the fairy tale tried out. Laurel McKelva Hand,
an artist like Rosamond (whose "fictions" were famous), ignores the
raven's warning to "Turn away, my bonny, / Turn away home." Like
her mother Becky, her stepmother Fay, like Rosamond and most
women, Laurel had to leave home to set out in life. The novel is
concerned with Laurel's return home, to change, emotional threat
and displacement—and, in this respect, as accurately reflects our
times as *The Robber Bridegroom* reflects the frontier of 1798.

Laurel's feelings about her "wicked stepmother" Fay echo Rosamond's wish that Clement should love her own mother best, not
her stepmother Salome (*Bridegroom* 29). Clement's feeling that both
his wives were somehow one is like Clint McKelva's dying "worn
out with both wives—almost as if up to the last he had still had both
of them" (*Daughter* 178). Rivers are connected with love and marriage
in both stories, as often they are in Welty fiction: Clement marries

Salome when they come upon the Mississippi; Rosamond, more ec-
statically, rides with Jamie on his red horse Orion into the winds of
love and arrives at a river flowing "as slow as sand" below (*Bridegroom*
65). And Laurel remembers her feeling that she and Phil would live
forever as they gaze down from a high elevation at the confluence
of the Ohio and Mississippi rivers, when all they see is "sky, water,
birds, light, and confluence. It was the whole morning world" (*Daughter* 186). Laurel's expectations were as archetypal as Jamie's and
Rosamond's. Despite these obvious similarities, it is Clement's vision
that "all things are double" which has the most crucial revival in
The Optimist's Daughter.

The method of the novel seems to transfer to the reader the
responsibility not to act too quickly "to finish things off" without a
second look at its method. The buried narrative voice is in the insistent
use of the words *hand, eye, cheek* and *foot* or words which name
or echo our physical doubleness and remind us concretely of the way
our knowledge is limited by the enclosure in self. We look with two
eyes, hear with two ears and hardly notice that we do—no more
than we notice how insistent is this language in the story.

Hasn't Welty seized these words of physical bilateralness, of
opposites and symmetries to call up in the reader a muscular as well
as a mental response? To suggest the source of our sense of doubleness
as well as its effect on language and perception? The vocabulary of
doubleness is a natural product of the story's viewpoint as Laurel
focuses on what is happening in the circumscribed world of loss, as
she examines painfully Clement's question, "And what kind of time
is this, when all is first given, then stolen away?" (*Bridegroom* 143).
The restricted language and setting are parallel to the restrictions
life imposes at times of crisis, when the self, at bay, has its being
through what is close up, seen, touched or remembered.

In the first 122 pages of a 208 page novel, the word *eye* is used
70 times; its use decreases in Parts Three and Four. *Look, see, watch*
or synonyms are used 148 times in One and Two, another 80 times
in Three and Four (excluding related words like *blazed, blind, read,
vision* and *book*). *Hand* is used 90 times altogether. *Hold* and *touch*
words are used 125 times; *cheek* is used 19 times, mostly in Parts
Three and Four. Wings of birds and birds are important, part of the
complex pattern of emotion and image which comes together at the
end (see pages 57, 111, 138, 154, 166, 180, 186 and 190–95). *Arms,
shoulder, shoes, heels* and *ears* are often repeated. One paragraph
will illustrate the art with which the words disappear into the text.
Hundreds of such paragraphs convince us of their deliberate use. "As
though he had all the time in the world, Dr. Courtland, the well-
known *eye* specialist, folded his big country *hands* with the *fingers*
that had always *looked,* to Laurel, as if their mere *touch* on the

crystal of a *watch* would convey to their skin exactly what time it was" (10).

Often the uses are idiomatic, sometimes metaphorical. We barely notice the "excruciatingly small, brilliant *eye*" of the doctor's instrument (13) or the eye in Miss Tennyson Bullock's opinion that daughters like Laurel "need to stay put, where they can keep a better *eye* on us old folks" (76). When the invaders, Fay's family, arrive at the wake, we slide over the eye in Mrs. Chisom's description of her son's suicide: ". . . stuffed up the door, turned on all four *eyes* of the stove and the oven. . ." (92). More than 350 *look, see, watch, wink, eye* words are blindstitched into the text as the story becomes more and more a story about the restrictions of vision and self. Laurel and Fay both behave at the wake and burial from inside the only vision each has.

Uses of *hand, hold* or *touch* are present from the opening sentences; in fact, Welty's revision from the *New Yorker* version insured just that when she revised the opening paragraph to begin: "A nurse *held* the door open for them. . ." (9). *Hand, hold, touch* words provide a close-up physical texture to the narrative: "Judge McKelva was a tall, heavy man of seventy-one who customarily wore his *glasses* on a ribbon. *Holding* them in his *hand* now, he sat on the raised, thronelike chair above the doctor's stool, flanked by Laurel on one side and Fay on the other" (9).

This opening paragraph above is an exercise in bilateralness— from the doctor's glasses, to his buttocks and flanks, to the opposed women at his sides. It seems also a vignette of the Judge's situation— his troubled physical vision, his reluctant inner vision—with the presence of Laurel on one side to remind him of his first wife Becky, and the presence of his second wife on the other side. Furtive uses of *hand* continue to press upon the reader a sense of touch and of "on the one hand, and on the other." In later chapters, *hands* and *touch* will have accrued and overlapping meanings.

During the wake at the McKelva home, townspeople, friends and near-strangers, and the outsiders, the Chisoms, gather. To Laurel their eyes invade Judge McKelva, and their voices distort the purity of his image as they recreate him to various preferred likenesses. *Walked, stood, stand, step, heel* and *foot* are used constantly in these chapters; there are multiple repetitions of *hand, eye* and *cheek* as church and cemetery are visited. *Cheek* sneaks its way into many a sentence: Fay holds her hand to her *cheek* (110) or Adele's loved *cheek* catches Laurel's eye. *Cheek* suggests "turn the other . . ." as it refers one time to Adele's life-giving touch, or to Fay's or Mr. Cheek's death-dealing touch (as Laurel perceives them). Mr. *Cheek*, the intrusive blunderer who could not get the bird out of the house, was Mr. Deedy in the *New Yorker* (and undertaker Freathy of the

New Yorker version became Mr. *Pitts* in the novel). It must be observed that old Mrs. Pease uses the expletive *foot!* twice in seven pages (pages 115–22).

After the chimney swift invades the house, Laurel escapes from its fearful presence into the peach satin betrayal of her father and Fay's bedroom. Trapped, she begins to face her parents' past and to touch her own. *Hand* is no longer discreetly sewn into the text, but takes over and recurs from one to many times on the pages which follow. Laurel touches objects Clint and Becky had made by *hand*, or she remembers the *foot* of the mountain her mother called home, "the light still warm on its *cheek*" (165) and her mother dying, saying, "If they try to *hold* me, I'll die" (168). Laurel knows that her mother's father, dying, had said the same thing: that her mother had not been able to save him, as she and Clint could not save Becky, and she could not save Clint. *Hold* and *death* grow close in association here, but *hold, hand* and *touch* associate equally with Laurel's memories of their lives lived together.

Birds and the *wings* of birds are related to Laurel's developing recognitions and the mounting impact of a montage of emotion and image combining with words and their associations in her mind. Laurel remembers her childhood fear of the pigeons at her grandmother's house "sticking their beaks down each other's throats, gagging each other. . ." (166). Her adult feeling about birds, including seagulls and swifts is bound up with her childhood fear of defilement, of generation conflict, and with the promise of death to the living.

By the end of Part Three, *touch* and *hold* have strong association with opposed meanings. Laurel remembers Becky's despair, "sewing on her *fingers*" (169); she remembers her father's horror of clash, he the optimist who had to be "helped to see the tragic" (172) and was unable to share Becky's despair; she remembers Becky, feeling betrayed, crying "Why did I marry a coward?", then taking her husband's *hand* "to help him bear it" (174). Becky, dying, had "*held* fast to their *hands*" and they held hers "long after there was nothing more to be said" (177). *Hands,* even before Laurel's memories of Philip *Hand,* her dead husband, *hold* onto life as death reaches out and the *hands* of time stop. This is a deepening of an earlier moment when Laurel, on the train, saw her own head, the *wings* of a seagull and the *hands* on the courthouse clock as a merged image (57). By the end of Part Three, the *hands* of life, the *hands* of death and the *birds* of childhood are a tangle of image, feeling and association.

In the most important revision of her story from the *New Yorker* version, Welty added about six pages of text in which, Laurel faces her personal past with Philip Hand; here the implosion of emotion and *hand, eye, hold, bird* imagery occurs. "Now, by her own *hands,* the past had been raised up" (181). Laurel weeps, thinking of Philip

Hand, and envisions him, *"eyes* wild with the craving for his unlived life" (181). She remembers that his artist's *hand* had "looked to her like the *Hand* of his name" (188). Laurel remembers her father asking Phil, home on furlough from flying in WWII, how close the Kamikaze had come to him, and Phil's reply, "About close enough to shake *hands* with" (189). The *hands* of death and the *wings* of the Kamikaze (which looks like a chimney swift in silhouette) *hold* Phil. The powerful montage of symmetrical and opposite word associations and images had coalesced. Laurel's emotions are a complex of childhood fear and love, fear of defilement by others or by time, fear of death, love of the *hands* of living that touch or make, of Phil's *hands* held now by death, and her recognition that "Surviving is perhaps the strangest fantasy of them all" (189).

In the last pages, Laurel's hands on life, freed, are the result of her discovery of many things, especially her own mortality. Her recognitions are the product of the rituals of death; the townspeople in their loving and sometimes overfamiliar attention have helped her follow out the path of grief for her parents, for Phil, for herself. The hands of the living, sure of the inevitability of death, become free. Welty ends her story, four words from the final period, with the word *hands.* Laurel is leaving Mount Salus on a plane. In an image curiously recalling Emily Dickinson's "Because I Could Not Stop for Death," Laurel is flying off (as in a carriage, with a courtly driver, past the schoolyard?). Adele, friend and schoolteacher, is outside with her children in the schoolyard. "The last thing Laurel saw, before they whirled into speed, was the twinkling of their *hands,* the many small and unknown *hands,* wishing her goodbye" (208). Perhaps it was the first time Laurel had discerned, truly, that "the Horses' Heads / Were toward Eternity—"

Laurel's consciousness seems more self-directed and less philosophical than Clement Musgrove's, but, like Clement, she has discovered the parallel roads of life and death. Her perception of the past, in this story shaped by *eye* and the *I,* is more limited than Clement's vision of past and present as one. If Clement's notions about doubleness and withholding judgment have been turned over to the readers of *The Optimist's Daughter,* they may surmise that Fay is but an obverse, left-handed version of Laurel because both women are unavoidably locked into self, as we are too; that tactless Mr. Cheek is an opposite to Adele; or that Roscoe Chisom who "just stretched himself out easy and put his head on a pillow and waited till he'd quit breathing" (93) is a mirror image of Judge McKelva's way of dying. Laurel knows she is "pursuing her own way through the house as single-mindedly as Fay had pursued hers through the ceremony of the day of the funeral" (205). If we are put off by Fay's constant reference of all events to herself, we finally realize that

Laurel, more genteely, does much the same thing. Fay is even a kind of Jungian shadow self for Laurel at the moment Laurel knows her own emotional truth to be as devastating as Fay's action in laying hands on the judge (156–7). Yet, withholding judgment comes hard to Laurel.

The simultaneity of past and present, of ugliness and beauty, of life and death, may have been clearer to Clement in his circle of stones than to Laurel in her circle of friends. Their question— Clement's and Laurel's—is the same: "And what kind of time is this, when all is first given, then stolen away?" and both must answer that the greatest double effect is life, which, as it gives, takes away. *The Optimist's Daughter* seems to be a fully experienced, modified yet extended version of Clement's insight that all things are double.

Notes

1. *The Optimist's Daughter* was published by Random House first in 1972, after an earlier version in the *New Yorker,* 15 Mar. 1969.

2. In addition to the many subtle changes in hand / eye vocabulary, and the addition of the important pages about Philip Hand, Welty often rearranged the order of conversation and event, expanded paragraphs, but cut material only infrequently. Typical is the change in the opening paragraph. The *New Yorker* version reads:

> Out of Chicago, suddenly here in New Orleans, Laurel Hand sat inside the windowless room where her father waited on the doctor who would examine his eyes. . . .

The book version reads:

> A nurse *held* the door open for them. Judge McKelva going first, then his daughter Laurel, then his wife Fay, they *walked* into the windowless room where the doctor would make his examination. . . .

Works Cited

Prenshaw, Peggy Whitman, ed. *Conversations with Eudora Welty.* Jackson: UP of Mississippi, 1984.
Welty, Eudora. *The Eye of the Story.* New York: Random House Vintage Books, 1979.
———. *The Optimist's Daughter.* 1972. New York: Random House Vintage Books, 1979.
———. *The Robber Bridegroom.* 1942. New York: Harcourt Brace Jovanovich, 1970.

General Essays

Eudora Welty

Several years ago Eudora Welty wrote to the *New Yorker* a witty letter, by no means so mild as on the surface it appeared to be, protesting against some observations on Southern writers that had been made by Edmund Wilson in the course of a review of William Faulkner's *Intruder in the Dust.* Like all Southern writers, Wilson had said, Faulkner was provincial; he was out of touch with contemporary currents of thought. His provincialism, Wilson granted, was in many ways an asset, but he went on to argue that Faulkner's remoteness from the great cities, which are the birthplace of modern fiction, had "apparently made it impossible for him to acquire complete expertness in an art that demands of the artists the closest attention and care."

This, Miss Welty objected, was like criticizing Cézanne because he lived in Aix rather than Paris. "Such critical irrelevance, favorable or unfavorable," she said, "the South has long been used to, but now Mr. Wilson fancies it up and it will resound a little louder. Mr. Faulkner all the while continues to be capable of passion, of love, of wisdom, perhaps of prophecy, toward his material. Isn't that enough? Such qualities can identify themselves anywhere in the world and in any century without furnishing an address or references." Mr. Wilson, she noted, tried to explain Faulkner's descriptive powers by saying that the Southern world is different and makes a different impact. She asked: "Could the simple, though superfluous, explanation not be that the recipient of the impact, Mr. Faulkner, is the different component here, possessing the brain as he does, and that the superiority of the work done lies in the brain?"

Although Miss Welty's Jackson is no great distance from Mr. Faulkner's Oxford, it was not mere regional patriotism that inspired her protest. She was expressing a philosophy of literature, a philosophy that is, of course, embodied in her own work as well as in William Faulkner's. Like Faulkner, and unlike most contemporary writers, she has spent the greater part of her life in the region in which she was

° From *College English* 14 (November 1952):69–76. Copyright 1952 by The National Council of Teachers of English. Reprinted with permission of the publisher.

born, and, again like him, she has found in that region all that she needed to exercise and challenge her talents. She would never condemn an author for being urban or cosmopolitan, but she would defend her own right, or the right of any other author, to be neither. Provincialism, she feels, is not a sufficient explanation of a writer's merits, nor is it inevitably a source of short-comings. A writer can be provincial in the geographical sense without being intellectually or aesthetically provincial: one does not have to live in cities, as Mr. Wilson seems to believe, in order to read and understand James and Proust and Joyce.

Miss Welty was born in Jackson, Mississippi, in 1909, and was educated at Mississippi State College for Women, the University of Wisconsin, and Columbia University. After working for a time in New York City, she returned to Jackson, and there she has lived, except for brief trips, ever since. Her first published story appeared in a little magazine, *Manuscript,* in 1936, and her first collection of stories, *A Curtain of Green,* was published in 1941. She has published four books since then: a novella, *The Robber Bridegroom;* another collection of short stories, *The Wide Net;* a novel, *Delta Wedding;* and a collection of related stories, *The Golden Apples.* Her work has been frequently honored: she once won second prize and twice won first prize in the O. Henry Memorial Award, and her work has also appeared in *The Best American Short Stories.* She was given an award by the American Academy of Arts and Letters in 1944.

Miss Welty has been even more faithful to her section of Mississippi than Faulkner has to his: a story is set in New York City, one in New Orleans, one in San Francisco, and everything else is close to the Natchez Trace. She has not, however, sought to create a region of her own, as Faulkner has done with his Yoknapatawpha County, and to that extent she is a less self-conscious regionalist than he. She has merely taken her material where she found it—i.e., not far from home. As Katherine Anne Porter said in the Introduction she wrote for Miss Welty's first book, *A Curtain of Green,* "She gets her right nourishment from the source natural to her—her experience so far has been quite enough for her and of precisely the right kind."

When *A Curtain of Green* appeared, in 1941, some reviewers quickly concluded that the author was one more Southern realist with a penchant for squalor. "Like many Southern writers," *Time* wrote, "she has a strong taste for melodrama, and is preoccupied with the demented, the deformed, the queer, the highly spiced. Of the 17 pieces, only two report states of experience which could be called normal." The statistics are probably accurate: the stories deal with such characters as a feeble-minded girl, a moonshiner and his faithless wife, a pair of poverty-stricken sharecroppers, a couple of hoboes, and a victim of dementia praecox. One story, indeed, "Clytie," seems

to present its once prominent family as a museum of Southern decadence: the father is paralyzed; one son has committed suicide;
another is alcoholic; one daughter is mad; and the daughter who has
been the mainstay of the family drowns herself in a rain barrel. This
might well be called Southern Gothic.

But if one reads carefully, it is apparent that Miss Welty is not
preoccupied with violence and horror, in the way that Erskine Caldwell so often is and not even to the extent that William Faulkner
sometimes is. The meaning of the story is never in the violence, nor
is the abnormality of the characters their important quality. Take,
for instance, "The Hitch-Hikers." Salesman Tom Harris picks up two
men along the road, one of them with a guitar. He feeds them, and,
when he comes to the hotel in which he intends to spend the night,
he makes arrangements for them to sleep on the back porch. But
suddenly word comes that one of the men has hit the other, the
guitar player, over the head with a bottle. The latter is taken to the
hospital, while the former is locked up in the hotel, the jail being
occupied by a Negro. The salesman goes to a party, as he had planned,
but it fails to distract him, nor does he respond when one of the
girls comes to the hotel for him. In the morning he learns that the
guitar player is dead. After listening to the other man's confession,
Harris gives the guitar to a little Negro boy and goes on about his
business.

The act of violence seems perfectly casual. "I was jist tired of
him always uppin' and makin' a noise about ever'thing," the assailant
says. And later: "He was uppity, though. He bragged. He carried a
gittar around." The murder is so casual in appearance that one is
horrified at the thought of what its real causes must be. The deeper
meaning of the story, however, is in the effect of the incident on
the salesman. After the party Harris tries to sleep.

> But it was too like other evenings, this town was too like other
> towns, for him to move out of this lying still clothed on the bed,
> even into comfort or despair. Even the rain—there was often rain,
> there was often a party, and there had been other violence not of
> his doing—other fights, not quite so pointless, but fights in his car;
> fights, unheralded confessions, sudden love-making—none of any of
> this his, not to keep, but belonging to the people of these towns he
> passed through, coming out of their rooted pasts and their mock
> rambles, coming out of their time. He himself had no time. He was
> free, helpless.

It is interesting that Miss Welty had used a figure comparable
to Harris as a symbol of rootlessness in her first published story,
"Death of a Traveling Salesman." This salesman, sick and lost, comes
upon a man and woman, the latter pregnant, living in primitive

poverty. It is the simplest, most basic kind of human association, and the salesman is moved by it.

> He wanted to leap up, to say to her, I have been sick and I found out, only then, how lonely I am. Is it too late? My heart puts up a struggle inside me, and you may have heard it, protesting against emptiness. . . . It should be full, he would rush on to tell her, thinking of his heart now as a deep lake, it should be holding love like other hearts. It should be flooded with love.

In this early story, which in some ways is reminiscent of Sherwood Anderson, Miss Welty is more explicit than she ever lets herself be in her later work. It is a tremendously effective story just the same, and, though the announced subject is death, the real theme is life.

Squalor, violence, and decadence have in themselves no importance for Miss Welty. They are merely facts, and facts, whether pleasant or unpleasant, are no more than means to an end. What matters in her stories is never the thing that happens but the effect of the thing on human beings. Her concern, in other words, is with states of mind, and her emphasis falls upon those emotional states that cannot be easily articulated. In "Clytie," for instance, the horrors are not intended to shock us; that would be all too easy to do; Miss Welty's task, far more difficult, is to show us their effect on Clytie. As Miss Porter says, "The very shape of madness takes place before your eyes in a straight account of actions and speech, the personal appearance and habits of dress of the main character and her family." In a simpler and even more memorable story, "A Worn Path," there is nothing at all except the details of an old Negro woman's journey to the city to get medicine for her grandson, but it gives us a sense of human fortitude that is almost unbearable in its sad intensity.

Miss Welty knows how, if ever an author did, to let facts speak for themselves, but she does not systematically refrain, in the Hemingway manner, from the direct account of emotional states. Although her later work is never so explicit as "Death of a Traveling Salesman," she does not hesitate to tell us what is going on within the mind of a character when it serves her purpose to do so. With beautiful adroitness, of which only a deliberate analyst can be conscious, she slips from the objective to the subjective, at just the moment to achieve the maximum of revelation. Her method varies to suit her themes: in "A Worn Path" everything is done with objective description and conversation; in "A Piece of News" there is a single, sudden illumination of the minds of Ruby and Clyde; in "A Curtain of Green" we are now outside and now inside the mind of the bereaved, bewildered Mrs. Larkin. So far as technique is concerned, her characteristic quality is just this perfect balance between the objective and the subjective.

In another sense her work is remarkably objective. As Miss Porter observes, there is only one story in *A Curtain of Green* that could conceivably be regarded as autobiographical, and in the second collection of stories, *The Wide Net,* there is not even one. Each story is an excursion of her imagination into the minds of others, and one finds in the two collections an extraordinary variety of subject matter. It is not merely that she writes about Negroes, poor whites, decayed aristocrats, the middle-class women of Southern towns, and, in *The Wide Net,* about the past as well as the present; her emotional range stretches from the poignant to the overwhelming, and from humor to the blackest tragedy. Nor do her stories always conform to the patterns that have been discussed. There is, for example, "Powerhouse," an enigmatic story of a Negro orchestra leader with a strong, wild rhythm in it, or there is "The Wide Net," with its fine colloquial style and country humor. Miss Welty's versatility baffles the pigeonholers.

Yet in all this variety there are, of course, persistent themes. The first is the mystery of personality, which Miss Welty perceives in two forms—the mystery of others and the mystery of self. The failure of human beings to understand one another, one of the perennial themes of literature, she treats often as tragedy and sometimes, as in "A Piece of News" and "The Wide Net," as comedy, though always with serious overtones. The mystery of identity, central in such a story as "Old Mr. Marblehall," figures in some degree in almost every one of her tales.

Closely related to this first theme is her second, the problem of what brings people together and what holds them apart. She writes about separateness in "Death of a Traveling Salesman," "The Hitch-Hikers," and many others, about love and separateness in "The Key," "A Worn Path," and "A Memory." In "A Still Moment," a kind of parable involving Lorenzo Dow the evangelist, Murrell the bandit, and Audubon the scientist, Dow thinks about separateness: "He could understand God's giving Separateness first and then giving Love to follow and heal in its wonder; but God had reversed this, and given Love first and then Separateness, as though it did not matter to Him which came first." At any rate, Miss Welty is saying, love and separateness are equally real; they are, perhaps, the great realities.

Some of Miss Welty's stories have been called obscure, and she would not try to refute the charge. She has said in one of her rare excursions into criticism:

> The fine story writers seem to be in a sense obstructionists. As if they hold back their own best interests. It's a strange illusion. For if we look to the source of the deepest pleasure we receive from a writer, how surprising it seems that the very source is the quondam

obstruction. The fact is, in seeking our source of pleasure we have entered another world again. We are speaking of beauty. And beauty is not a blatant or promiscuous quality: indeed at her finest she is somewhat associated with obstruction—with reticence of a number of kinds.

Miss Welty's short stories are not for inattentive readers; the best of them yield their meaning only to an effort of the imagination. But the effort is worth making. Speaking as a writer, Miss Welty has said, "In the end, our technique is sensitivity, and beauty may be our reward." This can be applied to the readers of Miss Welty's stories: sensitivity is what they must bring to them, and their reward is beauty.

In her Introduction to *A Curtain of Green,* Katherine Anne Porter spoke of the pressure that publishers exert upon short-story writers in order to get them to produce that more marketable commodity, a novel. This pressure she urged Miss Welty to resist. "There is nothing to hinder her from writing novels if she wishes or believes she can. I can only say that her good gift, just as it is now, alive and flourishing, should not be retarded by a perfectly artificial demand upon her to do the conventional thing."

Miss Welty was to come to the novel in her own time and her own way, but first, between the publication of *A Curtain of Green* and the publication of *The Wide Net,* she brought forth an experimental novella, *The Robber Bridegroom.* Located in Mississippi in the old days, it has elements both of the European fairy story and of the American tall tale. The central action is as implausible as anything in Grimm, and as plausibly narrated. The flat, poker-faced narrative, however, is enriched by a dry humor that delights in the absurdities that are being described, and it is interrupted by descriptive and meditative passages of great beauty and by colorfully fantastic episodes in which historical and legendary figures such as Little Harp and Mike Fink take part.

It is an engaging little story, and one feels that Miss Welty had a good time writing it, but the core of seriousness is not to be disregarded. In one of its aspects the novella is a parable on the theme of the mystery of personality. Jamie Lockhart, the robber bridegroom, plays two roles, and Rosamund Musgrove, his mistress, presents two personalities to him. Her father, Clement Musgrove, is single-minded in his simplicity, but it is suggested that his beautiful first wife and his ugly second wife are actually the same person. There are other ambiguities as well on which a curious mind can meditate.

The Robber Bridegroom has its excellences, but it was in *Delta Wedding* (1946) that Miss Welty was to show what she could do with the novel. The book is a triumph of sensitivity: the atmosphere of the Delta in September; the excitement and commotion of a household preparing for a wedding; the feeling of a crowded house; the feeling of a house full of children; the special quality of a particular and unusual family, the Fairchilds. It is a technical triumph, too: the constant, subtle shifting of the point of view to render the most that can be rendered.

Outwardly little enough happens. Dabney, second of the Fairchild daughters, is getting married to Troy Flavin, her father's overseer, a poor boy from up in the hills. The relatives gather, and there are parties, excursions, rehearsals. Dabney's Uncle George arrives, with the disconcerting news that Robbie, his wife, has left him, but she subsequently appears. Among the visiting relatives is little Laura McRaven, Dabney's nine-year-old cousin, who has recently lost her mother, and in the parts of the story that are told from her point of view we not only get a sense of the intense juvenile life that is going on but also, because of her responsiveness to everything that is unique in the Fairchilds and Shellmound, are given fresh insight into the adult world.

Gradually we realize that George, rather than Dabney, is the novel's central figure. On her arrival, Laura is told of an act of rather pointless heroism in which George has recently engaged. This act, as we later learn, or the pointlessness of it, is what has alienated Robbie. The scene of George on the railroad bridge with his feeble-minded niece is referred to again and again, until we perceive that it is the key to George's character and that George is the quintessential Fairchild. The outsiders, Robbie and Troy, meditate on the mysteries of the Fairchild character, and so does Laura, who is only half a Fairchild and finds Shellmound strange and wonderful. Even Ellen, the mistress of Shellmound, who has mothered half-a-dozen Fairchilds, is still an outsider, though she rests more easily with the enigma than the others. To the born Fairchilds, of course, there is no mystery; they accept George, as they accept themselves, without any conception that he or they could be different from what they are. Although we look through the eyes of many of the characters, we are never taken inside George's mind, and to the end he remains a mystery, though one that we constantly feel we are on the verge of solving.

If *Delta Wedding* is one of the finest novels of recent years, it is because Miss Welty's sensibility is equal to the burden she has imposed upon it, the burden of a sustained narrative. There is nothing higher to be said in praise of *Delta Wedding* than that it is just as good, and good in just the same way, as her best short stories. It is held up from beginning to end by unfailing insight into the subtle and complicated emotions of its characters and by a matchless gift for making us feel what they feel.

In *The Golden Apples* (1949) Miss Welty did not attempt that kind of sustained effort. The same characters figure in various episodes, and of some of them we have a cumulative revelation, but each episode stands by itself. It is, in part, a book about small-town life, and the quality of its understanding of small-town ways reminds one of Anderson and Faulkner. In another, more important aspect it is concerned with the mystery of personality. King MacLain, who periodically vanishes from Morgana, and who affects the imaginations of its people, is an obvious enigma, but he is really no more mysterious than Miss Eckhart the music teacher or Easter the orphan or either of his sons or Virgie Rainey or Loch Morrison.

The resourcefulness with which Miss Welty explores her mysteries is exciting to watch. Regarded simply as short stories, the episodes of *The Golden Apples,* with a single exception, belong with her best work. Take, for instance, "Music from Spain," in which Eugene MacLain is jolted out of his routine and into a state of heightened sensibility by an arbitrary act—slapping his wife's face as it happens— and spends a remarkable day in the company of a Spanish musician. Or there is the final story, "The Wanderers," with its wonderfully evocative portrayal of Virgie Rainey.

The title of the book is, of course, an allusion to a Greek legend, and so is the title of the first story, "Shower of Gold." And in almost all the stories there is some suggestion of myth. "Moon Lake," for example, which is in part an amusing account of life in a girls' camp, has its parable of death and resurrection.

I do not want to suggest that Miss Welty belongs to the school of authors who think that the retelling of an ancient legend makes a modern masterpiece. I am merely saying that her work has acquired something of the quality of fable. In *The Robber Bridegroom* and a couple of short stories she has deliberately created legends of her own, but these are less important than the tales in which the ordinary events of life in contemporary Mississippi take on the purity and— to use a reckless word—the universality of legend.

It is not easy to say how she has learned to do this. Even if Miss Porter had not told us, we would have no doubt that Miss Welty has read widely. She has learned, we can be sure, from many writers, but none of them has left a clear mark upon her work. Her admiration for her fellow-Mississippian, William Faulkner, is great, but his way of doing things is not hers. Nor is Henry James's way her way, though he is another writer she has certainly studied with great care. Her work has often been compared with that of Virginia Woolf and Katherine Mansfield, but the resemblances seem to me superficial. In the beginning, I suspect, she learned a good deal from Katherine Anne Porter, about both the shaping of a story and the manipulation of words, but she has followed her own path of development, so that today the individuality of her prose is as obvious as it is quietly asserted.

Although her work has been frequently honored and, with each volume, more and more highly praised, she has failed to win the approval of certain critics who are to be taken seriously, among them Diana Trilling, Isaac Rosenfeld, and Margaret Marshall. They agree with her admirers that she is greatly talented, but what she does with her talents distresses them. They feel, to begin with, that she exploits her technical virtuosity for its own sake, but their quarrel is larger than that. Mrs. Trilling, reviewing *Delta Wedding,* said that she disliked equally the literary manner of the book and the "culture out of which it grows and which it describes so fondly," and she accused Miss Welty of a lack of moral discrimination. Miss Marshall, after complaining about the "finespun writing" in *The Golden Apples,* summed up her indictment: "The book does, I suppose, convey the quality of life among the main families of Morgana, but this is its only accomplishment, and the quality of life among the main families of Morgana is, to speak rudely, not worth 244 pages."

Miss Marshall's comment, it seems to me, is not so much rude as narrow. If one begins with the assumption that life in a small Mississippi town is not worth writing about, one is likely to miss the larger implications of a book about such a town. (Hamilton Basso, a Southerner, has testified that Morgana "can be taken to represent not only all small Southern towns but the whole Deep South.") If, moreover, one has no sympathy with the kind of life that is being portrayed, one may easily call a writer who does like that sort of life uncritical. And, finally, if a way of life is distasteful, the skill a writer employs to evoke that way of life may seem wasted.

Miss Welty is, to be sure, a Southern writer, in the sense that the South is her subject matter, just as it is Faulkner's. Furthermore, again like Faulkner, she lives in the midst of the life she writes about. She is a writer with roots, a fact significantly reflected in all her work. But if she shares in the heritage of the South, she also shares in the literary tradition of Western civilization, and shares at least as fully and deeply as the most up-to-date New York intellectual. And not only that: she proves, as the good regionalists have always proved, that the deeper one goes into the heart of a region, the more one transcends its geographical boundaries.

Eudora Welty and the
City of Man
Elmo Howell°

When Jane Austen died in 1817, Walter Scott wrote a tribute in which he summed up the difference between her fiction and his own. He could do the "big bow-wow strain" like any now going, the marshalling of events and sweep of history, but not the intimate play of daily domestic life, which Miss Austen did so well.[1] Eudora Welty admires Jane Austen and owes much to her and indeed stands in the same relation to fellow-Mississippian William Faulkner that Austen stood to Scott. With little interest in history or social themes, she concentrates on the ordinary people of her country who go about the business of loving and hating and talking about their neighbors as if there were nothing more important in the world. But within this close range, she scrutinizes her subject and registers its vibrations with a tenderness of attention that places her closer to the heartbeat of her region than Faulkner himself.

If she shows greater variation than her eighteenth-century predecessor, it is not because her aim is different but because she lives in another age and her work inevitably shows it. Like Miss Austen, she remains aloof from social and political events of her time, but with one important difference. In spite of the French Revolution and Napoleon, England was confident and self-contained, and the Catherines, Elizabeths, and Emmas could go on flirting and finding husbands in a way of life that was apparently immutable. After two hundred years, even though Miss Welty's village remains intact, the world outside is not, and disturbing voices are beginning to be heard. Instead of writing about home and social ties, the old standbys of the English novel, young writers today are peering, in Miss Welty's words, through "knot-holes of isolation."[2]

She does not take much to isolation—as no one could who believes in the family as she does—but feels very keenly the plight of the individual who pursues his own dream, never quite going the whole way perhaps but suffering from loneliness even while playing his part in the family life. Thus in the midst of what appears light comedy, she shifts abruptly to the subjective, and at times in fact appears uncertain where her main interest lies, with the individual or the social circle he belongs to. She veers from characters like Miss Eckhart and Miss Julia Mortimer and the other seekers of "the golden apples" to the village at large, loud with the clatter of ordinary life. Jane Austen's interest could not have been so divided because her audience

° From *Georgia Review* 33 (Winter 1979):770–82. Reprinted with permission of the author.

would not have tolerated the private eye in fiction. She keeps passion offstage, concealed in a social mode, and so achieves a synthesis that Miss Welty's fiction lacks.

The gulf between "June Recital" and "Why I Live at the P. O.," for example, is very great indeed. One is in the major, the other a minor key. Miss Eckhart, Virgie Rainey, and Cassie Morrison are tragic figures, while in the other story Miss Welty is out for fun and the reader is not asked to consider what lies behind the old maid's spiteful antics. These disparities, however, are more apparent than real. In the long view, as one takes leave of a Welty story, the private voice is lost in the hubbub of family or community at large: the vision is essentially social. Whatever problems the individual may have—and they are sometimes very great indeed—can best be dealt with among those he knows best in some sort of conformity to the general pattern.

This public rather than private view sets her work in perspective, frames it in time and space and, like Miss Austen's, adorns it with the particularities of her culture, which to the outside world at least seems almost as remote as eighteenth-century Hampshire. She has not striven for these effects. She is too honest in the business of presenting life as it comes to her and to people about her, informed by a principle of civility and moral character handed down from the past. In this respect she is most Southern, more than in those light touches of speech and manner which have identified her with Mississippi; for if the Old South produced anything of note in the American experience, it was the conviction that living itself is an art, which requires careful fostering. Of all the Southern writers, Miss Welty is most sensitive to the grace of manner and to those dissonances that threaten from the outside. Such is the precarious balance of her world, where not much seems to happen except a lot of talk but where in fact she outlines in her own quiet way what being civilized is all about.

II

Although she describes herself as socially underfoot in Jackson and her friends think of her in that way, Miss Welty is a very private person with a bent for writing about private experiences, however much she participates in community life. Her most dramatic moments are in this vein, when like the poet she explores the inarticulate region of the mind and heart. She shows a predilection towards the character, usually female, who dramatizes her loneliness—like Cassie Morrison in "June Recital" and Shelley Fairchild in *Delta Wedding*—and wonders why nothing ever happens to *her* as other lives are being fulfilled. These characters are the still point of her drama.

Cassie cries out against the tragedy of Miss Eckhart and Virgie Rainey (neither of whom she loves), the suffering and shock of their lives, as she sits apart with her "girl's business" of dyeing scarves, remembering that on the hayride she allowed no one to touch her, even on the hand.[3] Shelley Fairchild keeps a diary on the eve of Dabney's marriage, unable to go directly to happiness like her younger sister, but gifted with a power of reflection that frightens and paralyzes. "Shelley was sickeningly afraid of life, life itself, afraid *for* life."[4]

This type of character is recurrent in Miss Welty's fiction—Nina Carmichael, Laura McRaven, Lexie Renfro, Laurel Hand are variations—but too passive to command much interest, even when, as in the case of Laurel, she is given a leading role. They are all sad people—*The Optimist's Daughter* is one of Miss Welty's saddest stories—because their lives are in some basic way unfulfilled, although before the world they acquiesce and carry on. But there are other lonely characters who excite more interest because they do *not* stand still, who lurch out at life, sudden, grotesque, and finally impotent, in a game they are obviously not fitted for. Miss Eckhart, the piano teacher of "June Recital," is anything but passive. She came to Morgana, Mississippi, and in spite of aversion to her foreign ways, set up a studio, took in pupils, and made a home for her old mother. For this she was respected, but later her private life became a matter of attention. At first, there was the crazy Negro in the hedge one night, "the terrible fate that came on her, that people could not forgive"[5]—they thought she should leave Morgana after that. Then there was Mr. Sissum, the shoe salesman, who remained completely unaware of Miss Eckhart's attachment; but at his death she behaved in a manner the whole town talked about. "In Mr. Sissum's life Miss Eckhart, as everybody said, had never known what to do; and now she did this"—pushed forward to his grave, nodding her head and making a strange sound, and ladies had to hold her. "After the way she cried in the cemetery—for they decided it must have been crying she did—some ladies stopped their little girls from learning any more music. . . ." (p. 55).

And finally Virgie Rainey. Virgie is the favorite pupil, not just because she is best but because she is not afraid of Miss Eckhart and knows how to handle her. The others are held back by something strange about her, the unfamiliar manners. When someone plays particularly well, for example, she never seems to notice but goes over to the bird cage and tells the canary something. " 'Enough from *you* for today,' she would call to you over your shoulder." Virgie pays no attention to all this, ignores the "Yankeeness," and breaks through to Miss Eckhart and wins her over by indifference and sheer impudence. She will not play until the all-important metronome is removed from before her, and Miss Eckhart unaccountably gives in—

because Virgie will be heard from in the world, she says. How can Virgie be heard from in the world, and where does Miss Eckhart think she is now? "The very place to prove Miss Eckhart crazy was on her own subject, piano playing: she didn't know what she was talking about" (p. 60).

And of course they are right. Virgie winds up as the town floozy, carrying on with sailors and playing the piano in the local picture show. And just as they thought, after taming her old mistress she abuses her. The final scene, where she cuts the crazed old woman being led off to a public asylum, is almost too painful to contemplate. Both are "human beings terribly at large—roaming like lost beasts," but Virgie takes hold of life in a way denied the older woman. Miss Eckhart tried and failed utterly. "Her love never did anybody any good."

Miss Julia Mortimer, the schoolteacher of *Losing Battles,* is a later version of Miss Eckhart. She never marries, and no one can imagine her ever having been in love, carrying a banner "like St. George," out for the dragon of ignorance in her country. But she wants to love, like the music teacher, and settles on student protégées who are to go on to the state Normal and become teachers to carry on the torch after her time. "Teach, teach, teach! Till I dropped in harness! Like the rest of 'em!"[6] These overtures come to nothing, and Miss Julia dies alone.

Only the life that sparkles around these sad, wasted lives, usually on a lower level of mind and character, makes them bearable at all. But Miss Welty takes Miss Julia and Miss Eckhart very seriously. With them her manner becomes tense and concentrated, she has absolute control. Even so, she will not wholly join with them and subscribe to their partial view when there is so much going on in the world that they cannot or will not see. They look out from a promontory over the heads of their neighbors, who figure not so much as fellow human beings as mere possibilities in some scheme of rearrangement. More than is good for them, they are touched by pride. The June recital is the one great event in the music teacher's year but only another occasion to the ladies of Morgana—like Miss Nell's rook parties—where they can dress up and come together. How much better for Miss Eckhart if she could enter lightly into these affairs, realizing that little girls of nice families take music lessons as a matter of course and that nobody takes them seriously, least of all Virgie Rainey, who is not nice at all and comes from a family that is hardly respectable. Miss Welty's irony is the more effective because it cuts both ways and because she herself at times hardly knows where her sympathies lie.

And so the reader has to move warily because he is concerned with a fundamental question which lies at the heart of Miss Welty's work: Is simple animal happiness enough, or must one be involved with those intangibles of character that she obviously admires in Miss Julia and Miss Eckhart? And what about those who seem to be left out altogether, to whom nothing ever happens? The questions are not answered—perhaps there is no answer—and so Miss Welty returns to the cheerfulness of social life. "There's something I think's better to have than love," says Edna Earle in *The Ponder Heart;* "that's company."[7] And for the long stretch, Miss Welty seems to agree. Since so often there is no rationale behind suffering, what is to be done except to recognize it with pity and turn back to life, where happiness is not evenly distributed but where there is a great deal for everyone if he will accept it. Beyond this charmed circle, disturbing cries are being heard in the novels of her contemporaries, but here at least it is still possible to live the good life. And the good life is the most important matter of consideration to Miss Welty.

III

British and American novels are intrinsically different, says Richard Chase, deriving from the principles on which the countries were founded, one on tradition and cultural accretion, the other on revolution. Until recently at least, British society as reflected in the novel suggested the normative view. Social man was the focus of interest, while the waifs and strays—"loners" of modern fiction—were kept in subordinate roles. Movement was towards reconciliation of opposites for participation in the general life, which found a place for the eccentrics of Scott and Dickens but not a Roger Chillingworth or Captain Ahab. No disturbing questions were left over at the end, where the villains were disposed of and the rest brought in to the comforts of hearth and home. Our own society is too new and too variously composed for such comforts, says Chase, and so the American novelists have broken away from the social to the individual consciousness. Instead of health and wholeness, they project a fragmented world where every man goes his own way.[8]

However just this observation may be concerning the American novel in general, it does not hold with the Southern novel, which has remained close to the pattern of the mother country. The bent towards allegory and the "heresy of the didactic," to use Poe's phrase, are New England attitudes which found no following in the South. Mark Twain is closer to the English, says F. R. Leavis, in spite of the frontier image than any other major American writer, including Henry James, whose heritage of Puritan introspection sets him apart from the tradition of Fielding and Dickens.[9] The South—and Mark Twain's Missouri was a part of the Old South—is the only section of the country with an unbroken cultural identity, which gives to its

novelists over a long period of time—Simms, Twain, and Faulkner—
a sense of continuity and values commonly held. It is only with this
distinction in mind that Eudora Welty's "Southernness" has any real
meaning. The regional manner comes natural to her, but she is most
Southern in choosing to write about a whole society, not a sick one;
for whatever the outside world may have thought about the South,
and Mississippi in particular, the people who live there have had no
doubts about it. To them, and to Miss Welty, it is a rational world
of checks and balances, informed by principles of conduct handed
down from the past.

Miss Welty does not insist on these matters, but her type of
comedy can exist only on a foundation of social order where certain
principles are quietly observed. Quietness is one of her virtues. In
"A Memory," she describes the impression made on a sensitive young
girl by a party of vulgar people who settle near her on the beach.
In loud, jeering voices, they seem "driven by foolish intent to insult
each other, all of which they enjoyed with a hilarity which astonished
my heart."[10] Even after they are gone, she feels "victimized" by the
imprints left in the sand by their ugly bodies, and looking away
towards the white pavilion, "I felt pity suddenly overtake me, and
I burst into tears."

In "The Burning," her only story about the Civil War, she
describes the destruction by the Federal Army of a home outside
Jackson, where two sisters, living alone with their servants, hang
themselves after the burning and the rape of the younger. Miss Welty
is not trying to revive old partisan feelings: the fate of the sisters is
symbolic. Not only a house is destroyed but the decency of life by
an intrusive element incapable of understanding what it destroys.
When a soldier rides a horse into the parlor where the ladies are
sitting, the elder sister turns indifferently to her maid: "Delilah, what
is it you came in your dirty apron to tell me?" The maid has come
on a homey errand: the eggs taken from the setting hen are "addled."[11]
And now this preserve of ordered life close to the natural world that
Miss Welty loves is to end in an orgy of horror. After the burning,
rape, and public humiliation, the drummer boy of the regiment catches
Miss Theo's peafowl, Marco and Polo, and wrings their necks in the
yard. "Nobody could look at those bird-corpses; nobody did." The
terrible pathos is not in the fate of the women but in the triumph
of a particular type of mind.

"The Burning" and the incident in "A Memory" are Miss Welty's
way of pointing up social values: men should be able to live, if not
with love, at least with civility and mutual respect. *Delta Wedding*
is her most elaborate expression of this ideal. As in most of her work,
the individual with his problems sometimes gets in the way—in this
case, characters like Laura McRaven, George and Shelley Fairchild;

but she never loses sight of the larger harmony of the Fairchild plantation, which becomes a microcosm of the South and in a larger sense of the civilized order. Not much actually happens in the novel, but out of the bustle of preparation for a wedding (covering about a week in the fall of 1923) the history of a family emerges covering five generations. The first Fairchilds came to the Delta in the first half of the nineteenth century. One son died in the Mexican War, others in the War Between the States, but the family survived and prospered. In 1923, Battle Fairchild heads the clan with his quiet Virginia wife and eight children, and Shellmound on the Yazoo is the center of a Fairchild world that reaches out in all directions from Memphis to Jackson. To Laura McRaven of Jackson, who feels the deprivations of living in the city, the handsome Fairchild cousins are the "sensations of life" and Shellmound is the center of the universe where all wonderful things happen.[12]

Laura enters the Delta suddenly and dramatically, as the Yellow Dog descends from the bluffs at Yazoo City and hills and trees give way and the flat cotton land begins. The fields shimmer in the heat "like the wing of a lighted dragon fly" while large clouds and specks of buzzards float over the immensity "as wide and high as the sun." The windows of the train are propped open with sticks of kindling wood, and sometimes yellow butterflies, which seem to race with the train, fly in one window and out another. And along the way, Mr. Doolittle, the old engineer whom everybody knows at Fairchilds, stops in an open field to pick "some specially fine goldenrod—for whom, she could not know" (p. 4).

Miss Welty believes in place in fiction and spends a lot of time with it—as important, she says, as plot and character[13]—which means first of all the feel of a particular landscape at a particular time of the year. The peculiar light on the cotton fields, goldenrod, and yellow butterflies mean fall, which gives the novel a reflective richness altogether different from the sudden and disturbing spring scenes of *The Optimist's Daughter,* for example. Miss Welty, at home with the changing moods of nature, is scrupulous with detail, though the casual reader might overlook how much of the gardener's heart is in her work. Flowers are a special province, the wild as well as garden variety, the enumeration of which becomes a kind of poetry: black-eyed Susan, Queen Anne's lace, Cape jessamine, spider lilies, crape myrtle, a rich panoply of roses—the Etoile, Lady Hillington, Maréchal Niel, and old-fashioned Seven-Sisters—the abelia bell with attendant hummingbird; and then the homey plants of Brunswick-town where the Negroes live: princess feather, false dragonhead, four o'clocks, okra, butter-bean vines along the porch and the cool umbrella of the chinaberry tree, where chickens fluff in the afternoon "with shut eyes in dust holes" (p. 127).

The names are not gratuitous, however, but take on cultural meaning, like the flora of Brunswick-town or the Christmas rose, rare in Mississippi, in Mary Shannon's portrait, drawn by her Fairchild husband (or was it Audubon?) how many generations ago. "I spend a great deal of time on my names," she says, because names suggest place and social standing, "especially in the South."[14] Flavin is a peculiar name," says Aunt Tempe, referring to Troy Flavin, the underbred overseer from the hills of North Mississippi who is to marry Dabney Fairchild (p. 111). Without the least impression of snobbery, the lines are drawn between classes as well as between races. The names of her Negro characters, very much a part of the Fairchild family, shine in their separateness: Partheny, Pinchy, Bitsy, Zell, Man-Son, Juju, Aunt Studney, Roxy, Sylvanus, Oneida, Sudy, and Pleas. All this is as it should be, Miss Welty suggests. Flavin is a "peculiar name," but Troy is no fool, and the Negroes, within the social arrangement taken for granted in the Delta, bear their own pride which has nothing to do with race.

But place involves more than the natural world or the people who happen to live there. It means rather the two together, after generations of interaction of one upon the other. Time is the important element. The present moment has meaning only in the larger perspective, and at Shellmound there are reminders everywhere of other generations of Fairchilds: the tremendous dictionary in the library that came through "high water and fire in Port Gibson"; the dark painting above the bookcase of Great-Great-Uncle George, murdered on the Natchez Trace; Marmion, the empty mansion across the river where James Fairchild was killed in a duel; Great-Aunt Mac still wearing mourning for her young husband killed at Shiloh, and Great-Aunt Shannon who talks conversationally with Uncle Denis and Aunt Rowena and Great-Uncle George, "who had all died no telling how long ago" (p. 13). Yet how lightly the past rests on the present. No one spends much time in the library at Shellmound ("there was so much going on in real life"), and the sorrows of the old aunts have worked through the years into singularities and dear possessions of the whole family. Great-Aunt Mashula Hines's dulcimer still hangs on the wall, her cookbook is still in use in the kitchen. "Oh, Mashula's coconut!" Aunt Tempe interrupts her flow of talk as she accepts a slice of cake on her arrival (p. 107); and the wedding cake is placed "right in the center of that large rose that's the middle of Mashula's cloth" (p. 201).

This legacy of the past is a source of pleasure and strength. Arriving from Inverness, Tempe is at first critical of the old-fashioned appearance of the house, the "high, shabby old rooms" that go unchanged through the years, with "little knickknacks and playthings and treasures" that remain on the mantel even during Dabney's wedding. But this, as Tempe knows, is a sign of life. "Oh, there's always so much—so *much* happening here!" (p. 190). She is a part of it, of course, with the commotion of her entrance leading a parade of boxes with Dabney's wedding gift, a forty-eight piece luncheon set. As for the marriage with the overseer, she is a little vindictive in her satisfaction, since her own daughter disappointed the family by marrying a Northern man and raising up "a lot of little Yankees in Illinois" (p. 107). "Oh, the mortification of *life*, Ellen!" (p. 104). But Dabney comes in to show her the wedding dress, nieces and nephews swarm around her to be hugged and sent away—and then comes the news that her brother George's wife (Robbie Reid, old man Swanson's granddaughter who used to keep the store) has had the nerve to leave her husband. Battle greets Tempe with a friendly spank, and then there is his wife Ellen, gentle and abstracted, and expecting again. Vi'let comes with a pitcher of lemonade, and other servants everywhere are carrying on their business: Howard pondering, indifferent, in the middle of the room over the position of the altar, his special charge; with the big feet of Bitsy and Bitsy's little boy hanging inside the room while they wash the windows, or carry on idly with someone outside. "If they knew Aunt Tempe could see their feet, they would be moving their rags" (p. 97). Shellmound, says Ruth M. Vande Kieft, is "as thoroughly lived in as any house in fiction or out,"[15] and that is because Miss Welty knows that life fully lived involves time and place and complex relationships with other human beings. The past is in it, and the future, and the present moment is always a shared experience, like Dabney's wedding, in which everyone in the family and on the plantation in some way plays a part.

Delta Wedding has been called a comedy of love, because that is the impression one brings away from it, the almost unreal extent to which kindliness, if not love, radiates from one character to another. But there is no false sentiment and no misconception about the surface tranquility; Miss Welty understands human nature too well. (In "Going to Naples," a half-cracked old man terrifies his fellow passengers on an Atlantic crossing with a tin whistle, "his joke and his privilege" to break up any island of peace with a screechy blast. "When your thoughts were all gentle and reassured and forgiving and triumphant— then it would be your turn: 'Tweeeeet!' "[16]) Miss Welty understands the precariousness of the quiet moment and of harmony among human beings, and so at Shellmound a current of opposition runs beneath the surface threatening at any time to break through. That it never does with serious effect is due to the deliberate care with which life is lived there. The informality of a large family is kept within bounds by a formal structuring of manners, nowhere stated but everywhere understood and taken for granted. The Negroes are impeccable in their relations with whites and with each other, their gentility is as real as that of the people they serve, but at the same time they suggest the possibility of violence, which must be watched and controlled. The white family has its own problems. Aunt Tempe bullies her husband and anybody else who allows her. Her granddaughter Lady Clare is a terror, and the feebleminded Maureen's unaccountable, hateful acts are darkly symbolic. "Harm—that was what Maureen intended. . . . It was the harm inside her" (p. 74). Even great-aunts Shannon and Mac indulge in petty malice, rivals in grief for their husbands and brothers killed in battle sixty years ago. And Dabney's happiness is built on the injustice done another girl, Troy's turned-off mistress who kills herself before the wedding.

All this is the real world of human nature on the loose, the tin whistle that threatens around the corner, but somehow kept under control among the Fairchilds. Nothing ever gets out of hand, and any private distress—like Shelley's fear and embarrassment over her younger sister's marrying before her—is concealed by the face the family as a whole puts up to the world. "We never wanted to be smart, one by one," Shelley says, "but all together we have a wall. We are self-sufficient against people that come up knocking, we are solid to the outside" (p. 84). Their success and happiness may look smug and proprietary, but Miss Welty has no qualms about it. The Fairchilds have achieved something rare and precious, and that is the point of her story.

It did not happen by accident. First, there is Troy Flavin, the "born overseer," with gun and long knife, who stands between the exquisite manners of Shellmound and the black bodies that sweat in the fields. A few minutes before the wedding, he shoots a Negro who draws a knife on him. Miss Welty does not blink at this ugly act of repression; it is the price to be paid for the security of the whole. But there is a higher source of discipline which the overseer's gun has nothing to do with: an acknowledgement that everyone is a member of the family and must take his part in a general responsibility. To past generations he owes respect, and to those to come a duty, and to members of his own generation, tolerance and restraint. This is the common lesson learned at Shellmound. And so they all move together in a controlled dissonance, each giving up a little of his own angularity to find step in the measured strain. *Delta Wedding* is Miss Welty's representation—a dream perhaps, but a dream in close conformity to the life of her region—of what it is like to live in a civilized order.

IV

Eudora Welty's achievement is wonderfully varied because of the susceptible nature of her mind, which takes life generously as it comes. Both joy and pain are in it, both intensely private, but at the same time part of a larger corporate experience. Life itself is a mystery to be gratefully received and lived with as much wisdom as one and his fellows can bring to bear on it.

Unlike most writers of our time, including William Faulkner, she has stayed clear of the timely topics, especially tempting to Southern authors, who for the last generation of social change have had an audience ready and waiting for them. The writer, she insists, must keep an eye upon the ages, not one disturbing season. She shows less interest in cataclysms that affect nations than in the private experience of living—the way a person greets a new day, or walks in a garden, or reacts to the face one meets on the street. In this large perspective, the social problems of her region are not important at all.

Writing in *The New York Times* a few years ago, John Bowen pointed out the fallacy of modern readers and critics in attaching importance to relevance in fiction rather than to excellence—because relevance is easy to recognize and excellence is not. Violence, war, social injustice are "important," whereas the quiet life well lived is not. Harriet Beecher Stowe is "important," as well as the countless modern writers who comment on some aspect of a faltering social order; Jane Austen is not. "I myself believe," says Bowen, "that a novel is first of all an object, as a play is, and that what is 'important' about it is its completeness."[17] It pertains, as Miss Welty says about the Austen novel, "not to the everchanging outside world but to what goes on perpetually in the mind and heart."[18] It sets up resonances and demands response. That is what happens when one comes face to face with excellence, the difficult province that Miss Welty has taken for her own.

Jane Austen has no interest in "important" subjects but can hold her own, says Lord David Cecil, with the acknowledged grand writers; because what she writes is set in its relation, not to an English village of the eighteenth century, but to the universe. "If I were in doubt as to the wisdom of one of my actions," he says, "I should not consult Flaubert or Dostoevsky. The opinions of Balzac or Dickens would carry little weight with me; were Stendhal to rebuke me, it would only convince me that I had done right; even in the judgment of Tolstoy I should not put complete confidence. But I should be seriously upset, I should worry for weeks and weeks, if I incurred the disapproval of Jane Austen."[19]

Eudora Welty, like Jane Austen, speaks with authority because she avoids theory and contention and sticks to the fact as she sees it in the world about her. And in Fairchilds or Banner Community in the hills or in China Grove—"the next to the smallest P. O. in the entire state of Mississippi"—the fact speaks for itself. Her people know or care little about what goes on in the world beyond, but they know each other, are functionally connected with each other and the place they live in, and from these associations have learned a great deal about how to live. They would not be able to express what they have learned, but that is Miss Welty's business. Their lives may seem unimportant when set against the big issues of the moment, but not to the reader whose ear is attuned to the quiet wisdom beneath the social comedy.

Notes

1. Joan Williams, ed., *Walter Scott on Novelists and Fiction* (London: Routledge & Kegan Paul, 1968), p. 8.
2. Eudora Welty, "The Radiance of Jane Austen," a lecture delivered at Millsaps College, December, 1968, Jackson *Clarion-Ledger*, 6 December 1968, p. 16.
3. Eudora Welty, *The Golden Apples* (New York: Harcourt, Brace and Company, 1949), p. 96.
4. Eudora Welty, *Delta Wedding* (New York: Harcourt, Brace and Company, 1946), p. 197.
5. *The Golden Apples*, p. 58.
6. Eudora Welty, *Losing Battles* (New York: Random House, 1970), p. 169.
7. Eudora Welty, *The Ponder Heart* (New York: Harcourt, Brace & World, 1954), p. 56.
8. Richard Chase, *The American Novel and Its Traditions* (Garden City, N.Y.: Doubleday, 1957), pp. 4–5.
9. F. R. Leavis, "Introduction," *Pudd'nhead Wilson* (New York: Grove Press, 1955), p. 14.
10. Eudora Welty, *A Curtain of Green* (New York: Harcourt, Brace & World, 1941), p. 152.
11. Eudora Welty, *The Bride of the Innisfallen* (New York: Harcourt, Brace & World, 1955), p. 29.
12. Eudora Welty, *Delta Wedding* (New York: Harcourt, Brace & World, 1946), p. 15. (Subsequent references to this work will appear in the text).
13. Eudora Welty, "Place in Fiction," *South Atlantic Quarterly*, 55 (January 1956), 57.
14. Toni Klatzko, "Eudora Welty Tells Students About Writing," Jackson *Clarion-Ledger*, 19 March 1962, p. 2.
15. Ruth M. Vande Kieft, *Eudora Welty* (New York: Twayne, 1962), pp. 93–94.
16. *The Bride of the Innisfallen*, p. 163.
17. John Bowen, "Speaking of Books: In Defense of the Unimportant Novel," *The New York Times Book Review*, 4 February 1968, p. 2.
18. Eudora Welty, "A Note on Jane Austen," *Shenandoah*, 20 (Spring 1969), 6.
19. David Cecil, *Jane Austen* (Cambridge: Cambridge University Press, 1935), p. 43.

Eudora Welty's Photography:
Images into Fiction
Suzanne Marrs[*]

Eudora Welty's photographs have long been admired, but have too seldom received critical and scholarly attention. Admirers of the photographs have erroneously assumed that Welty used only a rather primitive Kodak camera and that she took all her photographs between 1933 and 1936. Most interviewers of Welty have been unconcerned with her photography, essays about the photographs have inevitably been based on very few remarks by Welty, and scholars have typically examined only Welty's published photographs, not all of the 1,062 negatives held by the Mississippi Department of Archives and History. As a result, Welty's career as a photographer, the elements of change and continuity that characterize her photographs, and the relationship between Welty's photographs and her fiction require further study.

Eudora Welty grew up taking photography for granted. Her father was a camera enthusiast who took family and travel photographs, developed his own prints, and supported the efforts of two young men to establish the first camera store in Jackson, Mississippi. Christian Webb Welty might have expected his daughter to share his enthusiasm for photography, and indeed she did. For twenty years Welty would take and for many years print her own photographs, and when she ceased being an active photographer, Welty would carefully preserve her prints and negatives.[1] She began to take snapshots sometime late in the 1920s, perhaps in the summer of 1929 after she had graduated from the University of Wisconsin and before she became a graduate student at Columbia University. At that time she used a Kodak camera with a bellows, and she continued to use that camera until she purchased a more sophisticated Recomar Camera in 1935. The Recomar, however, proved expensive to use. It required film packs (3″ × 4″ negatives), not the more economical 116 film (2½″ × 4¼″ negatives) that the Kodak had taken. So late in 1936 she changed cameras once again. She bought a Rolleiflex camera (2¼″ × 2¼″ negatives) and used it until 1950. In that year she accidentally left the Rolleiflex on a Paris Metro bench, and annoyed with her own carelessness, she refused for many years to replace it. From her graduate student days until 1950, therefore, Welty was busy with a camera.[2]

Welty's activity with her cameras resulted not in one, as has been assumed, but in two New York shows. The first was sponsored by Lugene, Inc., Opticians at the Photographic Galleries in New York

[*] This essay was written specifically for this volume and is published here by permission of the author. A form of this essay appears in *The Welty Collection* (University Press of Mississippi, 1988).

City, the second by The Camera House in New York City. We know a good deal about the first show: held from 31 March to 15 April 1936, it consisted of forty-five photographs; twenty-nine of the originals are still with the Mississippi Department of Archives and History, and all of the photographs in this show were taken with the Kodak or Recomar camera. Samuel Robbins, who had worked on Welty's first show, contacted her when he moved from Lugene, Inc., to The Camera House and proposed a second show of her photographs. He requested photos of "poor whites," and his correspondence with Welty further indicates that this show of 6–31 March 1937 included photos of cemetery monuments.[3] It seems impossible to determine precisely which photographs were exhibited at this time, but a number of mounted, original prints held by the Mississippi Archives seem likely candidates.

Though publishers as well as galleries were interested in Welty's photographs, book publication of them was long in coming. In 1935 Welty submitted a collection of photographs to Harrison Smith and Robert Haas, Publishers; the collection met with praise but was rejected as an unprofitable undertaking.[4] In 1937 Covici-Friede rejected a work in which Welty had juxtaposed stories and photographs. This juxtaposition, Welty recalls, was artificial; the pictures had not inspired the stories.[5] She hoped that the photographs might interest publishers in her stories, but Covici-Friede foresaw commercial problems with such a combination. And in 1938 the Story Press rejected a collection of Welty photographs, fearing that the costs of producing this book would be prohibitive.[6] It was not until 1971, therefore, that Welty's photographs were published in book form; *One Time, One Place* came out that year.[7] Since then three collections of Welty photographs have been issued; the Mississippi Department of Archives and History's *Welty* (1977), edited by Patti Carr Black; Palaemon Press's *Twenty Photographs* (1980); and Lord John Press's *In Black and White* (1985).[8]

Despite the publication of four books of Welty photographs, few scholars have chosen to study them, and no one has looked at the evolution of Welty's career as a photographer or at the parallels between her development as a photographer and her development as a writer.[9] Welty's early photographs tend to focus upon encounters, upon small groups of people, while her later photographs more often depict landscapes and townscapes. But her photographs also show unexpected lines of continuity—pictures of parades and carnivals date from her use of the simple Kodak and extend throughout her years as a photographer; pictures of cemeteries date from her use of the Kodak, though the Mississippi Department of Archives and History holds no such negatives, and are prominent among the Recomar and Rolleiflex photographs the Department does hold. In fact, Welty once thought of publishing a book of cemetery photos and took many cemetery shots as a result of that persistent notion.[10] No more than twenty percent of Welty's photographs fall into these two categories, but her other photographic subjects varied with the years.

Welty's early photographs, those taken between 1929 and 1936 with the Kodak and Recomar cameras, suggest her fascination with the citizens of her native state. After returning from the University of Wisconsin and then from Columbia University, Welty seemed to rediscover her native land, to find a world of infinite variety close at hand. Welty predominately photographed people, people engaged in street-corner conversations, children at play, adults at work. A majority of these people were blacks, oppressed by white authority but free from white social conventions—a fact that may have prompted Welty the writer to pair black characters with white characters who were artists or wanderers. But Welty's photographs more often depict both blacks and whites as Southerners and as people, not as members of particular racial groups.

Welty's Kodak and Recomar photographs, for instance, often depict typically Southern stances, gestures, and encounters that she noted after her stay in the North—stances, gestures, and encounters that she had probably taken for granted before living outside the South. In 1953 Welty herself used these photographs to provide a picture of the region for Joe Krush, the illustrator of her novel *The Ponder Heart*. She sent him many of her early photographs and made comments on the backs of them. Some comments refer to white or black poses, but all discuss Southern ones. On the reverse of her photograph of a young black girl lying in a porch swing, she wrote: "Good Southern attitude" (no. 727). On the reverse of a picture of white people eating watermelon on the town square in Pontotoc, Mississippi, she wrote: "Man seated (1) on ground might look like Old Man Gladney—elastic bands on shirtsleeves, etc. big black hat, suspenders, sharp-featured country face" (no. 975). On the reverse of a snapshot of four black men leaning against a fence, Welty wrote, "attitudes" (no. 279). And on the reverse of her portrait of a white storekeeper, she wrote: "A country storekeeper, The face & clothes are usual for people on the street (+ hat) (panama) & the telephone is good" (no. 694). The typical sights of Southern life that Welty had documented in her photographs she sent along to Krush. Her fiction, of course, is filled with such typically Southern types. In fact, Welty's famed sense of place in her early fiction is established more through character and social behavior than through description of the physical setting. The three ladies in "Lily Daw" who gather at the post office while one of their number does up the mail might well be images from a Welty photograph. The conversational grouping of these women and storekeeper Ed Newton, as he strings up Redbird tablets in his store, might be as well. The depot gathering to bid Lily farewell also evokes the photographs. None of these images, however, emerges directly from the photographs. Welty did take her Kodak photographs before she wrote the stories later collected in *A Curtain of Green* (1941), though very few of her early stories bear an explicit relationship to them. But Welty's vision as a photographer and her vision as a story writer were similar: what interested her in one art form interested her in another.

Although the evocation of a region is important, there is a more profound connection between the 1929–36 photographs and the early stories. Most of Welty's Kodak and Recomar photographs are framed to emphasize relationships between individuals. Even the photograph titles from her Lugene Show emphasize this overriding concern. "Boast" (no. 971) is simply a picture of three boys sitting on a street corner, but Welty's title bestows a story upon this framed picture. Another picture of a young girl leaning against the porch post of her shabby home Welty has titled "Waiting" (no. 704), and this girl seems to be waiting for someone she loves or for someone *to* love. "Small Talk" (no. 711) is the photo of two men engaged in conversation, both amused by the talk, both perhaps amused by the repetition of an old story that has become more dear in its repeated tellings. "Dolls Alike" (no. 988) depicts two black girls with white dolls; Welty's title centers not on the obvious irony but upon the relationship of the two sisters who have dolls alike. "Sunday Errand" (no negative available) shows two boys carrying home chunks of ice, and suggests a story—the work and the pleasure involved in having iced tea and perhaps homemade ice cream once a week. "Spanking" (no. 477) shows a mother's frustration with her infant child. "Chums" (no. 713) depicts the friendship of two young girls. Welty carefully selected what to enclose within the frame of her camera's lens, and her "instinct and knowledge," she told a BBC reporter, "was to take a group of people whose being together shows something."[11] The same instinct and knowledge, she went on to state, governed her work as a writer. From the first Welty's stories focus upon relationships—the relationship between Lily Daw and the community of Victory, Mississippi, the relationship between husbands and wives in "Petrified Man," the relationships denied to Clytie, the two marriages of Mr. Marblehall, the relationships of the family members in "Why I Live at the P.O.," of Ruby Fisher and her husband in "A Piece of News," of Sonny and his wife in "Death of a Traveling Salesman." The mood of these stories, however, differs sharply from the mood of the photographs. Few relationships in the stories provide characters with emotional sustenance; few characters can understand or communicate with their friends or family members. As Robert Penn Warren long ago noted, "the fact of isolation, whatever its nature, provides the basic situation" of Welty's early fiction.[12] The photographs bear testimony to the need for love—romantic love, parental love, the love of friends—and at times these photographs show the difficulty of finding love and of transcending separateness—"Waiting," for example. But more typically the photographs are affirmative in implication. The Kodak and Recomar photographs and the stories in *A Curtain of Green* suggest the poles of Welty's thought—the need for love and the difficulty inherent in loving.

Although Welty's photographs taken in 1935–36 with the Recomar camera focused upon human interaction as did her earlier Kodak photos, Welty paid greater attention to landscapes and architecture with her second camera than with her first. Her photographs of the Big Black and Pearl rivers, of antebellum Natchez homes, of Raymond Courthouse, of Charleston, South Carolina, and of New York City suggest a shift in her photographic interests. With her third camera, her Rolleiflex, Welty took still more photographs of landscapes and townscapes. This is not to say that she ceased to photograph people after she bought the Rolleiflex late in 1936—her pictures of Holiness Church members, of Ida M'Toy, of parade watchers and participants, of state fair crowds and acts, and of New Orleans Mardi Gras revelers put that notion to rest. But the Rolleiflex photos focus upon the Old Natchez Trace region of Mississippi—upon the physical appearance of its small towns and upon the land formations and plant life of the region. Some time in 1940 Welty, having read Robert Coates's *The Outlaw Years,* John James Audubon's journals, Lorenzo Dow's sermons and autobiography, and J. F. H. Claiborne's *Mississippi,* went in search of the exotic world these books described. She saw and photographed Hermanville, Rocky Springs, Port Gibson, Grand Gulf, and Rodney, the hills overlooking the Mississippi River and the dense, vine-covered woods of these hills. This locale entranced Welty and became her central photographic subject.

In *A Curtain of Green* locale is important but not central. This work makes economical use of setting to develop the issues of love and separateness. The desolate hill country in "Death of a Traveling Salesman" suggests that R. J. Bowman is literally and figuratively at the end of the road. The flat, monotonous landscape of the Mississippi Delta reflects the nature of Tom Harris's uncommitted life in "The Hitch-Hikers." The stately homes of Natchez reflect the power of convention in "Old Mr. Marblehall." But the physical world claims few lines in these stories.

Of course, Welty was writing the stories to be collected in *A Curtain of Green* even as she was using her Recomar and her Rolleiflex cameras, and a few of these stories reflect the fictional equivalent of her increasing photographic interest in place. The Recomar photographs of New York City, for instance, depict the city's streets, its squares filled with pigeons, its shops and sidewalk markets, and they were taken only a short time before Welty wrote "Flowers for Marjorie," a story in which she made extensive use of the physical environment to emphasize the failure in the marriage of Majorie and Howard. Though Welty never consulted her photographs when writing, photographs provide exact parallels to descriptive passages in "Flowers for Marjorie."[13] Howard, sitting on a park bench next to other unemployed men, glancing at a drinking fountain a short distance away, looking at pigeons in the square, might be any of the men Welty photographed in New York City's Union Square (nos. 949, 953, 955, 957, 996, 997, 998, 999, 1000, 1004, 1037). And this New York City world has separated Howard from the natural world and from his wife:

> He walked up Sixth Avenue under the shade of the L, and kept setting his hat on straight. The little spurts of wind tried to take it off and blow it away. How far he would have had to chase it! . . . He reached a crowd of people who were watching a machine behind a window; it made doughnuts very slowly. He went to the next door, where he saw another window full of colored prints of the Virgin Mary and nearly all kinds of birds and animals, and down below these a shelf of little gray pasteboard boxes in which were miniature toilets and night jars to be used in playing jokes, and in the middle box a bulb attached to a long tube, with a penciled sign, "Palpitator—the Imitation Heart. Show her you Love her." An organ grinder immediately removed his hat and played "Valencia."[14]

In the city Howard encounters an unchanging environment of steel and concrete, of tawdry commercialism and unemployment—for him time seems to have stopped. Although Marjorie lives in the urban setting, she remains part of the natural world, of the world of time and growth and change—her pregnancy makes her part of that world. This difference from Marjorie is unbearable to Howard because he loves Marjorie—his love, in fact, increases his pain. And this difference from Marjorie has been precipitated by the young couple's move to the city. Welty thus places greater emphasis upon the physical world of her story here than she does in most of the *Curtain of Green* stories. Her photographic interest in the shade of the L (no. 1002) and in the shops she describes in "Flowers for Marjorie" (no. 953) parallels her increasingly emblematic use of place in her fiction.

So too does Welty's photographing of the Natchez Trace landscape parallel her emblematic use of that area in her fiction. Welty had photographed Natchez's First Pilgrimage in 1933 and had also photographed the great houses of Natchez with her Recomar. But through the lens of her Rolleiflex Welty looked not at Natchez itself but at the wilder region along the old trail that led to it. She came repeatedly to the Old Trace with her Rolleiflex. Her enlargements

No. 49. "Hamlet"
(Welty's title)

No. 925. Mardi Gras:
Death and Medusa

No. 0265. Friends

No. 1006. A cemetery near
the Natchez Trace

No. 853. Cemetery
monument. The inscription
reads: "He was an honor to
the earth on which he
lived."

No. 711. "Tall Story"
(Welty's title)

of photographs of Rodney's Landing date from 1940, and that year
marks both a photographic and a fictional concentration upon the
Old Trace. "A Worn Path," Welty's first published story with the
Trace as setting, was included in *A Curtain of Green*, but was written
in 1940, considerably later than most stories in that volume. In this
account of Phoenix Jackson's journey to obtain medicine for her
grandson, Welty's response to the Trace landscape was as direct and
intense, though not as expansive, as it would be in her later fiction
about the region. On the way to Natchez, Welty tells us, Phoenix
walks up through pine trees that cast dark shadows and down through
oak trees. She sees Spanish moss hanging as white as lace in the cold
weather. She passes small fields of dead cotton and corn. She walks
between high, green-colored banks. This beautiful Trace world, that
can be seen in so many of Welty's photographs (nos. 13 and 1022,
for example), makes the story believable—we believe in Phoenix
Jackson because we recognize and believe in the world that she
inhabits. But setting does far more than lend credibility to the story's
action. The natural world of the Trace is Phoenix's home, and its
qualities are to some extent her own. Her life has been relatively
untouched by "progress." She is not removed from nature but lives
naturally. She tells time by turning to nature. As Phoenix sets out
on her December trip to Natchez, she knows that it is "not too late"
for the mourning dove. As she travels on, she measures her progress
by the progress of the sun: " 'Sun so high!' she cried, leaning back
and looking, while the thick tears went over her eyes. 'The time
getting all gone here.' "[15] Later as she crosses a field, she is "Glad
this not the season for bulls" and that "the good Lord made his
snakes to curl up and sleep in the winter."[16] The rhythms of the day
and of the year constitute Phoenix's way of measuring time. Phoenix
herself seems almost to be a part of the natural world: "Her skin
had a pattern all its own of numberless branching wrinkles and as
though a whole little tree stood in the middle of her forehead, but
a golden color ran underneath, and the two knobs of her cheeks
were illumined by a yellow burning under the dark. Under the red
rag her hair came down on her neck in the frailest of ringlets, still
black, and with an odor like copper."[17] And Phoenix's love for her
grandson, love that sends her on a heroic quest for medicine, is
absolutely natural. It is as enduring as the daily and seasonal cycles.
Her love is innate. Even when Phoenix momentarily forgets why she
had traveled to the doctor's office, she is acting intuitively out of
love. And when she remembers her grandson and his ailment, she
states: "I not going to forget him again, no, the whole enduring time.
I could tell him from all the others in creation."[18] In "Some Notes
on River Country" Welty has asserted, "Whatever is significant and
whatever is tragic in its story live as long as the place does."[19] "A

Worn Path" shows us that Phoenix's love lives as long as its place does; her love is as enduring as the Trace itself. Welty's photographs of this landscape thus parallel her metaphoric use of it in fiction. Her interest had not moved away from relationships but had shifted to the way the external world can serve as a metaphor for those relationships.

The parallel between Welty's photographs of the Natchez Trace and her writing about the region is even clearer in *The Robber Bridegroom* (1942) and *The Wide Net* (1943), a novella and a short story collection set primarily in this area. And the parallels are most direct and revealing in "At The Landing," the final story in *The Wide Net* and a story set in Rodney's Landing and Grand Gulf. A photograph Welty entitled "Hamlet" in *One Time, One Place* shows Rodney's Landing—a two-story brick building with a back gallery, two one-story frame structures, and a man walking beside a dirt road carrying a large fish (no. 49). This image is part of "At The Landing":

> Under the shaggy bluff the bottomlands lay in a river of golden haze. The road dropped like a waterfall from the ridge to the town at its foot and came to a grassy end there. It was spring. One slowly moving figure that was a man with a fishing pole passed like a dreamer through the empty street and on through the trackless haze toward the river.[20]

The photographic image suggests the town's decaying nature, its lifeless quality, and these suggestions prove appropriate for Welty's story. She intensifies the image—the scarcely perceptible second man in the photograph is gone from the story, and even the man with the fish seems scarcely to exist as he "passes like a dreamer through the empty street." The isolation and lifelessness of the town suggest the threat it poses to Jenny Lockhart, the story's protagonist.

A second photographic image comes into the story with a similar impact. Welty writes,

> The cemetery was a dark shelf above the town, on the site of the old landing place when the ships docked from across the world a hundred years ago, and its brink was marked by an old table-like grave with its top ajar where the woodbine grew. Everywhere there, the hanging moss and the upthrust stones were in that strange graveyard shade where, by the light they give, the moss seems made of stone, and the stone of moss.[21]

Welty might well be describing her series of photographs of the Rodney cemetery. The "table-like grave with its top ajar" appears in negatives nos. 482 and 1006, and the image of hanging moss and upthrust stones calls to mind negatives nos. 32, 387, 748, and 749. Here Jenny's retreat to the cemetery seems a move away from love and life and the riverman Billy Floyd. Similarly, Welty's photo of a stile over a cemetery fence (no. 27 or 1058; *Welty*, 4) becomes in the story the point of indecision for Jenny: should she cross into the open sun and meet Billy Floyd or should she remain in the dark and shady cemetery where her grandfather permits her to go? She must choose between a lifeless but secure existence and a perilous quest for love.

A rather different image also unites photography and story. Welty's photographs of Mississippi River fishing nets (nos. 750, 1024) suggest this passage in her story: "A great spiraled net lay on its side and its circles twinkled faintly on the sky. Veil behind veil of long drying nets hung on all sides, dropping softly and blue-colored in the low wind, and the place was folded in by them."[22] The beauty of the nets belies, however, the danger they represent—the place seems "folded in by them" and Jenny's journey toward freedom and love is also a journey toward destruction. The photographs carry no such metaphoric suggestion, though the images are the same as the story's.

Still a final image in the story parallels a Welty photograph—but this photograph depicts people more than place. Her picture of a fisherman and his boys throwing knives at a tree appears in *One Time, One Place* and seems only slightly sinister—the activity itself is threatening, but it is after all a father-and-son entertainment, and the man and boys appear to be enjoying themselves (no. 752). Not so in the story. By the last light of day the men throw knives at the tree, and then after dark the boys do: "The younger boys separated and took their turns throwing knives with a dull *pit* at the tree."[23] This image is decidedly sinister. Jenny Lockhart has left the repressive but secure environment of The Landing and has ventured after Billy Floyd and in quest of love; instead she meets violence and destruction. The river men rape her, and the knife throwing suggests the violence that has become her lot. In "At The Landing" Welty's creation of setting directly parallels her framing vision as a photographer; the increasing importance of place as a way of developing and representing the nature of human relationships seems implicit in Welty's shifting emphasis as a photographer; she continues to photograph people engaged with each other—witness the shantyboaters—but she also sees the physical environment—the town, the cemetery, the fishing nets—in metaphoric terms. And this metaphoric stress upon setting does not vanish from Welty's fiction when she ceases to write about the Trace. The Mississippi Delta, the Irish city of Cork, and the Mediterranean harbor at Naples, for example, would receive similar emphasis and serve similar functions.

What unites all of Welty's photographs and much of her early fiction is scope. The well-framed photographic image is highly selective—it includes relatively little; it captures a single, decisive moment in time. In these terms, Welty's first two story collections seem photographic in nature. The shortness of elapsed time, the small cast of characters, and the taut structure in a short story resemble those very qualities in a photograph. Welty's subsequent fiction would often be more expansive. She would begin to write novels, and her stories would grow much longer. She would deal with multiple plots, with many characters, and with elaborately rendered landscapes, but she would continue to focus on a limited, decisive time span and to use images in her fiction that she had seen through the lens of her camera. In fact, the precise sorts of images that appear throughout Welty's work as a photographer appear throughout her work as a writer.

Welty's taking of cemetery photographs was consistent during her years as a photographer—she took such pictures with all three of her cameras, and images she photographed in the 1930s and 1940s appear not only in the fiction of those years but also in works of the sixties and seventies. The cemetery photographs Welty took with her Kodak are not part of her photographic archives—early in the thirties Welty and some friends posed with cemetery monuments and took a few humorous photographs of each other. But the cemetery photographs Welty took with her Recomar and Rolleiflex cameras are a major portion of the collection she has donated to the Mississippi Department of Archives and History. Why did Welty photograph so many cemeteries and why did she contemplate a book of cemetery portraits? Certainly she was amused by the Victorian sentimentality and excess to be found in the monuments, but beyond this must lie Welty's concern with time and mortality. "In the most unpretentious snapshot," Welty has written, "lies the wish to clasp fleeting life. Framing a few square inches of space for the fraction of a second, the photographer may capture—rescue from oblivion—fellow human beings caught in the act of living. He is devoted to the human quality of transience."[24] The many cemetery photographs are eloquent testimony to that same quality of transience and to the same need to rescue human life from oblivion. Time moves inexorably and life is short, Welty's cemetery photographs tell us. One of her earliest stories, "Magic," set in a Jackson cemetery beneath a cemetery angel that Welty had photographed, conveys a similar message.[25] Here a young girl is seduced—here she becomes a victim of her own illusions about love and is introduced to the reality of time's movement. But monuments Welty had photographed also appear in her fiction of later years. The cemeteries in *Delta Wedding* and *The Golden Apples* specifically parallel actual cemeteries Welty had photographed, as do the cemeteries in *Losing Battles* and *The Optimist's Daughter*. In *Losing Battles* Sam Dale Beecham's grave marker "had darkened, its surface like the smooth, loving slatings of a pencil on tablet paper laid over a buffalo nickel, but the rubbed name and the rubbed chain hanging in two, its broken link, shone out in the wet."²⁶ On Rachel Sojourner's headstone a small lamb "had turned dark as a blackened lamp chimney."²⁷ And on Dearman's grave is a shaft, "on its top the moss-ringed finger that pointed straight up from its hand in a chiseled cuff above the words 'At Rest.' "²⁸ All of these images we can see in Welty's photographs (nos. 1048, 787, 781). And in both the photographs she took in the thirties and forties and in this novel published in 1970, cemetery monuments are emblems of human mortality, life's one "irreducible urgency."²⁹ Jack Renfro knows that cemetery monuments will be worn smooth, blackened, covered with moss; for Jack, life's only source of continuity lies in love, not stone. When he looks at his grandparents' graves, he tells his wife, Gloria: "There's Mama and all of 'em's mother and dad going by. . . . Yet when you think back on the reunion and count how many him and her managed to leave behind! Like something had whispered to 'em 'Quick!' and they were smart enough to take heed."³⁰

Laurel McKelva Hand's visit to the Mount Salus Cemetery in *The Optimist's Daughter* brings her in contact with monuments very like those Welty had photographed thirty years earlier, and it helps to bring her in contact with a realization similar to Jack Renfro's. The funeral procession for Judge McKelva enters a cemetery

> between ironwork gates whose kneeling angels and looping vines shone black as licorice. The top of the hill ahead was crowded with winged angels and life-sized effigies of bygone citizens in old-fashioned dress, standing as if by count among the columns and shafts and conifers like a familiar set of passengers collected on deck of a ship, on which they all knew each other—bona-fide members of a small local excursion, embarked on a voyage that is always returning in dreams.³¹

The gates of this fictional cemetery recall Welty's photograph of a Port Gibson, Mississippi, cemetery gate (no. 860). The cemetery itself could well be Jackson's Greenwood Cemetery or the cemetery in Crystal Springs, Mississippi—both of which Welty photographed extensively. Here the old part of the cemetery offers comfort; the citizens of old Mount Salus seem to experience a sense of community in death as well as life. But this quality is entirely lacking in the new part of the cemetery where Fay elects to bury the Judge. Its rawness and its location on the edge of the interstate highway provide no sense of continuity or comfort. And Laurel ultimately realizes that life's only continuity and only meaning lie in love and memory.

Carnivals and parades also provide consistent images for Welty the photographer and for Welty the writer. Clearly the arrival of the circus was an exciting event in the life of small-town Jackson. Welty had attended parades and the state fair as a child, and as an adult she went on to photograph these events. Relatively few overt references to circuses and parades enter her fiction, but these few are significant, though they are also far removed from the high spirits and humor that typify the photographs. "Acrobats in a Park," probably written in 1934, deals with the way adultery threatens the solidity of a circus family. And "Keela, the Outcast Indian Maiden" recalls a circus sideshow in which a clubfooted black man is forced to eat live chickens—Welty heard about such a sideshow during her work for the WPA and that anecdote prompted her story. She also photographed numerous sideshow posters at the annual state fairs in Jackson—"Rubber Man," "Mule Faced Woman," "Frog Boy," "3 Legged Man," "Ossified Man" were among the sideshows that played in Jackson (nos. 117, 113, 481, 110, 469). But Welty's amusement with the posters does not betoken the mood of her story. The story deals with victimization—to his kidnappers, to the circus crowds, even to his own family, Little Lee Roy is scarcely human, a victim of the horrifying separateness that can exist among human beings. Welty's photographs of a pin-headed boy are her only carnival shots to suggest this horror (nos. 112, 115, 1011).

Actual parades as well as carnivals play a role in at least two of Welty's works. King MacLain, Katie Rainey tells us in "A Shower of Gold," is fabled to have ridden in Governor Vardaman's inaugural parade—a sign of the grandeur King holds for the hometown folk. More significantly, in *The Optimist's Daughter,* Welty uses an image she herself had photographed during a Mardi Gras parade (no. 925). Laurel Hand and Fay McKelva find themselves in New Orleans in the midst of this festival of indulgence that occurs annually before Lent, before the fasting and penitence that the crucifixion of Christ made necessary. Fay sees two revelers who embody the dark impetus of Mardi Gras: "I saw a man—I saw a man and he was dressed up like a skeleton and his date was in a long white dress, with snakes for hair, holding up a bunch of lilies."[32] But Fay does not see that these emblems of death and the Medusa are the harsh realities that inspire Mardi Gras. She longs for the celebration but cannot see beyond it as Laurel does.

The carnival of "Keela, the Outcast Indian Maiden" and the Mardi Gras costumes of *The Optimist's Daughter* notwithstanding, indirect, oblique, or figurative references to circuses and parades are more typical of Welty's fiction; in fact, they pervade it. In *One Writer's Beginnings* Welty comments on this motif in relation to a parade she saw as a child:

> In Davis School days, there lived a little boy two or three streets
> over from ours who was home sick in bed, and when the circus

came to town that year, someone got the parade to march up a different street from the usual way to the Fairgrounds, to go past his house. He was carried to the window to watch it go by. Just for him the ponderous elephants, the plumes, the spangles, the acrobats, the clowns, the caged lion, the band playing, the steam calliope, the whole thing! When not long after that he disappeared forever from our view, having died of what had given him his special privilege, none of this at all was acceptable to the rest of us children. He had been tricked, not celebrated, by the parade's brazen marching up his street with the band playing, and we had somehow been tricked by envying him—betrayed into it.

It is not for nothing that an ominous feeling often attaches itself to a procession. This was when I learned it. "The Pied Piper of Hamelin" had done more than just hint at this. In films and stories we see spectacles forming in the street and parades coming from around the corner, and we know to greet them with distrust and apprehension: their intent is still to be revealed. (Think what it was in "My Kinsman, Major Molineux.")

I never resisted it when, in almost every story I ever wrote, some parade or procession, impromptu or ceremonious, comic or mocking or funeral, has risen up to mark some stage of the story's unfolding. They've started from far back.[33]

Eudora Welty's career as a photographer is thus intimately related to her career as a writer. Though her photographs did not inspire her stories, though Welty never consulted her photographs when writing her stories, Welty's interests as a photographer parallel the course of her writing career, and taking snapshots left her with a store of indelible memories that would be available when she needed them. Her photographs of encounters prefigure her fictional concern with human relationships, with love and separateness; her increasing emphasis upon locale prefigures her increasingly detailed and emblematic use of setting in her stories and novels; and her photographs of cemeteries and parades prefigure the central role of these images in the symbolic structure of her fiction. Yet there is a side to Welty's fiction that is rarely conveyed by her photographs. She transforms photographic images when she translates them into language. Through what Patti Carr Black calls "the alchemy of Welty's genius and vision," images become words that illuminate life's terrors as well as its consolations.[34] The photographs' greatest value may thus lie in what they indicate about Eudora Welty's transcendent imagination.

Notes

1. While she was using her Kodak and Recomar cameras, Welty typically asked Standard Photo (Jackson, Miss.) to process her film and provide her with negatives.

She would then make her own prints. With negatives from her Rolleiflex camera, Welty seldom did her own printing.

2. Unpublished interviews by the author with Miss Welty, July 1985 and July 1987, Jackson, Mississippi; hereafter cited as Welty Interviews.

3. Eudora Welty Collection, Mississippi Department of Archives and History, Correspondence: 7.18.1936, 11.9.1936, 12.14, 1936; Photographs: Negatives and Prints, Z301. As the 1985–86 Scholar-in-Residence at the Mississippi Archives, I was responsible for cataloging all materials in the Welty Collection. Reference to the Eudora Welty Collection made by permission of the Mississippi Department of Archives and History.

4. Welty Correspondence: 04.02.1935.

5. Welty Correspondence: 11.01. 1937.

6. Welty Correspondence: 02.24.1938.

7. Welty, One Time, One Place (New York: Random House, 1971).

8. Welty, ed. and Introduction by Patti Carr Black (Jackson: Mississippi Department of Archives and History, 1977); Twenty Photographs (Winston-Salem, N.C.: Palaemon Press, 1980); In Black and White (Northridge, Calif.: Lord John Press, 1985).

9. Two important essays about Eudora Welty photographs appear in Eudora Welty, Critical Essays, ed. Peggy W. Prenshaw (Jackson: University Press of Mississippi, 1979). In one, "The Eye of Time: the Photographs of Eudora Welty" (389–400), Barbara McKenzie attempts to place Welty in the context of Talbot's The Pencil of Nature (1844–46) and Susan Sontag's On Photography (1977). She also discusses the similarities between photography and fiction as they appear in Welty's work: the symbolic dimension of place, the informal and therefore unconventional way of seeing that characterizes snapshots, the use of light, and a concern with time and mortality. Elizabeth Meese, in "Constructing Time and Place: Eudora Welty in the Thirties" (401–10), reports on her examination of Welty's entire photographic output, categorizes Welty's subjects, discusses the organization of One Time, One Place, and explores the role of photography in Welty's creative processes as a writer, arguing that the visual image triggers Welty's narrative impulse and that photography taught Welty the importance of gesture as a defining feature. Charles Mann, in a 1982 essay for History of Photography ["Eudora Welty, Photographer," in History of Photography 6 (1982):145–49], briefly comments on Welty's photographs and suggests that her concept of photography allies her with Jean-Luc Godard "who feels that film catches us in the act of dying, and with others who see the photograph as related to death" (149). In the past year two additional essays have focused upon Welty as photographer. In his brief article for America ["Eudora Welty's Eye for the Story," America, 23 May 1987, 417–20] Patrick Samway argues that Welty's photographs provide noteworthy portraits of women and that they tell us much about Welty's concern with human mortality. Louise Westling, in a more ambitious and expansive piece for Mississippi Quarterly ["The Loving Observer of One Time, One Place," Mississippi Quarterly 39 (1986):587–604], also pays special attention to photographs of women. Westling discusses "Welty's place among documentary photographers and writers" (588) and explores the "lyricism, mysticism, intimacy, and celebration" that differentiate her from those photographers (601).

10. Welty Interviews.

11. Patchy Wheatley, director, A Writer's Beginnings, British Broadcasting Company, 24 July 1987.

12. Robert Penn Warren, "The Love and the Separateness in Miss Welty," Kenyon Review 6 (1944):250.

13. Welty Interviews.

14. Eudora Welty, "Flowers for Marjorie," in *The Collected Stories of Eudora Welty* (New York: Harcourt, Brace, 1980), 102.

15. Eudora Welty, "A Worn Path," in *The Collected Stories of Eudora Welty* (New York: Harcourt, Brace, 1980), 143.

16. Ibid., 144.

17. Ibid., 142.

18. Ibid., 148.

19. Eudora Welty, "Some Notes on River Country," *The Eye of the Story* (New York: Random House, 1978), 299.

20. Eudora Welty, "At The Landing," in *The Collected Stories of Eudora Welty* (New York: Harcourt, Brace, 1980), 241.

21. Ibid., 243.

22. Ibid., 257.

23. Ibid., 258.

24. Eudora Welty, "A Word on the Photographs," in *Twenty Photographs* (Winston-Salem, N.C.: Palaemon Press, 1980), n.p.

25. Number 791; see also Albert J. Devlin, "Jackson's Welty," *The Southern Quarterly* 20 (1982):57.

26. Eudora Welty, *Losing Battles* (New York: Random House, 1971), 427.

27. Ibid., 428.

28. Ibid.

29. Eudora Welty, "Some Notes on Time in Fiction," in *The Eye of the Story* (New York: Random House, 1978), 168.

30. Welty, *Losing Battles,* 426.

31. Eudora Welty, *The Optimist's Daughter* (New York: Random House, 1972), 89.

32. Ibid., 43.

33. Eudora Welty, *One Writer's Beginnings* (Cambridge, Mass.: Harvard University Press, 1984), 37.

34. Black, *Welty,* Introduction.

Further Reflections on Meaning in Eudora Welty's Fiction   Ruth M. Vande Kieft*

Though I have been thinking and writing about Eudora Welty's fiction for over a quarter century and have always been on a search for meaning as the path to understanding and enjoyment of that fiction, the quest turned into a question about eight years ago when I first started looking into postmodern criticism. What I found was

* This essay was revised for publication in this volume and is published here by permission of the author and *The Southern Quarterly*. It originally appeared as "Eudora Welty: The Question of Meaning," *The Southern Quarterly* 20, no. 4 (Summer 1982):24–39.

that post-Saussurean linguistics, separating signifier from signified, author from text, and reader from both, had seemed to make the assumptions and practice of New Criticism untenable, symptomatic of literary imperialism; that "common sense" and "humanism" were evidences of ruling ideologies sinister because ignorantly espoused or guiltily unacknowledged by bourgeoise moralists and aesthetes alike. Meaning in literature—literature itself, it seemed—was being destroyed. Freudian and Marxist critics were stealing the text (no longer designated as "literature") from the author and her intentions, as well as an "implied" reader. I was shocked and appalled.

In the lecture and article[1] that came from out of my reading and ruminations, I referred to the work of Barthes, Lacan, Derrida and others as "a French disease rapidly spreading out of its American locus, Yale University." I viewed deconstruction with dismay, especially as I saw it practiced "close to home" in the work of a fellow graduate student friend of the fifties, now professor of English. Though I acknowledged and welcomed the existence of pluralism in criticism and indicated my own debts to the work of many excellent critics of Welty's fiction, I stated that the kind of critical pluralism I espoused assumed "the humanistic values which unite beauty and truth," as well as the "pursuit" of those values. In what followed in my article, most of which in turn follows here, I engaged in what I felt, and still feel, to be a practical defense of traditional values in criticism.

Yet several years, a book, an article, and a lecture later,[2] I find myself somewhat embarrassed not so much by the *substance* but rather the *tone* of this defense. I have come to feel, my Chicken Little cries to the contrary, that the sky has not fallen nor is likely to, even though we witness the proliferation of postmodern criticism, and Welty's stories have joined the sacred texts, from the Bible to Brecht, which appear to be appropriate subjects for deconstruction. There seems to be a healthy pluralism in criticism, as this collection of articles will no doubt demonstrate. Welty's stories have already proved themselves, happily, to be nothing like so fragile and in need of support and defense as I had feared they might be. Furthermore, I have learned that deconstruction has all along insisted both on preserving and undoing "traditional" meaning in texts. It needs the former to accomplish the latter; needs the assumptions and practice (largely expressive and realistic) of modern fiction, and a critical approach that assumes the ends of meaning and communication, in order to practice its own deconstruction. It retains the original "signs" under "erasure," even cultivating the rapid oscillation of hierarchical terms. It seems to approve of rapid change, instability, open-endedness, tolerance, benevolence; its mood is often winsome, if self-involved, in the exercise of a bold, yet quizzical, playfulness. In short, to deconstruct a text, I now perceive, does not mean to destroy it, nor even necessarily to attempt to. Yet the process is not entirely playful: it has serious business on its agenda. It can be well or ill-practiced, like any other critical approach.

Nor is deconstruction, when performed on Welty's fiction, an act as arbitrary as might first appear. A good many of her stories, and facets of her novels, are of the sort that Emile Benveniste called *interrogative,* raising questions difficult or impossible to resolve in the reader's mind, for example, about what is illusion and what is "reality," casting a doubt on the expressive / realistic fictional mode. Some of Welty's stories do not contain a clear authorial position, closure, and ostensible unity; they harbor a good deal of contradiction, embracing polarities; they can be extremely subtle, dense, even opaque. We know as well, from her having often said it, that she is a writer who enjoys taking risks, and this makes some of her stories experimental. He who runs may not always read a Welty story.

Many questions are asked by these interrogative stories. To what extent do Welty's ideas exist outside the realm of discourse of their Southern speakers when the point of view is dramatic ("outside" and dialogic)? What are the "shared worlds" of implied reader and narrator? What do we mean by "realism" and "fantasy" in stories that seem to be shifting the terms of discourse, as Welty does in "Powerhouse," "Old Mr. Marblehall," "The Burning," "The Purple Hat," and (some readers think) "A Worn Path"? What is "vulgarity" in Welty's fiction, and what are the implied attitudes toward it in any given story? What volumes of meaning occupy the space between Welty's legendary openness and availability to her public and her equally legendary reticence and privacy? Has her autobiography raised more questions than it has answered about her life in relation to her art? How broadly or narrowly do her stories mean what they appear to within the frame of their time and place, and what meanings inevitably change because of the movement of time, the changes in her Mississippi settings and the state's and its citizens' ongoing history and culture? What is one to make of the almost obsessive use and exploration of *mystery* and its variables and cognates in her fiction (the adjectives *secret, hidden, concealed;* that teasing image *curtain of green;* the tantalizing *enigma;* the terrifying *oblivion*)? These and related questions are enough to suggest the legitimacy, at least, of postmodern and deconstructionist readings of Welty's fiction, in the vanguard of which is the work of Danielle Pitavy-Soques, a critic appropriately French, intellectually rigorous, sensitive, and discerning.[3]

With an eye, then, on what is to come, as well as what is past, there is still every reason to assert our faith in the meaning of fiction as a source of humanistic values in Welty's fiction, if for no better reason than that she shares this faith. Her fiction, her theories and observations about it, as collected in *The Eye of the Story,* are brimming with assumptions and statements about value. She speaks of both beauty and truth—the artist's truth, imaginatively perceived; the story's truth, fidelity to life; and the need for readers to apprehend it by means of a willing imagination rather than by the use of some closed system of critical terms and norms which threaten to destroy the possibility of communication between writer and reader. Her motives for writing, she has stated, are celebration and love. The act of empathy, trying "to enter into the mind, heart, and skin of a human being who is not myself,"[4] is the means by which she seeks to fulfill her wish, to raise the curtain which separates human beings. She also implicitly accepts the notion of critical pluralism in that she thinks the story, once in its final shape, and published, becomes autonomous, in the public sphere. Then many things become clear: "how [the author] sees life and death, how much he thinks people matter to each other and to themselves, how much he would like you to know what he finds beautiful or strange or awful or absurd, what he can do without, how well he has learned to see, hear, touch, smell—. . . how he imposes order and structure on his fictional world; and it is terribly clear, in the end, whether, when he calls for understanding, he gets any."[5]

To be guided by what an author says outside his or her work is, of course, to commit the intentional fallacy. I confess to stumbling here, but I do so in order to become a better reader of Eudora Welty's fiction. Nor do I stop with *conscious* intent and meaning; we have every reason to assume the existence of unconscious meanings and explore them if understanding is thereby enriched.[6]

Most readers feel an affinity for the work of Eudora Welty. Considering its variety, one would have to be extremely narrow not to enjoy at least some of it. An affinity for the comedy in particular may be so strong as to make for a lack of balance in critical perspective—a *something too much* warned against in the delphic oracle. The comic is certainly her most popular mode and the enthusiasm with which it is greeted by college audiences is a cause for rejoicing.

An over-valuing of the comedy, though innocent enough, may lead to blind spots when it comes to Welty's more serious work. Or it may have results the other way around. This is where the other delphic maxim comes in: know thyself.[7] Readers may fall into all sorts of personal and group fallacies because they are from the South or North, of such and such a class, religious believers or agnostics, men or women, black or white, married or single, survivors of psychoanalysis or self-therapists, and so on. Accidents of nature and experience affect our explorations of meaning. Perhaps the best way to deal with them is forthrightly, as Peggy Prenshaw did in her introduction to her article, "Woman's World, Man's Place":

I feel somewhat uncertain of the boundary of my perceiving and the stories' showing. Teacher that I am, ordinarily I duck the old ontological problem and proclaim myself the ideal reader Cleanth Brooks has tried to teach us how to be. Now, however, an admission of wariness seems in order, for I am anxious about the topography I have mapped here, about the announcement that Miss Welty's fiction reveals a woman's world. It sounds distinctly like the report of a new feminist critic, but perhaps that is what I am.[8]

Such candor is refreshing and rare.

Meaning may be a problem because it is often difficult to catch precisely the tone of Eudora Welty's fiction, to determine what Wayne Booth would call the "reliability" of her narrators. Then there are rapid shifts between and among some of the traditional generic modes of comedy, tragedy, satire, farce, melodrama, fantasy, and so on. We know about the terror adjoining the comedy in her fiction, and it rarely seems possible to think of her stories as wearing, unequivocally, one or the other of the two masks of ancient Greek drama. But it is useful to do this, occasionally, by way of testing our critical truth. First, the comic mask.

It is always interesting to see what a critic makes of Eudora Welty's comedy—and encouraging, in a way, to remember that what might be called the Ur-blooper of Welty criticism was committed by the highly discriminating writer who first introduced Eudora Welty to the world in her introduction to *A Curtain of Green*. Katherine Anne Porter called the heroine of "Why I Live at the P.O." "a terrifying case of dementia praecox."[9] Even translating the diagnosis into what it would now be—paranoic schizophrenia—we are no closer to the truth of *that* story. The mistress of China Grove's P.O. is a case all right, but not a terrifying case history. The story *is* essentially comic; to approach it clinically or as anything but lightly amoral would, I think, be a mistake.

The Ponder Heart seems a crucial work in understanding Eudora Welty's comedy, often revealing as much about the critic as the comedy. Elizabeth Evans takes her first big dive into the canon by discussing Welty's comedy. She makes no shapeless flop in the water, however, as though to say, "Look, I've got to get wet *somehow!*" It is a neat dive into shallow water (later she gets in deeper). She shows full awareness that "the comic element must include almost all of [Welty's] work," that "it is often true that Miss Welty's way of being comic is a serious one," and that "individual works must also be examined from other perspectives."[10] It is significant that she considers *The Ponder Heart* from that perspective *only*, however, linking it with Southern humor, for example, and pointing out its use of exaggeration, comic migrations and comic effects of manners and clothing.

Michael Kreyling, who wades into his subject circumspectly, popping down the grotesques bobbing in the water—not Welty's grotesques so much as those of the distorted critical reactions to that early fiction—devotes no chapter to comedy in his study, which is to be expected, since he considers the work in chronological order and deals with the gradual development of her technique in the achievement of order. He is venturing toward what he calls "the main channel of Welty's work," and the comedy is not that. In the opening chapter he says about the two most famous of Eudora Welty's comic heroines: "Even though the beleaguered Martha of "Why I Live at the P.O." and the efficient, neurotic Edna Earle of *The Ponder Heart* are unforgettable, the more intricately fashioned stories, those based on the technique that searches for and waits upon the moment when separateness is abolished and wholeness is so intense it becomes a thing, are truer to Welty's overall achievement."[11]

In his chapter on *The Ponder Heart*, titled "Comedy's Adjoining Terror," Kreyling states of the novella, "the comic theme is so important . . . that it would be well to probe *The Ponder Heart* beneath the humor for the terrible story that Edna Earle refuses to tell lest the sky fall on her head."[12] Edna Earle's "terrible story" is that privately her "heart . . . is wrung with a thousand concerns for the orderly way of life she sees dropping into oblivion before her attentive eyes." She is a victim of the battle between self and society. Uncle Daniel's disorder and Bonnie Dee's eroticism, while the source of "a lot of laughter," are Edna Earle's private cross. The terror adjoining the comedy, Kreyling thinks, was badly traduced in the stage adaptation of the work, cheapening it to "a burlesque of rural types and manners."[13]

Cleanth Brooks, however, finds *The Ponder Heart* not only comic, but even "merrily absurd." He wastes no sympathy on Edna Earle, finding her "uncommonly good company." In her "exuberance and in her earthly complacency" she reminds him of Chaucer's Wife of Bath—"perceptive, on occasion even witty, and always the complete mistress of her own domain," as compelling a talker as the Ancient Mariner, a "high priestess of the oral tradition."[14] Other reactions are far more extreme. Robert Adams thought the characters of *The Ponder Heart* exhibited "all the squeaky energy and self-conscious buffoonery of television comedians."[15] Gilbert Highet considered Edna Earle none too bright. "The book is virtually a tale told by an idiot, and many may think it signifies nothing. . . . Edna Earle . . . is a ferocious bore." He interprets the book as a satire on Southern ladies "who (it would seem) believe that it is better to talk than to remain silent, because any silence is a social blunder. . . ."[16] Kingsley Amis failed to see anything at all funny in *The Ponder Heart*. His review contains a nasty parody of the speech of Southern women: "Uncle

Ponder is just the *most* adorable old character you-all ever saw in all your sweet life, full of the cutest and quaintest little ways, and if that ain't enough to make a *novel*, why you-all really must see the way the story (if you-all can *call* it that) gets told, just the cosy little friendly way I'm *talking* to you-all right now, hush my mouth."[17]

What is one to make of all this? Obviously personal preferences, and some deeply ingrained attitudes toward Southern women and their speech, are being expressed. In general, I would tend to trust a Southerner's reactions to Eudora Welty's comedy over a Northerner's. Good story telling, as she has pointed out, is a mutual enterprise: it requires the capacity to *listen* well. The form of the dramatic monologue asks of a reader a dramatic act. While reading, he or she must become the *listener* of the story; in the case of *The Ponder Heart*, the person whose car broke down, necessitating a stopover at the Beulah Hotel. The reader need give not an ounce *more nor less* than the person and occasion demand: in the case of Edna Earle, putting down one's book, lending a good ear, becoming absorbed in the unfolding tale, at least temporarily withholding moral judgment, having a ready laugh or murmur of sympathy. One must be silently *with* her while she speaks, lending support. One must *not* be listening with the third ear—not then. Cleanth Brooks would have made an ideal listener—I can see him sitting there at the Beulah Hotel enjoying every minute, merry eyes twinkling or watering with laughter, his face flexible and changing swiftly with the narrative flux. Elizabeth Evans would have made a good listener too, though more reserved, being of another generation of Southerners. Michael Kreyling would have listened attentively, laughed too, now and then, but when Edna Earle had finished her long tale he might have leaned over and asked, "Edna Earle, why are you so unhappy?" Gilbert Highet, in the unlikely event that he had been caught in Clay, Mississippi, with a broken down car, would have checked in at the Beulah, dined alone, retired to his room, read a book and written a review of it for the Book of the Month Club or the Reader's Subscription. Kingsley Amis would have asked Bodkin at the garage for the nearest bar, been reminded the state was dry, bribed Bodkin to get him the best jug of moonshine in the county, checked in at the Beulah, gone to his room, got bombed, and been awakened by a shocked Edna Earle to find he had burned out half his bed with an unextinguished cigarette.[18]

I am not implying that the critical faculties should be either completely or permanently suppressed in reading, certainly not in writing about Eudora Welty's comedy. Nor am I suggesting that *only* Southerners can truly enjoy this monologue. V. S. Pritchett seemed to, for one, and had some astute remarks to make about it.[19] I am simply stressing the importance of the two delphic maxims in the attempt to discover meaning in Welty's comedy. The writing of useful or interesting criticism about Welty's or any comedy, especially if its tone is genial and the moral and satiric elements are minimal, is extremely difficult: happy the critic who can do it well.

I now propose to lay down the comic mask and superimpose the tragic one—in some ways not only an arbitrary but a wrong-headed thing to do, since we know that comedy in some form appears in all of Eudora Welty's fiction. I oversimplify in order to pursue the question of meaning, by suggesting what I see as misemphases in critical approaches to Welty's serious fiction. Several of her stories seem to me essentially tragic—all those in which human suffering, even intolerable agony, are as palpable as on the mask of Greek tragedy; those in which the separateness triumphs over the love, and the characters and we are brought up against the snub-nose of non-meaning in the universe, or the finality of death. Such stories would include "A Curtain of Green," "Flowers for Marjorie," "A Still Moment," "Death of a Traveling Salesman," "The Hitchhikers," and uniquely among Eudora Welty's longer works, *The Optimist's Daughter*. The only relief from the pain with which I leave these stories comes from the lyric beauty, mystery and fascination of Welty's prose, the perception of some kind of order in the work itself and of truth seen and faced, some equivalent of the catharsis of pity and fear, despite the stories' lack of closure in the classical mode of tragedy.

The Optimist's Daughter, regarded by many readers and the author herself as Welty's best work, seems to me different from her earlier fiction in that "the judgment sunk in the work," to borrow a useful phrase from Flannery O'Connor, seems relatively clear and explicit. The abysmal selfishness and cruelty of Fay Chisom, as felt by Laurel Hand, seems unprecedented. For a critic to attack Laurel and leap to Fay's defense is to me about as perverse as to attack Cordelia and leap to the defense of Goneril and Regan. I am disturbed by what I regard as the exercise of a will*ful* imagination in the interpretation of this work.

With extreme trepidation I shall discuss the readings of two critics whose contributions to Welty criticism are considerable: Edward Hardy and Reynolds Price.[20] I admire both of these writers immensely, the latter especially in his fiction, poetry, and criticism. Hardy's essay on *Delta Wedding* opened up that novel to me, and the first part of the essay I shall consider, "Marrying Down in Eudora Welty's Fiction," seems perceptive in sorting out ambiguities and in placing judgment delicately. All the more strange that Hardy seems to go so wrong in his approach to *The Optimist's Daughter*. Hardy sees the crux of the problem, the "grave challenge" it presents to the reader, in how to distinguish Laurel Hand's "dominant and solid middle class, quasi-artistic consciousness" from the consciousness of

Eudora Welty. Having declared that "the last thing we should assume is that Eudora Welty, this most serenely detached of artists, has decided at last to commit herself to a mere heroine," he is free to find a "fundamental defect of vision" as well as "an instinct of self-preservation" in Laurel Hand, which leads her to total misunderstanding of Fay and her father's second marriage, and leaves her deluded to the end.

Hardy's initial assumption about authorial commitment seems to me arbitrary. It would also appear to be the polar opposite of Reynolds Price's about Laurel's reliability as a center of consciousness. Of her Price says, "I take Laurel's understanding to be also the author's and ours; there can be no second meaning, no resort to attempts to discredit Laurel's vision."

Hardy never denies Fay Chisom's vulgarity or selfishness—his chief point here seems to be that neither Fay nor Laurel either transcends the manners and morals of her class, nor descends beneath them. He credits Fay with a great deal of primitive, instinctive wisdom regarding the reason for Judge McKelva's eye injury and Dr. Courtland's method of treating it, making partly justifiable her screaming at him finally, "Thank you for nothing!" He finds Laurel as exclusively *self*-involved as Fay in concentrating on her parents' and her own marriage, and "her father's death only as it is related in the pattern of her experience to Philip's and her mother's and grandparents' deaths." He reduces the confrontation with Fay over the breadboard to a catty quarrel over possession, with exchanges of "boasts and insults with her on the issue of which is the better equipped by her upbringing for coping with widowhood and the hard facts of life in general." Since, Hardy argues, Laurel has never attempted to understand, forgive, or even *feel* for Fay as a real person, she has no right to accuse Fay of lacking feeling, and is only "dramatizing an argument that is essentially one with herself." The argument about the past and its meaning and the invulnerability of the dead becomes pointless as an exploration of truth on Laurel's part, and when Fay surrenders the breadboard as "one less thing to get rid of," Laurel, who must have the last word, again matches Fay's action by laying down the board and saying, "I think I can get along without that too." Hardy finds Laurel's final response "both spiteful and smug," and attributes the difference between the spoken words each woman uses in surrender of the breadboard to personal style. In her rejection of the breadboard and in burning the family mementos Laurel is suspiciously "*anxious* to dispose of the material reminders of her past." Hardy finds Adele Courtland, in her calm reasonableness and generous defense of Fay and the Chisoms, to be "the embodiment of the authorial presence."

The chief conflict in the novel, Hardy states, is Laurel's inner struggle to be reconciled to her father's death and the implications of his supposedly flawed character. The judge is commonly taken as unable "to face unpleasant facts about human nature"; the euphemism for this weakness is his self-assigned label of "optimist." Laurel is not the "tough-minded and scrupulous realist" she is usually taken for, but continually evades the truth, not only about her father and Fay, but about her parents' relationship and her own marriage. Hardy tops himself in exhibiting a will*ful* imagination in discussing the latter point, saying of Laurel that "she is quite evidently reluctant also to pursue certain implications of her own husband's behavior in seeking the most dangerous possible assignment in the war." This can only mean that Hardy suspects Philip to have been suicidal rather than courageous, and for the appalling reason that he preferred death to life with his bride. The final, damning evidence Hardy produces is Laurel's trying to attribute her father's fatal attraction to Fay to any motive, such as compassion or physical infirmity, rather than that of "his vulgar inclinations," the "appalling evidence" of which is "the pink-satined bed." Hardy concludes that "beyond any reasonable doubt" McKelva married Fay not in spite of but because she was vulgar, candidly selfish and sensual—as a relief from the impossibly demanding role of being the formidable Becky's husband. In her refusal to acknowledge the truth about her father's nature or to understand Fay, Laurel "fails in the final analysis to understand herself, and settles for the false comfort of an insight unworthy of her moral intelligence." She is "a person whose vision is tragically incomplete—rather than the heroine of a rather snobbish, and specious, moral comedy."

When it comes to this story's truth, Hardy's approach seems to me as wild as a drunken driver's. He seems right about only one thing: it is always a mistake to equate Eudora Welty with any of her characters, however sympathetically drawn—that is not the way she works. Laurel is a fictional projection, an imagined character so convincingly drawn that if the author has done her work and we are reading well, we come to accept Laurel's truth as the story's truth, related somehow to universal truth. Hardy seems right not to identify Eudora Welty with Laurel, though wrong to identify her with Adele Courtland, and wrong in his attack on Laurel's reliability in not taking account of many facts about who and what she is, chiefly her nature as an only child, the effect of her choices and background, what she has had to endure and must now endure in order *not simply to survive,* but survive in the only way either viable or worthy for a woman like that—in, with, and through the continuity of her love, which must be sustained in the way of the survivor—that is, through memory. Eudora Welty has seen to the believability of Laurel; under the circumstances then, we must see her *not* as a victim of self-delusion, but as the means to the disclosure of that story's truth—seriously distorted, I think, in Hardy's reading.

Reynolds Price produces a far better reading, sympathetic, clearly the product of a willing imagination and passionate response. He stresses the difference between this and Eudora Welty's earlier fiction in that the "onlooker" (which he sees as the characteristic stance of the narrator) does not end with a question and a look of puzzlement. In this work, says Price, "Mystery dissolves before patient watching—the unbroken stare of Laurel McKelva Hand. . . ." What Laurel sees is "that we feed on others till they fail us, through their understandable inability to spare us pain and death but, worse, through the exhaustion of loyalty, courage, memory. . . . Death and your own final lack of attention doom you to disloyalty." Laurel weeps in grief for love and for the dead because, Price says, it is "grief surely *that* love had not saved but harrowed her parents, a love she had not shared and now can never." This clarification of Laurel Hand is "finally merciless—to her dead parents, friends, enemies, herself: worst, to us."

So far, though I have some reservations about the meanings Price finds in the *New Yorker* version of the novella—whether, for example, the mystery is dissolved since to me it is deepened and darkened—I can learn much from his insights. But in the final paragraphs he leaves me, and I think the story, far behind. Laurel's final word, he says, might have been "fierce as her mother's":

> She might have said, "Show me a victor, and *actor* even." Or worse, she might have laughed.
>
> For there is at the end, each time I've reached it, a complicated sense of joy. Simple exhilaration in the courage and skill of the artist, quite separate from the tragic burden of the action. Joy that a piece of credible life has been displayed to us fully and, in the act, fully explained. . . . And then perhaps most troubling and most appeasing, the sense that Laurel's final emotion is joy, that she is now an "optimist" of a sort her father never knew. . .—that the onlooker's gifts, the crank's, have proved at last the strongest of human endowments (vision, distance, stamina—the courage of all three); that had there been any ear to listen, Laurel would almost surely have laughed, abandoning her weapon (as Milton's God laughs at the ignorance and ruin of Satan, only God has hearers—the Son and His angels). For Laurel has been both victim and judge—who goes beyond both into pure creation (only she has discovered the pattern of their lives—her parents,' Fay's, the Chisoms,' her friends,' her own) and then comprehension, which is always comic. All patterns are comic—snow crystal or galaxy in Andromeda or family history—because the universe is patterned, therefore ordered and ruled, therefore incapable of ultimate tragedy (interim tragedy is comprised in the order but cannot be the end; and if it should be—universal

pain—then that too is comic, by definition, to its only onlooker).
God's vision is comic, Alpha and Omega.

Price's ecstatic conclusion, whether in Johannine, Dantesque,
Miltonic, or Dilseyan vision he sees the beginnings and the endings
and feels himself, whether as reader or fellow writer, artist or believer,
caught up into a divine perspective, has taken us far from Laurel's
and the story's humble and far more earthly truth, from what to me
remains its essentially tragic vision. Price's reading ends not in a
serious distortion of meaning, like Hardy's, but simply takes off from
the terrestrial up beyond the ninth circle where Price laughs with
God and the angels, leaving us ordinary mortals far below.

Perhaps Price's and all our readings have been misled, to a greater
or lesser extent, by the title—perhaps a blunder in that beautiful
work. We have stretched and pummeled the word "optimist" to death
in assuming that Laurel has somehow to be made importantly *like*
her father, when she seems so much more like her mother, though
loving both deeply. *That* title somehow doesn't fit *that* story.

Having ceased to struggle with this dilemma, I now see the tragic
mask on the face of the novella more clearly because of Laurel's
discoveries: that no matter how much they *love* each other, people
cannot be saved *from* each other (even worse than their not being
able to be saved *by* each other); that the most ideal relationships can
be and usually *are* destroyed by time, fate, and the finitude of love's
capacity for longsuffering. And then I find such tragic waste in the
book, not only personal and private but broadly social in scope—the
dissolution of a whole Southern tradition of courageous, courteous
and kindly people living together in families and communities, of
people caring for each other and maintaining the dignified, orderly
relationships of Southern manners and morals. The novel seems to
me an elegy without an apotheosis—only Laurel's very tenuous, highly
personal one, experienced in her conviction that the meaning of her
life lay in the continuity of love, that "memory lived not in initial
possession but in the freed hands, pardoned and freed, . . . in the
patterns restored by dreams."[21]

The *best* part of the meaning we perceive in Eudora Welty's or
any other fiction, I think, is what spills over from the story into our
lives, enabling us to make connections—not only of our private
experiences with those of fiction, but the connections between literature, art and music; of our bonding, both within and beyond the
limits to time and place, with the whole human race. Of these
connections, deconstruction knows nothing. From this perspective,
The Golden Apples, flawed as it is, remains my favorite among her
works, an inexhaustible source of delight and truth. Delight starts
for me with its sensuous richness—evoked by the hummingbird that

sucks sweetness from my flowers each day in summertime. This golden book recovers for me the delights and terrors of my childhood. It feeds my passion for music—Beethoven and the Romantics; my fascination with myth and art—the statue of Perseus holding the head of the Medusa, with his vaunting right arm (one currently looms from the balcony over the great lobby of the Metropolitan Museum). *The Golden Apples* makes me ponder metamorphosis, heroism of many kinds, including success-in-failure—all of life's dualities. It makes me feel close to the Greeks because of their closeness to nature—or is it the other way around?

Very little of this personal meaning gets into critical writing; it is, quite simply, enriching, and urges us toward the revelation of the mystery of life.

Of the *best* meaning, then, private and personal, each of us must take his or her own measure, in Eudora Welty's or any fiction, while getting on to where we are going as readers and critics.

Notes

1. The lecture was given at a special session on Welty at the South Atlantic Modern Language Association in Louisville, November 1981. The article, titled "Eudora Welty: The Question of Meaning," appeared in *The Southern Quarterly*, 20 (Summer 1982), 24–39.

2. *Eudora Welty*, rev. ed. (Boston: Twayne Publishers, 1987). "Eudora Welty: Visited and Revisited," *Mississippi Quarterly*, 39 (Fall 1986), 455–479. " 'Where Is the Voice Coming From?': Teaching Eudora Welty." Lecture given at a conference on Eudora Welty at the University of Akron, September 17–19, 1987.

3. See especially Pitavy-Souques' article "A Blazing Butterfly: The Modernity of Eudora Welty," *Mississippi Quarterly*, 39 (Fall 1986), 537–560.

4. *The Collected Stories of Eudora Welty* (New York: Harcourt Brace Jovanovich, 1980), p. xi.

5. "Words into Fiction," *The Eye of the Story* (New York: Random House, 1977), p. 142.

6. In opening the door to "unconscious meanings" I have perhaps put a chink in my humanistic armor, capitulating to the Freudian deconstructionists who base the whole of their analytic work on exposure of concealed, unconscious meanings, slips and puns.

7. I allude to the two delphic oracles in my Akron conference lecture, and add a third maxim, "Don't be afraid to change your mind," phrased more memorably by the sage of Concord, "A foolish consistency is the hobgoblin of little minds."

8. Peggy Prenshaw, *Eudora Welty: A Form of Thanks*, eds. Louis Dollarhide and Ann J. Abadie (Jackson: Univ. Press of Mississippi, 1979), p. 47.

9. *A Curtain of Green* (Garden City, N.Y.: Doubleday, Doran, 1941), p. xvii.

10. Elizabeth Evans, *Eudora Welty* (New York: Frederick Ungar, 1981), p. 21.

11. Michael Kreyling, *Eudora Welty's Achievement of Order* (Baton Rouge: Louisiana State Univ. Press, 1980), pp. 12–13.

12. Kreyling, p. 106.

13. Kreyling, pp. 106–07.

14. Cleanth Brooks, "Eudora Welty and the Southern Idiom," *Eudora Welty: A Form of Thanks,* eds. Dollarhide and Abadie, pp. 14–15.

15. Robert M. Adams, "Formulas and Fiction," *Hudson Review,* 7 (Spring 1950), 145. For this and the following two references I am indebted to John Idol's collection of reviewer's reactions in his valuable article, "Edna Earle Ponder's Good Country People," *The Southern Quarterly,* 20 (Spring 1982), 66–75.

16. Gilbert Highet, Review of *The Ponder Heart, Harper's Magazine,* Feb. 1954, p. 97.

17. Kingsley Amis, Review of *The Ponder Heart, The Spectator,* 29 Oct. 1954, p. 534.

18. The high-browed reaction of Gilbert Highet, renowned classicist, is of course hypothetical and based solely on his reaction in the review. That of Kingsley Amis, as readers will recognize, is based less on his review than the behavior of his amiable hero, Lucky Jim.

19. V.S. Pritchett, "Bossy Edna Earle Had a Word for Everything," *New York Times Book Review,* 10 Jan. 1954, pp. 5–6.

20. John E. Hardy, "Marrying Down in Eudora Welty's Fiction," *Eudora Welty: Critical Essays,* ed. Peggy Prenshaw (Jackson: Univ. Press of Mississippi, 1979), pp. 93–119. Quotations are from Part II, pp. 107–19 *passim.* Reynolds Price, "The Onlooker, Smiling: An Early Reading of *The Optimist's Daughter," Shenandoah,* 20 (Spring 1969), 58–73. Price's essay was based on the *New Yorker* version of the novella, but Welty's revisions of the work do not seem to me to bear upon his response to the work in any significant way.

21. *The Optimist's Daughter* (New York: Random House, 1972), p. 179.

INDEX

311